ISLAND
ENDURANCE

Frontispiece 1: Inishark and Inishbofin. Aerial image from Galway Coastline Survey © 2014 by Peter Barrow. Surveys on behalf of Galway County Council, licensed under CC BY-ND 4.0.

Frontispiece 2: The village on Inishark. Aerial image from Galway Coastline Survey © 2014 by Peter Barrow. Surveys on behalf of Galway County Council, licensed under CC BY-ND 4.0.

IRISH CULTURE, MEMORY, PLACE
Oona Frawley, Ray Cashman, Guy Beiner, editors

ISLAND ENDURANCE

Creative Heritage on Inishark and Inishbofin

—⚏—

Ryan Lash

INDIANA UNIVERSITY PRESS

This book is a publication of

Indiana University Press
Herman B Wells Library 350
1320 East 10th Street
Bloomington, Indiana 47405 USA

iupress.org

© 2025 by Ryan Lash

All rights reserved
No part of this book may be reproduced or utilized in any form or by any means, electronic or mechanical, including photocopying and recording, or by any information storage and retrieval system, without permission in writing from the publisher.

First printing 2025

Cataloging information is available from the Library of Congress.

ISBN 978-0-253-07247-4 (hdbk.)
ISBN 978-0-253-07248-1 (pbk.)
ISBN 978-0-253-07249-8 (web PDF)
ISBN 978-0-253-07250-4 (ebook)

To my parents, Lucy and Bill. *E a tutti i miei parenti.*

Contents

Preface xi

Acknowledgments xv

Note on Irish Place-Names xxi

Introductory Maps xxiii

1. Alive in Ruins 3
2. Dynamic Endurance and Creative Heritage: A Taskscape Approach 26
3. Traces of Leo on Inishark 54
4. Pebbles, Pilgrims, and Sacred Order: Heritage in Inishark's Medieval Taskscape (c. 700–1300) 126
5. Cult, Commemoration, and Cooperation: Heritage in Inishark's Modern Taskscape (c. 1600–1960) 166
6. Tourists, Corncrakes, Cattle, and Craic: Heritage in Inishbofin's Contemporary Taskscape (c. 1960–2019) 210
7. The Enduring Challenge 256

Bibliography 279

Index 305

Preface

MY DOCTORAL DISSERTATION was planned as a study of early medieval island monasticism and its material and devotional legacies in western Ireland. As readers may come to suspect, over the years that project was infiltrated by sheep. This has made all the difference.

I first set eyes on the islands of Inishark and Inishbofin in the fall of 2007 during a research trip for an undergraduate course called Archaeology of Ireland at the University of Notre Dame. The conditions weren't right to land on Shark that day, so Dr. Ian Kuijt, our course instructor, led us around the loop-walk of Westquarter Mountain on Inishbofin. By the slant of a setting sun, the contours of the islands shared their history in shapes of shadow: the parallel lines of twentieth-century potato ridges, the circles of Bronze Age huts, the distant triangular silhouettes of empty homes on Inishark, and all around us, the walking shades of sheep and cattle, moving about the commonage and turning their heads to assess these unfamiliar figures on the road.

Unlike many of my classmates at Notre Dame, I had no Irish Catholic heritage to speak of, no real premise for a connection to Ireland apart from the given name Ryan, adopted from the surname of my Irish American godfather. It was the presence of the past in the landscape and its animal dwellers that caught me. It echoed with family stories I had heard, memories of rural experiences I missed by a generation or two: my dad milking cows as a kid on a Pennsylvania dairy farm and my mother's father, as a boy in central Italy in the 1920s, keeping watch over a flock of sheep through the night on a lonely hillside. These echoes rang out again over the years like the chimes of a bellwether, and my curiosity would follow.

In summer 2008, I returned to Ireland as a student researcher on Dr. Kuijt's archaeological field project, the Cultural Landscapes of the Irish Coast (CLIC). The team camped on Inishark for more than a week, pitching tents among the ruins of the village and becoming neighbors with the sheep who grazed there. Inishark was evacuated in 1960 and has seen little subsequent activity. The remnants of millennia of human dwelling have accrued on its landscape, casting more than telltale shadows of the past. That was the first of nine summer field seasons (2008–12, 2014–17) in which CLIC would return to the island to conduct archaeological surveys and excavations as well as oral history interviews with islanders from Shark and Bofin. Because of my interest in medieval studies, my role on the project gravitated toward the documentation of Inishark's early medieval monastic settlement. The results of preliminary excavations near Clochán Leo, a stone hut associated with the local Saint Leo, proved more promising than perhaps anyone anticipated. By piecing together archaeological discoveries, folklore, and antiquarian accounts, it might be possible to trace periodic reengagements with Inishark's monastic monuments from the early medieval period to the late twentieth century. Here was a chance to refine the too easy narrative of timeless tradition on Ireland's islands.

This topic emerged as the basis for a PhD project in the Department of Anthropology at Northwestern University, commenced in the fall of 2012. More excavations and more discoveries were to follow in coming years, but the greatest boons, personally and professionally, came from sharing time and work with islanders and their animals. The CLIC project and my role within it could never have developed as it has without the support of islanders. Ian's dedicated pursuit of community engagement by organizing open excavations and public heritage events at the Inishbofin Community Centre set the stage for conversations and collaborations that grew over the years, over tea, under weather, by campfires, across the bar, through pub sessions, and at work with animals.

In 2014, for the first time, Tommy Burke invited me to accompany himself and other farmers from Inishbofin to help gather and shear their sheep on Inishark. What that day gave me—and many, many subsequent days with Tommy and John Burke and Simon Murray—was a chance to know the landscape through work. Anthropologists are primed to recognize the power of ritual to influence people's perceptions of how they fit within the swirl of time, community, and cosmos. We are perhaps less well trained to imagine how practical, physical labor might do the same. Without deliberate strategy or intent, my participation in farming fundamentally shaped the course of my research. Fieldwork and farmwork increasingly converged.

Farmwork is what inspired me to examine how heritage and livelihood are entwined. It reminded me to understand transformations in ritual traditions against the backdrop of agricultural regimes that sustained island communities across time. Farmwork attuned my attention to the sensory and commemorative dynamics of human encounters with other-than-human agents, whether animals, materials, or environmental phenomena. It helped me to see possibilities for enchantment, poetry, and reflection in the course of daily routines of hospitality, seasonal cycles of labor, and elaborate choreographies of devotion. Farmwork changed my approach to writing. It inspired me (successfully or not) to imagine lived experience in the past with as much flesh and sweat and allusive possibility as experiences in the present. Farmwork honed a sensitivity to other ways of being in the world. Collaboration among farmers and dogs in the gathering of sheep and the practice of anthropology have more in common than might first appear. Both crafts are exercises in imagining the world from multiple perspectives simultaneously and attempting to formulate responses that take heed of the whole and might reshape it in turn. That, at least, is the idea. As experienced shepherds and researchers can attest, results may vary.

Preparing a book in the turbulence of late 2010s and early 2020s felt at times like the foolhardiness of raising the alarm about a blazing fire by commencing a ponderous lecture on the physics of combustion. Urgency brooks not exposition. These years have seen political unrest, pandemic, conflict, hate, and climate change all in acceleration. With the naïve ambition of a graduate student, I hoped to do research that would yield some small insight into the collective task of finding better ways to live together in the world. I remain convinced that we can learn from islanders' history and creativity—whether we find ways to live those lessons is another question. This book seeks to undermine old but stubborn fables about the timelessness of marginalized peoples. The history of the islands illustrates the capacity of human groups to adapt the resources of the past—monuments, memories, and traditions—to generate new possibilities for social resonance, cooperation, and livelihood. That history also demonstrates the limitations of creative heritage to confront broader structures of inequality and ideology. If we are to live the lessons from the islands' past, it will demand a dedication to collaboration between a diverse range of stakeholders, an openness to multiple perspectives, including the other-than-human, and a capacity to imagine new frameworks of belonging.

Memory demands exposition, and remembrance has its own urgency, even in the most trying times. So much of the research in this book would not have been possible without a bulwark of local knowledge, oral tradition, and embodied skill passed between generations, constantly renewed and remade in its reiterations. This book, I hope, by contributing something to that memory-keeping, will find a justification, even in times of urgency. Despite inevitable limitations, I have done my best to document and interpret aspects of the islands' archaeological and cultural heritage and to reckon what this small corner of human experience might tell us about human possibility. If nothing else, I ask readers to read this book as a record of my admiration for islanders and of the deepest gratitude for friends who shared their heritage and their work with me.

Acknowledgments

FIND A WINTER NIGHT without moon or clouds on the islands and look up for a carnival in celestial light. Writing acknowledgments is like mapping that night sky with only the stars of the constellations. Inevitably, countless who have given some glow will go unnamed. I thank first all those uncharted lights.

The research featured in this book would not have been possible without friends, colleagues, and collaborators on the Cultural Landscapes of the Irish Coast (CLIC) project. Ian Kuijt and Meredith Chesson have offered me more than fifteen years of intellectual guidance, encouragement, hospitality, patience, and friendship. I am immensely thankful for their mentorship. This book would certainly not exist without them. I also thank Ian for access to archaeological data and aerial imagery used in this work and Meredith for her tutelage during fieldwork, contribution to figures and plan drawings, and analysis of the CLIC ceramic database. Nathan Goodale, Alissa Nauman, Colin Quinn, Meagan Conway McDonald, Claire Brown, Maddy Bassett, Casey McNeill, Annie McNeill, Katie Shakour, Phil Lettieri, Lauren Marie Couey, Nicholas Ames, Sara Morrow, Erin Crowley-Champoux, Eugene Costello, Rachael Tracy, Alessandro Martellaro, and Kaatje Chesson have all enriched the joy and quality of CLIC's research. Special thanks are due to my comrades on the CLIC medieval team, Elise Alonzi and Terry O'Hagan, who have continually supported and enlightened me. John O'Neill and Franc Myles provided essential mentorship in the conduct of excavation. I also thank Franc for his aid in navigating the logistics of license applications, reporting, and artifact storage, as well as his hospitality over the years. I have learned a great deal from Michael Gibbons, Jim Higgins, and John O'Halloran about the archaeology of the islands and Connemara. CLIC is also much obliged to faculty and staff in Archaeology and the University of Galway for their support in artifact analysis and storage, particularly Kieran O'Connor, Joseph Fenwick, and Angela Gallagher. Linda Martellaro holds my undying gratitude for her logistical expertise and culinary virtuosity amid the challenges of keeping hungry excavation crews fed while camping on Inishark without electricity, refrigeration, or running water. Speaking for myself, rarely has one with dirtier fingernails feasted better than kings.

Financial sponsorship for CLIC's archaeological fieldwork has come from many sources. Initial support was generously provided by the John Tynan family, the Institute for Scholarship in the Liberal Arts, and the Office of Sponsored Research, University of Notre Dame. Fieldwork conducted for my doctoral project was funded by a Northwestern University Graduate Research Grant, a National Science Foundation Graduate Research Fellowship (1000135637), and a National Science Foundation Doctoral Dissertation Improvement Grant (1630141).

This book began as a doctoral dissertation for the Department of Anthropology at Northwestern University. There was no better home to nurture that process. My dissertation supervisor, Matthew Johnson, provided constant advocacy and thoughtful feedback on the earliest drafts of this work. Mary Weismantel's enthusiasm and encouragement influenced the approach and style of this book profoundly. She is partly responsible for holding open the gate that allowed sheep to wander in and out of this book at will. Constructive feedback from Cynthia Robin and Mark Hauser always alerted me to avenues for improvement. I am also grateful to Amanda Logan for encouraging writing that strives to convey experience and to appeal beyond academics. I always emerged more thoughtful and inspired after discussions with fellow archaeologists Kathryn Catlin, Eric Johnson, Sarah Breiter, and Doug Bolender. Many thanks are due to the department's administrative staff for their help: Tracy Tohtz, Nancy Hickey, and Will Voltz. I remain grateful for the fellowship of many friends from Anthropology at Northwestern, including Nazlı Özkan, Khadene Harris, Ruby Fried, Elizabeth Derderian, Elisa Lanari, Livia L. Garofalo, Calen Ryan, Aydin Özipek, Ashley Ngozi Agbasoga, Stephen Sullivan, Mariam Taher, and Kaelin Rapport. We shared lively times.

Postdoctoral fellowships from the College of Arts and Letters at Notre Dame (2019–20) and the Keough-Naughton Institute for Irish Studies in 2020–21 provided invaluable time, support, and inspiration to revise my dissertation into a book manuscript. Many offered support and camaraderie during this second stint at Notre Dame, including Beth Bland, Mary Hendriksen, Patrick Griffin, Colin Barr, Diarmuid Ó Giolláin, Mary O'Callaghan, Muiris MacGiollabhuí, Chanté Mouton Kinyon, and Nicholas Ames, certainly the world's best housemate. I am especially indebted to three readers who participated in a workshop sponsored by the Keough-Naughton Institute and provided feedback on an earlier version of this book. Tomás Ó Carragáin has been exceedingly generous in his encouragement over the years. Anyone familiar with the field will know that I'm only one of the harrowers of a row that he plowed. Audrey Horning offered vital advice for refining the discussion of Ireland and postcolonial theory and opened my eyes to loose ends and blind spots that I have endeavored to address. Ray Cashman offered thoughtful reflections and a boost of enthusiasm for this project at a crucial time. I am grateful for his encouragement to publish with Indiana University Press. I thank him, the series editors, Bethany R. Mowry, and all of the team for shepherding me through the process.

An Irish Research Council Postdoctoral Fellowship based at the School of Archaeology at University College Dublin (2021–23) provided additional support to develop research relating to the production sequences of early medieval cross-slabs. Aidan O'Sullivan, Brendan O'Neill, and Anita Radini offered valuable mentorship and opportunities for experimentation at the Centre for Experimental Archaeology and Material Culture. Conversations with Tadhg O'Keeffe, Nora White, Gary Dempsey, and Séighean Ó Draoi contributed significantly to my thinking on early medieval stone-craft and devotion during this fellowship. Thanks to Conor McDermot for his ever readiness to field questions and facilitate my research. I am grateful to Joanna Brück for fostering such a welcoming environment during the postdoc and for the friendships I made at UCD with Jess Beck, Tiber Falzett, Russel Ó Riagáin, Rory Connolly, Sonja Kacar, Kate Kanne, and Sam Kinirons. I have also been blessed in Dublin by the exquisite hospitality of Bell Pesto Cafe on James Street.

The last stages of manuscript submission were undertaken in Dublin as a postdoctoral research associate with the Clingen Family Center for the Study of Modern Ireland at Notre Dame. My thanks to the center for generously providing funds to support publication with color imagery. Shelley Deane provided much-needed heartening during this time. I am grateful to Mobeen Hussain, Ciaran O'Neill, Pegi Vail, Ciarán Walsh, and Patrick Walsh for providing their feedback on the discussion of the return of human remains from Trinity College Dublin to Inishbofin in chapter 7. Deirdre Ní Chonghaile has appeared now and again over the years on both sides of the Atlantic like a fairy godmother to lend her advice, experience, and energy and was a great support during the final throes of preparation.

My thanks to those individuals and institutions who provided access to materials and permission to reproduce images in this book. Jonny Dillon helped me to navigate Brían MacLoughlin's materials in the National Folklore Collection and Conor Ó Gallachóir provided transcriptions and translations of MacLoughlin's Irish notes. I am grateful to John Reader for sharing his memories of sheep gathering on Inishark in 1964 and for his generosity in allowing me to reproduce one of his photographs as a cover to this book. Aerial images from the late Peter Barrow, reproduced here with the kind permission of Galway County Council, set the scene for the islands better than words ever could. Lesley O'Farrell kindly allowed me to use a photograph that captures brilliantly an unforgettable sheep-gathering episode between Inishlyon and Inishbofin. All images unless otherwise credited are my own.

I thank my lucky stars I ever set foot on the islands. I have benefitted immeasurably from the generosity, hospitality, and wit of islanders. CLIC owes a debt of gratitude to Shark islanders Noel Gavin, Theresa Lacey, Leo Murray, and Martin Murray for sharing their time and stories with our team. On Bofin, Andrew Concannon, John Concannon, Matty Concannon, James Coyne, and Anne Day all shared valuable recollections and reflections on the past. Our team has also had the privilege of drawing from a wealth of locally curated oral history and heritage projects. Not least of these is Kieran Concannon's documentary *Inis Airc - Bás Oileáin*, a film that has become only more poignant, more enlightening, and more essential with repeated viewings.

The CLIC team has relied heavily on the skillful boat-handling and knowhow of Pat, Dermot, Seamus, and Harry Concannon, who transported CLIC teams safely over many years between Shark, Bofin, and other islands. We are also indebted to the many friends and crew members who helped us to offload equipment and artifacts without mishap.

We owe endless thanks to Aileen Murray, Fiona Murray, Simon Murray, Andrew Murray, and Donna Dever at the Doonmore Hotel for their hospitality, humor, and forbearance in dealing with CLIC field crews, especially when we arrived at the bar with the aroma of a week's digging on Inishark without a shower. Alice O'Halloran, Mary Day Lavelle, Luke Murray, Oileán Murray, Éibhe Murray, Róisín Murray, Dualtagh Murray, Béga Murray, Marcais Lavelle, Caolán Murray, Finnan Murray, Paddy Murray, Dylan Murray, Josh Levy, Zach Levy, Simon Cloonan, Michael Cloonan, Ciarán Ó Mathúna, Rory Gartlan, Joe Junker, and many, many more of Murray's staff members and patrons generated a lot of *craic* over the years. CLIC also enjoyed the kind welcome and hospitality of the folks at the Beach: Day's Bar and BnB, the Dolphin Hotel, the Inishbofin Hostel, the Inishbofin House Hotel, the Galley, Inishwallah, and the Saltbox.

Many at the Inishbofin Community Centre, Inishbofin Development Company, and Inishbofin Community Services Programme have facilitated CLIC's research, public presentations, and storage requests over the years, including Simon Murray, Margaret Mary O'Halloran, Tuuli Rantala, Hugh and Tara McMahon, Imelda Reidy, and Kevin Abeyta.

I am profoundly thankful for the friendship of Marie Coyne, Tommy Burke, John Burke, and Simon Murray. Marie and Tommy have shared so much of their talents, work, and knowledge. The course of this project and of my life would surely be duller things without them. Both have welcomed me into their homes and into the lives of their families. I am particularly grateful to Anne Burke, Emer Burke, Sean Igegeri, Dafe Igegeri, and the extended Burke family for welcoming me like one of their own. My thanks to John Burke for sharing his time, many fine feeds, and memorable moments, both charmed and dodgy. Simon Murray has been a trusty source of hospitality, conversation, and counsel, and I'm grateful for his having provided a close reading of this book prior to publication.

I thank all the other Bofiners who have ever shared farmwork with me or even a few memories about it, including Andrew Concannon, John Concannon, Pat Concannon, Seamus Concannon, Enda Concannon, James Coyne, James Coyne Jr., John Michael Coyne, Ryan Coyne, Dennis Burke, John Gerard Burke, Mary Davis, Pat Coyne, Jackie Jefferson, Austin Coyne, John Cunnane, Margaret Mary and Michael Joe O'Halloran, Henry Kenny, Paddy Jo King, Mairtin Lavelle, Paddy Lavelle, Francis Lavelle, Mary Lavelle, Willie Lavelle, Oisín Lavelle, Marcais Lavelle, Patrick Murray, Mick Murray, and Seamus Ward.

Endless thanks are due to Augustine Coyne for rescuing me from my foolishness.

Thanks to Malise Gibney for his tunes and his time. Thanks to Desmond O'Halloran for his Thomas Hardy references. Thanks to Sara Attanasi for her comradeship and indulgence of my sorry Italian. Thanks to Peadar King and Eamonn Day Lavelle for their warmth and brilliance. Thanks to Mary Ward for her hospitality and friendship. Thanks to Anne Prendergast for her ever-ready cheer. Thanks to Kartika Menon for her kindness and culinary prowess. Thanks to Fr. Declan Deasy for sending me the last postcard ever to reach Inishark. Countless others on the islands have contributed to this research and enriched my time with their presence. I thank them all for making space for me.

I thank my partner, Malak, for her love, patience, and embrace of the islands. Learning together with you is a gift.

The love of my family, near and far, has been a lodestar across these years of wandering and writing. Memories of my grandparents have swirled around me during fieldwork. I'm grateful to my grandpap Bill for providing my earliest experience of catching lambs and to grandma Audrey and her garden for fond memories of digging potatoes and eating peas and tomatoes fresh off the vine. My nonno Amedeo and his boyhood as a shepherd in Cervara has been almost ever present in my mind. I can only imagine his giggling at the sight of a grandson, gifted with all the education he never got, somehow back chasing sheep over a boggy hillside of an Irish island. I've been nurtured by the love of a large and cheerful family of siblings, aunts, uncles, cousins, nieces, nephews, and *parenti*. I'm indebted to them all. I was a late-arriving lamb to my siblings, Pace and Melissa, who have let me follow them around and look up to them and always responded with love and support and the strength of their example. Their partners, Sharmila and Barry, have done the same. I am grateful too for the joy brought to my life by my nephew and nieces, Amedec, Lena, Vinaya, and Totti. My parents, Lucy and Bill, have always indulged my curiosity, though it took me far from home. I have learned so much from their love, sensitivity, and fortitude. This book is dedicated to them.

Books and thanks are never finished, but they do come to an end. All of these people contributed to this work, though the arguments set forth are my own, and I reserve sole ownership of all flaws, shortcomings, and errors herein.

Note on Irish Place-Names

THE IRISH LANGUAGE was in decline on the islands of Inishark and Inishbofin as early as the late nineteenth century and now has not been spoken as a mother tongue on Inishbofin for many generations. This language shift is one of the fundamental features of the islands' history and a major complicating factor when attempting to reconstruct and transcribe local place-names. Throughout this book, I generally employ English transliterations of Irish place-names, particularly when a standard form is in common use (for example, Inishbofin for *Inis Bó Finne*). Some historical place-names appear with many variations in extant records, but have no standard form in common use. In some cases, for the sake of clarity, I have adopted a standard form that mimics existing conventions of transliteration on the islands (for example, I use Clochán Congleo rather than Cloghaun Congleo). The linguistic heritage of these islands is rich and complicated, and I hope that this book will inspire scholars with the right expertise to build on previous scholarship and conduct additional detailed analysis of surviving linguistic evidence from place-names, materials in the National Folklore Collection, and residual Irish features in local language use.

Introductory Maps

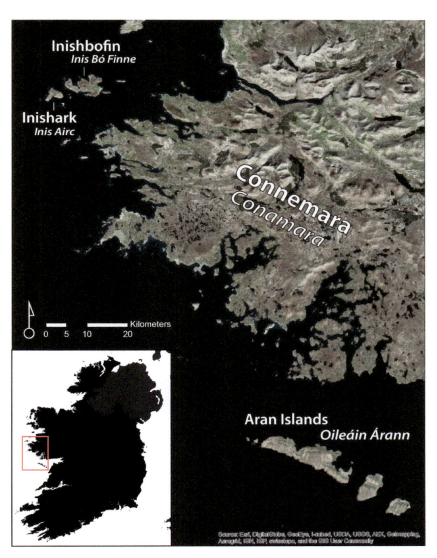

Map 0.1: The location of Inishark and Inishbofin in relation to the Connemara coast and the Aran Islands.

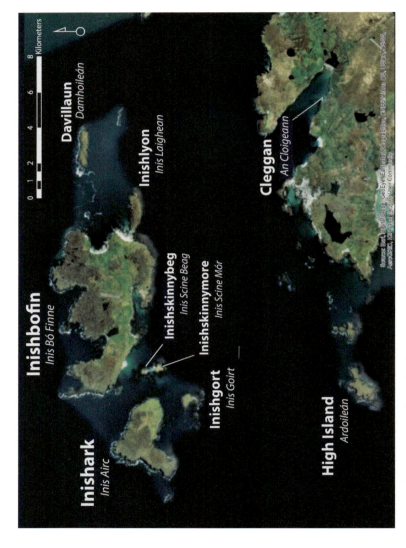

Map 0.2: Detailed view of the islands within the Inishbofin-Inishark archipelago as well as High Island and the pier at Cleggan, now the principal mainland harbor for Inishbofin.

ISLAND
ENDURANCE

Figure 1.1: Ruins on Inishark in a storm, June 2017.

ONE

ALIVE IN RUINS

INISHARK IS ALIVE IN RUINS. Seven and a half kilometers off the coast of Connemara in western Ireland, the island has had no permanent human residents since the last islanders left on October 20, 1960 (fig. 1.1). Yet, across a narrow stretch of water, the neighboring island of Inishbofin remains home to nearly two hundred people and harbor to thousands of tourists throughout the summer. From the western end of Bofin, you can look across the sound—*idir dhá bhaile*, "between the townlands"—and see on Shark the green fields and gray stones of the townland that was (fig. 1.2). Empty houses with collapsed roofs and drystone walls bare and bowing. Field walls of various makes and states of disrepair, bonded and abutted to one another in a pattern of interconnections that have outlived the reasons for which people assembled them. In the years since evacuation, the walls that once divided one household plot from another have become the everyday terrain of free-grazing sheep. Several times per year, farmers from Bofin travel to Shark to tend to their sheep, including a trip in summer to gather and shear them. I have gone along for six shearing trips in the summers of 2014, 2016, 2017, 2018, 2019, and 2022. Setting off from Bofin, these trips offer a circuit tour across a landscape where people have settled, built, refashioned, socialized, worshipped, and made a living where space is confined but materials and memories accumulate. Recalling one of those circuits provides a useful introduction to the history and archaeology of the islands as well as this book's main ideas.

AUGUST 28, 2016. THE GATHERING.

"At the old pier for half-eight" was the word from Simon. There was a lot to be done, and we had to get ourselves to Shark and gather all the sheep before the real work could even begin. I accompanied men from Bofin who have kept sheep on Shark for years: Simon Murray, his teenage son Caolán, and the two Burke brothers, John and Tommy. Three sheepdogs came with us: John's dog, Toby, and Simon's dogs, Eve and Risp. We set out in the crystal light of the morning in two crafts, a RIB (rigid inflatable boat) and an aluminum fishing boat, each powered with an outboard motor. Traveling across Inishbofin's harbor, we passed the ruins of a fortification, built in the wake of Cromwell's conquest of Ireland in the 1650s. The "Old Barracks" served as a garrison for Commonwealth soldiers and later as a prison for Catholic priests, some sent to the Caribbean as indentured servants. It was left to ruin by the early eighteenth century. In every corner of the barracks' outer walls there are cavities where, long ago, islanders removed the dressed blocks of imported limestone to use as building material or grist for limekilns. A monument of conquest and surveillance reduced to a hollowed husk from which islanders plucked to furnish their homes and fertilize their fields.

Bofin's harbor could never have escaped attention from conquerors, pirates, pilgrims, scholars, or tourists. About a mile long, it is among the finest and best sheltered in the west of Ireland. In contrast, Inishark offers only a ragged landing place (fig. 1.3). In 1873, the parish priest of Bofin described Shark to the inspector of Irish fisheries in spare poetry: "A crow could not land on it when it is blowing and a heavy sea running" (Brady 1873, 5). Today, the landing place is a narrow inlet between the crumbling remnants of a concrete pier and breakwater, both damaged during the raging storms of winter 2014. Outboard motors make landing easier than in the nineteenth and early twentieth centuries, when help was often needed from those on shore to haul the boats up to land. Even so, the landing place is often too treacherous to chance, especially with southeasterly winds. The storms that broke the breakwater have also eaten away at the cliffs above the pier. Atop these cliffs is a burial ground full of nameless gravestones in gray schist. A few sun-bleached bones peer out from the cliff face as the subsoil gradually peels away from the sod, leaving grassy overhangs. Villagers used this cemetery only rarely in the nineteenth and twentieth centuries, particularly for young children, the elderly, or anyone who died when the island was weather-bound. There was never a resident priest for Inishark, and most often the dead were ferried to Bofin for burial in the cemetery there. The risk of extended isolation by the weather, the fear of death without last rites, and the government's inability to provide new infrastructure were among the primary reasons that the last islanders relocated in 1960. There were no prospects to improve conditions for themselves and

Figure 1.2: The Old Barracks at the mouth of Inishbofin's main harbor was a garrison constructed in the wake of the Cromwellian conquest of Ireland in the mid-seventeenth century.

their children on the island. What could have gone one way—toward reinvestment and continued maintenance—went the other—toward mainland priorities—and now the shattering pier and eroding cliff are left to the gnaw of wind and water.

As the boat wavered gently near the landing, I scrambled up the wet rocks, helped unload equipment, and left the tying down of the boats to trustier hands. The men that brought me were then in their mid- to late forties, each a fount of local knowledge. I have learned a lot from them. Each was born after the evacuation of Inishark, but all could recite stories from the days when visitors would have been met at the pier and welcomed into homes for tea. Simon Murray worked for years as Inishbofin's

Above, Figure 1.3: The approach to the landing place on Inishark (2014).

Facing, Map 1.1: The approximate routes taken by gatherers in 2016 with arrows indicating the direction in which the sheep are encouraged to move. (1) The task begins by gathering all the sheep in the fields east of the village, pushing them north and east, and then sweeping around to corral them in the Lacey House, where Simon and Caolán can begin shearing. With those sheep gathered, the circumambulation of the island begins, (2) with Tommy hugging the coast while I keep to higher ground, driving the sheep downslope to the west or northwest. (3) While Tommy continues along the coast, hoping to gather all the sheep into an accumulating flock, John, his dog Toby, and I prevent any sheep from returning east and hold any sheep to the north in place until Tommy sweeps around the headland. (4) Next, Tommy continues to drive the flock along the coast while John, Toby, and I push any stragglers toward the coast and prevent the bolder sheep from breaking away. (5) Finally, the flock enters the eastern fields, and Caolán and Simon, with Risp and Eve, join us to slowly close in on the flock and sweep them around into the fenced area by the pier.

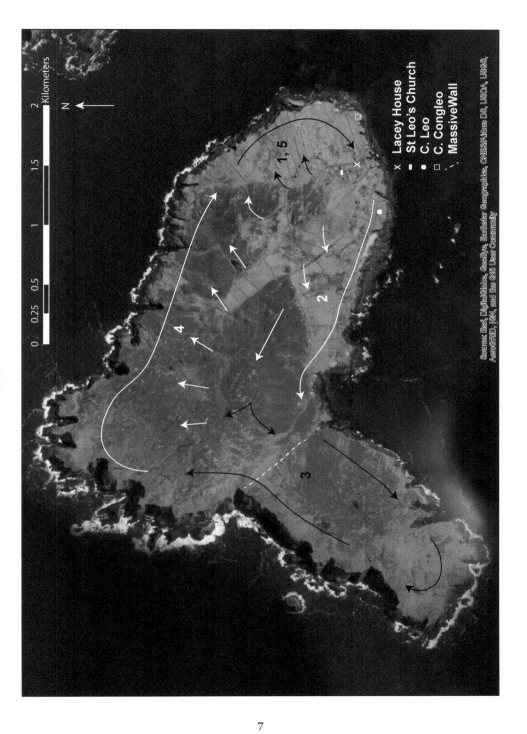

Community Development Manager, raising funds, representing, and campaigning on behalf of islanders. He has represented the Comhdháil Oileáin na hÉireann (the Irish Islands Federation) multiple times in committee meetings of the Oireachtas (the Irish Legislature). When his friends and fellow islanders need him, he never lacks for energy or intelligence. Simon has multigenerational kinship ties to Shark through his father's side and has been going to Shark since he was a little boy. His parents met when his mother was the schoolteacher on Inishark in the 1950s. John and Tommy Burke have no direct kinship connections to Shark but know a great deal about the island and its history from former islanders. John, who sadly passed away in 2024, used to fish and farm with former Shark islanders and their descendants, and he seemed to know every spit of rock in the seaways around the islands. Tommy carries oral history and genealogical knowledge that might be gone without him. He studied archaeology in college and offers guided walking tours around Shark and Bofin. He has a head for stories and the cunning to tell them.

To ensure all the sheep were gathered, we had to walk clockwise around the perimeter of the island, gathering the sheep as we went and finally penning them in a ruined cottage back near the pier. The circuit became a kind of time travel as we encountered the left-afters of many pasts, near and distant, well-remembered and half-forgotten.

As we walked up along the old grass-covered road, the ruined houses, sheds, and garden plots of the eighteenth- to twentieth-century village came into view. This village, the latest phase of permanent settlement on Inishark, was sustained with fishing and farming. Perceivable underfoot and in the variation in grass color were the old spade-dug ridges for sowing rows of potatoes. With quality land at a premium and labor plentiful, the introduction and shifting fortunes of potato cultivation transformed settlement patterns and demographics in the west of Ireland in the eighteenth and nineteenth centuries. There were over two hundred people living on Inishark in 1840, and the footprints of their dwellings and their labor endure. Much of the ground here was improved through human work. Walking along the road through the village, one can see how much higher the ground level is in adjacent fields. Season after season, villagers hauled up and heaped seaweed in their gardens, a practice that added nutrients to depleted soil and gradually increased soil depth.

There were hardly more sheep grazing on Inishark that day than there were people farming at its height in the mid-nineteenth century, but we met only a few stray ewes (pronounced "yoes" here) with their lambs in the village. One group looked down at us from a prominent knoll along the coast. The knoll is topped by a roofless stone hut known as Clochán Leo—"Leo's Stone Dwelling" (fig. 1.4). Leo is the patron saint of Inishark, reportedly the founder of an early medieval monastery on the island and the namesake of many islanders over the years. The medieval church on the island, renovated from a ruin in the 1880s, is dedicated in his name. In the nineteenth century, villagers celebrated St. Leo's Day on April 11 by visiting a series of monuments

Figure 1.4: Clochán Leo, the ruins of an early medieval stone hut associated with Saint Leo. Remnants of the historic village are visible in the background. Photo by Marie Coyne.

associated with him. Clochán Leo was the final stop, where some would pass the night sleeping in the ruined stone hut. Tracing the ritual tradition centered on St. Leo's monuments across different phases of settlement on the island was a focus of my dissertation research. I held my own tradition of sleeping within Clochán Leo at least one night while camping on the island for excavations. During those field seasons, I'd often walk through the village and turn to see the distinctive silhouette of Clochán Leo looming on the horizon. This day, it was backlit by the sun's flickering gold on the ocean. It had no place in our circuit, so we passed on.

At the western end of the village, we entered the old infield once used for rotations of potato and cereal crops. In the twentieth century, the infield was divided into strips, each apportioned to a particular household, with long stone walls running down a slope to the coast. There were many more sheep here, and Tommy and I spaced ourselves out to encourage them to flock as they moved west. From that point onward, the gatherers would have to work out of earshot of one another until the task was nearly done.

As we pushed beyond the infield, we came upon a greater stone wall of a different age and make. Constructed of larger stones atop a sod berm, this wall extends the entire width of the island, enclosing the western prong of Inishark. From a dip in the ground, one can see there was once a ditch on the far side that could have kept in livestock, perhaps for the island's medieval inhabitants. The old ditch has long since silted, and the sheep passed over easily. Beyond the great wall is the village's former outfield commonage of mountain and bog land, scattered about with the remnants of Bronze Age dwellings, burning features, and field walls whose era of use (some 3,200 years ago) seem immeasurably distant. So foreign did they seem to villagers that they were attributed to an ethnic other—the ancient "Danes" (MacLoughlin 1942; NFC 838, 107).

Continuing our circuit, we became the unwelcome "others" to creatures on land and in air. We entered a domain of birds who nested in sea-cliffs and on the dry high points of the outfield. Large black-backed gulls swarmed overhead. Periodically, they would make sudden swoops at the backs of our heads, diving low enough that I could hear the woosh of their wings cutting the air. The great skuas, predatory seabirds, opted for a frontal assault. They sped low at head height in strafing taunts that sometimes brought me to my knees. Afterward, I would gather myself and try again to take stock of the position of the sheep and my companions.

When we reached the westernmost end of the island, the delicate turn of the flock began. We needed to drive them along the northern coast of the island and, eventually, back toward the pier. Simon and John, with their dogs, had stationed themselves in the high ground in the center of the island to prevent the sheep from escaping back along the south. While Tommy kept the sheep moving by pressing on their western flank, I worked my way to the high ground overlooking the north coast. We had all become links in a chain that must move along with one another and with the flock to dissuade them from splitting. The task required a great deal of coordination and mutual awareness among the group. A mishap that split the flock could erase our work and force us to track back again. The further we went, the more we had to lose.

Just as the stakes began to rise along the north coast, the beauty of the day became more distracting. Clear skies and a low sun cast the entire silhouette of Bofin in high relief. The homes and guesthouses there were bright with whitewash. Cars drove across paved roads trailed by power lines. Such amenities are crucial attractions for a lively tourist trade that offers a temporary escape from mundane cares, if not all mundane comforts. Like other Irish islands, Inishbofin is a pocket of low population that makes an outsized contribution to Ireland's domestic economy through tourism.

Nevertheless, capturing government attention and maintaining sufficient public services is a constant campaign. Much of the repair work in the wake of the 2014 storms was undertaken by the islanders themselves. There are EU and Irish subsidies that provide some support for small-scale farming, but also environmental and economic regulations, especially regarding fishing, that deter traditional economies. The dynamic tension that exists everywhere between interconnection and isolation and between dependence and self-sufficiency is especially heightened on islands. In a few hours, one of the day's three ferry runs would bring in tourists from the mainland. Would there be guesthouses on Shark today if the village had endured a little longer and received more government investment? Would there be cars? Would that be better and for whom? Shark is a de facto preserve for rare birds, seals, and the archaeology of post-1800 life that is not officially protected by Ireland's heritage legislation. Even if well-meaning, regulations or development initiatives administered on a wide scale do not always make sense when applied locally. By a fluke of contemporary telecommunications, Shark notoriously offers a better mobile phone signal than most of Bofin. It's a sad irony. Prior to Inishark's evacuation, islanders campaigned for the installation of phone service to connect to the outside world. It never came, and in times of distress, when bound by weather, they had to resort to signal fires on a hilltop.

I wavered between appreciating the vantage of Inishbofin, keeping track of the sheep and gatherers, and finding secure footing in the uneven and boggy land. I usually wore an old pair of sneakers during farm work and had a tendency, amusing to my companions, of soaking my feet in disregard of bog or tide. "He's worse than the Buff," they would joke, alluding to a Bofin man that they had worked with when they were young. Nicknamed "the Buff" (short for Buffalo), Stephen Lavelle was a big, hardy man famous for always finding an excuse to get his feet wet during work. He had no children, but my companions recall him fondly among the generation above their own.

As our circuit turned south again, we entered the infield on the eastern side of the village. Now the advantage turned. At this point in the familiar circuit, old pathways, stone walls, and sheds came out of retirement. Ruin became infrastructure as dogs, gatherers, sheep, and stone walls entered into a new ensemble. The dogs sprinted alongside the flock, circling, withdrawing, pressing. The gatherers sometimes stood fast, sometimes spoke and walked calmly with their hands folded behind their backs. At other times, when the sheep were stubborn or bold, we thrusted out our arms, whistled, yipped, and hollered. I tried to keep to the top of the grass-covered field walls to seem more imposing to the flock and to keep a better vantage on the sheep and gatherers. Moving sheep here was like dancing with a hundred recalcitrant partners, with gatherers and sheep constantly recalibrating angles of engagement, vying for an advantage of position that would influence the movement of the whole. The sheep, albeit wilder than most, gradually fell into larger and larger groups until all were

Figure 1.5: Near the end of a gather in 2017 (step 5, map 0.1).

Figure 1.6: Christy Concannon and his dog driving sheep toward the village on Inishark in 1964. The island was evacuated only four years earlier. While the roof of the church had been removed, many of the houses remained habitable, and farmers would spend a few days on Shark to shear all the sheep and collect the wool. Photo by John Reader.

gathered into a continuous body. Huddling and hurrying on, they bleated a din and wended their way between tripartite hazards—the small, swift beasts; the tall, slow beasts; and the long stone ridges that never budge (figs. 1.5, 1.6).

At last, we returned to the main road leading up from the pier. The old grass-covered stone walls that lined the road were topped by wire fencing to prevent the sheep from hurtling. An enclosed segment of this road would act as our corral. As we closed in on the sheep, they filtered into a gap in the wire fence. Once all were in, we closed the gap behind us and exhaled collectively.

The next order of business was lunch, and the first topic of conversation was sheep. How many had been lost since winter... Did any escape the gather?... Did you see those brown-faced ewe lambs?... Do they belong to your ewe?... They're fine beasts....

Lunch was sandwiches, biscuits, potato crisps, confectionary, and soft drinks. As we settled in, the conversation switched from sheep to reminiscing about former trips to Shark and, eventually, the great characters from the islands known from living memory or oral tradition (fig. 1.6). As is so often the case, the conversation became a string of anecdotes. Linked one after the other by a uniting character or theme, most shared the same structure: an odd setting or scenario culminating in a memorably witty turn of phrase. I got the impression that virtually all of these stories were well-known to all—even I had heard one or two before in pubs on Bofin—but they recited them anyway with deftness and delight. These stories are means of identity-making and score-keeping, and not everyone comes out well. Who was clever, who was foolish, who generous, who mean, who a great worker, who slack? An emerging theme that day was the loss of fingers, and the final story about a man describing his injury over the phone to his wife finished with a brilliant, inadvertent pun.

As we regained our energy and one last story came to an end, we began the next task. We drove a portion of the sheep up the road into another area enclosed by wire and metal gates (fig. 1.7). Within the enclosure was a ruined two-room house whose long wall fronted the road (fig. 1.8). Decay and the aid of human hands had widened the door opening in the wall of the house. The two front windows on either side of the door were blocked up with stones from the surrounding field walls. We forced in as many sheep as would squeeze into the house and pulled a wooden pallet across the door opening. Within, decayed plaster, still showing the faintest signs of hand-painted decoration, clung to the walls. Here and there were streaks of the red, blue, and green spray paint that farmers used to mark the sheep after shearing. The floor was dirt, the original surface long since covered with accumulated sheep dung. In 2016, this was one of the few early twentieth-century houses on the island with a roof almost entirely intact. Even so, the walls were coated in dark brown mildew. In the chaos of the crowd, two sheep worked their way into the fireplace. They stood stark still with

Figure 1.7: Sheep gathered within the pen outside the Lacey House. The pointed gables of Teampaill Leo, St. Leo's Church, stand in the background (2016).

their heads obscured up the flu. The "chimney sweeps," as they were soon dubbed, were surreal and sad. It was around this hearth, like many in the village, that food had been prepared, tea enjoyed, visitors entertained, joys celebrated, and sorrows endured. It was in this house that Thomas Lacey had remained for one night on his own after the other islanders had evacuated the island on October 20, 1960. He had lost two sons and a nephew in a drowning accident on Easter Sunday eleven years earlier and spent that final night alone mourning their loss and the loss of his home. For the next six hours, it was to keep us out of the sun while the men from Inishbofin sheared and I did my best to help out by fetching and marking the sheep and then packing their fleeces (fig. 1.9).

Figure 1.8: The Lacey House outfitted as a sheep pen (2016).

As the work proceeded, I began to recognize how much more the house offered besides shade. The lintel above the door was a shelf, keeping bottles of 7UP and sheep dip clean and ready to hand (fig. 1.10). The blocked-in front windows allowed enough space for the cord of Simon's electric shears to reach his petrol-powered generator that we had brought from Inishbofin. Meanwhile, the sills of these windows held spray cans and the metal hand-shears when not in use. A wooden pallet that blocked off the second room to the right of the fireplace allowed us to quarantine two rams that would return with us to Bofin.

This cycle of use and reuse is an old story on the islands. Before St. Leo's Church was renovated in the 1880s, islanders used the collapsing medieval shell as a cattle

Figure 1.9: John Burke hand shearing in the Lacey House while Simon Murray, aided by his son Caolán, uses an electric shears powered by his generator brought to the island (2016).

pen. After the island's abandonment, the local priest ordered the roof removed. This may have been done to officially desacralize the building and discourage a return to the island. It had one other unforeseen consequence: storm-battered sheep have preferrd to take shelter in the old houses with their roofs at least partially intact. Over the years, this has meant that layers of sheep feces have accumuleted to a greater extent on the floors of the houses while the concrete floor of the church has remained relatively clear. It was for this reason that our archaeological field team had used the church in previous years to pitch portable canopies for the camp kitchen. For a long

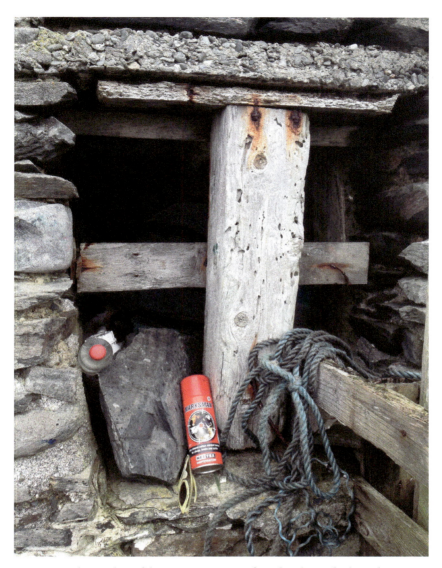

Figure 1.10: The window of the Lacey House, reinforced with wood salvaged from an old pallet, becomes a convenient shelf. Farmers often joke they would be lost without salvaging the wood from pallets and the twine from hay bales to build impromptu enclosures.

Figure 1.11: Outside the western window of the Lacey House, Toby rests after his part in the gathering taskscape has ended. A jut of green, Clochán Leo breaks the plain of the horizon just to the left of the roofless ruined house.

time here, and in more ways than one, people have converted ruined infrastructure into an infrastructure of ruins.

After an hour or so, we finished processing the first batch of sheep in the house. After we dosed and castrated the lambs, we would drive a new batch of sheep into the house and repeat the cycle. Contemplating the hours of work before us, I bent to gather a fleece from the dirt, and the sun through the rear window caught my eye. Squinting, I saw Clochán Leo on its knoll, still a ruin, still looming (fig. 1.11).

—⁂—

We tend to describe ruins by what they cannot do. A house built to shelter a family becomes a ruin when it can no longer carry out that function. Ruins are former infrastructure more durable than the ensemble of people, animals, plants, and tasks they were built to sustain. And yet, ruins are constantly finding their way into new ensembles. This book is about the making and remaking of such ensembles. Drawing from fifteen years of archaeological and ethnographic research on Inishark and Inishbofin, I hope to show what ruins can do.

My approach is grounded in the view that human lives are intimately and unavoidably enmeshed with the lives of others—not just other humans but other-than-human animals, plants, environmental forces, and even inanimate materials. In recent years, a diverse body of theory often classified as "posthumanism" has exerted its influence across the social sciences and humanities (Bennett 2009; Cipolla et al. 2022; Ferrando 2019). This work challenges fundamental assumptions of human exceptionalism—that is, our supposed distinction as agents par excellence, the supreme doers, thinkers, and feelers who exert our agency on "lesser" life-forms and on the dull, inanimate matter of the world. Living amid climate crises and global pandemics makes the flaws of this kind of thinking impossible to ignore. But even a closer look at the prosaic daily tasks of maintaining livelihoods can lay bare the follies of anthropocentrism.

Take the circuit described above. One useful concept for analyzing our work that day is taskscape. The term was coined by Tim Ingold (1993), but I will take some liberties with his original formation. Taskscape is a spin on landscape. If landscapes are collections of interlocking features, taskscapes are collections of interlocking actions. We encounter small-scale taskscapes every day without fail, if not without failure. Indeed, we become particularly aware of taskscapes when they break down. Anyone who has helped young children get ready for school after a snoozed alarm, endured a broke-down vehicle on a road trip, or kept a garden in a drought knows the feeling. One small oversight, poorly timed action, unwise word, faulty piece of equipment, or change in the weather can have repercussions that ripple outward and inhibit our capacities to achieve desired ends. Human action is always caught up in an interplay of more-than-human factors. Islanders who work by sea, season, weather, and tide appreciate this better than most.

We can also think about taskscapes on a broader scale, as the whole collection of actions and elements that make human dwelling on the landscape possible. Although some elements of landscapes are relatively durable, landscapes are constantly in the process of becoming, constantly shaped by sequences of actions that occur over different timescales. Tasks undertaken by humans are not alone in shaping landscapes, even if we sometimes exert outsized capacities in transforming them. Various climatic, hydrological, and geological processes render the earth and impinge on the actions, perceptions, and livelihoods of humans and animals (Ingold 1993, 163–64). The fall of rain, the growth of grass, the grazing and defecating of sheep, the development of roundworm larvae within sheep feces, the control of worm burden with medication, the modification of ruined buildings for gathering and shearing sheep, and the maintenance of pastoral and maritime skills are all actions, among many others, that afford a particular pattern of human dwelling on the islands today. As an anthropologist, I see it as my goal to understand "the tasks of human dwelling in their proper context within the process of becoming of the world as a whole" (Ingold 1993, 164).

So where does this leave our ruins? Ruins are more than the leftovers of defunct taskscapes. Ruins can give life to new and altered forms of dwelling. The work of human livelihood is constantly in flux. Even the most hallowed traditions and the necessary cycles of food production are intermittently and unpredictably affected by new conditions. This dynamism is the inevitable outcome of interlocked tasks dependent on a wide range of beings, materials, and environmental phenomena both near and far. Imagine how the tasks of gathering sheep change in foul weather or with a collapsed field wall or with a gate left open or with an untrained dog (or untrained American PhD student). Within dwelling taskscapes, the potential for wavering between infrastructure and ruin is great. More often than not, humans enlist ruins into reconfigured taskscapes. This is evident in the way that former village infrastructure on Inishark periodically facilitates the gathering of sheep. More distinctively, on Inishark ruin is latent infrastructure at the particle scale. Most of the island's structures are made from common building blocks—irregular mica schist stones. The history of the village on Inishark could be told in part by tracing the constant reassembly of its infrastructure by recycling slabs from abandoned houses to new walls and from redundant walls to new houses.

There are other less obvious ways in which ruins become new infrastructure. The physical presence (or absence) of ruins affects our capacity to remember (or forget) the past (Beiner 2013, 32; Gordillo 2014; Trouillot 1995; Van Dyke 2019; Whelan 2004). It matters a great deal to islanders and visitors to Inishbofin that the ruins of Inishark are still there, still carving the silhouette of the island to the west. Their presence evokes the generations of neighbors and relations that lived there and the circumstances of the island's evacuation. For Bofiners, the ruins of Shark are a reminder of that ever-looming threat of depopulation. As Simon Murray put it in his presentation before the Oireachtas in 2021, Inishark is "the shadow that stalks us all the time, the possibility of the lights going out on another island."

Just like infrastructure in active use, ruins can shape human habits of thought, commemoration, affiliation, and cooperation. In the expedition described above, the tasks of gathering consisted of a series of actions in sequence that relied on both material infrastructure (i.e., the fence lines and repurposed cottage) and social relations (i.e., collaboration and coordination among gatherers and dogs to elicit desired movements among sheep). From this perspective, the telling of old stories cued by the ruins is arguably a vital component of the gathering taskscape. Along with the reciprocal exchange of conviviality in pubs on Inishbofin, these stories reiterate the relationships of friendship, kinship, mutual obligation, and shared history and identity that islanders activate in collaborative tasks. Even with the renovated infrastructure in place, the gathering expedition is not possible without the simple willingness of my companions to work together. Work needs a will and a way. The modification of the ruined village provides the infrastructural means of gathering. The memories that the ruins evoke help to provide the will.

This book builds from these core observations about ruins and works to examine the relationship between material things, heritage, and community endurance. The taskscape of gathering described here is just one component of a larger taskscape of dwelling, a collection of practices that sustains the livelihoods of Inishbofin islanders. As I have applied a taskscape analysis to the gathering expedition, this study applies a taskscape analysis to examine community endurance on the islands. Endurance is possible when material infrastructure exists that facilitates both the social relationships and practical tasks necessary for community members to make a living. My central questions are these: How can material things—and especially material heritage—act as infrastructure within dwelling taskscapes? How can heritage cultivate perceptions of belonging that make a community's livelihood socially, economically, and politically feasible?

To address these questions, I will examine three separate phases of settlement on the islands: the medieval ecclesiastical settlement on Inishark (c. 600–1300), the modern village settlement on Inishark (c. 1750–1960), and contemporary settlement on Inishbofin (c. 2014–23). Though separated by centuries, people living in each period engaged with the material traces left by previous dwellers and, in turn, left (and continue to leave) material traces for future generations. What links each period is the recursive rendering of inherited landscapes into new dwelling taskscapes, the assembly of new materials, and the conversion of old ruins into active infrastructure. Heritage exists in the present and addresses the future but in some way carries over from the past. Heritage, as I understand it, includes both materials—ruins—and the embodied knowledge and skill that emanate from engagement with those materials. Tracing the creation, maintenance, and adaptation of heritage to different dwelling taskscapes across time is the thread that links my analyses of early medieval monasticism, nineteenth-century pilgrimage, and contemporary heritage tourism and pastoralism.

This book proceeds as follows: Chapter 2 positions this study in its historiographic and theoretical context. I begin by tracing the history and intellectual genealogy of primitivist tropes in anthropology and in writing about western Ireland in particular. I then describe how engagements with postcolonial thought, indigenous perspectives, memory theory, and posthumanism help to better scrutinize cultural change and persistence across time, particularly with reference to Irish pilgrimage traditions. Building from these insights, I define a taskscape approach and argue how the concept can reframe discussions of primitive persistence into more nuanced and productive analyses of dynamic endurance and creative heritage.

The empirical backbone of this book, chapter 3 offers a virtual tour of the monuments associated with Saint Leo on Inishark. This overview draws together my own archival research with surveys and excavation conducted with colleagues on the Cultural Landscapes of the Irish Coast (CLIC) project, directed by Dr. Ian Kuijt. For each monument, I provide an account of its appearance in the landscape today, an analysis of relevant archaeological and historical evidence, and a summary of its use and development across time. I reserve special attention for Clochán Leo. Among all the monuments on Inishark, excavations here provide the most detailed chronology of periodic activity, hiatus, and renovation stretching from the early medieval period into the twentieth century. Indeed, the site offers among the most significant records of the development of a modern *an turas* "pilgrimage" tradition from the left-afters of early medieval devotion.

Building on the data presented in chapter 3, chapters 4 and 5 apply a taskscape approach to consider how St. Leo's monuments framed experience, evoked the past, and fostered different social and economic relations across many centuries. The foundation of this analysis is identifying how the use of monuments changed across time—as centers of veneration and healing, as respected or forgotten landmarks, and even, in some cases, as sources of stone to be recycled into new buildings. Throughout, I will employ premises gathered from historic texts and folklore to consider how the material characteristics of monuments in the landscape channeled capacities for movement, interaction, memory, and affiliation among people living, working, and worshipping on Inishark. As far as is possible, I will track how transformations in the use of monuments correlate across time to changes in the island's dwelling taskscape, particularly the methods, political context, and social organization of agricultural production.

Chapter 4 considers the monastic settlement on Inishark (seventh to thirteenth centuries). During this period, a monastic community designed monuments to accommodate their daily devotions as well as the devotions of lay pilgrims. Examining excavation evidence alongside hagiographic texts, I attempt to reconstruct the material settings, spatial dynamics, and embodied experiences of medieval ritual. Evidence for the use of natural objects—especially water-worn beach pebbles—suggests that encounters with environmental forces represented a crucial aspect of ritual practice. I will argue that pebbles evoked the divine governance of the natural world and highlighted the shared devotional aspirations of monks and pilgrims to be rendered spiritually by God. Nevertheless, the form, configuration, and regulation of access to ritual monuments also reinforced the sacred status and authority of monastic men. By channeling worshipers' movements, commemorations, and access to sacred objects, monks positioned themselves as mediators of sanctity and salvation. Such a status allowed monks to leverage their claim to the agricultural labor and produce of affiliated lay clients. In short, medieval devotional practices engaged cosmologies while supporting the particular socio-economic relationships required by the monastic community's agro-pastoral regime.

Chapter 5 considers the afterlife of monastic ruins on Inishark in the modern period (seventeenth to twentieth centuries). Despite a dearth of surviving evidence for settlement activity on Inishark between the thirteenth and eighteenth centuries, periodic reengagement with ruined monuments carried forward some knowledge of the island's monastic heritage. As the island was resettled in the late eighteenth century as a fishing and farming village, islanders incorporated the ruins of St. Leo's monastery as focal points in annual communal celebrations of St. Leo's Day (April 11) and in periodic performances of private devotion. Fragments of nineteenth- and twentieth-century folklore stigmatize the destruction or misuse of Leo's monuments—whether simply by recycling stone for building material or by weaponizing their supernatural power against neighbors. I suggest that the villagers' collective curation of Leo's monuments buttressed a system of collective agricultural and land tenure that prevailed on the island until the mid-nineteenth century. In the later nineteenth century, visits from a parish priest became more regular, and the restored medieval church became the new venue of officially sanctioned communal ritual. Nevertheless, islanders continued to venerate Clochán Leo, which they visited periodically, sometimes holding picnics that redeployed the familiar foodways and ceramic wares of household hospitality. Despite the erosion of collective agriculture and the decline of the pilgrimage tradition, islanders found new ways of generating experiences of social resonance and belonging.

Differences in the quality and resolution of evidence between the medieval and historic period will naturally impact the conclusions I can draw from each era. Nevertheless, what will become clear is the dynamism of the tradition of St. Leo's veneration and its associated ritual practices. In the medieval and modern periods, ritual monuments played a role in defining the heritage of communities that sustained—at least for a time—viable dwelling taskscapes amid extreme environmental conditions and political economic adversity. Islanders in the twentieth century could not overcome the economic and environmental constraints that led to the evacuation of Inishark, but creative heritage played an important role in making the village's difficult and dangerous dwelling taskscape socially feasible for nearly two centuries.

In chapter 6, I return to Inishbofin to consider the role of heritage within islanders' continuing efforts to endure. I juxtapose the insights of my archaeological analysis with participant observation of heritage tourism and small-scale pastoralism on Inishbofin in recent years. The stable—and thus far sustainable—model of tourism that islanders have developed is based on annual extended stays by repeat visitors. As with monks and pilgrims in the early medieval period, the relationship between locals and tourists is characterized by both integration and distinction. Material heritage once again provides part of the necessary infrastructure for maintaining social and economic relationships amid and between islanders and visitors. I argue that various forms of heritage tourism on Inishbofin accentuate visitors' sense of belonging and shared experience with islanders, which in turn supports the pattern of extended stays by familiar visitors year after year. However, the tourist market simultaneously incentivizes and complicates local engagements with heritage and the viability of islanders' livelihoods. Tourist traffic and conservation regulations can complicate the practice of small-scale pastoral farming. An important source of income to sustain year-round residence on the island, subsidized farming can also play a significant role in the stewardship of the island's cultural and ecological heritage.

In chapter 7, I review this book's principal findings and consider how they resonate with recent developments, including Covid-19 and the highly publicized campaign to repatriate human remains stolen from Bofin in 1890 and kept subsequently in the Old Anatomy Department of Trinity College Dublin. I close by considering some wider implications. I suggest that taskscape analyses can effectively confront primitivist tropes by revealing how people creatively adapt their heritage to changing circumstances, using the past to foster continuity as well as transformation. Ironically, it is precisely the creativity of heritage that can present the illusion of timelessness. More generally, to approach questions of sustainability, we need theoretical frameworks that allow our focus to oscillate between posthumanist premises and humanist empathy for the lived experiences of individuals. A shifting perspective, I suggest, is necessary to build analyses that attend to other-than-human forces without obscuring realities of inequality and the potential human costs of sustainability initiatives. This theoretical point comes with an obvious methodological corollary: the capacity to synthesize multiple perspectives demands active collaboration with a wide variety of stakeholders. When researchers and policymakers consider future heritage policy and agri-environmental planning for islands, the perspectives and priorities of islanders must be at the heart of the decision-making process. Islanders have at once the most intimate knowledge of island landscapes and the most at stake in their futures.

There will be, I hope, valid lessons in tracing historical trajectories over long timescales with a mixture of archaeological and ethnographic research methods. Creative heritage—by making the past present in ways that generate social resonance, belonging, and innovation—can be an essential aspect of sustainability and one that anthropologists should explore in the past and present.

TWO

DYNAMIC ENDURANCE AND CREATIVE HERITAGE

A Taskscape Approach

INISHBOFIN, SEPTEMBER 2016. THE WHITE COW AND THE CROOKED MOUTH.

Names hold memories. The name Inishbofin is transliterated from Irish, Inis Bó Finne—"Island of the White Cow." *According to one version of a local legend, in ancient days the island was enchanted, shrouded in mist and meandering in the ocean, unknown and unfastened to the world. Then one day, two fishermen lost their way in the fog and found themselves beside a rock, whereupon they landed and lit a fire. The flames burnt away the mist and the enchantment, revealing the island and finally fixing it in place. It was not the end of magic. The fisherman had landed on a narrow, rocky belt of land with the ocean on one side and a lake on the other. As the darkness lifted, they beheld the approach of a hag, driving a white cow before her. She forced the animal all the way into the lake and struck it with a stick, and the cow was immediately turned into a rock. Objecting to what he had seen, one of the fisherman confronted the woman and struck her a blow in rage, and at once, she and he were likewise turned into stones. The lake and the island thereafter took their names from the white cow.*

Variants of this legend disagree on which and how many characters turned to stone and entered the lake (Browne 1893, 36; Concannon 1997, 1; MacLoughlin 1942, NFC 838, 426). There is no parallel legend to explain the name of Inishark—Inis Airc—nor even agreement on the name's meaning (Mac Gabhann 2014, 710; Neary 1920, 221). The legend of the white cow may seem strange—in 1942 the visiting folklorist Brían MacLoughlin deemed it with some derision "the well-conceived story of some local half-wit" (1942, NFC 838, 426). MacLoughlin is half-right. Whatever its origins and author, in imagery and plot, the legend conjures a series of oppositions—between seen and unseen, fixed and unfixed, settled and unsettled, known and unknown, named and unnamed. It is the imaginative interplay of these oppositions that gives the legend an enduring resonance. To know is to name, and to name is to remember. In this regard at least, so long as the legend circulates, it proves itself true.

My plan in the fall of 2016 was to remain on Inishbofin through the end of the year and use the quiet, dark days of winter to finish our team's excavation reports and begin writing my dissertation. I rented the Tower Cottage, so named because it stands adjacent to a nineteenth-century navigation tower along the lower strand of the island's main ring road. A second tower stands farther upslope behind the cottage. The towers were positioned to aid boat handlers in finding the safest approach into the harbor. When at the helm, you align your course with the towers, which will to your eyes appear to stack, one atop the other. You make a temporary constellation of these fixed marks and your own wandering craft to find the clear line that avoids the hazards of submerged rocks at the harbor mouth.

But "Tower Cottage" is a relatively new name, applied after its conversion from a farm building into a rental cottage for visitors. Such places on Bofin often retain the names of the last people who used or dwelt in them. And so, to those who know, I was sitting in Josie's Barn, failing to summon that focused stupor of writing, when Tommy came by and asked if I wanted to go "for a spin." Himself, John, and Simon had spent the afternoon ferrying weaned lambs from the old pier on Bofin to Davillaun, an uninhabited island to the east. Davillaun (Damhoileán, "Ox Island") is high, dry, and thick full with grass. The remnants of a large stone enclosure and hut structures suggest that herdsmen and women may have managed livestock there as far back as the early medieval period. For my friends that day, there was only one more run left to make on a fine evening, with not many left to enjoy in the dwindling year. As the crow flies, Davillaun is only two kilometers from the nearest point on Bofin (map 0.2). Our voyage was much longer—by boat, one has to navigate the contours of coastal footprints and the restless waters that made their shape. Simon brought his timber currach accompanied by Tommy, and I went with John in his aluminum fishing boat.

When mapping travel or geographic relationships, islanders have a distinctive way of assigning prepositions to directions of movement. In conversation, Inishbofin islanders may speak of being "in the island" or "on the island" somewhat interchangeably, but when it comes to travel, the prescribed usage is clear: you come "in" to the island and go "out" to the mainland. Each of the cardinal directions likewise has a standard preposition. Our journey to Davillaun took us "back" (west) to exit the harbor, then "over" (east) along the south coast of Bofin past the farthest reach of Inishlyon (Inis Laighean, "Spear Island"), then "down" (north) to Davillaun. With the lambs aboard, it took the better part of an hour to reach the landing cove at Davillaun (fig. 2.1). I hopped from boat to shore and pulled the bowline. My friends had timed the task on the flowing tide to ease the transfer of lambs to land. Now at

Figure 2.1: John Burke and Rebel returning from Davillaun, their passengers safely grazing ashore (2021).

nearly high tide, the lambs, with some little encouragement, ran onto the rocky shore without stirring much salt water.

We took off from the cove, never having tied down or shut off the outboard motors. Weeks earlier, John and Simon's nephew Luke had set out from this spot with about twenty hoggets aboard. Hoggets are sheep between one and two years old and, notoriously, a little wild. Midway on the journey back to Bofin, one sheep had panicked and jumped out of the boat—and six others followed. I had the story from Luke afterward. John, on the till of the outboard motor at stern, had coolly maneuvered the now ill-balanced boat to each of the floundering sheep, then lifted them—and the extra pounds of water in their sodden wool—over the gunwale. At each lift, Luke had to counterbalance the boat and prevent it from capsizing by leaning his weight over the gunwale opposite John. They retrieved every hogget. John's words to Luke when they finally got to shore: "That was fucking dodgy boy."

Our return journey was simpler, though memorable to me. As I watched the currach tear off to retrace the route we had taken east of Inishlyon, John steered his boat toward the eastern coast of Bofin. In the open water, he suddenly idled the motor and left the boat to drift calmly while he took his time to roll a cigarette, his back curled to cradle it from the wind. When he turned the throttle again, to my surprise, he continued a direct course toward Bofin. As we continued, I recalled a place-name Tommy had taught me—Béal Cam, "the crooked mouth," a particular gap between the chain of rocks in the intertidal zone that extends from Bofin to Lyon. The water here can be shallow enough for a boat to bottom out, and the mouth is navigable only when the tide is right. I turned back to John and he smiled in the comfort of a fresh cigarette and a shortcut. I wouldn't have guessed the line of approach through the gap in a thousand tries. No navigation towers here, but subtler cues in angles of rock and water. As we neared the chain of rocks, John turned the boat sharply and directly toward one of the larger exposed rock faces and then idled the motor, and we slowed to the speed of conserved momentum. Just as the bow looked like it might kiss the face of the rock, he turned the till sharply again and twisted the throttle to pull us through the gap without a scrape on side or bottom. We had made a kind of Z maneuver that had cut out a third of the time of our homeward journey. The experience remains in my memory as a gift, a marvel of heritage enacted. To find this path was beyond John's individual intuition. It was the achievement of generations of knowing, naming, and remembering. It was experience shared, passed down, and now put to use in a performance of embodied skill: to know the dance of hand, throttle, craft, rock, tide, and time to chance a cut through a pathless sea.

—⁂—

Outsiders have long viewed rural western Ireland as a place unmoved by the currents of time—a kind of cultural preserve to behold people and practices that have not endured elsewhere. For an anthropologist, to discuss heritage in western Ireland is to call forth the old familiar ghouls that stalk the history of the discipline—colonial ideology, religious prejudice, social evolutionary theory, scientific racism, and romantic nationalism (Egan and Murphy 2015, 134–35). Each of these intellectual traditions has cast the Irish, whether in admiration or disdain, as primitive. One of the goals of this book is to shake off primitivist tropes and reframe patterns of endurance as products of creative heritage.

The concept of taskscape facilitates this rethinking. A taskscape approach forefronts how human livelihoods and lived experiences emerge from our existence within a world of interdependent beings, materials, and environmental forces. The shoreline of Inishbofin, like all the world we inhabit, comprises elements that in human eyes seem remarkably stable and others that appear incomprehensibly variable. As such, the endurance of any phenomenon—whether a stone, a place-name, a shortcut, or a social formation—is necessarily a dynamic process wherein the enduring thing must address a world perpetually in motion. Against a stiff current, a boat may appear stable on the surface of the water, but beneath, the propeller is spinning mightily to hold the position. Likewise, the illusion of timelessness and primitive survival is sustained by a hidden dynamism: the creativity of heritage.

What is heritage? The episode above offers many possible examples—legends, place-names and naming customs, conventional directional prepositions, enduring monuments, and embodied skills. In an expansive view, heritage includes all that may be inherited from the past into the present. Heritage comprises the material remains of the past, the conventional practices that descend from or engage the past, and the shared embodied knowledge generated from those engagements. In other words, heritage emerges from and in turn shapes human participation in taskscapes. Though heritage develops from a past context, it can offer material or conceptual frameworks for addressing the present in all of its unpredictable variability. This is where the possibility for creativity in heritage lies—in guiding us to find a useful resonance between past experience and new conditions. John was no fossil. He worked in London when he was young and fished salmon off Alaska in his fifties. He knew the names of countless landmarks around Bofin's shoreline and how they appear and disappear with the tide. But he also knew how to work GPS apps on his phone when the fog was too heavy even for all his tricks. The maintenance of heritage need not fix one in anachronism. Rather, it can show us how to find a dance with the old steps for new tempos and unfamiliar melodies.

Before we explore this alternative framework, we must first confront some stubborn ideas that won't stay quiet in the grave. This chapter begins with a review of primitivist tropes in the history of writing and scholarship about Ireland.

Irish pilgrimage traditions in particular will demonstrate the challenges at play in deciphering patterns of continuity and change across time. Building on postcolonial and so-called posthumanist approaches, I will then better define my use of taskscape and suggest how it can help to model the dynamism of endurance and the creativity of heritage.

FAMILIAR GHOULS—PREMISES OF IRISH PRIMITIVISM

In one form or another across time, the trope of the primitive and savage other has proved a favorite excuse for inexcusable colonial violence, dispossession, and inequality (Said 1978; Spivak 1985). At its base, the trope is a form of essentialism that ascribes an archaic character and an incapacity for change to some group of "others." European colonialism of the fifteenth to twentieth centuries led to the propagation of this trope on a global scale and its intellectual crystallization as the basis for scientific disciplines concerned with human variation throughout time and across the globe (Launay 2018; Trigger 1997, 110–45). The case of the Irish can shed light on both the prehistory of primitivist colonial tropes and the ideological legacies that continue to disfigure understandings of heritage and endurance.

The development of primitivist ideas about Ireland maps onto the distinctive political history of the island, which was at various times occupied by, incorporated into, and partially liberated from more powerful dynasties and imperial polities centered in Britain. As many scholars have noted, Ireland fits somewhat oddly alongside other postcolonial nations (Carroll and King 2003; Flannery 2007; Horning 2013; Said 2003; Scanlon and Kumar 2019). The complexity and ambiguity of Anglo-Irish relations across time means that the processes and legacies of colonial discourse and dispossession both parallel and diverge from colonial dynamics in Africa, Asia, Australia, and the Americas. Stated plainly, though people with Irish ancestry were at various times victims of colonialism, they and their diaspora have also participated in colonial projects and slave economies as soldiers, settlers, overseers, and slave owners (Draper 2013; Hussain et al. 2025; O'Kane and O'Neill 2023; Rodgers 2007; Wright 2019). This mixed experience of subjugation by, struggle against, and collusion with colonial projects can diverge in important ways from the experiences of people of color who were—and often remain—more systematically and enduringly oppressed by regimes of capitalist extraction and white supremacy. Yet, there remains some validity in comparing and contrasting how tropes of primitivism operated in writings about the Irish alongside other indigenous and colonized groups. Rather than simply drawing an equivalency, the juxtaposition helps to delineate more finely the different legacies of colonial and racist discourse around the world. It might also contribute to anticolonial political solidarity based on analogous, though not equivalent, histories of racialization and otherization (Power et al. 2017; Sackett 2021; White 2023).

The trope of Irish primitivism goes as far back as the conquest of areas of eastern Ireland by Anglo-Norman lords in the late twelfth century. In the *Topographia Hibernica* (Topography of Ireland), Gerald of Wales, a Cambro-Norman ecclesiastic and apologist for the invasion of Ireland, depicted the Irish as barbarous and stalled in an archaic state of social development. His writings prefigure a fundamental assumption echoed in later writings about the Irish and other indigenous groups around the world: that the persistence of older forms of social organization and technology betray an inescapable stasis, a lack of capacity for the kind of civilization cultivated by invaders. "In the common course of things, mankind progresses from the forest to the field, from the field to the town, and to the social condition of citizens; but this nation, holding agricultural labour in contempt, and little coveting the wealth of towns, as well as being exceeding averse to civil institutions—lead the same life as their fathers did in the woods and open pastures, neither willing to abandon their old habits or learn anything new" (Forester 2000, 70).

Later writers took up similar themes to justify subsequent phases of colonial endeavors. Edmund Spencer's *A Vewe of the Present State of Irelande*, written in 1598 but not published until 1633, speaks to the era of renewed conquest and plantations under Tudor and Stewart dynasties. Spencer deemed the Irish, in their ancestry and customs, "the most barbarous Nation in Christendome"; reckoned that the descendants of Anglo-Norman settlers, the "Old English," had degenerated in their adoption of Irish ways; and suggested that the desolation of famine would offer the means of finally bringing the Irish to submission (Hadfield and Maley 1997). From the sixteenth century, English conquests in Ireland took on a new religious dimension in the wake of the Reformation of the English church. The Catholicism of the native Irish and the Old English set them in opposition to the ambitions of the Tudor rulers in England and in accord with England's Catholic rivals on the continent. Oppression of Irish Catholics became particularly severe during the Cromwellian invasion of Ireland in the mid-seventeenth century (see chap. 5). Interestingly, one plank of anti-Catholic critique posited a primitivist interpretation of popular Catholic devotions. Writing in the early eighteenth century, John Richardson, a Protestant rector from County Cavan, explained Irish Catholic pilgrimage focused on holy wells and springs as a relic of prehistoric paganism (Richardson 1727, 163). This ancient heritage of idolatry persisted, he claimed, because the backward and superstitious Catholic church had failed to repudiate it.

Obviously, scholars have explored whether English colonial endeavors in sixteenth- and seventeenth-century Ireland provided practical or ideological models for initiatives in the new world (Canny 1998; Horning 2013). Ideologically, colonists in both contexts could certainly deem indigenous people as primitive, savage, and heathen. However, as Horning's detailed assessment of the archaeological and historical evidence shows, parallel tropes of primitivism did not translate to equivalent realities of interaction. Compared to Native American groups, the Gaelic Irish's Christianity (however maligned by Protestant colonists) and deep history of cultural exchange with Britain afforded greater opportunity for hybridization and accommodation alongside brutal violence (Horning 2013, 353–55).

Despite important distinctions in application, colonial stereotypes about the Irish and other indigenous groups were mutually influential. Views of Irish primitivism were reinforced and reframed by scientific theories generated amid colonial encounters between Europeans and indigenous people with vastly different forms of social organization, technology, and cosmology. Nineteenth-century theories of social evolution depicted indigenous societies and European colonial powers as, respectively, the most primitive and most advanced stages of human social evolution. Indigenous groups were conceived as living fossils, stuck in a primitive stage of human evolution from which Western colonial societies—industrialized, capitalist, Christian, and raced as white—had long ago advanced. This social evolutionary framework became the common theoretical denominator of the nascent disciplines of anthropology, archaeology, and folklore (Johnson 2019, 180–200; Lucas 2012, 19–24; Trigger 1997, 110–45). The material culture, lifeways, kinship networks, and even physiologies of certain groups were all deemed "survivals" that could be used to interpret the distant past (Gazin-Schwartz and Holtorf 1999, 7–9). In short, early social evolutionism glossed cultural difference as temporal distance.

The emerging science of race spun a similar deception, by dividing the continuous spectrum of phenotypic variation into discrete categories that could themselves be plotted on a hierarchy of archaic to evolved. The most extreme theories posited wholly separate origins for different races (Blakey 2020, S183). Craniometrics—measuring skulls—became a favored method within early anthropology for delineating racial categories and origins, even into the twentieth century (Gravlee et al. 2003; see Blakey 1987 and 2020 for the role of American anthropology in buttressing racial inequality). Yet, already in the mid-nineteenth century, Frederick Douglass (1854) recognized how the dubious logic of race science, so evidently contorted by prejudice, offered justification for the institution of slavery. Interestingly, Douglass compared the appearance of the

Irish poor with enslaved African American plantation workers to repudiate contemporary perceptions of race. Douglass had traveled to Ireland for four months in 1845–46, on the eve of the catastrophic failure of the potato crop in 1847 (Kinealy 2021). Among the crowds of common people that came to Douglass's speeches, there was already sufficient destitution to leave an impression on his mind: "Never did human faces tell a sadder tale. More than five thousand were assembled; and I say, with not wish to wound the feelings of any Irishman, that these people lacked only a black skin and woolly hair, to complete their likeness to the plantation negro. The open, uneducated mouth—the long, gaunt arm—the badly formed foot and ankle—the shuffling gait—the retreating forehead and vacant expression—and their petty quarrels and fights—all remined me of the plantation, and my own cruelly abused people" (Douglass 1854, 30–31).

The point of Douglass's comparison is to illustrate that physical traits and behaviors often cited as evidence of African Americans' racial inferiority were actually the consequences of oppressive social and labor conditions that could equally victimize anyone. This insight, although often uncredited, prefigures frameworks in contemporary biological anthropology that trace how even socially constructed categories of difference can create real embodied consequences (Gravlee 2009). Nevertheless, in the late nineteenth and early twentieth centuries, scientific studies of the Irish population operated with the more naive, nefarious, and common assumption that cranial morphology revealed racial ancestry.

A Race of Celts

The history of employing anthropometrics to shed light on the origins of the Irish race best illustrates the multivalent political implications of investigating primitivism in western Ireland. In the nineteenth century, scholars ascribed the origins of Ireland's distinctive linguistic and cultural heritage to prehistoric migrations of Celtic people from the continent. The use of *Celtic* as a linguistic category for the affinity between languages spoken in Ireland, Scotland, Wales, the Isle of Man, Cornwall, and Brittany was an innovation of the eighteenth century, and the linking of these modern languages with prehistoric migrations remains highly controversial (Collis 2017; James 1999; Patterson et al. 2022; Sims-Williams 2020). Yet, the notion of an ancient race and ethnolinguistic culture preserved in early Irish literature and art offered a compelling narrative that articulated neatly with older tropes of Irish primitivism and emerging romantic nationalism (Gardiner 2011, 708–12). To nineteenth- and twentieth-century anthropologists, craniometrics offered a methodology for identifying the traces of a purported Celtic ancestry.

As a source of both living and skeletal specimens, Inishbofin did not escape anthropology's era of head-hunting. The English researcher Alfred Cort Haddon, initially trained in comparative anatomy and zoology, developed interests in ethnology, folklore, and craniometrics during his expedition to the Torres Straight Islands in 1888–89 (Walsh 2023). In 1890, as part of a survey of Irish fisheries, Haddon and his colleague Andrew Dixon visited Inishbofin. There, on the night of July 16, they crept into the ruins of St. Colman's Abbey and stole thirteen cranial fragments curated in a niche by the altar of the ruined medieval church (Quiggins 1942, 70–71). In the following years, Haddon and his colleague Daniel J. Cunningham founded the Anthropometric Laboratory of Ireland, based in what was then the museum of Comparative Anatomy at Trinity College Dublin. Haddon deposited the skulls there, where they would remain for 133 years (more on this story in chap. 7).

Undertaken with the encouragement of Francis Galton, a pioneer of the eugenics movement, the Anthropometric Laboratory's aim was to "unravel the tangled skein of the so-called 'Irish Race'" (Cunningham and Haddon 1891, 36). In 1892, Haddon and his Anglo-Irish colleague Charles R. Browne traveled to the Aran Islands to collect craniometric data from islanders. It was only the first of many craniometric studies on western islands perceived to be remote and therefore liable to preserve the last vestiges of a primeval Irish race, relatively undiluted by later invaders. As Emma Dwyer (2009) notes, the supposed isolation of rural people in Irish and British highlands and islands was a common narrative that propelled tropes of primitivism, ignored rural people's engagements in global economies, and was undermined by the very presence of researchers themselves.

Haddon and Browne stopped short of deeming islanders as pristine survivals and suggested likely admixture with Cromwellian era troops (Haddon and Browne 1892, 826). Browne would later travel to a series of other islands along the west coast, including Inishbofin and Inishark in 1893. One of the photographs taken during his expedition shows Browne, calipers in hand, measuring the cranium of an islander on Inishbofin with the aid of officers of the Royal Irish Constabulary (fig. 2.2). The image captures the complicity of science as well as Anglo-Irish intellectuals in the racialization of a particular subsection of subjects in Ireland—that is, impoverished western islanders.

Interestingly, Haddon and Browne's work would feed back into Romantic views of islanders as quickly disappearing relics of a lost world (Ashley 2001; Ferguson 1853). The controversial playwright John Millington Synge visited the Aran Islands between 1898 and 1901. From a wealthy Anglo-Irish background, Synge was fascinated by what he saw as the cultural residue of ancient paganism

Figure 2.2: Irish medical doctor and anthropologist Charles R. Browne, with assistance from officers of the Royal Irish Constabulary, collects craniometric data from islanders on Inishbofin in 1893. TCD MS 10961/4, Fol. 5v. Courtesy Trinity College Library Digital Collections Department.

and the racial atavism displayed by the islanders. "These strange men with receding foreheads, high cheek-bones, and ungovernable eyes seem to represent some old type found on these few acres at the extreme borders of Europe, where it is only in wild jests and laughter that they can express their loneliness and desolation" (Synge 1966 [1907], 140).

The notion that Ireland—and particularly the west of Ireland—preserved an otherwise disappearing Celtic linguistic, cultural, and racial heritage became central to certain strands of Irish nationalism (Johnson 1993; Nash 1993; Ó Tuathaigh 1991). Following independence for southern Ireland, Celtic cultural identity and romanticization of rural western Ireland became a central organizing principle of Éamon de Valera's Free State Government (Fallon 1999, 19–21). Between 1932 and 1936, the Department of Anthropology at Harvard University, facilitated by the Free State Government, launched a multidisciplinary study of the racial and cultural heritage of the Irish. The project produced seminal research in archaeology and social anthropology, including some of the first comprehensively published systematic excavations in Ireland (O'Sullivan 2003, 21) and Arensberg and Kimball's (2001 [1940]) ethnographic portrait of rural County Clare. Notably, the third prong of the project, led by the physical anthropologist Ernest Hooton, included a craniometric survey of ten thousand men and two thousand women across all thirty-two counties of the island of Ireland, as well as comparative measurements of prehistoric skulls (Hootan et al. 1955; O'Neill 2022). If earlier craniometric studies in Ireland entwined Romantic and colonial discourses, the Harvard Irish Mission was informed by contemporary discourses of conservative nationalism and eugenics (Carew 2018). Hooton, the overall director of the Harvard Irish Mission, was a member of the American Eugenics Society, and Adolph Mahr, the Austrian-born director of the National Museum of Ireland at the time, was the local group leader of the Nazi Party in Ireland (it is worth noting that Hooton wrote decisively against the Nazis and their interpretation of racist science in the late 1930s) (Carew 2018, 52–54).

Enduring Primitivism

Within the fields of archaeology and geography, influential scholars in the early to mid-twentieth century continued to operate with an assumption that Ireland, and particularly the west of Ireland, offered exceptional preservation of primitive European society. R. A. S. Macalister, professor of Celtic Archaeology at University College Dublin from 1909 to 1943, argued on archaeological grounds for an Iron Age Celtic invasion in Ireland, which, due to the lack of Roman influence in Ireland, had left behind a Celtic culture now disappeared from the Celts' continental homelands. Taking persistence of memory for granted, Macalister employed legends written by monks in early medieval manuscripts and contemporary folklore to interpret pre-Christian, Iron Age culture. He argued the case for continuity in grandiose terms: "The importance of Ireland is that, thanks to the 'time-lag,' it has rendered to Anthropology the unique, inestimable, indispensable service of carrying a primitive European Precivilization down into late historic times" (Macalister 1949, x).

E. Estyn Evans, the first chair of the Geography Department at Queen's University Belfast, cited the authority of this quote in his *Irish Folk Ways* (Evans 2000 [1957], 12). Evans likewise saw Ireland's "historic literature, language and social organization" alongside its "folklore and folk customs" as illustrative of "the marginal survival of archaic elements of the Indo-European world" (1957, xiv). Yet, Evans deployed a more nuanced explanatory framework for cultural continuity and change based on underlying geographic characteristics. By studying "regional and social evolution as a continuous interaction between people and their environment" (Evans 1957, xi), Evans simultaneously stressed varying regional cultures within Ireland and the role of peasants as agents maintaining the vitality of traditional technologies, customs, and values (Graham 1994, 187–93).

Following his death in 1989, scholars have debated whether Evans's work—particularly his emphasis on the distinctiveness of Ulster in relation to the rest of Ireland—was motivated by an implicit unionist agenda or merely a lack of explicit discussion of the political context of his work (Evans 1999; Graham 1994; Stout 1996). Whatever the case, the existence of the debate highlights how certain premises—particularly cultural continuity among the rural Irish in marginal environments—resonated with both nationalist and unionist political ideologies. Tropes of primitivism in Ireland made strange bedfellows of otherwise opposing political positions. Whether premised on a naked will to conquest, religious bigotry, social evolutionary theory, the science of race, romantic nationalism, or anthropogeography, the notion of a deep, persistent, and sometimes timeless heritage abounds in Irish historiography.

PERSISTENCE OR INVENTION—AN IMPASSE

The development of social theory in the twentieth century challenged the primitivist assumptions embedded in the foundations of anthropology, folklore, and other disciplines. Some of the most substantial contributions have come from postcolonial criticism and through engagement with and scholars from indigenous and marginalized communities who problematize essentialist viewpoints (Blakey 2020, S186-87; Colwell 2016; Said 1978; Spivak 1985). These critiques, justly leveled, complicate investigations of enduring traditions and social formations.

Crude essentialism has been contested on many fronts. Race and craniometrics have been invalidated over and over as essential metrics of human difference, even as scholars acknowledge how the social construction of racial categories and enduring racism has generated real, embodied inequalities in health (Boas 1912; Harrison 2019; Gravlee et al. 2003; Gravlee 2009). Meanwhile, scholars have become increasingly conscious of how colonial and nationalist discourses have shaped scholarly work, particularly assumptions about social continuity over long time frames (in the case of Ireland, see French 2013; Horning 2017; Mytum 2017; O'Sullivan 1998). Two foundational works in the late twentieth century highlighted how perceptions of continuity and primordial heritage afforded the formation of modern nation states. Benedict Anderson

(2006 [1983]) argued that the rise of nationalism did not reflect the inevitable fluorescence of primordial ethnic loyalties but rather the construction of "imagined communities"—that is, frameworks for belonging premised on perceptions of a distinctive history and identity rather than daily face-to-face encounters or shared socioeconomic standing. Published in the same year, a volume edited by the historians E. J. Hobsbawm and T. O. Ranger (2012 [1983]) outlined a similar constructivist perspective. Their notion of "invented traditions" refers to cultural practices recent in origin but construed to appear as if inherited from time immemorial (1983, 1–2). The illusion of antiquity plays a crucial political role, allowing such traditions to presage, legitimate, and naturalize contemporary formations of national identity and political integration.

Such theoretical developments problematize archaeological examinations of cultural persistence. Outside a social evolutionary framework, existing traditions and folk beliefs among indigenous or rural groups cannot be taken for granted as windows into the deep past. As such, scholars have focused greater attention on the tensions and contradictions between archaeological and folklore evidence, rather than assuming that they sing in unison. In some cases, to contest primitivist claims of continuity can act as a decolonizing practice—one that archaeologists are advantageously positioned to enact (Robin 2006). Archaeological evidence can sometimes provide empirical grounds for evaluating claims of continuity and for repudiating the anachronistic projection *into the past* of folklore, ethnohistory, or other political narratives *concerning the past*.

The search for survivals latent in folklore, traditional narratives, and the beliefs of communities in the present or near past is increasingly rare and must be undertaken with care (for a thought-provoking example, see Thompson 2004). Instead, the dominant trend is to seek modes of combining archaeology with traditional knowledge without assuming the pristine maintenance of ancient knowledge or practices by descendant communities. Gazin-Shwartz and Holtorf almost utterly dispense with the question of ascertaining the temporal provenance of folklore accounts (1999, 14). They locate the value of folklore not in the preservation of information from the past but in offering alternative perspectives that "counter our tendency to portray everyone in all time as versions of ourselves" (Gazin-Schwartz and Holtorf 1999, 5). In North America, proponents of indigenous archaeology and engagement with local and descendant communities have made similar arguments. Namely, archaeologists are bounded by their own cultural, political, and disciplinary biases. Hence, casting out for a greater diversity of perspectives and interpretational possibilities makes for better scientific inquiry (Colwell 2016; Colwell-Chanthaphonh et al. 2010, 233–34; Clark and Horning 2019; Fowles 2010, 461–62; Haraway 1988; La Roche and Blakely 1997; Marshall 2002, 217–18).

If not actually premised on essential primitivism, archaeology that incorporates traditional knowledge to interpret the past may risk reproducing primitivist narratives. Alternatively, demonstrating the adoption of new practices across time risks undermining claims of distinctive heritage, which can sometimes provide economic opportunity or legal protection to indigenous, rural, or other marginalized communities (Silliman 2014, 60–61; see Spivak 2008 and Kurzwelly et al. 2020 on strategic essentialism). The Anishinaabe scholar Gerald Vizenor has suggested casting indigenous histories in terms of "survivance" (1998, 2008). As a means of nuancing accounts of indigenous endurance that neither deny agency nor minimize the reality of historical oppression, survivance signifies the struggle to maintain community livelihood and integrity and to repudiate domination and victimhood (Vizenor 1998, 15). Notably, this struggle can include the blending of old and new—the adaptation of inherited knowledge and practices to new circumstances and the creation of new identities and traditions, premised on and coherent with the past (Silliman 2014, 58–66; Velie 2008, 147). This is a vitally important insight that casts light on the path ahead.

In short, to examine claims of continuity means navigating challenges both epistemological and political. Recent scholarship has identified essential questions and offered routes of analysis: How does one interweave archaeological, ethnohistoric, and folklore evidence to reconstruct the past? How does one produce accounts of continuity and change that do not reproduce the ideological lifeblood of different forms of political domination, exploitation, and marginalization? What does continuity have to do with survivance or sustainability? The example of Irish pilgrimage traditions illustrates these challenges particularly well and establishes the need for a novel approach to the creation and maintenance of heritage. If considering the history of Irish pilgrimage traditions risks reviving some primitivist tropes, it also provides an opportunity to generate more nuanced accounts of heritage and endurance that may shed light on present challenges of sustainability.

An Turas—"The Journey"

Most Irish pilgrimage traditions include a distinctive genre of devotion known as *an turas*, "the journey," "pilgrimage" (plural *turasanna*). This is characterized by procession to a sequence of outdoor stations to carry out prescribed motions and prayers. The primary sources of knowledge relating to Irish pilgrimage traditions come from folklore, antiquarian, and travelers' descriptions of practices conducted primarily (but not exclusively) by Catholic laypeople at different sites between the eighteenth and twentieth centuries (Croker 1824; Hardy 1840; Richardson 1727; Stephens 1872). Such pilgrimages customarily involved visiting particular places associated with a saint of local or national renown on his or

Figure 2.3: St. Colmcille's Well, Glencolmcille (*Gleann Cholm Cille*), Co. Donegal. According to a description of the turas collected in 1886, "Everyone must bring three stones up the steep hill, and on reaching the well you must go round it three times on the right-hand side, and each time you go around a stone must be flung on the heap of stones round the well" (Price 1941, 75).

her feast day, named *pattern* days (from Irish *pátrún*, meaning "patron"). In some notable cases, such as the mountain Croagh Patrick and the island pilgrimage site of Skellig Michael, pilgrimage might entail an arduous journey across difficult terrain or ocean water. In other cases, pilgrims needed only to visit local ruins of early medieval churches and monasteries to carry out a turas circuit, in which they prayed and circumambulated at a number of stations. The prescribed

Figure 2.4: Pilgrims perambulating *deiseal* around St. Patrick's Bed (*Leaba Phádraig*), August 2016, on the peak of Croagh Patrick (*Cruach Phádraig*), a mountain along the west coast of Co. Mayo. The site of an early medieval ecclesiastical settlement, the mountain has been associated with Saint Patrick from at least the seventh century and attested as a place of Christian pilgrimage from at least the twelfth century (Corlett 2014, 42; Morahan 2001; Walsh 1994). Some believe that the tradition of Christian pilgrimage developed out of prehistoric, pre-Christian devotions centered on the mountain (Corlett 1998).

direction of circumambulation, or rounding, was often *deiseal*, literally *right-hand-wise*—that is, clockwise. Participants and folklore collectors commonly glossed deiseal as sun-wise—that is, according to the apparent path of the sun across the sky in the northern hemisphere (Ferguson 1879). Various kinds of

Figure 2.5: A leacht on St. MacDara's Island (*Cruach na Cara*) during a regatta in July 2015. This stone platform, mounted by an imported limestone upright, featured as one of the stations in the traditional turas circuit. The sailboats in the background, Galway hookers, compete in a race by circling the island in the direction of the sun, mimicking the *deiseal* choreography of the pilgrimage circuit.

built monuments and landscape features have acted as turas stations, including holy wells, *leachta* (stone platforms), shrines, stone cairns, carved stone crosses, and stone basins (bullauns) (Ray and McCormick 2023) (figs. 2.3–2.5). Folklore accounts indicate that certain monuments garnered specialized uses for curing particular ailments of the body, restoring fertility, or ensuring the health of livestock (Ó Giolláin 2005, 16–17). In the present, people still sometimes visit traditional turas sites on annual pattern days, though carrying out the full sequence of procession, prayer, and rounding is now rare, and tourism increasingly draws visitors with different religious motivations and cultural backgrounds (Ray 2011, 280–82).

The origins and development of turas traditions have remained a point of enduring controversy. As mentioned above, Protestant observers in the eighteenth and nineteenth centuries interpreted turas traditions as developing from ancient pre-Christian customs and objected to what they saw as the pagan excesses of lay Catholics' intensely embodied devotions focused on natural phenomena (Richardson 1727, 137). Catholic clergy sometimes shared this view. In 1840, Phillip Dixon Hardy, a Protestant polemicist convinced of the immorality of Irish pilgrimage practices, could cite remarks of the Catholic priest Rev. Charles O'Connor concerning the ritual practices of Catholic peasants in County Roscommon: "And so thoroughly persuaded were they of the sanctity of those pagan practices, that they would travel bare-headed and bare-footed, from ten to twenty miles, for the purpose of crawling on their knees round these wells, and upright stones, and oak trees, westward, as the sun travels, some three times, some six, some nine, and so on, in uneven numbers, until their voluntary penances were completely fulfilled" (Rev. Charles O'Connor, quoted in Hardy 1840, 100). The primitivist view that turas traditions embodied a persistent, savage paganism articulated with the racist, social evolutionary framework that set the Irish alongside other colonized groups. In a travelers' guide to Ireland, Samuel Carter and Anna Maria Hall assessed Irish pilgrimage traditions in nakedly racist terms: "the most ignorant and savage of the tribes of Africa have few ceremonies more utterly revolting" (Hall and Hall 1841, 282).

Recent scholarship has repudiated the primitivist view of turas traditions, albeit with various degrees of nuance and empirical evidence. Carroll's (1999) study of holy wells and turas practices—significantly influenced by the notion of invented traditions—argued strongly against their pre-Christian origins. Carroll argued that turas practices originated only in the sixteenth and seventeenth centuries as the melding of the collectivist, kin-based ethos of rural Ireland with Counter-Reformation theological and liturgical developments emanating from the Council of Trent (Carroll 1999, 133). Paralleling the nationalist reframing of racial science, the hypothesized Celtic origins of turas traditions took on a positive valence in the context of Celtic Revival and romantic nationalism that staked Ireland's national identity in a Celtic heritage. Accordingly, Catholic priests, who formerly disdained and actively suppressed turas practices, began to participate in their revitalization in the nineteenth and twentieth centuries

(Taylor 1995, 64–75). While Carroll did not fully consider the historical and archaeological evidence for prehistoric and medieval antecedents to turas practices, his work highlights the dynamism of traditions, their creative adaptation to new social circumstances, and contestation over their political valences.

More recently, Celeste Ray (2014) uses evidence from within Ireland and beyond to suggest that holy well venerations in Ireland do indeed owe something to antecedent pre-Christian practices. She offers a nuanced syncretic view of turas practices as hybrid traditions that incorporate elements that originated in various historic contexts. Today, the purported pre-Christian heritage of turas traditions remains attractive to participants, particularly to neo-pagan and Celtic reconstructionist groups, but also to people critical of the historical and contemporary influence of the Catholic Church in Irish society (Butler 2015; Lash 2018a; Power 2015; Ray 2011, 280–82).

If purported links to paganism and Celtic heritage (whatever *Celtic* is taken to mean) remain controversial, recent archaeological research has demonstrated material continuities and historical connections between turas traditions and early medieval forms of devotion (Corlett 2012, 2014, 85–9; Herity 1995; Nugent 2020; O'Sullivan and Ó Carragáin 2008; Ó Carragáin 2009b, 2013). The clearest and most comprehensive evidence for the ancestry of a modern turas tradition in early medieval pilgrimage liturgies comes from the early medieval monastic settlement on Inishmurray, a now uninhabited island off Sligo Bay. A large cashel (stone enclosure) at the center of the island contains the monastery's most sacred structures, including the principal church and shrine chapel dedicated to St. Molaise, while a circuit of ritual monuments run along the coast. The nineteenth-century turas began at the cashel and proceeded to each of the satellite monuments before pilgrims returned again to the cashel (Heraughty 1982). Excavations of a series of leachta platforms that acted as stations in the modern turas suggest that they were originally constructed as part of a single initiative around the end of the first millennium CE (O'Sullivan and Ó Carragáin 2008, 316–17). Ó Carragáin's (2009b) careful synthesis of material and textual evidence illustrates how the modern turas tradition emerged from the monuments and practices initially developed as part of penitential liturgies that combined monks residing on the island as well as visiting pilgrims.

How does one begin to interpret archaeological evidence for the early medieval foundations of modern turas traditions without succumbing to old primitivist tropes or simply discounting any possibility of continuity of practices and commemoration over many centuries? As summarized above, recent work indicates some necessary points of attention: the political affordances of heritage (invented or otherwise) and the need to see patterns of continuity and change in the context of communities' struggles to maintain integrity and livelihood in the midst of adversity. I think we can go further still by focusing squarely on that aspect of turas traditions that has made them so controversial: their relationship to the natural world. I suggest that an approach centered on the concept of taskscape can develop previous insights by attending to human lived experience and livelihood within environments animated by other-than-human forces. This frame, I suggest, provides a means of recognizing endurance as dynamic and heritage as creative.

My approach emerges from a context of lively debate on the prospects of so-called posthumanist thought.

A TASKSCAPE APPROACH

Posthuman Premises for Human-Oriented Problems

Posthumanism is an umbrella term that refers to a variety of theoretical approaches that seek to undercut the anthropocentrism (human-centered bias) of much Western scholarship since the Enlightenment. Under particular scrutiny are a series of conceptual oppositions that uphold human exceptionalism: nature vs. culture; subject vs. object; human vs. animal; animate vs. inanimate. Instead, posthumanism adopts a *relational* perspective. Relationality is the premise that interactions are generative. Many familiar categorical distinctions (like those dichotomies listed above) almost always obscure relations of mutual influence and intimate interconnection. Rather than viewing humans as exceptional subjects acting upon inert matter, relational analyses explore how human capacities for action, perception, and intention emerge from encounters with other life-forms and vibrant materials that can act back (Bennett 2009; Watts 2013). *Material vibrancy* or *agency* refers to the potential of materials—whether they are living or sentient—to make a difference in the world, to create effects and impact the course of events. This kind of agency emanates, in part, from how things get tied up with one another in relationships of dependence and mutual construction.

The game Jenga well illustrates material vibrancy and relationality. The fate of the increasingly precarious tower relies on the changing configuration of blocks and their shifting balance of potential energy, the steadiness of the players' hands, and the vibrations of air molecules set off by players' shouts and movements. Feelings of nervous anticipation, solidarity, or competitive antagonism as the game goes on do not originate solely within the human players themselves but emerge over time from the whole assemblage of blocks, bodies, and atmospheric conditions (on *assemblage*, see Antczak and Beaudry 2019; Bennett 2009; Crellin 2020; DeLanda 2006; Deleuze and Guattari 1987).

Of course, the most prescient contemporary example of relationality in action is human-driven climate change. The now popular concept of Anthropocene attempts to evoke humans' agency and vulnerability as actors enmeshed within a global environment drastically altered by our activities (Latour 2014, 5–6, 17) Amid rising sea levels, unprecedented heat waves, and increasingly violent storms, the division between nature and humanity and the ascription of agency only to sentient beings becomes philosophically and politically untenable (Kohn 2015, 312).

If propelled by reflection on contemporary ecological conditions, posthumanism draws inspiration from earlier threads of relational thought. This includes previous developments in material culture studies, such as object biography, materiality, memory studies, and Peircean semiotic approaches (Appadurai 1986; Miller 2005; Preucel 2010; Van Dyke 2019), which highlight the diverse ways material things affect social interactions, commemorations, and meaning-making. Less often recognized is the significance of antecedent and affinal perspectives in threads of indigenous thought and scholarship (Cajete 2000; Kelechi Ugwuanyi 2020, 266–67; Ramos 2012; Todd 2016; Willerslev 2004; Crellin et al. 2021).

Unsurprisingly, posthumanism has generated considerable controversy and debate, with some scholars insisting that it tends to elide issues of power and culpability and potentially even reiterates aspects of colonial thought (see Fowles 2016; Hauser 2015; Van Dyke 2015). These cautions are justified and should inform applications of theory. Following Barad (2007) and Cipolla (2018), I contend that posthuman premises—such as relationality and material vibrancy—may help to better frame and formulate responses to human-oriented problems. Again global climate change proves an instructive example—posthuman premises help to define the shape of a phenomenon that threatens human well-being. Taskscape, I suggest, offers a perspective that can shift emphasis back and forth between posthuman relationality and humanist attention to the lived experience of people who act day to day to sustain livelihoods and to reproduce or contest different forms of community and inequality. As I see it, the precise strength of a taskscape approach is to understand how human capacities for memory, affiliation, and livelihood are generated from interactions with materials and environments animated by other-than-human forces.

Taskscape Defined

As originally outlined by Tim Ingold (1993), the concept of taskscape represents an attempt to reconcile phenomenological and ecological approaches to the environment, a theme Ingold has continually addressed in his subsequent works

(Ingold 2000, 2010, 2011, 2012, 2013, 2015, 2017). In a general sense, *taskscape* is an alternative term for landscape that emphasizes the dynamic production of the inhabited world by various kinds of action. As *landscape* typically refers to an array of interrelated features, *taskscape* refers to an array of interrelated activities (Ingold 1993, 158). Although some elements of landscapes are relatively durable, landscapes are constantly in the process of becoming, constantly rendered by collections of tasks that occur over different time scales and with different temporal rhythms. Taskscapes are not restricted to living things but also include various climatic, hydrological, and geological phenomena that render the form of the landscape and impinge on the actions, perceptions, and livelihoods of life-forms (Ingold 1993, 163–64).

Methodologically, taskscape plays to archaeology's strengths by beginning from simple inferences about how the material and spatial properties of landscapes manifest different kinds of movement and vitality. Accordingly, archaeologists have deployed the concept to model how the logistics of past settlement and subsistence practices shape the landscape and structure dwellers' interactions, embodied knowledge, and perceptions of nonhumans (Logan and Dores Cruz 2014; Moore and Thompson 2012; Rajala and Mills 2017). My application of the concept to reframe analyses of continuity in terms of dynamic endurance emanates from Ingold's original declaration of the concept's utility.

Ingold insisted that the essential goal of taskscape analyses is to situate "the tasks of human dwelling in their proper context within the process of becoming of the world as a whole" (Ingold 1993, 164). This means recognizing humans simultaneously as biological creatures enmeshed in flows of energy and matter and as social beings whose perceptions of identity, place, time, and the past emerge through multisensory experiences of dwelling in landscapes. As a framework for inquiry, taskscape maintains the means of human livelihood as a central component of analysis. If taskscape refers generally to "the becoming of the world as whole," one can speak of certain collections of tasks from a human perspective. Thus, I will use *dwelling taskscape* in this book to refer to the set of tasks that make human livelihood in the landscape feasible. Dwelling taskscapes always include practices of subsistence and necessarily human and other-than-human actors. But, as we saw in chapter 1, dwelling taskscapes can also include other activities, such as practices of ritual, conviviality, or commemoration, that shape experiences and foster social relationships. Taskscape should make us think equally about ecology and lived experience, subsistence and subjectivity, energy as well as affect. Analyzing functional articulations between subsistence practices and traditional practices of commemoration and ritual provides a means of understanding turas traditions in particular historic contexts and of evaluating their contribution to community endurance. Below, I outline the value of taskscape to model two key concepts in this book: dynamic endurance and creative heritage.

Dynamic Endurance

In the simplest terms, *dynamic endurance* refers to the capacity to persist across time despite changing conditions. As usual, it is easiest to understand this concept by considering the taskscape of a single practice. Consider a team of rowers propelling a currach in rough waters. Their endurance is not the inevitable outcome of some essential fixed nature, nor is it the maintence of power, determination, and an unvarying sequence of movements. Their endurance requires the application of will and coordination that must respond to fluctuations in wind and wave action and the creeping fatigue of their limbs. The team may persist in their rowing, but this persistence is not stasis.

Now we can zoom out to consider the taskscape on the scale of human dwelling. A taskscape approach asks how enduring cultural features or social forms operate within the collection of practices that make human livelihoods possible. These collections are variable and changing. As such, endurance must be a dynamic process in which the old persists only by rearticulating with constantly evolving social and ecological circumstances. By situating human dwelling in the broader context of the becoming of the world, a taskscape approach is in essence an ecological framework. This attention to ecology and the vibrancy of environments highlights the dynamism of endurance. As stable and indefatigable as they might seem as landmarks, the rocks at Béal Cam, where John took his shortcut, are in fact eroding at so slow a pace that only many lifetimes of experience could see it. Other aspects of the environment—sea and weather conditions, soil chemistry, grass growth, fungal infestations of subsistence crops—fluctuate more rapidly or respond more immediately to human interaction. Human endurance, whether of customs, traditions, subsistence practices, or social formations, always occurs in relation to an environment that is deceptively or conspicuously but inevitably dynamic.

Yet, enduring communities are dynamic in another sense. Communities rely on the constant rearticulation of patterns of experience, perceptions of social order, and regimes of subsistence. A taskscape approach asks us to consider how subsistence practices articulate with a wider range of human interactions in the landscape. The continuation of any social formation across time will necessarily depend on tasks that derive food energy. Yet, the vitality of subsistence regimes also relies on notions of social order and forms of political collaboration or oppression. Consider how British rule, *laissez-faire* economic theory, and primitivist stereotypes about the Irish compounded the effects of potato blight in the mid-nineteenth century into mass famine, death, and migration

(Gray 2021; Ó Gráda 1995). The challenge of endurance is not just the challenge of adapting subsistence regimes to turbulent environments. Subsistence practices and their social contexts are always mutually constituted. The challenge of enduring human livelihood is always also a challenge of maintaining viable social and political relations. Recent work in historical and political ecology make this eminently clear in case studies from around the world (Catlin and Bolender 2018; Chase and Scarborough 2014; Costanza et al. 2007; Hartman et al. 2017; Liu et al. 2007; Morehart 2011; Van der Leeuw and Redman 2002).

If we are concerned with the endurance of human livelihood on the landscape, then we must consider how that endurance derives from changes or continuities in how humans relate to one another. In other words, how are ecologically sustainable livelihoods made socially and politically feasible? A taskscape approach seeks answers in patterns of human experience, in sensory and commemorative engagements with landscapes. It is a commonly cherished notion in archaeology that humans' interactions with materials—whether objects, architecture, or landscapes—can play a fundamental role in reiterating or transforming human relations. Materials influence social relations by evoking the past, structuring movements and visibility, and segregating or integrating different people and activities according to social categories of difference such as age, class, gender, or race (DeMarrais et al. 1996; Smith 2003). As many scholars have explored, landscapes and built environments generate experiences that can routinize and naturalize existing social and political relations and their associated subsistence regimes (Beck et al. 2017; Beck and Brown 2012; Joyce 2004; Whitridge 2004). In short, the endurance of dwelling taskscapes relies on articulations between strategies of food production, social and political relations, and patterns of lived experience, often furnished through embodied encounters with material things.

This book, of course, is concerned particularly with patterns of experience that engage with, emanate from, or reference the past. A taskscape approach can also sharpen analyses of how the curation of old materials and traditions can foster forms of identity, belonging, and cooperation.

Creative Heritage

The scholarship on heritage is vast and contested. One influential perspective, outlined by Kirshenblatt-Gimblett (1995, 2004), identifies heritage as a metacultural category—that is, as a form of cultural expression in the present concerned with a form of cultural expression from the past. Within this framework, heritage is marked out as a valued aspect of the past, precisely because the context in which it emerged has disappeared or is disappearing. To some, this discursive highlighting is precisely what distinguishes heritage from other forms, even quite old traditions, that remain largely taken for granted within normative culture (Jackson et al. 2020). In cultural policy, the legislative protection of heritage, whether tangible or intangible, also acts as a discursive marker for cultural forms deemed either as extraordinary contributions to global human achievement or as essential to the integrity or identity of certain cultural groups (Coombe 2009). As such, on a national or international scale, what becomes enshrined, valorized, and preserved as heritage is necessarily fraught with competing interests, political ideologies, and unforeseen consequences—not least because an idealized past can offer belonging for some and exclusion for others (Grama 2013; Hafstein 2018; Meskell 2020).

Though I recognize the analytical value of more restrictive definitions of heritage, I will operate with a more expansive view of heritage and one more familiar from the word's colloquial connotations. Simply, heritage comprises anything inherited from the past into the present. To study heritage is to examine how human interactions with the world create durable legacies that inform how we engage new circumstances. I will use *heritage* to refer to the enduring material traces of the past (stuff), traditional practices that emerge from or engage the past (actions), and the shared narratives and embodied knowledge generated from those engagements (knowledge). Each of these forms of heritage, tangible and intangible, relies on and influences the others, and all can act as resources for addressing the future (see Cashman et al. 2011, 2–4, for a similar approach to tradition).

A taskscape approach to heritage begins by recognizing how landscapes materialize the past. The traces of discrete actions or wider processes that occurred or commenced in the past endure materially in the present. This is as true of Neolithic passage tombs as it is of yesterday's footprints left in the mud. As such, Ingold insists that any act of dwelling in the landscape can be an act of remembrance (1993, 152–53). Sharing this observation, memory studies in archaeology, anthropology, and related disciplines have explored how social forms of remembering and forgetting are enacted through engagements with artifacts, architecture, monuments, and landscapes (Basso 1996; Van Dyke and Alcock 2003; Van Dyke 2019). In other words, material heritage can act as infrastructure for staging traditional actions and for generating more intangible forms of knowledge about the past (Nic Craith and Kockel 2016). Yet, the transmission of the past, in material and in memory, is never perfect, total, or neutral. Memories and narratives attached to material heritage, as well as the materials themselves, are clearly subject to revision, suppression, and distortion across time, often intentionally to suit particular political interests (Beiner 2018; Trouillot 1995; Van Dyke 2009). In some cases, political factions may intentionally modify the landscape to accentuate, fabricate, or elide certain aspects of the past. Such inscriptive practices of commemoration, such as monument construction, are often undertaken as part of political projects that advantage some groups at the expense of others (Connerton 1989, 75–78). In other cases, repeated and habitual encounters with material heritage can generate nondiscursive, embodied, and durable dispositions that are resistant to change (Connerton 1989, 72–78; Mills and Walker 2008). These so-called incorporating practices of commemoration (Connerton 1989, 72–74) operate sometimes without intent or explicit awareness.

Inscriptive and incorporating practices necessarily work together: indeed, ideologically motivated ideas about the past operate most effectively when incorporated as unconsidered bodily habits. In the case of turas traditions, the construction of a shrine monument to commemorate the saintly dead could be taken as an inscriptive practice designed to perpetuate the memory and veneration of a particular figure who brings esteem to a monastery. The conventional choreography of pilgrimage, like the circumambulation of a monument, may be taken as incorporative practices that cultivate a particular embodied disposition of respect toward the shrine. We will consider such examples more deeply later in this book. The crucial point I wish to make here is that taskscape forces us to think of heritage not just as enduring materials but as the embodied skills, know-how, and dispositions that emanate from engaging with material things in both mundane and ceremonial practices.

A taskscape approach also highlights how perceptions of heritage are often entwined with perceptions of relationality. Inhabiting taskscapes means confronting not only the past but also a multitude of other-than-human elements, forces, and life-forms. The materialization of the past in the landscape is also of necessity a materialization of relationality. A deep footprint in hardened mud tells you about not only human action in the past but also the interactions of moisture, soil, footfall, and atmosphere. The erosion of a stone carving or the slow collapse of a drystone house represents former human interactions with materials and ongoing interactions among those materials and the elements and the force of gravity. As such, engaging the landscape provides an opportunity not only for reckoning relationships to the past but also to "the becoming of the world as a whole."

The character and choreography of turas traditions make them particularly liable to spur such reckoning (Lash et al. 2023). Commentators have long noted in disdain and wonder how turas traditions attune practitioners to environmental phenomena, often fostering sensorily intense experiences of devotion. Ubiquitously outdoors and open to the weather, turas monuments include natural features (trees, stones, wells) that worshippers engaged by rounding in accordance with the movement of the sun. As we will see, folklore accounts from the nineteenth and twentieth centuries warn of sharp changes in the weather resulting from the misuse or mistreatment of turas monuments in the context of oath-taking, malediction, or theft. Obviously, the forces of the sun and the sea were vital factors in different dwelling taskscapes across time, and perhaps this begins to account for the enduring resonance of the natural features and choreography of turas traditions (Lash 2018a, 294–95).

Encounters with material heritage in the taskscape can offer sensorily heightened, memorable, and evocative experiences of engagement with the past and the vibrancy of the world. Jane Bennet has dubbed this mood of intense and lively engagement as "enchantment" (Bennett 2001, 111; Lash 2018a). Whether through inscription or incorporation, these experiences of enchantment can foster perceptions of relationality—that is, perceptions of how one fits within models of social, temporal, or cosmological order (Lash et al. 2023). By naturalizing particular perceptions of relationality, heritage can work to perpetuate patterns of inclusion, exclusion, communal solidarity, or political hierarchy. In this way, material heritage, traditions, and their embodied consequences may contribute to the viability of social formations and their capacity to endure. Of course, heritage is also liable to do the opposite.

Heritage is creative because it is reliably evocative but materially, semiotically, and ideologically malleable. It is a resource that can be deployed by individual and collective creativity to find resonance in a new context. As Glassie writes of tradition, heritage is a "means of deriving the future from the past" (2003, 192) and "flowers in variation and innovation" (1993, 9). A taskscape approach to creative heritage is, I hope, an antidote to primitivist tropes. As I will illustrate, the enchantments generated by similar movements and materials in pilgrimage traditions had very different ideological resonances and political consequences in different historical contexts.

A closer look at the long history of engagement with the past on Inishark and Inishbofin will illustrate how dynamic endurance is born of creative heritage. The next chapter begins this journey in the traces of St. Leo on Inishark.

THREE

TRACES OF LEO ON INISHARK

INISHARK, JUNE 2012. MIND'S EYE TO CARVEN STONE.

One of the things that impressed me most when our team first camped on Inishark for excavations was the hours that stretched between night and day. In June, at that latitude, and with nothing but the expanse of the ocean to obstruct the setting sun, full dark wouldn't come until after midnight.

Sensing the tail end of the long twilight, I left the few members of our excavation crew remaining at the campfire, gathered my sleeping bag from my tent, and walked west to spend the night in Clochán Leo. The stomping of startled hooves greeted my approach, and I felt a pang of guilt at disturbing the sheep who had settled for the evening on the knoll. The sheep had left some traces of their presence in the clochán—thankfully not recently. I kicked the dried dung away with my boot, cleared a spot to lay out my sleeping bag, took off my boots, and zipped inside. The stone walls, still standing to three feet, stayed the wind, muffled the gentle wash of the tide on the coast below, and hemmed the scope of my vision to count the few stars emerging in the sky above.

With imagined stones, I extended the walls upward and over me, remaking the corbelled roof that once had been there. It seemed precarious work, even with stones quarried from thin air. As it was, there was barely enough room to lie diagonally and avoid the few wall stones that had collapsed inward at some point in the past. I hoped none of their fellows would decide to join the fallen that night. How many had slept here before me in the last century and centuries beyond, in fear, in hope, and in whatever else? However much we may wish it, there is no summoning the experiences of the past. By sleeping there, I wanted only to take a share, somehow, in an old

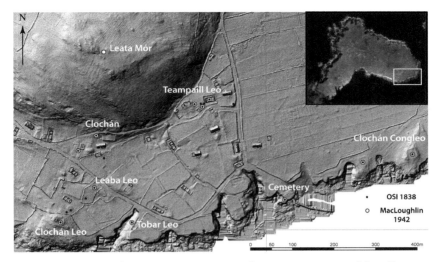

Figure 3.1: Location of monuments superimposed on a LiDAR image of the village on Inishark. Monuments listed on the 1838 Ordnance Survey (OS) map are marked by small black dots. Larger black circles indicate monuments recorded by MacLoughlin in 1942.

Figure 3.2: William Bald's Map of Mayo (c. 1816) with "K Leo," "Old Church," "Leo's Cove," and "Cloughanahinlow" highlighted. Courtesy of the Mayo County Library.

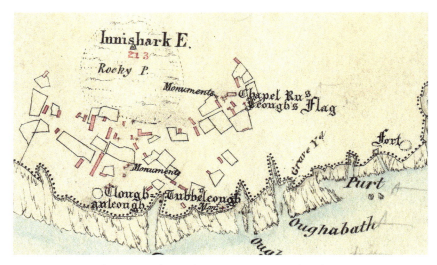

Figure 3.3: First Edition Fair Plan Ordnance Survey Map of Inishark. National Archives OS/105B/249/1. Reproduced with the kind permission of the director of the National Archives.

tradition almost forgotten, to lay my body where others had lain theirs. Archaeology, in its own way, is a mode of remembering. What we call rituals are often the same. I wanted to remember in action, not just in mind's eye.

One blessing came—a merciful rain woke me the next morning in sparse little droplets. The excavation crew had our breakfast, prepared by Linda Martellaro, the team's magisterial cook and logistics wizard, in the skeleton kitchen set up in the shell of St. Leo's Church. Camping on the island for a week meant bringing in all necessary food, water, and equipment. It was a big undertaking and one impossible without the Inishbofin Ferry Company, their captains and their crews. The knowledge and deft boat handling of Pat, Dermot, and Seamus Concannon always ensured that we could disembark safely in a notoriously difficult spot. We would pitch our tents around the village, which again saw light and life as the old pathways took new foot traffic, the distinctive shape of crumbling gables became navigating landmarks, and we embellished the night with cheer and laughter around an open fire. That day, June 12, was our last day of fieldwork before heading over to Bofin for a few nights to restock our supplies and reacquaint ourselves with the pleasures of the indoors: showers, toilets, warm beds, and freshly pulled pints (almost never in that order).

But before leaving, we would open a new trench outside Clochán Leo. Throughout the day, as we laid out the excavation area and removed the initial layers of sod, the weather periodically lost its mercy and lashed us with rain. Knowing the comforts

Figure 3.4: Franc Myles, *left*, had encountered quartz pebbles during excavations at monastic sites on Illaunloughan (Co. Kerry) and High Island (Co. Galway). Terry O'Hagan, *sitting*, recognized immediately the importance of the quartz and its careful documentation. Photo by Meredith Chesson.

that awaited us, we continued with abandon, sopping wet and soiled. Franc Myles, a senior archaeologist on the crew from Dublin, set the pace with palpable excitement, digging through the deluge, the old shaft of a pickax fractured in his hands from the torque of dislodging collapsed stones beneath the sod.

Only a few inches down, our trowels began to scrape against a flagstone surface, the gray schist painted near black with wet soil. But now and then our trowels would catch a new marvel—pebbles small and round that screamed in white behind their

Figure 3.5: View facing west of the Clochán Leo Complex under excavation (2012). Photo by Meagan Conway.

Figure 3.6: The first of the cross-slabs uncovered from the Clochán Leo Complex in 2012. Photo by Meagan Conway.

muddy coats (fig. 3.4). A small strip trench in this location the summer before had revealed a few quartz pebbles, but we could not anticipate the scale we would uncover. Franc had excavated quartz pebbles surrounding graves and shrines at the island monasteries of Illaunloghan, County Kerry, and High Island, whose outline was still visible from Clochán Leo in the haze on the southern horizon. Here again they were, pebbles like pearls, smoothed by the tide's churn and washed into coves, collected and brought here, long ago covered and now uncovered at a site ascribed to an early monastic saint and visited by pilgrims into the twentieth century.

A few days later, having restocked and returned to Shark, we commenced clearing the flagstone surface and methodically removing displaced stones (fig. 3.5). Tommy Burke had joined us, and the crew had fallen into the trance of excavation. By and by, Tommy's words broke the spell of silence. "Ah, Meredith," he said, calling gently to another senior archaeologist on the crew, Dr. Meredith Chesson, "I think I have something here." By his tone, I could tell he had. I rushed over and saw beneath him what had lain hidden for centuries—the paired and bending lines of an elaborate carved cross traced by the cling of dirt to the channels cut into a schist flagstone. It would take another excavation in 2017 to decipher the full chronology of the site, but in that moment, the early medieval history of Clochán Leo had woken again from mind's eye to carven stone.

—⚬⚬⚬—

TRACES OF TRACES

The coast of Connemara is riddled with the reputed traces of saints. Some monuments are indeed the remnants of monastic settlements founded in the early medieval period (c. 400–1100 CE). The start of this epoch in Ireland is typically defined by the spread of Christianity, the concomitant development of literacy, and the appearance of Ireland's earliest textual sources from the fifth century. The era would see many developments, yet throughout the period, Irish society remained gravely hierarchical, organized by kinship and status and reliant on mixed agriculture and pastoralism (Charles-Edwards 2000; Ó Cróinín 2017; O'Sullivan et al. 2014). Monasteries, staffed by men in religious orders but supported and visited by various types of lay men and women, were at once important social, political, economic, and religious institutions. They served as primary vectors for the promotion of literacy, learning, and the binding of Christianity to a new cultural and ecological setting. Within early medieval cosmology, Ireland lay on the western fringe of a globe centered spiritually and geographically on Jerusalem, the site of Christ's crucifixion and resurrection (Charles-Edwards 1993; O'Loughlin 2004). Christian asceticism—forms of penitential devotion imitating Christ and conceived as a voluntary exile from temporal comfort—had emerged through engagement with the arid landscapes of North Africa in the fourth century. In Ireland, it found a supreme new venue: Ireland's western islands, wracked by wind and rain, lapped by a broad and restless ocean on the edge of the edge of the world (Picard 2009).

The patrons and founders of Ireland's island monasteries are variously recorded in medieval annals, hagiographies, and later legends. We know a great deal about the circumstances surrounding the foundation of St. Colman's Abbey on Inishbofin around 668, or we know at least how one Anglo-Saxon historian framed the story less than a century later. In other cases, we have only oral traditions and folk practices developed over centuries and only much later put into writing. To examine the origins of monasteries in coastal Connemara is often to examine the tracing of traces, how people centuries after the medieval period found and spun the threads of centuries past. The ruins of monasteries remained venues of devotion in the postmedieval period, including the forms of pilgrimage discussed in the previous chapter.

The monastery on Inishark is particularly obscure, and we are left to work backward through time to uncover its history. Extant medieval annals, hagiographies, and martyrologies offer not a whiff of a Saint Leo of Inishark. Yet, for islanders in the nineteenth and twentieth centuries, the reality of St. Leo and of his former presence on the island was there to behold on the surface of the land. In April 1942, Brían MacLoughlin visited Inishark to collect local traditional knowledge on behalf of the Department of Irish Folklore. Proficient in Irish and English, MacLoughlin came from Ballynew, near Cleggan, the nearest mainland port to Inishark and Inishbofin. As a witness to the state of St. Leo's cult within two decades of the island's evacuation, he will serve as a guide for our survey in this chapter. His notes suggest that islanders were forthcoming in pointing out traces of the past that any visitor would likely never notice without local direction. One such trace was to be found on the bedrock of the mound on which Clochán Leo is set.

> An oval shaped hollow, measuring 3 inches in length and seems to have been artificially constructed: this is supposed to be the impression of the saint Leo's foot. This impression in the solid rock is, according to the inhabitants of this island, the greatest proof of the Saints having been in this island. That this heel shaped impression was constructed by the hands of man, is instantly disbelieved and the suggestion abandoned as sheer nonsense by the islanders: their belief being that as a living memorial to the saintliness of Leo this impression of is foot was allowed to be thus created in solid rock. (MacLoughlin 1942, NFC 839, 3–4)

When interviewed by members of the CLIC project in 2009, Inishark-born Martin Murray recalled putting his heel in the imprint with other young boys in the 1950s. Myself and my colleagues have never been able to positively identify the supposed footprint. Memory is work, and we can lose what is left to atrophy. Despite all the details MacLoughlin recorded, it is clear from his account that a pilgrimage tradition held in honor of St. Leo had begun to decline by the

Figure 3.7: Photograph of Clochán Leo from the Browne expedition (1893). TCD MS 10961/4, Fol. 8r. Courtesy Trinity College Library Digital Collections Department.

mid-twentieth century. Islanders showed him the former location or ruined foundations of pilgrimage monuments that had been destroyed and other ruins that they could not explain at all.

Forty-nine years before MacLoughlin's journal, Charles Browne recorded the following description of the turas on Inishark from Michael Lavelle, a resident of Inishbofin (fig. 3.7): "There is yet shown a ruin called Cloghan Leo, in which he [St. Leo] is said to have dwelt; also fourteen stations, to each of which on certain days these people make a holiday, and pray there for the day. There is also a blessed well, called Thobar Leo, at which they pray; and after praying during the day, they go and sleep in the place mentioned above [Cloghan Leo], but it is now almost to the ground" (Browne 1893, 359).

These two glimpses into the veneration of Leo suggest that to perform the turas was to (re)trace the presence of Leo on the landscape, to put your body where his body had been. To a great extent, islanders maintained the tradition of St. Leo's turas through mimesis—the reenactment of past deeds over and over. As the excavation evidence presented here will show, the process of mimesis created opportunities for the formation of a conventional choreography of devotion as well as for novelty and improvisation.

This chapter will offer a tour of the monuments—lost, found, remembered, and half forgotten—associated with Leo, the modern turas, and the island's monastic heritage. It draws from the results of excavations undertaken by the CLIC project alongside historic maps, antiquarian, folklore, and oral historic accounts gathered throughout the nineteenth and twentieth centuries. In uncovering the reality of an early medieval monastic phase underlying Leo's turas, our team had not demonstrated the uncanny persistence of a timeless tradition but rather the traces of people leaving and following traces—islanders engaging the remnants of the past and leaving behind some sign of their presence for subsequent islanders to confront. No location on Inishark demonstrates that pattern so clearly as Clochán Leo.

THE CLOCHÁN LEO COMPLEX

Clochán Leo is set near the high point of a ridge near the coast, with the ground sloping downward in all directions. The ruined stone hut, standing c. 1.5 m above the ground surface, is round externally, but its internal dimensions are more polygonal (1.9 m N–S × 2.6 m E–W) (fig. 4.7). The gentle overhang of stones in the upper reaches of the wall reflects the line of a former roof of corbelled stone. The entrance to the hut is a half-meter gap in the eastern wall. The hut stands at the western side of an oval-shaped enclosure (17.7 m N–S × 16.5 m E–W) entered through a gap in the northeast, toward the village. Ranging from 0.75 m to 1.25 m in thickness, the enclosure consists of multiple courses of massive stones, much larger than those that make up the field walls of the nineteenth-century village. Antiquarian and folklore accounts from the nineteenth and twentieth centuries refer predominately to the hut, Clochán Leo, or use that name to refer to the entire complex. For clarity, I use *Clochán Leo* to refer to the hut itself and *Clochán Leo Complex* (CLC) to refer collectively to the hut, the enclosure, and other features excavated within.

Our team undertook excavations at the CLC in 2011, 2012, and 2017, as illustrated in figures 3.8–3.11. Preliminary excavation reports were submitted to the National Museum, and fuller accounts will be published in a future edited volume. Here I will lay out the broad strokes of the development of the CLC from the early medieval period till the late twentieth century.

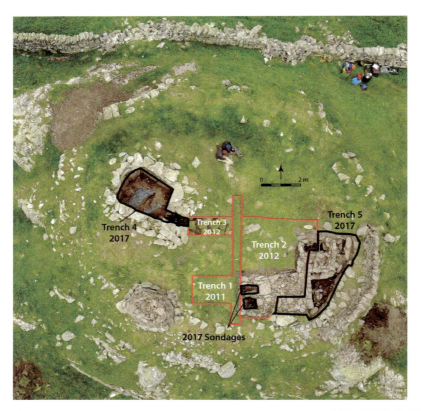

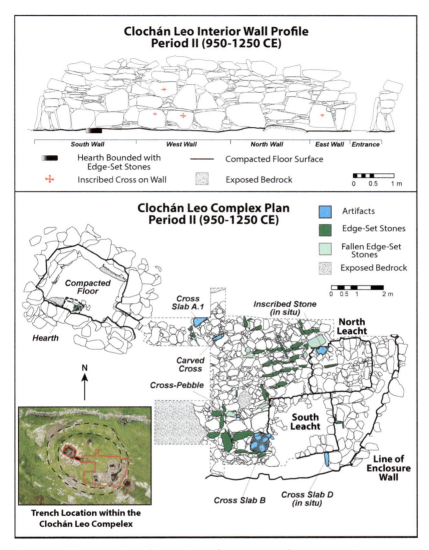

Facing top, Figure 3.8: Trench Locations of 2011, 2012, and 2017 excavations at the Clochán Leo Complex.

Facing bottom, Figure 3.9: Excavations of the Clochán Leo Complex underway in 2017. Photo by Ian Kuijt.

Above, Figure 3.10: Composite plan drawing of the excavations (2011, 2012, 2017) at the Clochán Leo Complex, showing features present in Period II. Figure produced by author, Meredith Chesson, and Elise Alonzi.

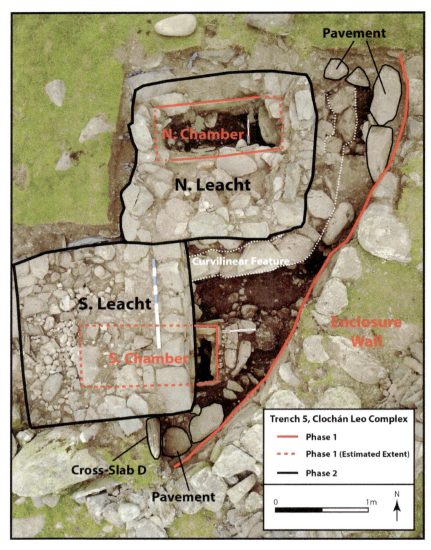

Figure 3.11: The chronology of features within Trench 5 at the Clochán Leo Complex.

Earliest Traces

The earliest evidence of human activity on site comes from a fragment of charred barley chaff recovered from a subsoil deposit just above the bedrock. The fragment yielded a radiocarbon date in the Iron Age, between 357 and 170 BCE (UBA-40622, 2175 +/− 22 BP). Cereal grain processing, if not cultivation, existed to some extent on the island prior to any monastic occupation. Whatever the character of Iron Age settlement on Inishark, the earliest monastic foundation entailed some engagement with the residue of previous human occupation.

The earliest and most enigmatic structural feature on site is a curvilinear alignment comprised of four courses of large stones (fig. 3.11). This feature was buried by a subsequent soil context of dark brown humic clay, which included an isolated willow charcoal fragment radiocarbon dated to 600–665 CE (UBA-40621, 1404 +/− 28 BP). Thus, the curvilinear feature, whatever its full form and function, appears to have been built prior to the seventh century. Whether it represents the earliest traces of monastic activity on Shark is unclear. It does, however, allow for the possibility that some form of ecclesiastical establishment existed on Inishark prior to Colman's well-recorded foundation on Inishbofin in the late seventh century.

CLC Period I: c. 650–950

The CLC initially took form between the seventh and tenth centuries. A combination of stratigraphic evidence, scientific dating, and comparative sites indicate that the clochán, the enclosure wall, and two stone-lined, gravel-filled chambers represent features built during Period I (figs. 3.8–3.11). The presence of these features would structure subsequent building and devotional activity within the complex for centuries thereafter.

Before laying the foundations of the clochán, builders—perhaps teams of monks alongside lay affiliates—prepared a compacted surface of orange-brown soil. Laid directly atop bedrock, the compacted surface acted as both foundation and floor surface within the clochán. The base stones of the clochán's wall rest atop the compacted surface and, in some cases, directly upon exposed bedrock. Finely fitted flagstones paved the threshold of the clochán's entrance.

A sample of hazel charcoal collected from the interface of the compacted surface and the underlying bedrock yielded a calibrated radiocarbon date of 599–674 CE (UBA-36757; 1393 +/− 32 BP). The charcoal does not represent an in situ hearth or any activity that may be directly associated with the construction of the clochán. Rather, it appears to have been redeposited from elsewhere during the preparation of the compacted surface. Nevertheless, the radiocarbon date suggests that the construction of the clochán *could* have begun as early as the seventh century. Corbelled, stone-roofed clocháns more typically date from the eighth century onward, though there are early exceptions (O'Sullivan et al. 2013, 115–16). While the clochán's initial construction dates to the early medieval period, the present structure formed through centuries of collapse and, most likely, partial reconstruction, tidying up, and stabilization during subsequent periods of occupation.

As such, it is difficult to date the three crosses incised on three large stones that make up the internal face of the clochán's western wall (fig. 3.10, below fig. 3.21). Though each cross is similar in size (less than 10 cm), one cross has a subtly different design with flared terminals. The traces of a fourth cross appear on the internal eastern wall of the clochán to the north of the entrance. Although each cross may date to the early medieval period, they may also have been carved subsequently or even accumulated over centuries across the long history of the clochán's use as a scene of devotion.

How did people use the clochán during Period I? Despite its small size, the clochán could have acted as an oratory for a small congregation. However, as a setting for mass, the clochán is irregularly oriented with its entrance on the eastern end. The difficulty of discerning the function of Clochán Leo during Period I is compounded by a lack of evidence for the extent of monastic settlement on the island during this time. Does Clochán Leo truly represent the initial core of a small monastic community that later developed into something more extensive? Or is it simply the best-preserved aspect of a more expansive early monastic landscape? Later folklore associates the hut specifically with Saint Leo and his practice of solitary ascetic devotion. Early medieval saints' lives include references to such features, typically as a refuge for saintly figures set at some distance from their monastery's core buildings (Plummer 1910: I, 141; II, 136–37). Archaeological research has identified possible hermitages at Iona, Inishmurray, County Sligo; Glendalough, County Wicklow; Skellig Michael, County Kerry; and Toureen Peakaun, County Tipperary (Bourke et al. 2011, 13–4; Ó Carragáin 2009, 216; 2010, 269–71; 2017b). Clochán Leo may indeed represent one of the earliest features of a monastic settlement, possibly used for individual ascetic devotion and later commemorated as the refuge of a founding saint.

As the clochán was built upon an introduced deposit, stratigraphic information could not definitely demonstrate the chronological relationship between the clochán and other features within the CLC. Yet, on the east side of the complex, the base layer of the enclosure wall rests within the clay deposit that included the willow charcoal fragment dated to the first half of the seventh century. As such, the enclosure wall likely also represents a primary feature of the complex built in association with the clochán in the late seventh or eighth century.

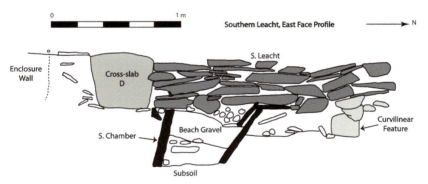

Figure 3.12: (*Above*) The southern chamber and curvilinear feature underlying the southern leacht. (*Below*) Profile drawing showing the edge-set stones of the southern chamber, in-filled with layers of beach gravel. The southern chamber was covered by the southern leacht in Period II.

Two other features within the enclosure originated between the seventh and tenth centuries: the southern and northern chambers excavated in Trench 5 (fig. 3.11). The southern chamber was only partially excavated as it lay beneath a later stone platform (see southern leacht, Period II), so its total dimensions remain uncertain. The exposed portion of the feature consists of thin edge-set

Figure 3.13: The northern chamber under excavation encased within the northern leacht.

stones that appear to define one end of rectangular chamber (fig. 3.12). The chamber was constructed by cutting into the underlying clay and digging down to bedrock. Edge-set stones were then inserted along the perimeter of the cut and then in-filled with fine beach gravel intermixed with winkle shells and small water-worn quartz pebbles (fig. 3.12).

The northern chamber (fig. 3.11), much like the southern chamber, is defined by edge-set stones and in-filled with beach gravel intermixed with quartz pebbles and winkle shells (figs. 3.12, 3.13). In the case of the northern chamber, the gravel deposit contained many small irregular schist flags and terminated by blending into a dark black soil deposit that rests above the bedrock. This stratigraphic superimposition of beach gravel atop subsoil suggests that the northern chamber originated during Period I as a counterpart to the southern chamber. Subsequent building work in Period II entailed some modification of the northern chamber, when it was encased within a stone platform (see northern leacht below).

One artifact found in association with the northern chamber also dates to Period I. The stone (approximately 38 cm × 30 cm × 7 cm), found directly atop the gravel fill of the chamber, bears a faint inscription in Insular script, a form of

Figure 3.14: The inscribed stone in situ (marked by the trowel) immediately atop the gravel fill of the northern chamber (2012). Photo by Meredith Chesson.

writing dated from the seventh to ninth centuries (Duncan 2016, 217–19) (figs. 3.14, 3.15). The text is tantalizingly ambiguous. It reads *beo*, followed by a space and then linear cuts that indicate attempts at either additional letters or shapes. These additional cuts might be read as the letters *in* executed at a smaller scale, yielding either *beo in* (Latin, "I bless in") or a possible Irish personal name, Beoín ("little life"). However, in my view, the stone flaked during production, erasing the bottom portion of these additional figures and obscuring what the creator intended. Believe me, try as we might and despite initial excitement, we could not propose *Leo* as a valid possible reading.

Most inscribed stones from ecclesiastical settlements are formulaic commemorations from mortuary contexts that implore the reader to pray for a named individual (Higgins 1987, 136; Okasha and Forsyth 2001). Hence, one might be tempted to bend an interpretation to meet this expectation. However, I am not confident that the inscription should be taken as fully realized and intentionally produced for placement in its find context. The likeliest possibility—based on

Figure 3.15: The inscribed stone. Photo by Terry O'Hagan.

the insertion of the stone face down and the attempts at additional script—is that the stone is a practice piece, possibly by a novice. The deposition of the stone in its find context might have been entirely incidental to the intended inscription. Thus, as a source of dating the northern chamber, the stone is dubious as its position may not represent a primary context.

Full excavation within the northern chamber and partial excavation of the southern chamber produced no datable artifacts, but their apparent form allows speculation concerning their original function. People clearly invested considerable labor and care in collecting and depositing the beach gravel to fill the chambers. Although no skeletal material was recovered from either chamber, in form and orientation, the fully excavated northern chamber is conspicuous in its affinity to a grave setting. Early medieval lintel graves, such as those excavated on High Island (*Ardoileán*), likewise consist of rectangular chambers, oriented east–west and lined with edge-set stones (Scally 2014, 303–11). Notably, three of these graves on High Island (Graves 2, 6, and 7) appear to have been built as pseudo-graves, empty of skeletal material, despite the presence of decorated headstones, footstones, and recumbent slabs (Scally 2014, 84–87). Textual and material evidence from early medieval Ireland suggest that ecclesiastical communities sometimes consecrated cenotaph monuments—symbolic graves—to evoke the presence of a saint's power without the physical presence of their corporeal relics (Ó Carragáin 2017a). Against this background, it is possible that the two chambers at the Clochán Leo Complex were intentionally constructed as cenotaph monuments. We will consider this possibility further in the next chapter.

In sum, the construction of the clochán, enclosure, and southern and northern chambers occurred between the seventh and tenth centuries. These components, whether the products of a single building initiative or episodic development, comprised the CLC during its initial period of use.

Combining a hermitage with two pseudo-reliquary monuments, the CLC could have facilitated both individual and communal forms of devotion. While individual penitents could have prayed within the clochán for extended periods of time, congregations of monks, and possibly lay pilgrims, could have visited the cenotaphs in the course of processional rituals, held periodically to commemorate particular feast days.

CLC Period II: c. 950–1250

A major phase of renovation at the CLC, likely between the tenth and early eleventh centuries, significantly altered material fixtures within the complex. Yet, this renovation was also an act of monumental commemoration that marked the presence of preexisting features (figs. 3.10, 3.11). This work included the construction of two leachta (stone platforms) associated with the underlying cenotaph chambers, the laying of a flagstone pavement, and the production of a series of decorated cross-slabs. These actions seemingly represent a campaign of infrastructural development designed to facilitate pilgrimage activity within the CLC.

The two leachta built in Period II are similar in appearance but different in their construction and in their relationship to the Period I chambers. The southern leacht was built directly atop the exposed surfaces of the southern chamber and the early curvilinear alignment (figs. 3.10, 3.11). Builders made the leacht by laying multiple courses of flagstones to create a rectangular box structure (1.75 m E–W × 1.9 m N–S) c. 30 cm high that they then in-filled with tightly packed rubble and quartz pebbles.

The plan of the northern leacht, although similar in dimensions (1.9 m E–W × 1.7 m N–S), is less formally linear than the southern leacht. Whereas builders simply constructed the southern leacht atop the Period I southern chamber, they designed the northern leacht to *encase* the Period I northern chamber and in-filled the rest of the structure with rubble and beach gravel (fig. 3.13).

What accounts for these differences in construction? I think that encasing the northern chamber in this way was necessary to ensure that the two new leachta would be similar in form and elevation. As excavated, the two leachta appear preserved to their original height and are practically identical in elevation where they abut one another. On the contrary, the elevation of the edge-set stones defining the top of the southern chamber is 26 cm lower than those defining the northern chamber. This difference in elevation is nearly identical to the difference in elevation (24 cm) between sterile soil deposits excavated beneath the two chambers. Hence, uneven natural topography likely accounts for the different elevations of the southern and northern chambers. The construction of the southern leacht *atop* the southern chamber and of the northern leacht *around* the northern chamber corrected this difference in elevation, creating two features that nearly approximate one another in plan and elevation.

Period II renovations also included the laying of a flagstone pavement within the complex (figs. 3.5, 3.10, 3.16). To the east of the leachta, the pavement consists of a series of flagstones somewhat haphazardly placed to cover the area between the leachta and the enclosure wall. Rather than totally dismantling the preexisting curvilinear alignment, they merely incorporated some of the stones into the new pavement. Significantly, the pavement did not cover the eastern end of the southern chamber, which would have remained visible at the foot of the southern leacht. To the west of the leachta, the pavement was more ordered in design and elaborate in creation. Initially, builders laid beach gravel, quartz pebbles, and schist flags to create a level surface. Upon this foundation, they laid the upper pavement of flagstones carefully set between parallel alignments of edge-set stones. This two-layered pavement would have facilitated drainage between gaps in the flagstones and through the gravelly matrix below, perhaps discouraging water from pooling in the complex after periods of heavy rain.

The Period II pavement also extends westward to the entrance of the clochán (see fig. 3.10). The pavement is less regular here, with gaps between flagstones exposing underlying soil deposits. In one of these gaps, excavators uncovered the fragment of an annular soapstone piece, so finely carved that it might have been lathe turned (see fig. 4.14). The piece appears unfinished and might have been intended as a loom weight or spindle whorl that broke during production. It's one of two soapstone pieces related to textile production uncovered at the complex (see chap. 4, p. 161).

A series of cross-slabs found within the CLC likely date to the same phase of renovations in Period II (figs. 3.17, 3.18). Only one of these, Cross-slab D, was

Figure 3.16: View facing east showing the Period II pavement still scattered with quartz pebbles. The figure in the center is kneeling atop the southern leacht while the figure on the right stands atop the enclosure wall of the complex.
Photo by Meredith Chesson.

found in situ immediately adjacent to the southern leacht and apparently set in place during the construction of the leacht and pavement (figs. 3.10, 3.11). The slab, a thick and heavy water-smoothed stone, includes a double-lined cross with flared terminals on its eastern face. Given the stone's placement, this design would have been visible only from the eastern side of the leachta. The other cross-slabs from the CLC, all found ex situ, feature so-called expansional cross designs (a reference to the cross's expanded terminals). Cross-slab A was found ex situ in two fragments, one outside the clochán entrance and another amid collapse within the clochán itself (figs. 3.10, 3.17, 3.20 below). The design consists of an equal armed expansional cross with a central disc boss within which is incised a Maltese-style cross. A similar but more intact cross-slab (Cross-slab

B), discovered by Tommy Burke, rested atop the pavement where it appeared to have slid from atop the southern leacht and broken in situ (fig. 3.17). Cross-slab C, the fragment of another expansional cross—though not likely equal armed—was found face down ex situ amid collapsed stones within the clochán (figs. 3.18, 3.20 below).

Once again, comparison with other monastic sites illuminates the likely circumstances surrounding the production of the cross-slabs and the Period II renovations. Expansional cross designs are known from early medieval monastic sites across the country, including Clonmacnoise, Co. Offaly; Inis Cealtra, Co. Clare; and Inchagoill, Clonfert, and High Island, Co. Galway (Higgins 1987, II, 342–43; Swift 2003, 118). The nearest comparable pieces to Inishark come from High Island, where expansional cross designs appear fourteen times on thirteen cross-slabs (Maddern 2014, 187). Four of these slabs are incorporated into the grave settings of three individuals whose skeletal material yielded calibrated radiocarbon dates between the late ninth and early eleventh centuries (Maddern 2014, 194–96; Scally 2014, 228–30). A closer look at the context of two of these graves in particular—Graves 3 and 4—suggests that their enshrinement represents an attempt to generate a cult surrounding two recently deceased holy men in the early eleventh century. Each grave, lined by upright stones and fitted with a paved floor, included the remains of an elderly man interred upon and covered by thin layers of sand. The nearly identical date ranges for each individual (Grave 3: 980–1025 CE; Grave 4: 980–1023 CE) suggest that their entombments in carefully constructed chambers represent near contemporary initiatives (Scally 2014, 73–78). Either skeleton might represent the remains of Gormgal, *prim-anmchara Erenn* ("chief soul-friend of Ireland"), a churchman of sufficient note to have his death on High Island recorded in the annals in 1017/1018 (Moran 2014, 25–26; Scally 2014, 300). The deaths of the individuals in Graves 3 and 4 appear to have inspired a major building campaign on High Island, possibly designed to facilitate devotion of their cult by monks and pilgrims. This campaign included the construction of High Island's first masonry church, the elaboration of three preexisting graves with carved-stone settings, and, significantly, three newly built pseudo-grave chambers (Graves 2, 6, and 7) (Scally 2014, 303–11). These pseudo-graves may have been purposely built as cenotaphs to commemorate figures who died at sea or were known to be buried elsewhere (Scally 2014, 309; Ó Carragáin 2017a). One of these pseudo-graves, Grave 2, was covered by a recumbent slab bearing an expansional cross design. In all, the evidence suggests that at least some of the expansional crosses on High Island were produced during the eleventh century as part of an initiative to create the necessary infrastructure for the veneration of the saintly dead:

Figure 3.17: Two expansional cross-slabs from the Clochán Leo Complex. *Left*: Cross-slab B. *Right*: Cross-slab A. The larger scale bars are 40 cm, and the smaller scale bars are 30 cm.

Figure 3.18: *Left*: Cross-slab C fragment. *Right*: A stone notched to create a cruciform shape. The larger scale bars are 40 cm, and the smaller scale bars are 30 cm.

both recently deceased holy men whose corpses were interred on site and more temporally or geographically remote figures evoked by means of empty graves.

Perhaps a similar cult-building renovation was undertaken by the monastic community on Inishark. The Inishark expansional slabs are sufficiently similar to their High Island counterparts to be products of the same floruit of cross-slab production centering around the early eleventh century. Both communities, if not dedicated to the same patron, likely shared a history of interaction characterized by the exchange of ideas, objects, personnel, and repertoire of craft works and technologies. It is possible that the early eleventh century building phase on High Island was paralleled by a near contemporary refurbishment of the CLC. Both initiatives included the reconfiguration of preexisting features and the creation of new infrastructure and artwork to facilitate the veneration of graves or pseudo-graves.

More than seven hundred water-rolled quartz pebbles excavated from atop the pavement in the CLC may represent direct evidence of a boom in pilgrimage traffic. A number of coves and pebble beaches on Inishark still offer harvesting points for tide-worn quartz, including the cove just east of Clochán Leo where once was St. Leo's Well (see below). Several excavations from across northern Britain and Ireland demonstrate that people deposited quartz stones in graves and on pilgrimage monuments during the early medieval period (Hill 1997, 472–73; O'Sullivan and Ó Carragáin 2008, 270, 320; Marshall and Walsh 2005, 87–89). Medieval hagiography references both the healing capacity of white stones and the turning of sacred stones to swear oaths and enact curses (Anderson and Anderson 1991, 398–405; Maddern 2014, 198). These early medieval practices influenced later turas traditions in which pilgrims marked their journeys to shrines by depositing stones or rotating distinctively shaped or decorated "cursing stones" in order to swear an oath or enact a blessing or curse (Corlett 2014, 84–85; Higgins 1987, 18–24; O'Sullivan and Ó Carragáin 2008, 335–41; Whelan 2018, 123–26).

In addition to the quartz, excavators also uncovered a cross-inscribed granite pebble atop the pavement near the find spot of Cross-slab B (figs. 3.10, 3.19). Rounded by water, the bottom side of this pebble has been polished even more, likely from rubbing or turning on a stone surface or within the palms of hands. This pattern of polish is also apparent on the Clocha Breca, the famous cursing stones on Inishmurray. Unlike those stones however, the granite pebble comes from an excavated context, where it has likely been buried for at least two centuries. As such, one can assign its wear pattern more confidently to practices that certainly predate c. 1700 and potentially belong to the early medieval period. Admittedly, the quartz pebbles and the cross pebble cannot be dated with absolute precision. While the deposition of quartz as pilgrims' offerings may have

Figure 3.19: The granite cross-inscribed pebble excavated from the Clochán Leo Complex.

begun directly following the refurbishment of the CLC, pilgrims likely continued to deposit the stones in subsequent centuries as the complex remained intermittently visited and venerated. By gathering and depositing water-rolled stones, pilgrims left traces of their journeys through objects that themselves embody histories of movement and transformation through natural forces. We shall return to this idea in chapter 4.

The development of new infrastructure to facilitate pilgrimage traffic within the complex is perfectly compatible with the continuation of personal or communal monastic devotion within the complex. The clochán itself could continue to function as an ascetic cell for the periodic meditation of members of the monastic community, penitents, or even pilgrims. Within the clochán, excavations revealed a possible hearth set against the southern wall of the structure (fig.

3.10). The feature comprises alignments of edge-set stones accompanied by a few dozen small quartz pebbles. The edge-set stones are fire-reddened and define a small rectangular area of burning. A fragment of hazel charcoal collected from this burnt deposit yielded a calibrated radiocarbon date between 1163 and 1252 CE (UBA-40623, 840 +/− 22 BP). This hearth, likely used for small, periodic, and temporary fires, perhaps provided a suitably meager amount of heat for a hermit or penitent praying overnight within the clochán.

The fully developed Clochán Leo Complex of Period II, with its pseudo-reliquary leachta and stone cell, is best interpreted as a pilgrimage shrine and ascetic refuge that could have accommodated visiting lay pilgrims as well as a hermit or anchorite. Indeed, it is possible that proximity to an ascetic undertaking devotions within the clochán was part of the attraction for pilgrims.

CLC Period III: c. 1250–1600

There is no tightly datable evidence relating to activity within the CLC between c. 1250 and 1600. However, evidence from elsewhere on Inishark suggests the endurance of an ecclesiastical community of some sort on the island, potentially as late as the seventeenth century. As such, the CLC likely remained the focus of devotion in the thirteenth to seventeenth centuries, but perhaps less frequently. These visitors may have continued to deposit quartz, manipulate the cross pebble, venerate the leachta, and pray within the clochán. It is possible that one or more of the crosses incised into the walls of the clochán date from this period.

CLC Period IV: c. 1600–1750

Period IV is marked by both the reemergence of datable material evidence for activity within Clochán Leo and the beginning of its dilapidation (fig. 3.20). The subsequent history of Clochán Leo represents a kind of ongoing combat between loss and retrieval and between gravity and memory—the slow, continuing decay of the clochán and the encroachment of sod periodically interrupted by people intervening to find, save, or make a trace of human presence for future visitors to behold.

Sherds of seventeenth-century ceramics embedded into the clochán's compacted floor surface suggest that the structure's roof remained intact and its original floor level maintained at the outset of Period IV. Although difficult to identify with certainty, these likely include rim sherds of an apothecary cup and a Surrey Whiteware jug and body sherds of an unidentified vessel with a hand-painted geometric design (fig. 3.20) (N. F. Brannon, personal communication, 2017). Evidently consumption, likely of medicinal and alcoholic substances, featured in visits to Clochán Leo at this time.

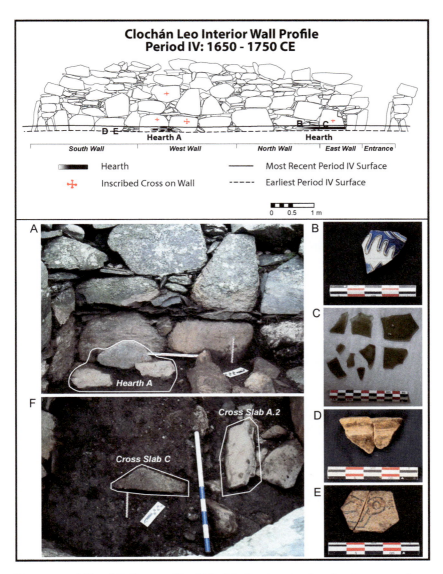

Figure 3.20: (*Above*) Rollout profile of Clochán Leo interior showing the accumulation of deposits during Period IV. (*Below*) A: Hearth in southwestern corner of western wall with inscribed crosses; B: Westerwald sherd found associated with hearth in northeastern corner; C: Case glass sherds found associated with a hearth in northeastern corner; D: Ceramic rim sherd associated with the earliest Period IV surface; E: Painted ceramic sherd associated with the earliest Period IV surface; F: Location of Cross-slab C (*left*) associated with most recent Period IV surface and Cross-slab Fragment A.2 (*right*) associated with the earliest Period IV surface and a metal object both covering part of the clochán's medieval hearth. Figure produced by Meredith Chesson and author.

Evidence of consumptive practices likely marks the transition from liturgies overseen by ecclesiastical officials to pilgrimage traffic primarily undertaken by laypeople in a context of Catholic suppression. On Inishbofin, British Commonwealth soldiers occupied a military garrison and prison for Catholic clerics following the Cromwellian conquest in the 1650s (Kuijt et al. 2015; Walsh 1989). It is hard to imagine that occupation of the neighboring island did not disturb devotional practices on Inishark in some way, and intentional destruction is not out of the question. A layer of collapsed stones covered the clochán's packed floor and the seventeenth-century ceramic sherds. Included amid the anonymous stones of this layer were two ex situ fragments of the early medieval Cross-slabs A and C.

Cross-slab fragment A.2, found face up above the medieval hearth feature, fits snuggly to Cross-slab fragment A.1, which was discovered face down amid collapse outside the clochán entrance (figs. 3.10, 3.17, 3.20). Resting atop fragment A.2 was a heavily corroded hunk of ferrous metal, possibly an assortment of multiple objects bound together through corrosion. This could represent a cluster of offerings left by pilgrims. Another cross-slab fragment (Cross-slab C; figs. 3.17, 3.20) was found face down amid nearby collapse. Were these cross-slab fragments brought inside the clochán for safekeeping and later lost amid neglect and collapse between the seventeenth and eighteenth centuries? In the deposits that buried the fragments, artifacts are intermixed with layers of collapse, suggesting that people visited the clochán only periodically during this era, perhaps primarily for annual pilgrimages.

Artifacts associated with these later deposits include a pipe stem, remnants of woven fabric, and fragments of olive-green case bottles—rectangular bottles typically used to ship gin in the seventeenth and eighteenth centuries (Munsey 1970, 84–86) (fig. 3.20). A few additional fragments were also found amid dislocated collapsed stone covering the early medieval pavement to the east of the clochán. There is otherwise no clearly datable evidence for Period IV activity outside of the clochán. Presumably, a combination of stone collapse from the enclosure wall, soil formation, and sod had begun to obscure early medieval features outside the hut.

In the southwestern corner of the clochán, there is evidence of repeated periodic burning. Someone built a simple stone-lined hearth at the western wall of the clochán, against a wall stone bearing one of the carved crosses (fig. 3.20). This hearth feature overlays an earlier deposit of charcoal and ash, and a subsequent deposit of charcoal and ash rested upon it. Even as collapsed stone continued to bury the clochán interior, people left traces that acted as cues for subsequent visitors to reiterate earlier practices.

The latest deposits from Period IV include a layer of stones that extended irregularly across the interior of the clochán. This appears to be collapsed stones that visitors arranged into an irregular pavement. Amid this pavement, we uncovered a single sherd of heavily decorated Westerwald stoneware, likely for a drinking vessel produced between the late seventeenth and eighteenth centuries (Gaimster 1997, 252–53; fig. 3.20).

CLC Period V: c. 1750–1960

Period V comprises the era of the historic village settlement on Inishark. Slow decay punctuated by periodic reengagement continued. A new bounty of historic artifacts attest to the importance of consumption and conviviality centered on the clochán (fig. 3.21).

Outside of the clochán, much of the complex had become overwhelmed with collapsed stone and vegetation by the nineteenth century. Excavations uncovered a substantial amount of displaced stone from atop the Period II pavement east of the clochán. These would have fallen from the clochán's roof and may have been intermittently cast here as visitors reentered and cleared out the clochán. A few small sherds of historic whiteware ceramics indicate that some of this collapse occurred during the nineteenth century. The depth of collapse on the eastern end of the leachta nearly reached the height of the leachta platforms themselves. Hence, following sod formation, it would have been difficult to identify the presence of the leachta here. Indeed, visitors' accounts from this period make no mention of them.

Within the clochán, continued collapse and soil formation buried the informal pavement established during Period IV and wholly obscured the lower two of the crosses cut in the clochán's western wall. A concentration of ash within the southwestern corner of the clochán suggests that burning continued in this area, possibly in the context of overnight vigils associated with customs reported in the nineteenth century (Browne 1893, 359). The uppermost deposits prior to the topsoil and sod included a layer of stone collapse that may represent an informal pavement that extended through the clochán entrance and eastward into the area of Trench 3. A variety of historic artifacts date these deposits to the nineteenth and twentieth centuries. Several artifacts likely represent devotions commonly associated with turas traditions: four nonmatching white glass buttons, possibly left to mark pilgrims' journeys; and a single multifaceted white glass bead, likely from a rosary (fig. 3.21). Several small schist stones with notches or perforations may represent weights for fishing lines, perhaps deposited in gratitude for or in hopes of securing fortune at sea (fig. 3.22).

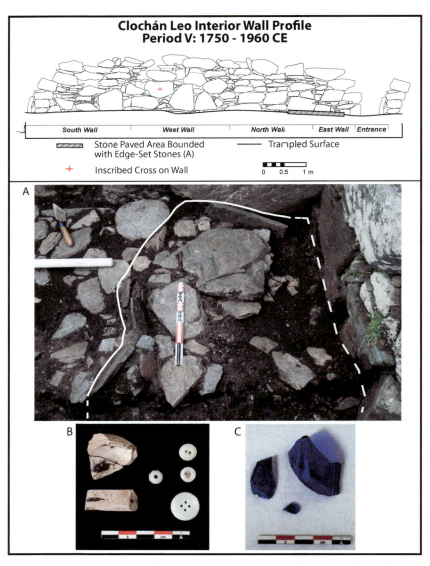

Figure 3.21: (*Top*) Rollout profile of the interior walls of Clochán Leo in Period V, marking the location of a stone platform. (*Bottom*) A: Stone paved area lined with edge-set stones on the western and northern edges; B: Fragments of pipe stem and bowl, one rosary bead, and three buttons; C: Blue glass sherds from a small medicine bottle. Figure produced by Meredith Chesson and author.

Figure 3.22: One perforated and three notched schist stones from Period V deposits.

Glass and ceramic vessel fragments testify to the consumption of alcohol, medicine, food, tobacco, and tea at the clochán, either on St. Leo's Day or on other occasions. Two identifiable glass vessels include a cobalt blue bottle commonly used for medicinal products and a vessel for Bovril, a salty meat extract paste spread on toast or diluted with hot water to drink or flavor soups. Sherds of sponge and transfer-print decorated serving vessels correspond with material excavated from historic houses on Inishark and in this context likely represent the remnants of picnicking activity (see chap. 5, fig. 5.8). We will consider this ceramic assemblage and the important commemorative and sensory elements of picnics at Clochán Leo in chapter 5.

The remarkable stratigraphy of activity at Clochán Leo spans the seventh to the twentieth centuries and provides a chronological framework for assessing the other traces ascribed to Saint Leo on Inishark. Other monuments, while similar in form and origin, appear not to have garnered the same pattern of enduring reengagement.

THE RECTANGULAR ENCLOSURES

There are two other enclosures on Inishark that recall the Clochán Leo Complex in their form and setting. Each stands atop the cliff-faced southern coast of the island, east of the pier (figs. 3.1, 3.23, 3.24). When approaching Shark from Bofin by boat, the first rectangular enclosure (c. 13.8 m E–W × 13.3 m N–S) comes into view atop a prominent knoll. At the southwestern corner of the enclosure, the rounded lump of a collapsed and overgrown clochán can be seen. This clochán

Figure 3.23: View looking southwest of the Clochán Congleo Complex. The Western Enclosure is visible top right between the two coves that cut into the shoreline. From footage by Ian Kuijt.

is recorded in the field name books that accompanied the 1838 Ordnance Survey, with three variants of its name provided: *clocán á cɔingleo*; *Cloghaun congleo*; "Congleo's stone house." To avoid confusion, I will use Clochán Congleo to refer only to the stone hut. To refer to the combination of clochán and enclosure, I will use the Clochán Congleo Complex, or more simply, the Congleo Complex. Around 100 m to the west of the Congleo Complex are the ruins of a second quadrangular enclosure (c. 13 m E–W × 13 m N–S) that we will call the Western Enclosure. Both the Congleo Complex and Western Enclosure include entranceways marked by pairs of upright stones in their southern and western sides.

Unlike Clochán Leo, these enclosures scarcely figure in extant folklore and never clearly in association with Saint Leo. But who is Congleo? Mac Gabhann, assessing the place-name variants recorded in 1838, renders the name as *Choingleo* and suggests that it might be a variant of the holy name Leo (2014, 715). If Congleo was once remembered as some disciple or counterpart to Leo, the name never appears elsewhere in extant folklore accounts after 1838. In 1942,

Figure 3.24: View looking southwest of the Western Enclosure. From footage by Ian Kuijt.

MacLoughlin recorded the site's name as *Clocán a' Coinnleora* (NFC 838, 114). MacLoughlin posited that the name was a reference to the shape of a nearby cove known as *fuaiġ a' Ċoinnleora,* "cove of the candlestick" (1942, NFC 839, 1). This cove is comprised of many narrow channels that converge into one, akin to the converging arms of a candelabrum. MacLoughlin was fond of finding shapes in the landscape to explain place-names, and this interpretation appears to be his own, rather than the suggestion of an island informant. My colleague Terry O'Hagan has observed that the root noun *coinnleoir* can also mean "candle bearer" or "acolyte." In this case, *Clocán a' Coinnleora* might be better interpreted as "the stone dwelling of the acolyte."

Latent religious resonances encoded in the inherited place-name may echo the history of the complex as a scene of devotion. If islanders once ascribed the clochán to a forgotten figure named Congleo or to a nameless religious devotee, by the mid-twentieth century the site was not regarded as sacred. Islanders either did not know or were not willing to tell MacLoughlin about the origin of

Figure 3.25: The Clochán Congleo Complex under excavation in 2016 showing the density of quartz pebbles blanketing the pavement.

the enclosure, and his words suggest a degree of apprehension among islanders in sharing details of the monument's associations.

> There is not the slightest scintilla of information regarding this mound or clochan to be had from the inhabitants of Inishark. (It was on the outskirts of this mound that cake-dances which were common in the island during the years in which 'poitin' was being manufactured, were held. I may here repeat that those cake dances were held, not on Sundays but on weekdays, and he or she who failed to sacrifice his or her work on that day, and participate in the cake-dance, held himself, or herself up to the opprobrium and contempt of his or her neighbours). (MacLoughlin 1942, NFC 839, 2)

Cake dances were dance competitions in which the winning partners were awarded a cake (Ó Dubda et al. 1941). MacLoughlin's phrase "I may here repeat" suggests that islanders were keen to indicate that these events, which likely included the drinking of *poitín* (unlicensed homemade whiskey), were not held on Sabbath days.

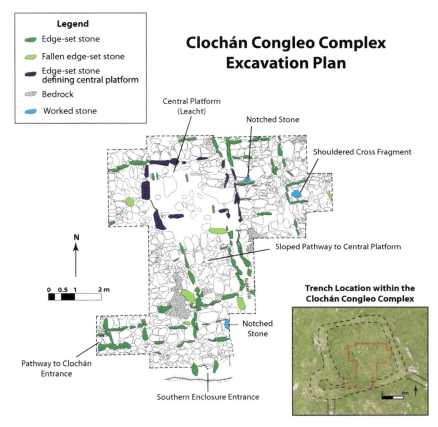

Figure 3.26: Plan of 2016 excavations at the Clochán Congleo Complex showing the pavement with the quartz pebbles removed.

Excavations centered on the Clochán Congleo Complex in 2016 and the Western Enclosure in 2017 revealed that the haziness of the folklore record belies common features and methods of construction that link the sites to Clochán Leo and the island's early monastic heritage.

The CLIC team excavated a single large trench within the Clochán Congleo Complex in 2016 (figs. 3.25, 3.26). While excavations revealed scant few datable artifacts, striking similarities with the Clochán Leo Complex suggest that the Congleo Complex developed in the period c. 700–1200. Beneath a thick layer of sod, we discovered a centrally positioned leacht (3.5 m E–W × 2.1 m N–S) surrounded by a substantial flagstone pavement topped with thousands of water-worn quartz pebbles. The leacht appears to have been a primary feature

Figure 3.27: View facing east of the stone-lined chamber partially excavated. Defined by edge-set stones on the north and south, the chamber was in-filled with gravel and capped by a layer of flagstones and quartz pebbles. The flagstone capping and gravel fill are still visible in place under the small scale bar.

that dictated the form of the surrounding pavement. The leacht is a complex structure that recalls the cenotaph leachta at Clochán Leo. To center the monument, builders constructed a rectangular stone-lined chamber, oriented E–W and measuring 2.1 m by 0.32 m (fig. 3.27). The chamber contained neither skeletal material nor artifacts but was in-filled with beach gravel. The chamber was then capped by a layer of flagstones and the edifice of the leacht constructed in the form of double alignments of edge-set stones on three sides. There is no clearly defined southern edge of the leacht, which instead articulated with the surrounding pavement. The rest of the leacht platform was constructed by stacking layers of quartz pebbles and flagstones atop the underlying chamber. The leacht, as excavated, stood no more than 30 cm above the height of the surrounding pavement. The combination of leacht and underlying gravel-filled chamber evokes the remains at the Clochán Leo Complex. However, in this case, the leacht and chamber appear to have been constructed as part of a single building initiative.

Likewise, the construction and orientation of the pavement suggest that it was laid as part of a cohesive design scheme that included the leacht, the enclosure, and the clochán. The double edge-set stone alignment that defines the eastern edge of the leacht extends south, defining the eastern edge of a sloped pavement that descends toward the southern entrance of the enclosure (figs. 3.25, 3.26). Another discrete pathway defined by edge-set stones leads from the base of this sloped pathway westward toward the entrance of the clochán (fig. 3.26). To the east of the leacht, crisscrossing alignments of edge-set stones define a series of rectangular pavement contexts. Again, this method of pavement construction matches that observed at the Clochán Leo Complex. In the easternmost area of the trench, the fragment of a simple but exceptionally well-crafted stone cross was found (figs. 3.26, 3.28).

Most extraordinarily, thousands of water-worn quartz pebbles lay thickly on all areas of the pavement (figs. 3.25, 3.29). While the quartz found within the central chamber and leacht had to be deposited at the time of construction, the quartz atop the pavement might have been deposited at any time after construction. Perhaps builders laid the quartz en masse after the completion of the pavement. This might explain the origin of the crisscrossing alignments of edge-set stones as a method designed to secure the quartz pebbles in place as an integral element of the pavement. An alternative interpretation is that the quartz at the Congleo Complex accumulated over time—possibly over centuries—as monks and pilgrims visiting the complex deposited the pebbles to commemorate their devotions. Either interpretation remains a valid possibility that accounts for the unusual density of quartz within the complex. Interestingly, the nearest places

Figure 3.28: The shouldered cross from the Clochán Congleo Complex. The scale bar is 30 cm in length.

to access quartz pebbles are the channels of the nearby *fuaiġ a' Ċoinnleora*, suggesting that the place-name connection between the natural feature and the complex may relate to former devotional practices rather than simple proximity. In all, our team counted 7,996 quartz pebbles that we excavated from the pavement or from within the leacht.

The lack of closely datable materials from the Congleo excavations means that the complex can be dated only by way of its similarity to the Clochán Leo Complex. Due to the affinity in construction and layout to the refurbishment of the Clochán Leo Complex in Period II, the Congleo Complex likely represents a near contemporary initiative. Perhaps the renovation of the Clochán Leo

Figure 3.29: Quartz pebbles in situ atop the pavement at the Congleo Complex.

Complex acted as a model for the development of the Congleo Complex—or vice versa. Both complexes, when fully developed, combined a pilgrimage shrine with one or more pseudo-graves and a hut suitable for ascetic devotion.

In 2017, the CLIC team undertook a small test excavation of the sub-rectangular Western Enclosure (figs. 3.24, 3.30, 3.31). The test trench, 12.1 m² in area, extended from the western entrance way toward a sod-covered eminence within the enclosure. Removal of the sod revealed the eminence to be a rectangular platform, likely a leacht. This feature (c. 1.5 m N–S) comprised a rectilinear alignment of stacked stones in-filled with rubble. A paved pathway defined by flagstones and edge-set stones led from the western entrance toward the leacht.

Figure 3.30: View of the Western Enclosure excavation facing east toward the hillock where the Clochán Congleo Complex stands.

Of the 144 quartz pebbles removed from the small test trench, the densest concentration clustered atop this pathway. Beyond this pathway, there were few pavement stones in place, and bedrock or subsoil lay immediately below the sod in much of the excavated area. Apart from small fragments of heavily rusted ferrous metal, excavators uncovered no artifacts from the trench. The combination and configuration of features exposed at the Western Enclosure suggest that people also built and visited this complex as one feature in a multifocal ritual landscape in the early medieval period.

The configuration of features excavated at the rectangular enclosures suggests that, like the Clochán Leo Complex, they were developed initially sometime between the seventh and twelfth centuries as focal points of pilgrimage and asceticism. Notable is the dearth of stone sculpture at the rectangular enclosures compared to Clochán Leo. This difference may represent their relative standing as sacred foci within the early medieval landscape, with Clochán Leo clearly reigning supreme. Yet, the density of quartz found at the Congleo Complex does suggest a substantial amount of pilgrimage traffic to a site that also

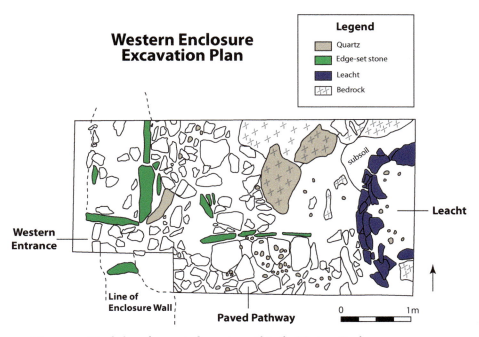

Figure 3.31: Final plan of excavated remains within the Western Enclosure.

appears to have derived its sanctity from the presence of a cenotaph monument and a resident ascetic.

While Clochán Leo remained intact and a focal point of at least periodic veneration, there is no unambiguous material evidence that people continued to visit the Congleo Complex or the Western Enclosure for the purpose of veneration or devotion in the postmedieval period. Despite folklore related to cake dances, excavations at the Congleo Complex recovered only twenty-two ceramic sherds from no more than four distinct vessels dating from the mid- to late nineteenth century and a single white glass bead. The clochán at the Congleo Complex is now totally covered in sod and appears to have dilapidated and collapsed to a much greater extent than Clochán Leo. Islanders in the nineteenth and twentieth centuries maintained Clochán Leo, but Clochán Congleo appears not to have garnered such attention and may even have been partially recycled for stone. Future excavation might clarify the story. Evidence of activity at the Clochán Leo Complex in the seventeenth and eighteenth centuries was almost entirely confined within the clochán itself. Clochán Congleo may harbor such postmedieval evidence yet undiscovered, or perhaps the monument's early dereliction has left early medieval surfaces and artifacts intact beneath the collapse awaiting excavation. At present, the balance of evidence suggests that different patterns of activity at these complexes intensified over time. Reengagement with Clochán Leo reproduced memories and maintained the visibility of remains over centuries. Disuse of the rectangular enclosures allowed the sites to fall into disrepair and obscurity as sod gradually blanketed the quartz-strewn pavements.

TEAMPAILL LEO, ST. LEO'S CHURCH

With its high, broad gables mounted by concrete crosses, St. Leo's Church is easy to pick out among the gray ruins on Inishark (fig. 3.32). The building (12.6 m E–W × 6.78 m N–S, external dimensions) is the product of multiple phases of medieval and modern building and refurbishment. When MacLoughlin visited

Figure 3.32: The eastern gable of Teampaill Leo.

in 1942, the church was still in good working order and served by monthly visits from the priest on Inishbofin. The building was said to encase more than a few traces of the island's monastic heritage.

> Until four years ago, when the church underwent reconstruction, a window five feet high and ten inches wide, said to have been constructed during the time of Leo, still retained its original position. On the apex of the east gable was also a stone cross of archaic construction, but to one not acquainted with the original cross, the cross at present on this apex could easily deceive one, as the ancient cross is now encased in a cement coating. I have heard on one occasion only that this cross did not originally belong to the church, but was found in a nearby garden at the time the church was first being reconstructed. Within the little chapel are still to be seen a small stone flag, engraved in which is a cross, and another large stone resembling a water-font and believed by the inhabitants to have served as a baptismal font during the days of Leo. (MacLoughlin 1942, NFC 839, 8–9)

While the concrete cross retains its position on the eastern gable, the cross-engraved flagstone and stone water font have disappeared. Excavations and a building survey by our team have made new discoveries that reveal the church's primary phases of development. These findings illuminate later medieval and early modern activity that is otherwise difficult to discern on Inishark.

An Early Medieval Antecedent?

No part of the church's building fabric dates as far back as the seventh century and perhaps not even before the twelfth century. Prior to the mid-eleventh century, most churches at minor ecclesiastical sites were constructed of organic materials and are rarely preserved in the archaeological record. There may well have been a timber church in the location of the extant Teampaill Leo when the Clochán Leo Complex took shape, but we cannot know for certain.

Leo's Church Period I: c. 1150–1250

The basic footprint of the extant St. Leo's dates between the mid-twelfth- and mid-thirteenth-century building campaign. This is based on the dimensions of the building as well as in situ and ex situ architectural fragments. The sill of an in-filled window surround, carved of local soapstone, is visible in the external eastern gable wall. A survey by Terry O'Hagan uncovered a punch-dressed round-headed window arch, also in soapstone, stashed in a cottage to the east of the church (fig. 3.33). The material and estimated dimensions of its aperture suggest that it matches the in situ sill. This sill and arch likely correspond with the window mentioned by MacLoughlin as dating from Leo's time. In reality, the splayed style of the round-headed window arch can be tentatively dated

Figure 3.33: Round-headed soapstone window arch, recovered from a house east of Teampaill Leo.

between 1150 and 1250 (Lash 2020). The construction of a church of this size suggests the need to serve a fairly large congregation of worshippers in the late twelfth and thirteenth centuries. This may mark an intensification of focus on lay devotion on the part of Inishark's ecclesiastical community.

Leo's Church Period II: c. 1250–1700

In the next major phase of construction, workers rebuilt the southern and western walls by using the original base courses of the Phase I church as a plinth (i.e., a foundation that juts out from the line of a wall). The rebuilt walls include dressed soapstone blocks used as quoin stones (in the southwestern and southeastern walls) and to surround a southern entranceway (fig. 3.34).

This phase of building likely belongs to the late medieval period. Across Connemara, a series of late medieval parish churches with dimensions similar to St. Leo's Church likewise include southern entranceways. Indeed, the late medieval parish church on Inishbofin also includes a southern entrance and dressed soapstone for aperture surrounds.

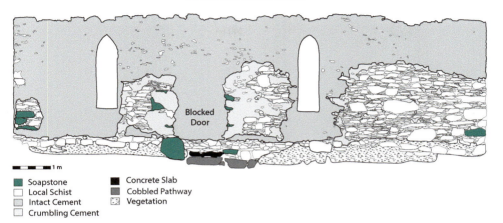

Figure 3.34: Profile drawing of the southern wall of Teampaill Leo, showing the soapstone quoins and doorway surround associated with the Phase 2 rebuilding. Figure produced by Elise Alonzi and adapted by author.

Like other medieval parish churches, St. Leo's acted as a focal point of burial. Five trenches excavated along the perimeter of the church exposed at least ten graves (fig. 3.35). Analysis of a small sample of skeletal material collected from graves along the eastern wall in Trenches 1 and 2 revealed a mixed deposit of fragments from multiple individuals (and animals) whose original burial context is unclear. A small fragment of crania from Burial I in Trench 1 yielded a date of 1478–1637 CE (UBA-41067 338 +/− 23 BP). This adult individual was buried with their head immediately adjacent to the base of the eastern wall. Similarly, an ex situ fragment of a juvenile's right ischium from the vicinity of Burial III yielded a date of 1444–1624 CE (UBA-41068, 385 +/− 24 BP). Trench 3 exposed a rectangular stone leacht platform built adjacent to the southern wall and above at least one burial capped by flagstones. This leacht may have been installed to mark a particular burial. Without further investigation, it is impossible to say when burial in this area commenced and how far the cemetery extended. Most of the exposed burials appear to have been dug to align with the footprint of the church and thus likely date from c. 1150 onward.

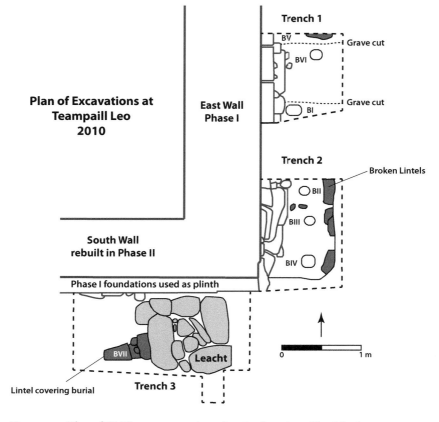

Figure 3.35: Plan of CLIC 2010 excavations showing location of burials along the eastern wall of the church as well as the leacht capping a grave near the southeastern corner of the church.

Leo's Church Period III: c. 1700–1881

Sometime between the eighteenth and early nineteenth centuries, St. Leo's Church fell into disuse and decay as the island's ecclesiastical community dissolved. The earliest inhabitants of the historic village on Inishark, developed from c. 1750, are likely to have had virtually no regular access to priests on the island. In 1838, the church was recorded as "in ruins." When the antiquarian George Kinahan visited in 1869, portions of the north, east, and south walls remained intact (Kinahan 1870, 203). Kinahan's unpublished notes, later referenced by Browne, indicate that islanders used the church as a cattle pen and had even repurposed a cross-inscribed flagstone to form a trough against the church wall (1893, 365). The building retained its association with a saintly past, but this did not prevent its reconfiguration into infrastructure for tending livestock.

Leo's Church Period IV: 1881–1960

The restoration of the ruined edifice into a functional church occurred sometime during the tenure of Father James Rabbitte as priest on Inishbofin (1881–84). Restoration work required the rebuilding of the western wall, most likely with the entrance present there today. The soapstone eastern window and the southern doorway likely also remained intact in the renovated building. Indeed, excavations revealed a cobbled path leading from the sill of the southern doorway to an entrance (now blocked in) through the enclosure wall surrounding the church. The church enclosure wall first appears on the twenty-five-inch Ordnance Survey (OS) map of 1898. Thus, the cobble path and the church enclosure wall may both have been installed alongside the restoration work of the 1880s. The accounts of both Browne and MacLoughlin mention that a stone cross—Leac Leo—was taken from somewhere in the vicinity of the church and mounted on the eastern gable during the 1880s renovation. In 1893, Browne described the church as whitewashed and slated for use.

MacLoughlin's account mentions another phase of restoration in about 1938, which obscured the presence of the eastern window. If not in-filled earlier, the window was now blocked in and plastered over, as was the southern entrance. The cross mounted on the eastern gable appears to have been covered over in concrete and the church reroofed. A cement floor was laid in the interior and a raised platform installed on the eastern end with a socket to hold a wooden altar. The pointed arch windows visible in the extant building likely belong to this phase of restoration. They once held stained glass. According to Andrew Concannon, one of the men from Bofin who served as an altar attendant for masses in the 1950s, a granite font, mentioned by MacLoughlin (1942, NFC 839, 9), stood to the left of the western entrance inside the church. A small wooden confessional was set along the northern wall. Other fixtures included statues of saints and stations of the cross, which islanders performed on those Sundays when weather forbade passage between Shark and Bofin. After the island's evacuation, many of the fixtures within the church were removed as part of its decommission, including the altar and confessional. The priest at the time, Fr. Flannery, distributed the stations of the cross plaques to the last families resident on the island. Sometime before 1964, Flannery also instructed a few men from Inishbofin to deroof the church, the timbers from which were brought back to Inishbofin and reused in roofs. Subsequently, islanders from Inishbofin occasionally used the church as a pen to hold sheep during shearing expeditions on Inishark.

TOBAR LEO, ST. LEO'S WELL

Around 100 m east of Clochán Leo, a deep cut in the cliff edge leads down to a cove: *Oughleo*, or Leo's Cove. Many footfalls have worn a path that wends down to a narrow ledge on the cliff face where once stood Tobar Leo, St. Leo's Well (figs. 3.1, 3.36). This was one of the few monuments still actively visited by the last generation of islanders. Coastal erosion and lack of maintenance claimed the stone setting of St. Leo's Well sometime in the late twentieth century, but the ledge is often left damp by an active spring. MacLoughlin writes:

> A few yards north of the holy well is a spring well. A large stone lies to the north of the holy well and some small flags indiscriminately placed help to complete the surrounding wall, which is about one foot high. Within the well can be seen buttons, pins and small pieces of cloth, which are some of the tokens left by the visiting pilgrims. The following tale is common among the islanders. A pilgrim to the holy well, having remained in a friend's house on the island, was once sent to the spring well in Leo's cove to fetch some water, and owing to the proximity of the two wells the stranger filled his vessel with the water of Leo's well. It followed however that the water, after considerable time, failed to boil. This was no surprise to the people of the house when it transpired that the water was taken from Leo's well. Local tradition has it that such water will refuse to serve any purpose, if used for domestic or cooking purposes. As the eleventh day of April is held as St. Leo's Day, it is on this day that the majority of the island population perform the annual pilgrimage to Leo's Well, but such pilgrimage can also be performed on any Friday or Sunday throughout the year. (MacLoughlin 1942, NFC 339, 6–7)

MacLoughlin received a detailed account of the procedure for completing the pilgrimage to St. Leo's Well from a seventy-three-year-old woman of Inishark called Máire Garbh (MacLoughlin 1942, NFC 838, 30–31). The text is at times ambiguous, but the complex choreography can be summarized as follows:

1. Kneel at the holy well and recite the Ave Maria and Glory to the Father seven times. Keep a count of the prayers by making a mark on one of the stones surrounding the holy well (MacLoughlin observed these marks during his visit).
2. Drink three drops of the holy well's water.
3. Go to the nearby spring well and wash your feet. Gather seven small stones.
4. Walk barefoot around the holy well seven times while reciting the Ave Maria and Gloria seven times. Throw one of the seven small stones into the well after every circuit to keep a count of your roundings.

Figure 3.36: The eastern cliff face of Leo's Cove, showing the path that once led down to St. Leo's Well and the pebbly beach below.

5. Take three sips of water from the holy well.
6. Fill a shell (presumably a large seashell, from a limpet or scallop) with water from the holy well and circle it around your waist three times in the name of the Father, the Son, the Holy Spirit, and St. Leo.
7. Leave a belonging at the well. Women typically left the pin or tassel from their shawls.

MacLoughlin's notes repeatedly reflect the special association of Leo's Well with women as agents of blessing, healing, or cursing. Women were the group most likely to perform a pilgrimage to the well and might even have undertaken the journey vicariously on behalf of children abroad. The following excerpts from MacLoughlin's Irish notes were translated by Conor Ó Gallachóir.

> It is said that the water from the well is holy, some of the islanders have a tradition of sending some of the water to relatives in America but this could not be done without undertaking the pilgrimage first.... When water cannot be sent to your relatives, they are sent a small stone from the well, in a letter. This old woman [i.e., Máire Garbh] tells me that she got news from her son who was sick in America once and she went and done the pilgrimage to Leo's Well and then she hoped to send him some of the water; she got a small carton, she plunged it into the well, she put the carton into a letter and sent it to America to him. (MacLoughlin 1942, NFC 838, 31–32)

Another of MacLoughlin's informants on Inishark, seventy-six-year-old Tomás Ó Cluanáin, testified to fishermen's devotion to Leo as a guarantor of safety at sea. The following is Ó Gallachóir's translation of Ó Cluanáin's words:

> There is not one day in the year that a boat from this island goes over and back past Leo's Well, that every single person on the boat doesn't bless themselves, say a prayer, Saint Leo is asked to take them home safe. Everyone in the boat kneels—takes off their cap and kneels—in honour of the Saint, passing the well. The first thing that's said when they're laying nets at night: "We put them out under the protection of Leo".... Not only do the boats of this island kneel for Leo's Well, someone from each boat takes three drops of salt water into the boat in the hope that the saint will save them from the sea. (MacLoughlin 1942, NFC 838, 59)

The power of Leo's Well might also be manipulated to cause misfortune. Draining the well and casting the water into the tide could work up the sea. Ó Cluanáin related to MacLoughlin that he once encountered a woman near St. Leo's Well who asked him as he passed whether his son would be on the sea that day. When he told her that his son would be returning from Cleggan, she became startled and began to cry. Tomás reassured her that if the day remained calm, his boat would return safely. "But the day became rougher but the men came home safe. The woman was probably supposed to drain the holy well in the hope to drown someone" (MacLoughlin 1942, NFC 838, 361, translated by Conor Ó Gallachóir).

Ó Cluanáin's suspicions resonate with a story purportedly collected on Inishark and published by Lady Jane Wilde in 1888:

There was a woman of the Island of Innis-Sark who was determined to take revenge on a man because he called her by an evil name. So she went to the Saints' Well, and, kneeling down, she took some of the water and poured it on the ground in the name of the devil, saying "So may my enemy be poured out like water, and lie helpless on the earth!" Then she went round the well backwards on her knees, and at each station she cast a stone in the name of the devil, and said, "So may the curse fall on him, and the power of the devil crush him!" (Wilde 1888, 71)

We will have occasion to consider this tale more deeply in chapter 5.

Does St. Leo's Well represent another endurance of early medieval devotion? It is possible, but impossible to confirm. There are no visible remains of the well's stone setting, and indeed the entire area might now be lost to the sea. The labeling of this cove as Leo's Cove on the Bald Map of Mayo (1809–16) demonstrates an early association of this location with the saint. John O'Donovon's research, gathered during the first edition Ordnance Survey in 1838, explicitly associates the cove with the ascetic devotion of St. Leo himself. "Uaim leó ... St Leo's Cave, on the south shore of the island. St. Leó is said to have spent much of his time in meditation in this cave" (Herity 2009, 163). Whether or not Saint Leo visited the cove, it is the nearest and likeliest source for the quartz pebbles found within the Clochán Leo Complex.

LEABA LEO, ST. LEO'S BED

Many early medieval monastic sites include some feature described as a saint's *leaba*, or "bed." Such monuments can vary in form from unworked stones to decorated grave settings. If there is a shared characteristic, it is that they generally look like an uncomfortable way to spend an evening—which is, of course, the point. *Leaba* may refer figuratively to a saint's final resting place, but it is often used to identify the scene of some penitential exploit of spending nights in severe discomfort. The link between graves and penitential beds is not mere euphemism. The archetype of all Christian hermits—St. Anthony the Great—sought isolation within tombs where, as his hagiography contends, he was tormented by demons. Asceticism, as penitential devotion, was not only a preparation for death; it was also often enacted through the imitation of death.

The many shades of meaning attached to leaba is complicated further on Inishark, as the folklore sources are inconsistent on its application. The place-name Leaba Leo, "Leo's Bed," has done a pilgrimage of its own, seemingly wandering between different monuments across time. MacLoughlin remarked upon the name's association with both Clochán Leo and a large irregular flagstone east of the church. Yet, to the last residents of Inishark, Leaba Leo referred to a separate monument entirely—an oval-shaped leacht set in a field enclosure along the road that runs through the center of the village (figs. 3.1, 3.37). The best-preserved leacht on the island, Leaba Leo is a grass-covered platform (1.5 m E–W × 1.0 m N–S × 0.2 m high), atop which rests a granite font, or bullaun (Irish: *bullán*) (fig. 3.38). MacLoughlin had more to say about this object: "Its surface is concave and is consequently looked upon by the islanders as a font used for the purpose of baptising.... I have heard some of the islanders call it an 'umar *Bapte', but this name has not been traditionally handed down, but the inhabitants find this name to be appropriate owing to is striking resemblance to the baptismal font" (MacLoughlin 1942, NFC 838, 12–13).

When asked about the monument during a visit to Shark in 2009, Martin Murray, who grew up on the island, remembered the bullaun as a wart well. "I remember when I was a young lad I used to have warts on my finger. There used to be water in that. I used to come down there and pray and dip our hands in that, and after a few days the warts were gone."

Bullaun stones are notoriously difficult to date with precision but occur commonly at early monastic sites and even seem to appear in some medieval hagiography (Hamlin and Kerr 2008; Plummer 1910, II, 35–36). The bullaun on Leaba Leo may well be even more ancient, as it appears similar to a prehistoric grinding stone used to shape stone tools or process cereal grains. Our team conducted a small test trench around Leaba Leo in 2011, followed by larger-area excavations to the north of the monument in 2015. The results, set alongside historic maps, illuminate how a medieval monument has endured despite many transformations in its immediate landscape setting.

Like other early medieval monuments on Inishark, Leaba Leo was built to occupy a visually prominent position. The leacht is constructed along an east-to-west ridge that creates a border between ground sloping gently upward to the north and ground sloping steeply downward to the south. Builders dug to the bedrock and constructed the leacht atop a particularly elevated shelf. They seem also to have introduced a deposit of gray, sandy clay atop the bedrock, likely to create a level surface for the monument's foundations. We recovered a fragment of a blue glass bead from this soil deposit, immediately above the bedrock (fig. 3.39). Glass beads are fairly common finds from early medieval settlement sites (O'Sullivan et al. 2014, 231). Whatever the exact circumstances of its deposition, the bead's find spot implies that the monument's initial construction belongs to the early medieval period. The leacht, however, may have been altered or rebuilt over time. The northern foundation of the leacht comprises large, edge-set stones. The base of the southern side of the monument is less well defined and appeared as a heap of irregularly shaped stones. Either this represents a

Figure 3.37: Leaba Leo with Clochán Leo on the horizon.

secondary phase of rebuilding or builders constructed the southern side of the monument differently from the outset.

There is one other exceptional find from the site that ties the leacht to the medieval period. The circumstances of its deposition also illustrate the messy, confused, and confusing encounters with medieval heritage within the historic village. Sometime in the mid-nineteenth century, islanders built a house less than two meters north of Leaba Leo (fig. 3.40). This development is demonstrated starkly on six-inch (1838) and twenty-five-inch (1898) Ordnance Survey Maps: on the first, Leaba Leo and another nearby monument are shown in unenclosed ground; on the second, the area has been enclosed by a field plot, and a three-celled structure stands north of Leaba Leo (see fig. 5.4). Excavations in 2015 centered on this house and its relationship to Leaba Leo (Conway 2019). While construction of the house did not damage Leaba Leo, it did displace artifacts and deposits associated with the leacht's early history. For example, excavators uncovered more than two hundred quartz pebbles from the area between the leacht and the house. These may originally have rested atop the leacht

Figure 3.38: Detail of the bullaun stone atop Leaba Leo, with the cavity holding water after a rain shower.

Figure 3.39: Blue glass bead excavated at the base of Leaba Leo. Photo by Meagan Conway.

Figure 3.40: The house adjacent to Leaba Leo under excavation in 2015.

itself. However, a more extraordinary object was found within the foundation trench of the southern wall of the house. Amid the cobbles in-filling the trench was a heavy, smooth, and distinctively shaped pebble incised with a compass-made cross-of-arcs design (fig. 3.41). Tiny pinpoint depressions in the stone mark where the craftsperson positioned and repositioned the compass point to draw the concentric circles and intersecting arcs. The incisions of the design are variable in depth, and it is unclear whether the stone was ever properly finished before it was damaged. The stone is a micro-taskscape in itself, but I will reserve this discussion for the next chapter.

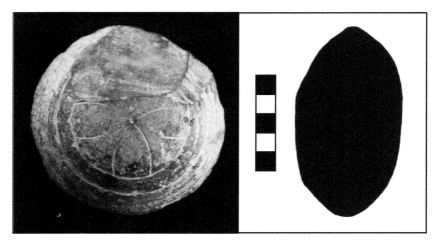

Figure 3.41: The compass-incised nodule excavated from the foundation trench of the nineteenth-century house adjacent to Leaba Leo.

The closest parallels for the stone found outside Leaba Leo are three stones uncovered during excavations of the monastic settlement on High Island. Two of these stones are incised with concentric circles with marks apparent from the compass used to render the decoration. One of these stones includes a cross design within the innermost circle on one face (Maddern 2014, 210–11). Excavators uncovered the stones amid rubble covering the graves adjacent to the eastern end of the church. Thus, while the context is not clearly datable, it appears they must have been deposited during the later phases of occupation on High Island, from the twelfth to fifteenth centuries.

Handheld X-ray fluorescence identified the High Island pebbles as ironstone nodules (Cotter 2014, 160). Nodules of this shape form naturally through the "precipitation of iron carbonate or oxide in pore spaces during diagenetic alteration of organic-rich sedimentary rocks" (Cotter 2014, 160). In other words, they form as the mineral components of liquid solutions solidify within cavities of certain kinds of stone under certain conditions. Ironstone nodules in particular are common in coal soils in Co. Carlow and Leitrim but also along the Shannon in South Clare. The Inishark stone is likely also a nodule or concretion formed through similar geological processes. However, it is larger than the High Island nodules, and handheld X-ray fluorescence revealed a relatively lower percentage of iron. As such, it may have originated from a different source.

Another well-known parallel for the Leaba Leo nodule comes from Temple Brecan on Inishmore (*Árainn*). That stone was found at *Leaba Bhrecáin*

("St. Brecan's Bed") beneath a recumbent stone slab bearing the inscription *SCI BRECANI*, "of Saint Brecan." The find in question was found among a number of beach-smoothed pebbles at a depth of four feet. Likely another ironstone nodule, the stone includes a simple inscribed cross on the top and an inscription along the side that reads *OR DO BRAN N-AILETHER*, "pray for Bran the pilgrim" (Higgins 1987, 16, 23, 137, 145–46).

It is striking that the closest parallels for the Inishark nodule come from sites associated with the bodies of holy men, as either actual graves or places of penitential sleep. Against this background, the Inishark nodule was most likely once associated with Leaba Leo, possibly resting atop the leacht. Worshippers in the early medieval period may have turned or manipulated the stone as part of processional liturgies that visited the monument. Perhaps the nodule was displaced or damaged during the decline of the island's ecclesiastical occupation in the seventeenth century and lost to memory.

More than any other of Leo's monuments, Leaba Leo demonstrates the tension between the endurance and loss of memory; between the desire to preserve medieval heritage and the demands of building on what was at times a crowded island where suitable space was limited. The leacht, likely first constructed sometime between the tenth and twelfth centuries, was never destroyed but simply encroached upon by household infrastructure and activities. Inhabitants of the village never ceased to venerate the monument, even if they were ambivalent about its name and origins.

OTHER FRAGMENTS LOST, FOUND, AND REMEMBERED

The monuments discussed so far are those that figure most prominently in folklore records or that have produced the most significant archaeological findings. Yet, there are other fragments of Leo's Cult that appear, disappear, and reappear in texts, in oral history, and in the landscape. In some cases, triangulating between historic maps, folklore and antiquarian accounts, and archaeology can reconstruct their chronologies of veneration, commemoration, and destruction, if not of their ultimate origins. Their stories, if sometimes foggy, help to scrutinize the development of devotional traditions on Inishark and their reception and reconfiguration in the historic village.

Leo's Bell

Ironically, the only named relic of Leo that appears in the earliest reference to his cult on Inishark—St. Leo's Bell—is also among the first reported lost. The entirety of Roderic O'Flaherty's reference to Inishark in his *A Chorographical Description of West or hIar-Connaught* (1684) reads as follows: "Inishark is of the same property with Bofin and the saint therein worshipped, St Leo; of whose reliques is a bell there extant" (Hardiman 1846, 117). James Hardiman, who edited O'Flaherty's work in 1846, noted that the bell had long since disappeared.

Handbells were familiar objects to ecclesiastical communities in early medieval Ireland and Britain (Bourke 2020; Stevens 2012, 126–31; Willmott and Daubney 2019). Bells served a variety of practical and liturgical functions, such as ringing calls to prayer throughout the day and marking crucial moments in the mass. Some bells survive because they were curated as associative relics of patron saints and even encased in reliquaries of precious metals. The *Tripartite Life of St Patrick* (c. 900) refers to Patrick's use of a bell to ward off demons, a story perhaps written to explain the existence of a bell cult by the tenth century (Stokes 1887, 115). *Clog Dubh*, St. Patrick's Black Bell, is associated with the pilgrimage mountain of Croagh Patrick, whose distinctive conical silhouette can be seen on the Mayo mainland from Inishark on clear days. In the nineteenth century, and possibly for many previous centuries, the Geraghty family curated the bell and brought it annually to the pattern day on Croagh Patrick (O'Flanagan 1926, 81). Various accounts from the late eighteenth and nineteenth centuries indicate that worshippers might touch or kiss the bell to ensure healing, forgiveness of sins, or the truth of legal oaths (Corlett 2012, 83; Otway 1839, 324; Stevenson 1917, 174). Now in the National Museum of Ireland, the bell's manufacture likely dates between 700 and 900 (Bourke 2020).

There is no compelling reason to doubt that Leo's Bell was also an early medieval artifact. Its curation into the seventeenth century suggests that the island's monastic heritage remained integral to the identity and authority of whatever kind of ecclesiastical community persisted on Inishark in the late medieval and early modern periods. It's hard to say whether O'Flaherty's report reflects the existence of an active ecclesiastical community on Inishark. The second half of the seventeenth century was a tumultuous time on the islands. As evidence from Clochán Leo shows, veneration of Leo's monuments persisted in the seventeenth and eighteenth centuries despite the suppression of Catholic devotion and the apparent dereliction of whatever kind of ecclesiastical community had claimed descent from the early medieval monastery. Local laypeople continued to maintain and adapt stories, practices, monuments, and objects associated with Leo in the absence of ecclesiastical elite. Memory endured despite institutional disintegration.

Oddly enough, the story of the fate of Leo's Bell underscores the role of ordinary islanders as the worthy inheritors of Inishark's sacred heritage. In 1893, Charles Browne recorded the following explanation for its absence.

The Bell of Inishshark. There once was a marvellous brass bell in Inishshark, which was preserved with the greatest care, as it had at one time belonged to St. Leo, the patron saint of the island, about which the following legend is related. A French ship came to the island, the crew of which plundered the place, and took away the bell; but their theft did not prosper with them, for they had not well got it on board before very rough weather came on, and the vessel began to sink. Suspecting that the bell was the cause of their misfortune, they threw it into the sea, and the ship was saved. Next morning, when some of the islanders were searching for sea-weed on the shore, they found the bell lying broken among the rocks. This relic has long ago disappeared, having been cut up into pieces which were worn as amulets, most of which have been taken to America, but it is said that some are still kept as great treasures by some old people in Inishbofin, who refuse to show them to anyone. (Browne 1893, 362)

Stories about ill-fated attempts to steal relics form a genre that occurs commonly in relation to islands with early medieval saint cults (Westropp 1911, 54). Conventionally, such stories oppose the rapine and presumptiveness of outsiders with the insider knowledge and respect of locals as worthy curators of heritage. This contrast is particularly stark in the story of Leo's Bell—while the outsiders' attempt to take the bell invites misfortune and is inevitably thwarted, the islanders continue to break up the bell and emigrate with the fragments as good luck talismans. Terry O'Hagan once offered a speculation that has continued to haunt me. He imagined that somewhere in Clinton, Massachusetts, or Pittsburgh, Pennsylvania—major destinations for Shark emigrants in the nineteenth century—there is yet some inconspicuous fragment of brass-coated iron, handed down and curated now without clear explanation, tucked away at the back of drawer.

Leac Leo and Other Cross-Slabs

Almost every antiquarian and folklore account from the nineteenth and twentieth centuries mentions a carved stone known as *Leac Leo*, "Leo's Flagstone." Unfortunately, these accounts are often inconsistent with one another regarding the form and (former) location of the stone.

The first edition OS map (1838) shows Leough's Flag southeast of the church (fig. 3.42). The notes scribbled in the field name books collected with this survey list Leac Leo as "A small stone cross 6 links {c. 1.2m} high" situated at the "E End of Inish Shark, 1 chain {c. 20m} S.E. of a Chapel." John O'Donovan, relying on a "very enlightened native of Inishbofin" named John Moran as an informant, provides almost no further detail (Herity 2009, 163): "A stone cross called Leac

Figure 3.42: Detail of the Fair Plan 1838 Ordnance Survey Map of Inishark (National Archives OS/105B/249/1) showing Teampaill Leo in ruins, four monuments east of the church, and another monument likely indicating "Leough's Flag" to the southeast. Reproduced with the kind permission of the director of the National Archives.

Figure 3.43: *Leac na naomh* (*right*) set atop an altar against the eastern internal wall of the small church on Caher Island (2015).

114

Leo or St Leo's flag. This lies a short distance to the S.E. of Leo's little chapel, and is of similar character with *Claidhmhin Chathasaigh*, and *Leac na naomh*, of which I spoke when treating of the parish of Kilgeever."

Notably, the two objects offered as comparisons to Leac Leo seem not to have been similar in appearance to the cross or even to each other. The affinity recognized by O'Donovan may have had more to do with the uses of the stones in question—he elsewhere describes *Leac na naomh* ("stone of saints," a natural conglomerate stone of many colors, fig. 3.43) and *Claidhmhin Chathasaigh* (a cross-inscribed pillar) as stones used to elicit the truth or vindicate the innocent from unjust judgments (Herity 2009, 160–61, 163–64). O'Donovan writes of Leac na naomh on Caher Island (*Oileán na Cathrach*):

> Whenever any one on the west shores or on the islands in the vicinity of Caher, find themselves aggrieved or scandalized openly and wrongfully, they have always recourse to the miraculous powers of this stone to elicit the truth. They first fast and pray at home for a fixed time, imploring that God through the intercession of St Patrick and the other saints who blessed this flag would bring about some occurrence, which would shew that they were wronged on such occasions, and after the fasting and praying are over they sail over to Caher and turn Leac na naomh. After the flag is turned the weather immediately becomes unfavorable, and storms and hurricanes most frequently ensue, to the great destruction of boats and currachs, and some event is, ere long, brought about, which shews clearly to the eyes of all the neighbours, that the character of the person who turned the Leac, had been unjustly and wrongfully attempted to be blackened. This may be shewn in various ways, such as great misfortune happening to the scandalizer, or in case of theft, the real thief being discovered, &c. (Herity 2009, 159)

This stone, like Leo's Bell, was also said to have assailed a French ship with turbulent seas when the crew attempted to remove it from the island (Westropp 1911, 54). Given the affinities between folklore relating to Caher Island and Inishark and O'Donovan's comparison, it seems likely that Inishark islanders likewise endowed Leac Leo with supernatural powers of adjudication.

From here on, things get confusing. Kinahan, who visited in 1869, does not mention Leac Leo by name but refers to a cross "much broken and disfigured" (1870, 204). He later noted to Browne that during his visit, a cross or coffin lid was set up against the wall of the church to form a trough (Browne 1893, 365). It is unclear whether this cross is the same or different from the one he described as broken and disfigured.

Browne, for his part, introduces more detail and more confusion: "The stone cross, Leac Leo, is now mounted on the east gable of the church; it is said to have carved on one side of it a chalice, and on the other a human figure, supposed to represent a bishop, with hands extended. There is another cross in the church which is of much finer workmanship, and is probably the true Leac Leo" (Browne 1893, 364–65).

It is again unclear whether the cross of "finer workmanship" is to be identified with the cross (or crosses) observed by Kinahan. As discussed above, the mounting of a cross atop the eastern gable of St. Leo's Church likely followed its restoration in the 1880s. This accords with the twenty-five-inch OS map (c. 1898), which lists the former location of Leo's Flag as somewhere east of the church. Father Neary, a priest stationed on Inishbofin, adds further confusion in his 1920 account. Neary describes a cross, which he calls Leach-Leo, as bearing the image of a bishop with outstretched arms but claims that a different cross, Crois Leo, stands atop the eastern gable (1920, 220–21).

At the time of MacLoughlin's visit, the cross atop the eastern gable had been covered in concrete. However, MacLoughlin mentions two other crosses, supposedly discovered in recent years at Clochán Leo and subsequently brought to the church for safekeeping. One had already gone missing at the time of his visit, "the probability being that it was inadvertently placed in the building" (MacLoughlin 1942, NFC 839, 5) during its renovation.

MacLoughlin made a sketch of the larger flag, which corresponds with a stone captured in home-video footage taken in 1948 or 1949, which shows an island man holding the stone for the camera while standing outside the eastern entrance of St. Leo's Church (Higgins and Gibbons 2018, 70). Like other crosses excavated at Clochán Leo, the flagstone, broken at the top, bears a double-lined cross with expanded D-shaped terminals. The current whereabouts of this stone remain unknown.

Amid these contradictory accounts, a few things are clear. There were certainly more early medieval cross-slabs on Inishark in the past than survive today. One particularly venerated stone, which may have depicted a bishop, once stood somewhere in the vicinity of the church and was mounted atop the restored church in the 1880s and subsequently covered with concrete. Islanders, at various stages, curated at least three and possibly four other cross-slab fragments in the church, two of which had been discovered in Clochán Leo in the twentieth century.

Other Stations

The number of stations in Leo's turas almost certainly fluctuated across time, with generally fewer monuments actively maintained, visited, and venerated as the history of the village unfolded. In addition to Leo's Church, Clochán Leo, and Leo's Well, the fair plan (proof copy) of the 1838 OS map of Inishark includes twelve red crosses, labeled simply *Monuments*, that appear to indicate the location of turas stations (fig. 3.3). Indeed, some of the crosses clearly correspond in location with ruins shown to MacLoughlin more than one hundred years later (figs. 3.42, 3.44). It is impossible to say whether these monuments had each featured in the early medieval pilgrimage landscape or whether they accumulated more incrementally throughout the long postmedieval history of the turas. Yet, by triangulating between folklore, maps, and archaeology, we can reconstruct something of the changing engagements and landscape settings of these unnamed monuments in the nineteenth and twentieth centuries.

The 1838 map shows one monument—apparently, Leac Leo—southeast of the church and four monuments in the area west of the church (fig. 3.42). The location of Leac Leo given on the 1838 map appears to correspond with a rocky mound still visible today. If Leac Leo was removed from this area subsequently, the mound itself was never disturbed or ransacked. In contrast, there are no obvious signs of monuments west of the church today, but in 1942 MacLoughlin was shown the ruins of at least two former pilgrimage stations in this area:

> Immediately west of Leo's chapel—about 20 yards distant—and at the southeast corner of the gable of Patrick Murray's dwelling house is a stone flag firmly placed in the earth and the upper portion of which stands 3 feet above the surface. It is not known if this shrine was of greater dimensions or at one time as the site of a more voluminous stone-heap, but the tradition exists—and I have this tradition from the owner of the garden in which the stone stands and he acquired the information from his mother—that in former times it was customary for pilgrims to perform a pilgrimage at this very stone. About 20 yards due south of this stone can be seen two small upright flags, placed in a semi-circular position, which it is said are the remaining fragments of another ancient shrine. Both these shrines are in the same garden. Somewhere near these shrines was found the stone-font, which is now in the custody of Leo's chapel and I have also heard it being said that in this very garden, was exhumed the stone cross which dominates the apex of the east gable of Leo's chapel. (MacLoughlin 1942, NFC 839, 14)

MacLoughlin's account suggests that construction of new houses in this area in the late nineteenth and early twentieth centuries involved the repurposing of stones from turas monuments, now enclosed within a garden plot. Islanders removed and relocated fixtures of these stations—the granite font and possibly a carved cross—into the church, and the stations were seemingly abandoned as stations in the turas circuit.

The 1838 map shows five monuments in the center of the village between Clochán Leo and the foot of Cnoc Leo (figs. 3.3, 3.44). One monument, still apparent today, appears to be a ruined and overgrown clochán, which MacLoughlin also observed (fig. 3.45): "The pile of stones in its present form stands four feet

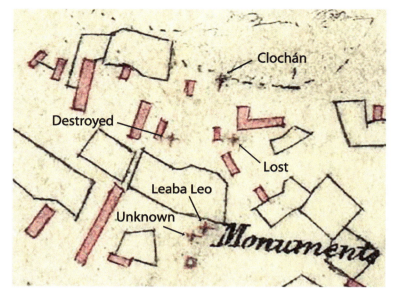

Figure 3.44: Detail of the Fair Plan 1838 Ordnance Survey Map of Inishark (National Archives OS/105B/249/1) showing the cluster of monuments in the center of the village and Leaba Leo and another unnamed monument to the south. Reproduced with the kind permission of the Director of the National Archives.

high, and is treated most reverently by the islanders, its stones having been refused for use in the construction of a road. Tradition has it that the monument was in former times a place of pilgrimage, as were many of the monuments in the neighbourhood" (MacLoughlin 1942, NFC 893, 11).

Islanders' apparent refusal to repurpose the stonework of the clochán contrasts with the fate of another nearby monument.

> About fifty yards to the south west of the above mentioned monument at the south gable of a barn, may be seen the foundation stones of another sacred monument: there on four large stones constituting the remaining orthostats thereof. The story exists amongst the inhabitants that about eighty years ago, a certain family ... when building a new dwelling-house removed the stones from this monument for the purpose of constructing a pathway from the old to the new dwelling; which accounts for is non-existence at present. This family, it is said, has been ever since, the victims of ill luck and misfortune, and that all sorts of unworldly things were at that time haunting this family in their new dwelling-house. (MacLoughlin 1942, NFC 893, 11–12)

Figure 3.45: A stone feature at the base of Cnoc Leo, likely a ruined clochán as described by MacLoughlin.

The divergent fates of these two monuments highlight an ambiguity in islanders' perception of pilgrimage stations: the monuments are at once convenient sources of building material and places of potentially dangerous supernatural power. The latter story implies a proscription against disturbing sacred monuments and provides an instance of the misfortune invited by such a transgression. As such, the circulation of the story—purportedly for nearly a century—might have reinforced apprehension about disturbing monuments, even as the memory and material aspects of the turas tradition continued to decay.

Figure 3.46: Leata Mór during excavation, facing south.

MacLoughlin recorded one final monument that is absent from the 1838 map.

> On the very apex of 'Cnoc Leo' are the apparent remains of a monument which is called 'Leata Mór'. It seems to have been rectangular in shape, measuring nine feet long by six feet wide, with four small stone flags standing on edge, one at each corner of the foundation. Perhaps because of this monument being associated with Leo, that the hill on which it stands was given the name 'Cnoc Leo'. (Leachta = any heap of stones whether sacred or other origin.) The presumption exists that this may have been a tomb, but such a belief could easily have been created by this monument's being so inaccessibly isolated from the many others at the base of 'Cnoc Leo', and thereby permitting the sacred knowledge of its origin to fall into oblivion. (MacLoughlin 1942, NFC 893, 10)

Interestingly, former islander Martin Murray, when interviewed in 2009, echoed the idea that the hill was the site of St. Leo's burial. Ironically, a small trench excavated here in 2016 found only evidence of activity that postdates the island's evacuation by at least twenty-five years (fig. 3.46). Beneath the thin layer of sod, excavators recovered only two artifacts: a 1986 Irish hunter horse twenty-pence piece and an extremely worn salmon ten-pence piece, the date of which appears to read 1993. Whatever the origins of Leata Mór, it appears to have attracted at least two separate visits or visitors, perhaps even a former islander, who decided to leave a trace of their journeys. And there the traces remain. After recording and photographing the coins, I slipped them back under the sod when we backfilled the trench.

The Cemetery

The last destination on our journey has been a final resting place for islanders, perhaps over many centuries. The cemetery is set atop an eroding cliff face immediately west of the landing place on Inishark (figs. 3.1, 3.47). Stone walls enclose the cemetery on its northeast and northwestern sides, but elsewhere the extent of the cemetery continues to contract as the crumbling cliff edge succumbs to the elements. Our team has monitored the progression of erosion since 2008. Year to year, stone grave settings and skeletal fragments appear in the cross-section of the cliff face. Three separate caves undercut the cemetery promontory by many meters, and the ocean will soon make the cemetery an island of its own. The surface of the cemetery undulates in the lumps and hollows of approximately sixty-six graves. The grave settings, now largely covered by grass, are generally comprised of rectangular stone cairns or platforms with upright stones at their head and foot. One grave near the northeastern corner of the cemetery is still largely free of grass and provides a hint at what the sod

Figure 3.47: The cemetery on Inishark viewed from the west. The cliff face is undermined by systems of eroding tunnels. Photo by Ian Kuijt.

conceals elsewhere (fig. 3.48). The grave consists of a rectangular cairn of schist flags and beach cobbles. A long ditch, possibly an old enclosing feature, runs along the northern side of the cemetery, dividing the cemetery promontory from the rest of the island. Although there is no evidence that islanders associated the cemetery with St. Leo or incorporated it into ritual circuits, the cemetery nonetheless served an important commemorative role as a burial place for certain groups. Its positioning immediately adjacent to the pier meant that it was also an important landmark in the daily lives of islanders.

The antiquity of the cemetery is uncertain. It appears on the Bald Map of c. 1809–16 and almost certainly predates the village (fig. 3.2). Indeed, the cemetery appears to have been only infrequently used during the occupation of

Figure 3.48: A grave on the northern edge of the cemetery is less overgrown than the others and composed of a rectangular cairn of stones. Photo by Ian Kuijt.

the historic village. The field name books recorded in tandem with the 1838 Ordnance Survey list the site as "a grave-yard in which few ever buried." MacLoughlin repeated this claim over a hundred years later: "Few people are interred in this cemetery, save young children, and elderly folk whose desire it is to be buried here, or those who, owing to the intervention of rough weather, cannot be brought to the Parish Cemetery in Inishbofin" (MacLoughlin 1942, NFC 893, 20).

Validating these accounts, survey and assessment of the eroding cliff edge in 2010, 2014, 2016, and 2018 revealed skeletal material from adults, subadults, and possible infants. The use of the cemetery for infants begs comparison with the phenomenon of *cillíní*, special-purpose burial grounds developed across Ireland from at least the seventeenth century and continued into the twentieth century (Murphy 2011). Typically reserved for unbaptized children or others denied burial on consecrated ground by the Catholic church, cilliní are commonly sited on earlier monuments such as disused ecclesiastical settlements or ringforts. On Inishbofin, a cillín is located on the western part of the island within a circular enclosure commonly associated with St. Scaithín (Kuijt, Lash, et al. 2015, 28; Gibbons and Higgins 1993). Islanders used the cemetery until the early twentieth century. Representatives of the Catholic church may have considered such places marginal and unorthodox. However, Eileen Murphy's (2011, 415–25) oral historical and archaeological research indicates that local communities, and particularly bereaved parents, often treated and perceived cilliní as sacred places appropriate as resting places for loved ones. Considering the intermittent inaccessibility of Inishark and the absence of resident clergy, the coastal cemetery is likely to have served as a kind of multifunctional cillíní. Though used especially for unbaptized children, bodies washed ashore, and those who died when weather prevented transport to Inishbofin, islanders might simply decide that themselves or their loved ones were better off remaining on their home island. Though most apparently preferred the cemetery surrounding St. Colman's Abbey on Inishbofin—officially sanctified ground—the coastal cemetery on Inishark presented a valid alternative.

Archaeological survey as well as the broader comparative context suggest that the foundation of the cemetery could belong to the medieval period. Two carved stones incorporated as headstones on separate graves are similar in form to examples from known early medieval settlements (Higgins 1987) (fig. 3.49). Of course, the cemetery on Inishark may not represent the primary context of these stones. Inhabitants of the historic village may have taken these stones

Figure 3.49: Two carved crosses in the cemetery on Inishark. Photos by Ian Kuijt.

from other early medieval landmarks on the island. Yet, established use of this area as a lay burial ground in the medieval period might explain why islanders living in the historic village settlement appear never to have buried their dead alongside the ruins of St. Leo's Chapel. This circumstance is especially unusual considering that people from Inishbofin throughout the nineteenth century and unto the present day continue to bury their dead in the cemetery surrounding the medieval ruins of St. Colman's Abbey (Coyne 2008). Perhaps the settlers of the historic village already knew the coastal cemetery as a burial ground for laypeople by the end of the eighteenth century.

In 2016, oak charcoal was collected from a streak of burned deposits 110 cm long, 3–5 cm thick, and 110 cm below the ground surface. Stratigraphically below all exposed burials, one charcoal fragment from the feature yielded a calibrated radiocarbon date of 1023–1160 CE (UBA-36756; 943 +/– 33 BP). The cause of the burnt deposit remains obscure, yet its stratigraphic position suggests the earliest burials must postdate the mid-eleventh century at least.

TRACES IN TASKSCAPES

Social memory, like archaeology, relies on the tracing of traces. As this survey has shown, some traces endure while others, by time, elements, or disregard, can be lost—sometimes for good, sometimes only to be found again. In the next three chapters, we will examine how islanders' tracing of traces has created forums for presenting the past, engaging other-than-human forces, and generating frameworks for belonging in changing taskscapes across time.

FOUR

PEBBLES, PILGRIMS, AND SACRED ORDER
Heritage in Inishark's Medieval Taskscape (c. 700–1300)

INISHARK, 1050. A PEBBLE'S PILGRIM.

The days have grown noticeably longer as summer approaches. The weather has turned fairer and the seas calmer. Today the wind is steady, pushing clouds that arrive to sprinkle rain and then pass away to unveil the sun again. To monks and pilgrims gathered at Clochán Leo, the wind carries a chill, the faint, plaintive calls of seals on the water, and the listless rise and fall of waves against the coast. The monks are garbed in white habits for the occasion of a feast day in which laypeople can visit sacred places more commonly reserved for the daily devotions of the island's monastic community. Some pilgrims are clients of the monastery, tenant farmers who live on the island and owe a portion of their labor and its produce to the monks. Others have come from off island, traversing the seas to achieve some blessing from the monks of Inishark.

Within the clochán, an aged monk kneels in prayer. His legs bend with strain, but his lips move through the Latin psalms with the swift deftness of old habit. He has spent a week leading up to this feast day praying in solitude within the cell. The seclusion purges his sins in penance and drains his mind of all but the eternal. The clochán stays the wind and his senses of the world beyond. Yet his brothers and these pilgrims know he is there, a vanguard of faith in this cave-like dwelling that cuts the horizon. His joints ache from long nights within the cell, where the cold would wake him in the dark, and he would pray and pass again into a restless sleep.

Within the enclosure, two pilgrims kneel at the eastern end of one of the twin leachta. Each holds a quartz pebble, smooth and whiter than the monks' habits. They place their pebbles on the leacht, alongside a large flagstone on which a cross has been drawn out in relief by carving away the stone stroke by stroke. Their pebbles

Figure 4.1: The Clochán Leo Complex during a feast day celebration around 1050. Illustration by Eric Carlson.

will join many others left by pilgrims in the past. Some remain atop the leacht, and others have fallen to rest on the flagstone pavement. Beneath their knees, the pilgrims can see traces of a grave-like chamber filled with gravel and quartz pebbles and now capped by the leacht. From their position, they can just make out the figure of the hermit kneeling in his cell, one of the many holy men who have hallowed this place since its foundation by the monastery's patron many generations ago. Opposite the pilgrims, a monk stands to hear their prayers and their requests. The two pilgrims are tenants of the monastery, come to settle a dispute over the injury of a ram and to seal the agreement by solemn oath. The animal was prized for his fine white fleece, the lambs he made for the monks' Easter meals, and the spotless wool his offspring produced to be spun for the monks' feast-day cloaks.

As the monk blesses their accord with the ringing of a handbell, one of the pilgrims takes in his hands a flat, granite pebble resting atop the leacht. Like the quartz the pilgrims have brought, the granite pebble is wave-carved but also bears the marks of human hands. The top of the stone shows a simple chiseled cross; beneath, the rubbing and turning of the stone in pilgrims' hands have worn the surface even smoother. Each pilgrim, one after the other, will turn the stone in his palm to seal the oath.

Outside the enclosure, a group of pilgrims waits to enter the complex. Some approach from their dwellings on the western part of the island. Others approach from a nearby cove to the east, carefully scaling the cliff edge with their white stones. A monk stands by the entranceway of the enclosure to hear requests and monitor entry. A woman waits, one hand clasping a pebble, the other resting on her swollen belly. Her husband stands nearby with her firstborn child. He is only five and may yet become a foster to the monastery to learn their scripts, their lore, and their ways. She remembers the difficulty of his delivery, and she is frightened of the labor to come. The monks of the island, vowed to celibacy, commonly avoid interacting with women who are not their kin. Her movements on the island are more heavily regulated than her male counterpart's. Her family will request entry, but her access may well be refused, regardless of what she and her family have given over the years: their toil in sowing and harvesting grain, tending animals, and spinning wool. They have always ceded some portion of their "first fruits"—the firstlings of their flock and even of their own families—as tribute to the monastery. These men, with their shorn heads and snowy habits, hold the well-being of herself and her children in their hands, with the power to grant her encounter with this sanctified place. As the monks' eyes turn toward her, she feels sweat gathering on her brow and nervously rubs the quartz in her hand, the white stone still wet and glistening from the ebbing tide.

—∞—

The scene above combines the results of archaeological excavation with insights from early medieval hagiography, canon law, and penitentials. My intent is to illustrate how a taskscape approach focuses attention on the interactive movement of human and other-than-human bodies, materials, and forces. As discussed in chapter 2, a taskscape approach considers how living in landscapes situates humans temporally and relationally. How do encounters with particular ensembles of bodies, materials, and environmental phenomena generate a sense of one's place in time, in space, and in relation to other beings and forces that animate the world? How do these experiences, in turn, contribute to the maintenance of communal formations and their associated dwelling regimes?

In the last three decades, scholars have significantly revised understandings of the church in early medieval Ireland. Previous scholarship presumed that the majority of ecclesiastical settlements were occupied by formally monastic communities of celibate men and paid little attention to evidence of interactions with laypeople (Ryan 1931; Kenney 1929). Increasingly, however, scholars emphasize the diversity of early medieval ecclesiastical settlements, with many church sites likely having no formal resident monastic community but instead serving small local kin groups. Moreover, textual evidence suggests that laypeople often worshipped at ecclesiastical settlements alongside men and women in religious orders (Etchingham 1999, 363–45; Charles-Edwards 1992; Ó Carragáin 2015). Even monasteries—those ecclesiastical settlements comprised primarily of men in religious orders—often possessed landed estates where laypeople dwelled, labored, and, as dependent clients, owed food renders to their monastic landlords. Recent excavations at Irish ecclesiastical settlements indicate various levels of investment in agriculture, craft, monastic practice, lay worship, and pilgrimage (O'Sullivan et al. 2014; Corlett and Potterton 2014). To confront these findings, recent work, particularly by Tomás Ó Carragáin, uses theories of memory and materiality to reexamine early medieval ritual. Ó Carragáin's research has demonstrated how the built settings of ecclesiastical settlements evoked the past, materialized templates of sacred order, and structured the movements of lay and ecclesiastical worshippers (Ó Carragáin 2003, 2007, 2009, 2010, 2013, 2021).

A taskscape approach extends previous research on the early medieval ritual in three important ways. First, it considers how the material traces of past activity can structure future actions by affording commemoration as well as innovation. Below, I discuss the role of clocháns and leachta as monuments that facilitate the cultivation of heritage by summoning distant times and places to the here and now. Second, it considers different peoples' multisensory experiences of both built environments and other-than-human forces. In addition to monks, I will emphasize laypeople's experience of work and worship on Inishark. In particular, I will consider worshippers' encounters with the power of the ocean as materialized in stone. Third, it contextualizes devotional practices in terms of a wider assortment of dwelling tasks. Specifically, I will suggest how ritual experiences contributed to the maintenance of the political relations and subsistence practices that sustained monastic settlements as viable forms of dwelling.

CULTIVATING (A ROMAN?) HERITAGE—MONUMENTS OF COMMEMORATION AND EVOCATION

The capacity of objects, architecture, and landscapes to evoke the past has become a dominant theme in early medieval archaeology (Bradley 1987; Semple 2013; Williams 2006; Williams et al. 2015). Scholars have examined how secular and ecclesiastical elites selected and modified the material settings of ritual to construct narratives of the past amenable to their claims to authority (Gleeson 2012; Bhreathnach 2014). For example, the reuse of prehistoric earthen monuments as places of assembly, burial, and inauguration in early medieval Ireland and Anglo-Saxon England allowed elites to forge connections to mythic pasts, bestowing a venerable heritage on contemporary authority (Newman 2011; Pantos and Semple 2004; Williams 1997). The status and identity of Irish ecclesiastical communities also relied fundamentally on their heritage, particularly their affiliation with saintly founders. An eighth-century legal text, *Córus Bésgnai*, declares that the independent status of a church settlement relied on the possession of its founder's relics (Etchingham 1993, 154). Relics might be corporeal or associative—that is, the physical remains of a saint's body or material objects used/touched by a saint. Thus, communities could rely on a diverse array of material strategies for constituting their heritage, such as curating liturgical items (e.g., bells, croziers, codices) or constructing shrine monuments over founder burials. The incentive to reiterate continuity with founders from the age of conversion may even account for the distinct uniformity and conservatism of church architecture in early medieval Ireland. The vast majority of pre-Romanesque masonry churches built in Ireland between the tenth and twelfth centuries are simple rectangular, one-chambered buildings, with a short length to breadth ratio, steeply pitched gables, a west entrance, and usually a window in the south and east wall (Ó Carragáin 2010). Not only do these churches appear to adhere to a simple template inherited from their timber predecessors, they also sometimes include skeuomorphic features, that is, deliberate translations into stone of elements integral to timber architecture (Ó Carragáin 2007; Ó Carragáin 2010, 26–28; see O'Keeffe 2023a for an alternative view). Ó Carragáin has interpreted this conservative continuity of church form as a deliberate strategy for maintaining a connection to the reputed founding saints of ecclesiastical settlements, for whom church buildings acted as associative relics (Ó Carragáin 2007; 2010, 149–56). Rebuilding in stone thus provided the opportunity to make present what was absent, to create a more durable replication of a patron's original church building (fig. 4.2).

The wider landscape and built settings of early church sites could also evoke a heritage rooted in more remote places and in longer-term histories. Early medieval ecclesiastics imagined Ireland on the far western margins of a world with Jerusalem as its central point. This geographic position accorded with Ireland's place in Christian salvation history—it was, for a time, imagined as the farthest frontier of Christianity's spread from the scene of resurrection in Jerusalem and beyond the bounds of the Roman Empire (Charles-Edwards 1993). The famed monastery of Iona in the Inner Hebrides, through the example of its built environment and the writings it produced, was a significant force in propagating conceptual frameworks that construed monastic settlements as mirrors of the earthly and heavenly Jerusalem (Campbell and Maldonado 2020). The seventh-century *De Locis Sanctis* (*Concerning the Holy Land*), compiled by Adomnán, ninth abbot of Iona, established Jerusalem's cosmological centrality and its built environment as a template for contemporary monasteries. Adomnán describes the Aedicule (the tomb of Christ) as "the center of the world," and a plan accompanying the text in a ninth-century manuscript depicts the Anastasis Rotunda surrounding the aedicule as a series of concentric circles (Ó Carragáin 2003, 142–43). This layout accords conspicuously with early medieval Irish

Figure 4.2: The church on St. MacDara's Island (*Cruach na Cara*), Co. Galway, demonstrates in extraordinary fashion the capacity of masonry churches to evoke timber precursors. The stone roof of the church includes skeuomorphs of shingles, end rafters, and finials. It is shown here during *Féile MhicDara*, St. MacDara's Festival, in 2016 as the crowd gathers for an open-air mass outside the church.

ecclesiastical settlements, which commonly position a settlement's most sacred features—principal churches and reliquary shrines—at their core, within multiple concentric boundary features (O'Sullivan et al. 2014, 145–48; fig. 4.3). Indeed, an eighth-century collection of canon law specifically prescribes three boundaries surrounding any sacred site. As we shall see later in this chapter, this concentric spatial template mapped onto a model of sacred hierarchy that operated at multiple scales and in multiple domains. For now, suffice it to say that concentric settlement layouts embodied a spatial template that mimicked

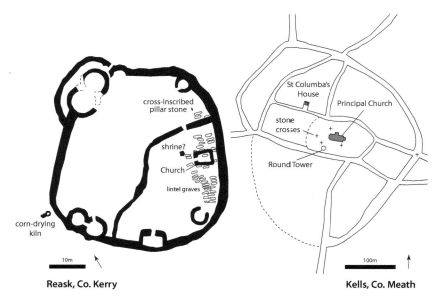

Figure 4.3: Concentric plans at two mainland sites: Reask, Co. Kerry, a small church settlement that likely served a local kin group (after Ó Carragáin 2010, 226), and Kells, Co. Meath, a major monastic-episcopal centre (after Ó Carragáin 2010, 264).

the supposed form of the Temple Complex of Jerusalem, evoked a cosmology that put Jerusalem at the center of the world, and, more fundamentally, relied on the association of sanctity with bounded space.

This model of concentrically ordered sacred space also informed perceptions of Ireland's Atlantic islands. Before the Christianization of Iceland around the year 1000, these spits of land in a vast ocean were the westernmost fringe of the frontier of Christendom. Oceanic islands like Inishark and its neighbors in Connemara became simultaneously ideal locations to dramatize the spiritual trials of ascetic exile and to demonstrate the manifest destiny of Christianity's promised spread (map 4.1). As landmasses surrounded by water, islands came ready-made as bounded entities that could be embellished with additional forms of concentric enclosure. Two of the island monasteries closest to Inishark and Inishbofin—High Island in Co. Galway and Caher Island in Co. Mayo—include small churches and reliquary monuments surrounded by multiple bounding features including stone enclosure walls, natural features, and strings of satellite leachta (figs. 4.4, 4.5). These sites are picture-postcard examples of early

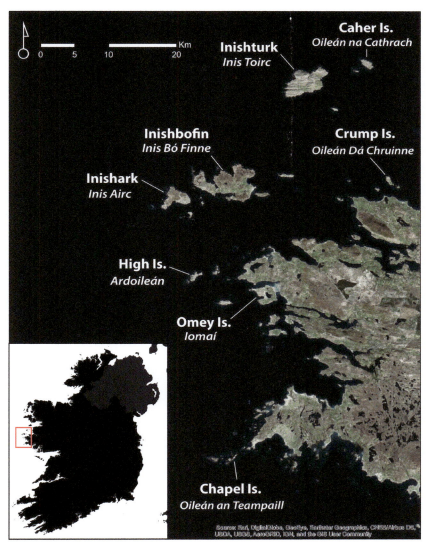

Map 4.1: Islands off the coast of northwest Connemara that preserve remnants of medieval ecclesiastical settlements.

Figure 4.4: Caher Island, Co. Mayo, about 19 km northeast of Inishark. The small church and a reputed founder's burial are surrounded not only by a rectangular enclosure wall but also by strands of stone enclosure walls and cross-topped leachta monuments that trace the ridge line that bounds the site in a natural amphitheater.

Irish monasteries, seemingly built to observe a concentric model of sacred order. Boundaries of ocean, earth, and stone cultivated the impression that these ecclesiastical settlements were sacred centers on the edge of the world.

How did Inishark's monastic community construct and convey its sanctity, its illustrious heritage, and its connections to Christian history? Interestingly,

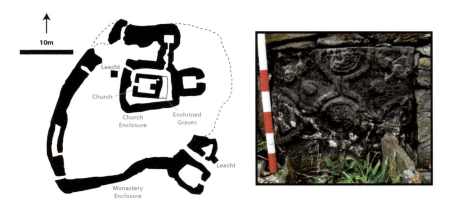

Figure 4.5: (*Left*) Simplified plan (after Marshall and Rourke 2000, 48) of the main monastic complex on High Island, Co. Galway, about 6 km south of Inishark. The small church and a series of elaborately decorated grave settings stood within a small rectangular enclosure. The church enclosure was itself surrounded by an immense stone cashel enclosure wall, perhaps originally 1.5 in height. Leachta marked the entranceways between boundaries—outside the southern entrance to the monastery enclosure and outside the entrance to the church enclosure. (*Right*) The headstone of Grave 4, set into the exterior eastern wall of the church on High Island. The grave contained a male over 55, whose bones radiocarbon dated between 980 and 1025 CE (Scally 2014, 73–78).

the layout of devotional monuments on Inishark is less neatly concentric than other island monasteries in its immediate vicinity. As such, relative to its neighbors, Inishark's landscape did not clearly evoke the familiar model of sacred space associated with Jerusalem. Instead, Inishark's monastic community relied on a distinct combination of built features and objects that could evoke the presence of a founder saint and allow for the imitation of his exemplary devotion.

St. Leo's association with various places, monuments, and objects on the island cannot be dated with absolute certainty. However, the early medieval origins of a cult specifically ascribed to a figure called Leo is a valid possibility. This ambiguity notwithstanding, folklore and archaeology demonstrate how the monastic community on Inishark cultivated a sacred heritage through the construction and curation of certain material things. The bell mentioned by Roderic O'Flaherty in 1684 might well have originated in the early medieval period as a liturgical item, subsequently curated as an associative relic of a founder. Likewise, nineteenth-century folklore depicted Clochán Leo, Leo's Cove, and

Leaba Leo as places that Leo's body had physically encountered. These associations are entirely in keeping with medieval hagiographies, which often tie particular objects or monuments visible at the time of writing to events in the saint's lifetime (for examples, see Ó Carragáin 2009, 217).

In some cases, there is good reason to take these associations as valid accounts. For example, the *Vita Columbae*, written within a century of St. Columba's death, repeatedly refers to a hut on Iona that Columba used for writing. Mid-twentieth-century excavations atop a hillock known as *Tòrr an Abba*, Hill of the Abbot, revealed the stone footings of a timber structure that was subsequently burned, covered with pebbles, and eventually surmounted by the plinth base for a standing cross (Fowler and Fowler 1988, 182–98). Recent radiocarbon analysis of charcoal from the burnt hut puts its construction during the lifetime of Columba. The building may well represent Columba's hut, which was subsequently commemorated in Adomnán's *Vita* and by the installation of a standing cross (Campbell and Maldonado 2017).

Clochán Leo provides a possible parallel to the commemoration of Columba's cell on Iona. The construction of Clochán Leo belongs to Period I of building activity within the complex that takes its name from the hut. As we saw in the last chapter, a fragment of hazel charcoal from the floor surface of Clochán Leo suggests that the hut might have been constructed as early as the late seventh / early eighth century. This evidence, as well as its position on the high point of the hillock, implies that the clochán was a primary feature of the complex and perhaps the initial structure around which the complex took shape during Period I (seventh to tenth centuries). Later folklore associating the clochán with a founding saint may well accord with early medieval tradition and possibly even with the clochán's actual origins.

Even at the point of construction, the clochán could evoke a deeper heritage of ascetic devotion. Early medieval Irish hagiographies associate anchorites and recluses with caves and stone dwellings (Dowd 2018; Manning 2005). This association is derived from earlier depictions of hermits in the deserts of North Africa, men whose exploits in the third and fourth centuries provided the inspiration for subsequent forms of Christian asceticism. As a cavelike stone shelter, Clochán Leo afforded not only physical isolation and hardship but also the recollection of the earliest exemplars of Christian asceticism. Even the first hermit to dwell within Clochán Leo could have perceived his actions as imitating venerable archetypes. Each subsequent generation of monks to pray within Clochán Leo enhanced the depth of this heritage for those who would follow after. To pray within Clochán Leo, to ache from restless nights, and to feel the chill of the stone shelter was to come closer not only to an abstract ideal of penance but to the experiences of other worshippers in the past. As a stone monument prominently visible in the landscape, Clochán Leo could evoke the monastery's foundation by a saint who had imitated the example of the desert fathers here on the western edge of Christendom. The stone shelters of Clochán Leo and Clochán Congleo allowed the faithful to embody an ascetic heritage of many exemplars near, far, recent, and ancient.

Like clocháns, leachta also afforded commemoration and the construction of heritage through the performance of devotions. Leachta were ubiquitous features at early medieval ecclesiastical settlements; they took many forms and served a variety of functions in early medieval and later devotional traditions. In form, they can range from simple rectangular platforms to more irregular cairns of stone. Archaeology, hagiography, and folklore depict leachta as multifunctional monuments including Eucharistic altars, prayer stations in penitential circuits, platforms for laying out the deceased prior to burial, grave markers, and cenotaphs (Ó Carragáin 2017a; O'Sullivan et al. 2014, 161–64). Of course, some of these uses are not mutually exclusive. A leachta marking a special grave might have functioned on some days as an altar for the liturgy of the Eucharist and on others as a nodal point in a penitential circuit. The tasks afforded by leachta on Inishark may have been just as diverse. The nineteenth-century turas tradition on Inishark suggests that leachta may also have been incorporated as prayer stations in early medieval penitential circuits. Excavation at Teampaill Leo, St. Leo's Church, uncovered a simple, nearly square stone platform capping a grave at the southeastern corner of the church building. Leachta within the Clochán Leo and Congleo complexes capped rectangular, stone-lined chambers. The dimensions and east–west orientation of these chambers are too reminiscent of graves for the affinity not to have been essential to their design. As such, these chambers add force to Ó Carragáin's (2017a) suggestion that many leachta acted as surrogate or symbolic tombs commemorating figures buried elsewhere.

Hagiographic and archaeological evidence offer additional parallels. A twelfth-century vernacular life of Colman of Lynn depicts the saint dividing his monastery's cemetery into sections focused around the tombs of saints buried elsewhere (indeed, saints not even deceased at the time of the episode) (Meyer 2001, § 42). Inishmurray Island, Co. Sligo, offers two archaeological examples of leachta likely serving as cenotaphs or symbolic tombs within enclosed complexes. The leacht at Ollamurray, dedicated to the Virgin, may have evoked Mary's empty tomb in the Valley of Josaphat. Meanwhile, the larger of two leachta at the enclosed cemetery complex known as Relickoran (Odrán's cemetery) probably represents a re-creation of Odrán's famous tomb on Iona. An episode from a twelfth-century life of Columba depicts Odrán as a follower of Columba who volunteers to be the first one buried on Iona, thereby consecrating the island and establishing a cemetery on the periphery of the monastic complex for laypeople (Ó Carragáin 2009, 209). Notably, excavations at Relickoran on Inishmurray indicate a burial community mixed by gender and age (O'Sullivan and Ó Carragáin 2008, 259–63, 280–85). Hence, dedication of a symbolic tomb to Odrán would have evoked not only Inishmurray's links to Iona but Odrán's role as an intercessor for the lay dead. Indeed, once constructed, burials began to cluster around the leacht that purportedly represented Odrán's tomb (O'Sullivan and Ó Carragáin 2008, 261).

As discussed in chapter 3, the nearby monastery on High Island provides additional parallels for purpose-built cenotaphs. Refurbishment of the monastery on High Island in the middle or late eleventh century included the construction of a masonry church and the incorporation of both preexisting graves and new pseudo-graves into the eastern wall of the church (Scally 2014, 303–11). Ó Carragáin raises the possibility that the pseudo-graves, rather than commemorating monks lost at sea, may have been dedicated to holy individuals revered by High Island's monastic community—most notably their reputed founder, St. Féichín, whose remains lay in Fore, Co. Westmeath (2017a).

In the last chapter, I argued that the refurbishment of the church and tombs on High Island was generally contemporary with the Period II refurbishment of the Clochán Leo Complex and the construction of the Congleo Complex on Inishark. Commemoration of the past and the construction of cenotaph monuments were essential to the design of each complex. Building activity on High Island and at the Clochán Leo Complex included the restructuring of earlier features. On High Island, this meant adjusting the stone settings of preexisting graves. On Inishark, this included the construction of the southern leacht atop the northern chamber and the encasing of the southern chamber within the northern leacht. Though the preexisting chambers were clearly visible to builders during Period II, their precise origins and dedications might have been subject to reinterpretation. I suggest two possible narratives of development: the northern and southern chambers were initially built as cenotaphs during Period I and never held human remains, or the chambers may originally have been built as graves that were subsequently exhumed and refilled during the Period II renovations. In either case, Period II renovations commemorated the presence of the chambers by surmounting them with leachta—an action likely undertaken to promote the complex as a pilgrimage shrine. The Congleo Complex likely also first took its fully developed state during the eleventh century. The focal point of the complex was once again a leachta, this time designed to encase a rectangular stone-lined chamber oriented east–west and filled with gravel.

To interpret these building initiatives, one must attend to the capacity of cenotaph leachta to evoke the past in the present, but also to summon distant places to the here and now. "*Leachta* provided a way to interweave reminiscences of distant sacred topographies into the local landscape. They could express alliances with and allegiances to important Irish saints and could symbolically cancel out the great distances between the local site and the great *civitates* of Christendom such as Jerusalem and Rome" (Ó Carragáin 2017a).

Against this background, I hypothesize a connection between the cult of St. Leo on Inishark and the presence of pseudo-reliquary monuments on the island. The papal connotations of the name *Leo* would have held ideological significance during different phases of ecclesiastical reform in the early medieval period. For example, during the seventh century, controversy arose in Ireland and Britain concerning the appropriate method for calculating the date of Easter. Some churches, particularly those affiliated with the Columban tradition of monasticism that spread from Iona, calculated the date of Easter with an eighty-four-year table (McCarthy and Ó Cróinín 1988). Troublingly, this method could yield a different date for Easter than an alternative set of tables devised by Dionysius Exiguus in the sixth century, practiced more widely throughout Christendom, and specifically endorsed in a letter to Irish clerics by Pope John IV in 640 (Corning 2016; Dailey 2015, 54–5). Clear reflections of the seventh-century Easter Controversy in the place names and monuments of the Irish landscape are vanishingly few (for likely instances, see Ó Carragáin 2017 and 2018; O'Hagan 2012). Yet Colman's foundation on Inishbofin may be the most conspicuous example. As documented by the Anglo-Saxon historian Bede, St. Colman, former abbot of Lindisfarne, founded his monastery on Inishbofin after his failed defense of the eighty-four-year Easter table against the Dionysian method at the Synod of Whitby in 664 (Bede, *Historia ecclesiastic gentis anglorum* book IV, chap. iv). Against this background, the juxtaposition of Colman on Inishbofin and Leo on Inishark begs contemplation. Radiocarbon dates from Clochán Leo allow for the possibility that the monastery on Inishark originated before, during, or in the immediate aftermath of Colman's lifetime. Counterposed with Colman's die-hard Columban community on Inishbofin, a papal name like Leo on Inishark at the turn of eighth century could have signaled allegiance to papal authority and a Roman paschal calendar.

But who was Leo? Marie-Therese Flanagan (2010, 108–11) has noted the fashion among Irish churchmen in the twelfth century to select Latinized stylings of their names that evoked former popes and possibly signaled enthusiasm for contemporary reforms initiated by the papacy. Such naming practices would also have held discursive weight during the earlier paschal controversy. Thus, *Leo* might have referred to an Irish monk of the late seventh / early eighth century who adopted the papal name. However, the number of apparent cenotaphs used as foci of veneration on Inishark also raises the possibility that the cult of Leo referred to St. Leo the Great himself, whose corporeal relics could not reasonably be claimed to reside on the island. Tantalizingly, April 11, the feast day of St. Leo on Inishark in the nineteenth century, corresponds with the date of St. Leo the Great's burial in the basilica of St. Peter as recorded in the sixth-century *Liber Pontificalis* (Davis 2000, 40). As such, one must consider the possibility that one of the three cenotaph monuments on Inishark was interpreted as a symbolic tomb for St. Leo the Great. If the monastery was initially founded in honor of Leo the Great, then either of the Period I chambers at the Clochán Leo Complex might have been built specifically as a cenotaph for him. Alternatively, association with St. Leo the Great may represent an innovation associated with the Period II (eleventh-century) revitalization of the monastery. In this case, one of the preexisting Period I chambers may have been reassigned to Leo the Great.

It is impossible to ascribe dedications for the Inishark cenotaphs with certainty. If compelled to wager on a speculation that uses the evidence at hand, I would propose the following. Maybe the twin leachta at the Clochán Leo Complex were built to commemorate two separate figures: (1) St. Leo the Great and (2) St. Leo the monastery's founder, who perhaps adopted the name in tribute to the famous pope. Meanwhile, the shrine at the Congleo Complex might have commemorated another figure renowned as a counterpart, devotee, disciple, or even heir to the monastery's founder. In this case, the shrine complexes of Inishark could trace the community's heritage across multiple generations of saintly personas on the island and reach even further back in space and time to identify with an illustrious pope. Albeit speculative, this interpretation accords with material strategies of commemoration documented at other early medieval monasteries. Whether or not a vita was ever written of a St. Leo on Inishark, it was primarily through commemorative ritual practice that his cult was propagated and his spiritual authority invested in the island landscape. By presenting one of the cenotaphs on Inishark as a symbolic tomb for a papal Leo, the monastic community on Inishark would have offered pilgrims on the margins of Christendom an opportunity to engage with the sacred power of the primal see of Rome.

Leachta that served as cenotaphs for religious elites could also foster imitation of their holy examples. Reflection on and imitation of death were among the primary goals of undertaking ascetic seclusion. Although from a different cultural context, the thirteenth-century *Ancrene Wisse*, a Middle English guidebook for anchoresses, explicitly equates the anchor-house with the grave of the anchoress and instructs her to "each day scrape up the earth of their graves, in which they will rot. God knows, the grave does a lot of good to many an anchoress" (translation from Hostetler 1999, 201). For anyone enclosed in Clochán Leo, the cell's opening would have directed their gaze—and perhaps the focus of their contemplation—toward the leachta as monuments to both holy forebears and their own desires for salvation after death.

For monks, building monuments meant producing the infrastructure for devotion, commemoration, and evocation. By summoning distant times and places—including illustrious pasts and imagined futures—clocháns and leachta could situate worshippers spatially and ideologically within the history of asceticism and contemporary debates over paschal calculation and the authority of Rome. Monks, of course, had a vested interest in cultivating a venerable heritage that would support their claims to status and command the attention of lay pilgrims. Yet, by engaging with monuments and leaving material traces of their own, pilgrims also played a role in commemorating the past and expressing their own place in the world.

ENCOUNTERING THE DIVINE THROUGH STONE AND TIDE

Pebbles and Peregrinatio

In addition to built monuments, encounters with smaller stone objects—both worked and unworked—were an essential component of ritual practices on Inishark in the early medieval period. Pebbles figured prominently in the actions undertaken at leachta. The cross-inscribed granite pebble once likely sat atop a leacht in the Clochán Leo Complex, just as the nodule with a compass-made cross of arcs design once likely sat atop Leaba Leo. Drawing from medieval hagiography and later turas traditions, I have imagined in the vignette above how the granite pebble might have been used by pilgrims to swear oaths. Excavations at the Clochán Leo and Congleo Complex also uncovered thousands of water-rolled quartz pebbles. In some cases—such as the pebbles in-filling the leacht at the Congleo Complex—people must have deposited quartz pebbles during the construction of monuments. However, the majority of quartz pebbles come from atop pavement contexts, on which they must have been laid following the completion of building work (fig. 4.6). The deposition of stones and other objects at pilgrim shrines in later turas traditions, as well as the ubiquity of votive offerings in medieval pilgrimage practices, suggest that early medieval pilgrims on Inishark deposited quartz pebbles to mark their journeys to leachta and shrine complexes. A taskscape approach unlocks the symbolic potential of these objects by placing them in the context of a sequence of actions that included both humans and other-than-human forces.

Most analyses of quartz in early medieval ritual focus on color. Biblical precedent and hagiographic tradition associate whiteness with spiritual cleanliness, humility, and healing (Hadley 2011, 297, 300; Hill 1997, 472; Holloway 2011;

Figure 4.6: View facing west of the Clochán Congleo Complex during excavation in 2016. A total of 7,996 quartz pebbles were exposed during excavations, with the majority found atop the pavement. As seen above, the pebbles stand out starkly in wet weather and would have been even more prominent when not coated in the dirt that buried them in the post-medieval period.

Thompson 2002, 240). The *Vita Columbae* (book III, chap. 13) mentions the monks' custom of wearing white habits to mark feast days. Irish writers in particular defined a form of piety, white martyrdom, achieved not by dying for one's faith but by leading a life of ascetic self-denial and chastity (Stancliffe 1982, 40). In the light of these sources, the deposition of white stones in or on the graves of men or women could act to display their status as saintly individuals. Deposition of quartz on top of shrines enhanced their visibility and demarcated their sanctity by providing a visual contrast with the surrounding landscape. Moreover, proximity of the pebbles to corporeal relics may have served to sanctify the pebbles themselves as a type of secondary relic. Hence, quartz deposited in locations made sacred by the presence of corporeal relics or the living body of an ascetic may have taken on new potency as a vector for spiritual purification if touched. On the small island monastery on Illaunloughan in Co. Kerry, quartz

Figure 4.7: Waves crashing and pebbles churning in one of the channels of the *fuaiġ a' Ċoinnleora* adjacent to the Clochán Congleo Complex. Quartz pebbles would have been available to pilgrims here and within St. Leo's Cove adjacent to the Clochán Leo Complex.

pebbles decorated a multitiered stone gable shrine that encased the exhumed skeletal remains of two adults and one child. Radiocarbon dates placed the human remains between the late seventh and late eighth centuries, but some of the quartz may have been deposited subsequently, as the shrine was refurbished in the eleventh century (Marshall and Walsh 2005, 62).

White stones with spiritual properties are also mentioned in early medieval written sources. Adomnán's *Vita Columbae*, composed in the seventh century, describes a white stone endowed with miraculous properties: "[Columba] took a white stone from the river, and blessed it for the working of certain cures, and that stone, contrary to nature, floated like an apple when placed in water" (Anderson and Anderson 1991, 398–405). The riverine source of the stone suggests a smooth, water-worn pebble. The origins of the stone's occult properties are, however, somewhat ambiguous. It is unclear whether the stone possessed the power to heal and to float on water prior to Columba's blessing or only afterward.

This account, when set alongside archaeological evidence, suggests how stones notable in their color, physical properties, proximity to holy bodies, and interactions with water may have mediated perceptions of sanctity and spiritual power. With a handful of exceptions, in a corpus from Inishark that amounts to nearly nine thousand pebbles from Clochán Leo, Congleo, and Leaba Leo alone, all of the quartz stones are water-worn, rounded and polished by the sea's churning. Thus, the taskscape they represent includes not only the collection of pebbles from the shore but also their modification by the waves (fig. 4.7). How might this history of formation have informed pilgrims' experience of the pebbles?

As Petts (2019) has recently argued, the spread of Christianity into Ireland and Britain required the remapping of biblical and scholarly interpretations of maritime phenomena (generated in Christianity's Mediterranean heartland) to a North Atlantic environment with far more extreme tidal dynamics. Water imagery in general, and the metaphorical use of the ocean in particular, abound in early Irish texts (Muhr 1999). Drawing from a long tradition of biblical exegesis, authors portrayed water as a manifestation of divine agency and as a mechanism of penance or spiritual trial that leads to salvation. The separation of the waters above and below the firmament, and God's creation of the earth on the latter, is a crucial component of the Genesis narrative. Seventh- and eighth-century authors in Ireland and Northern England—including Bede—sought to understand the predictable cycle of tides as linked to lunar cycles and, ultimately, revelatory of God's governance of Creation (Petts 2019, 12–14; Smyth 1996, 241–62). Apostolic and early Christian writings drew explicit links between the sacrament of baptism and the Old Testament stories of Noah's flood and the Israelites' crossing of the Red Sea, in which water is a source of both punishment and salvation (Muhr 1999, 200–03). These sources, likely combined with pre-Christian cosmologies, informed the early Irish genre of *immram*, in which sea journeys to otherworldly islands constituted physically and spiritually perilous trials (Dumville 1976; Wooding 2000).

These notions informed real-world behavior. Divine agency controlling the action of the sea was a central premise underlying seaborne ascetic wandering, known as *peregrinatio pro amore dei*, "pilgrimage for the love of God" (Charles-Edwards 1976, 46–53; Johnston 2016, 42–43). The *Navigatio sancti Brendani abbatis*, which may be as early as the eighth century, dramatizes this ascetic ideal of surrendering to God's will via sea voyage. At one point in his journeys, Brendan instructs his followers: "Brothers, do not fear. God is our helper, sailor and helmsman, and he guides us. Ship all the oars and the rudder. Just leave the sail spread and God will do as he wishes with his servants and their ship" (O'Meara 1981, 10). Such feats of piety find corroboration in other written accounts. The Anglo-Saxon Chronicle records the arrival in 891 (version A, or 892, versions BCD) in Cornwall of three Irishman in a boat without oars: "They had left secretly, because they wished for the love of God to be in foreign lands, they cared not where. The boat in which they traveled was made of two and a half hides, and they took with them enough food for seven days. And after seven days they came to land in Cornwall" (Whitelock 1979, 200–01).

In an era where the zealous could put out to sea to place themselves in God's hands, we can expect this archetype of asceticism to resonate in other domains. Rendered by the tide's churning and cast on island shorelines, quartz pebbles mirrored the actions of these wandering pilgrims who likewise submitted themselves to the divine caprice of the ocean. For pilgrims to Inishark, gathering quartz pebbles from coves and depositing them within shrines may have constituted an alternative expression of these devotional aspirations. The wave-carved polish and gleaming white of quartz offered a striking embodiment of the process of penitential pilgrimage: surrender to the transformative power of divine forces and the state of spiritual purity thereby achieved. Early medieval Irish penitentials and hagiography attest to the practice of praying or passing a night while submerged in water as an act of penitential devotion (Ireland 1997, 53–61). Against this backdrop, early medieval people would have been particularly liable to recognize an analogy between the watery transportation and transformation of the quartz stones and their own spiritual journey to the island. Notably, this ideal of penitential devotion could apply to both lay pilgrims visiting Inishark and the ascetics who prayed more regularly within the stone huts at the shrine complexes. In early Irish texts, peregrinatio has many resonances, connoting a self-imposed penitential exile that could be embodied by both travel and hermetical isolation and stability (Hughes 1960, 148; Johnston 2016, 40).

Monks' and pilgrims' tactile encounters with quartz pebbles may have generated a sense of shared expressions of ascetic devotion. The configuration of the quartz pebbles would have shifted as monks and pilgrims walked around quartz-strewn surfaces. This was particularly true at the Congleo Complex, where the entirety of the pavement was blanketed in pebbles. To walk on the uneven and unstable configuration of pebbles required visitors to focus more than usual bodily attention on the placement of each footfall. Visitors would have perceived the shifting of pebbles underfoot, the clinking sounds of their collisions, and, perhaps, the traces of pathways created by the patterned displacement of pebbles by previous processions. Each new visitor could recognize their own participation in the molding of a complex by many different worshippers over time. When depositing white pebbles as individual offerings, pilgrims embellished the depth of memory and meaning at complexes already made sacred by the presence of other holy objects, monuments, and bodies.

Stone-craft and Rumination

Attuning our attention to the formation of stone through other-than-human forces also enhances analysis of early medieval stone-craft. The study of early medieval sculpture has traditionally been dominated by stylistic and iconographic interpretations. While immensely fruitful in creating typologies and chronologies, these analyses tend to emphasize design form over the processes of production, the material properties of lithic materials, and their interactions with other environmental forces (though see Gefreh 2017 and Williams et al. 2015). Following the taskscape of production for carved stone objects illuminates possible links between early medieval craft and devotion.

As with Columba's floating stone, early medieval Christians would have invested meaning in the occult properties of conspicuous stone formations. In *De Mirabilibus Sacrae Scripturae, Concerning the Miracles of Sacred Scripture*, the seventh-century writer known as Augustinus Hibernicus suggests that unusual or unprecedented phenomena reveal the majesty of God's power over creation: "Therefore if among created things we see anything new arise, God should not be thought to have created a new nature, but to be governing that which he created formerly. But his power in governing his creation is so great that he may seem to be creating a new nature, when he is only bringing forth from the hidden depths of its [existing] nature that which lay concealed within" (Carey 1998, 53).

This excerpt offers a framework for scrutinizing the distinctive black nodules excavated on High Island and Inishark. As naturally occurring formations, uncanny in their shape, polish, and density, the nodules presented worshippers with conspicuous examples of the divine governance underlying all nature (fig. 4.8). The Inishark nodule was certainly singled out for special treatment in terms of acquisition, transport, and decoration. Indeed, the geometric cross design incised on the Inishark nodule also evokes divine Creation. Spoken by Wisdom personified, Proverbs 8 depicts God the creator as deploying geometric skill: "When he [God] prepared the heavens, I [Wisdom] was there: when he set a compass upon the face of the depth: When he established the clouds above: when he strengthened the fountains of the deep: When he gave to the sea his decree, that the waters should not pass his commandment."

The notion of God the creator as geometrist and architect also manifests in medieval imagery, such as the divine hand wielding a compass in the eleventh-century Eadwi Gospels from Winchester, England. Moreover, medieval compilers and commentators of classical and Late Antique geometric texts exalted

Figure 4.8: (*Left*) The nodule excavated near Leaba Leo. The colored dots indicate tool marks made by the point of a mason's compass. The color of the arc indicates which dot was used as the setting for the stable leg of the compass when the lines were incised. (*Right*) A full cross-of-arcs design superimposed on the Inishark nodule.

geometry as a means of modeling Creation (Zaitsev 1999, 531–32). The creator of the compass-made cross design might have seen his own task, aided by geometric knowledge and skill, as a representation of the divine act of Creation.

The creation of cross-slabs also entailed encounters with the forces of Creation as manifested by the formative power of the ocean. Despite variation in color and texture, each of the cross-slabs excavated from the Clochán Leo Complex is derived from the fine-grained, highly foliated Ballynakill Schist, which constitutes the primary bedrock of Inishark, nearby Inishgort, and the southern side of Inishbofin. This schist is particularly prone to flaking along its foliations and is irregularly angular when harvested by quarrying or from eroding bedrock deposits. Such stones compose the vast majority of postmedieval houses and fieldwalls on Inishark. In contrast, each of the cross-slabs from Clochán Leo are exceptionally smooth and flat along their faces and edges, though irregular in shape. This degree of smoothness is impossible to achieve through quarrying or carving and must be the result of erosion through water. Like the quartz pebbles, the stones used for the cross-slabs found at Clochán Leo were taken as tide-worn flagstones from the shoreline. While Inishark has many accessible coves where it is possible to harvest quartz pebbles, there are no stoney beaches where large flagstones are readily accessible. Consultation with local people and survey of the shorelines within the Inishbofin-Inishark archipelago have identified the likeliest source: a flagstone storm beach on Inishgort (*Inis Goirt*), the

Figure 4.9: A storm beach on the southern side of Inishgort is a likely source for the flagstones used to produce the cross-slabs excavated on Inishark.

small island immediately south of Inishark (fig. 4.9). To harvest this raw material for cross-slabs would have required detailed knowledge of the local littoral environment and the transportation of stones by boat to Inishark. Notably, two of the stones selected for cross-slabs—Cross-slab B and Cross-slab D—include quartz veins within their fabric.

Experimental archaeology has also shed light on the practicalities of carving on schist beach flagstones. In 2021–23, as a postdoctoral fellow at the Centre for Experimental Archaeology and Material Culture (CEAMC) at University College Dublin, I undertook a series of experiments to test different tool sets and techniques to carve the schist flagstones like those used on Inishark. The premise was simple: learning to carve cross-slabs would generate a more refined capacity to interpret the original artifacts in terms of material selection, tool markings, production sequence, labor investment, and embodied skill. The results suggest variation in the skill and experience of early medieval carvers and hint at the work of novice practitioners.

Cross-slab B is outstanding in its execution, in terms of both its relative symmetry and its regularity. Moreover, prior to carving, the raw schist flagstone was split longitudinally to yield a particularly flat face to bear the carving. This must have been a delicate operation, particularly considering the quartz vein that runs through the stone, but the result is a relatively thin and light object despite its broad surface area. Cross-slab A, in contrast, is a much bulkier stone and bears traces of mishaps during production. During carving, a large fragment of the flagstone flaked off, probably from a heavy blow. This compelled the carver to complete one terminal of the cross at a lower surface level than the rest of the

Figure 4.10: High contrast view of Cross-slab A produced for the CLIC project through laser scanning by the Discovery Programme (available online: https://sketchfab.com/discoveryprogramme/models). The dotted white line shows the line of the fracture that occurred during production. This flaking episode created a fault line on the surface of the stone and accounts for the irregularity of this terminal. The white arrow at bottom right indicates an abandoned line of carving—specifically, an initial border for the relief space that was subsequently reset nearer to the central disc. Note how the extent of the relief space in this quadrant varies from the other three quadrants of the design.

Figure 4.11: The central disc of Cross-slab C deviates from the other expansional crosses excavated at Clochán Leo. (*Left*) Detailed view of the central disc of Cross-slab C; (*top right*) Simplified schematic view of the carved lines that constitute the central disc of Cross-slab C; (*bottom right*) Simplified schematic view of the carved lines that constitute the central discs of Cross-slabs A and B.

design. This break during production, as well as a natural striation in the face of the stone, resulted in this terminal having a distinctive asymmetrical form compared to the other three (fig. 4.10). There is one other hint at the limitations of the carver's prior experience and perhaps a lack of a systematic technique. The delineation of the relief space (i.e., the area in which the surface of the stone must be carved down to a lower level) in one quadrant of Cross-slab A appears to have been begun at one point and then abandoned. This reduction of the relief space may have been undertaken to decrease production time. We have only a small fragment of Cross-slab C, but the surviving design is even more irregular, with the central disk of the cross deviating considerably from the pattern apparent on Cross-slabs A and B (fig. 4.11).

Based on timed experiments, I estimate that the design of Cross-slab A could have been carved in as little as four to six hours, with wider variation possible depending on the experience and skill level of the carver. The patterns of error on Cross-slabs A and C seem to suggest carvers who had little, if any, previous experience or developed technique. Cross-slab C may never actually have been finished. The inscribed stone from Period I, although earlier than the cross-slabs, likewise appears to represent a novice creation and potentially a trial piece. As such, we need not see early medieval stone carving as a craft exclusive to an elite segment of monastic artisans. Cross-slab A and the carved granite pebble could both have been produced by relative novices given access to appropriate tools. We must therefore acknowledge the possibility that some stone-craft from Inishark could represent the work of pilgrims or penitents who produced carvings as part of their temporary visits to the island. Whatever the case, the taskscapes of early medieval stone-craft on Inishark entailed various physical encounters with other-than-human agency. This included the seafaring necessary to acquire materials, the power of Creation manifested by the sight of uncanny nodules and tide-hewn flagstones, and the affordances and recalcitrance of schist in the process of carving. Early medieval stone-craft on Inishark reveals a preference for the acquisition of stone materials conspicuously rendered by other-than-human forces. I suggest that working such materials in processes of craft offered another opportunity for monks and pilgrims to ruminate on their relationships to divine Creation.

In sum, sea-born and seaborne stones were key players in devotional and craft practices on Inishark. Encounters with these stones could position worshippers in relation to fellow worshippers in the past and to the divine forces that rendered the world and cleansed the souls of the faithful. Pilgrims actively shaped the form and commemorative capacity of shrine complexes by depositing quartz pebbles and perhaps even by carving cross-slabs. If monks constructed leachta to cultivate a venerable heritage of sanctity, pilgrims' offerings added a new material framing that signaled their contribution to the island's heritage of devotion. By embodying the transformative power of divine force, quartz pebbles may also have signaled the shared devotional aspirations of monks and lay pilgrims. Nevertheless, it is important to recognize how ritual actions could express social differences as well as devotional affinity. To explore the social, political, and economic consequences of early medieval ritual on Inishark, it is necessary to contextualize these practices within the dwelling taskscape of the island's monastic settlement.

TASKS OF DEVOTION AND DWELLING

How did devotional practices fit within the larger dwelling taskscape of Inishark's monastic settlement? In recent years, scholars have begun to explore the articulation between ritual experiences, political economy, and the agricultural regimes of ecclesiastical settlements in early medieval Ireland (Etchingham 2006; Fitzpatrick 2006; Ó Carragáin 2006; 2014; 2021). Such an analysis must begin with a recognition that early medieval Ireland was a profoundly unequal society organized according to manifold distinctions of status, kinship, and gender. The surviving corpus of early Irish law codes, largely dated on linguistic grounds to the seventh and eighth centuries, legislate for a society that includes both free and unfree individuals (Kelly 1988). Enslaved people, whether born into servitude or taken captive in war, were exploited for their labor and as commodities of exchange. The various grades of freemen were distinguished by their wealth, rights, and privileges and obligations within relationships of clientship. Property-owning free classes—including kings, lords, and corporate institutions like monasteries—made grants of land or livestock to lower-status clients, who in return owed their labor, produce, and obligations of service and hospitality. The vast majority of people, free and unfree, were directly involved in the work of food production. Pastoralism, particularly of cattle raised for both meat and dairy products, features heavily in law codes, which often define legal status categories and clientship relations in terms of livestock (Kelly 1997). Yet, paleoenvironmental data and archaeological findings of water mills and corn-drying kilns demonstrate the importance of cereal crop cultivation (barley, oats, rye, and wheat), particularly from the eighth century (O'Sullivan et al. 2014, 179–80; McCormick 2008). Some of the earliest dated water mills come from ecclesiastical settlements, and church institutions may initially have enjoyed exclusive access to water-powered milling technology and expertise (O'Sullivan et al. 2014, 207–08).

Ecclesiastical communities were not merely devotional associations. They were corporate entities with their own wealth, property, and dependent clients. No comprehensive parish system existed in Ireland before the twelfth century. Nevertheless, early medieval legal texts demonstrate at least an aspiration to serve the laity at large and outline a contractual relationship in which clerics administered spiritual services (baptism, confession, eucharist, burial on sacred ground) in return for alms paid by laypeople (Charles-Edwards 1992; Sharpe 1984). In practice, this system of exchange may have applied most commonly to *manaig*, who were dependents attached to ecclesiastical estates (Etchingham 2005, 81–83). Manaig is simply the plural form of Old Irish *manach*, "monk," and sources from the time do not always make clear distinctions between the dependents of monasteries and those living under formal monastic vows (Flechner 2017). Perhaps distinctions were not always so clear in reality. Just like the dependents of secular elites, manaig could vary considerably in legal and economic status. Manaig might be nobles or commoners. The lowest status manaig might be expected to supply their labor directly on ecclesiastical estates as serfs. For others, clientship obligations meant paying rent in the form of food renders and supplying a certain amount of direct labor (Etchingham 1999, 363–454; Ó Carragáin 2014, 267). Some texts suggest that manaig might also supply fosters to the church—that is, offer a child to be educated and trained by the ecclesiastical community and perhaps eventually join their ranks (Etchingham 1991,

115–16). In the case of (at least in theory) formally celibate communities, fosterage allowed monasteries to replenish their membership with suitably learned individuals.

Even if some church dependents enjoyed relative wealth and status in a starkly unequal society, clerics maintained spiritual authority superior to other social classes. The seemingly reciprocal exchange of produce/labor for spiritual services presumed an ideology of sacred hierarchy that privileged the status and lifestyles of clerics over members of the laity. Legal prescriptions for the design of ecclesiastical landscapes strive to uphold this sacred hierarchy by regulating laypeople's access to sacred places and interactions with clerical groups. An excerpt from an eighth-century collection of ecclesiastical law, *Collectio Canonum Hibernensis*, prescribes three concentric divisions at holy sites: the outermost *sanctus* (sacred), the intermediate *sanctior* (more sacred), and the innermost *sanctissimus* (most sacred). While only clerics could access the sanctissimus, laypeople, regardless of gender, and even those guilty of sexual sins could access the outer boundaries.

> There ought to be two or three *termini* (enclosures) around a holy place: the first in which we allow no one at all to enter except priests, because laymen do not come near it, nor women unless they are clerics; the second, into the streets the crowds of common people, not much given to wickedness, we allow to enter; the third, in which men who have been guilty of homicide, adulterers and prostitutes, with permission according to custom, we do not prevent from going within. Whence they are called, the first *sanctissimus*, the second *sanctior*, the third *sanctus*, bearing honour according to their differences.
> (Doherty 1985, 59)

The ubiquity of concentric boundaries at early Irish ecclesiastical settlements embodies this model of sacred hierarchy. Ecclesiastical communities designed landscapes not only to evoke cosmological notions and to cultivate heritage but also to legitimate their claim to people's labor, produce, and reverence. The built settings of ritual must be seen as infrastructure that facilitated both devotion and the reproduction of political economic relationships.

If founded in part to facilitate extremes of asceticism, even island monastic settlements relied on manaig living either on island or on affiliated mainland estates. A variety of archaeological evidence sheds light on their actions and influence at island monasteries. Paleoenvironmental and faunal evidence indicates that island monasteries, such as Iona and Illaunloughan, Co. Kerry, had access to food sources brought from off island, possibly collected from manaig working on mainland estates (Bourke et al. 2011, 465; Murray et al. 2004, 183). The frequent presence of water mills on both mainland and island sites indicates a capacity to harness the labor of and process the grain for sizable populations in the surrounding landscape (O'Sullivan et al. 2014, 203–09). The built settings of ritual also attest to social diversity at ecclesiastical settlements. The internal dimensions of churches can distinguish those serving small monastic communities from those that could serve larger mixed congregations (Ó Carragáin 2009). Burial patterns are also telling. Gender-inclusive cemeteries situated on the periphery of monastic landscapes, such as Relickoran on Inishmurray, likely reflect burial grounds accommodating manaig on the margins of holy sites (Ó Carragáin 2013, 28–29). Ecclesiastical fosterage is difficult to identify through skeletal remains alone. However, excavations have identified potential fosters in the form of juvenile individuals buried alongside adult men on monastic cemeteries on the islands of Illaunloughan and Skellig Michael, Co. Kerry (Bourke et al. 2011, 376; Marshall and Walsh 2005, 84).

Previous archaeological fieldwork on island ecclesiastical settlements in Connemara sheds light on the lives, labors, and burials of manaig. Features of the monastic enclosure on High Island suggest only a small community of monastic inhabitants: a tiny church (3.5 × 3.15 m, internal) and a few cells suitable to accommodate a small monastic community. However, the island also includes the remains of a horizontal mill, likely built in the ninth or tenth century (Marshall and Rourke 2000, 55). Making this mill functional was a massive undertaking of landscape manipulation, requiring the production of a reservoir, feeder stream, millpond, raceway, and bypass channel (Rynne 2000; Scally 2014, 48–49). Rynne (2000, 212) estimates that the mill would have held the capacity to support a population of fifty to seventy inhabitants on the island—much more than could be accommodated within the monastic cashel. Survey of the island beyond the monastic cashel uncovered possible dwelling huts, garden plots, and a large stone wall running the length of the island (Scally 2014, 40, 46). This wall could be interpreted as a symbolic boundary, part of the multiple concentric enclosures of the monastery, and/or as a barrier for managing grazing livestock on the island. Sheep, likely raised on the island, dominated the faunal assemblage during the monastic phase on High Island, though cows and pigs were also represented (Scally 2014, 241–43). Pollen and macro-floral remains attest to the cultivation (and possible import) of cereal grains, primarily barley but also wheat and rye (Scally 2014, 264–47; 313–14). The inhabitants of the monastic cashel thus appear to have been able to draw from the labor of manaig possibly living on the island or on the mainland. It is not inconceivable that flour produced by the mill on High Island was believed to have inherited something of the sacred potency of the island's monastic community. Part of the incentive for rendering grain to the monastery may have been the opportunity to have the blessing of some portion returned to manaig for their own use.

The physical remains of the monastic dependents who supported the High Island community may reside on the nearby (4 km) intertidal island of Omey (*Iomaí*). Medieval hagiography and later folklore ascribe the foundation of both communities to St. Féichín, perhaps a reflection of an actual institutional link between High and Omey Islands in the early medieval period (Moran 2014, 21–22). The early medieval landscape of Omey is not as well preserved as High Island, but the character and configuration of extant ecclesiastical features suggest a center for lay worship. The extant late medieval parish church, which contains some early medieval fabric, has dimensions suitable for a large congregation (13.6 × 6.6 m, external) (Ó Carragáin 2010, 313). Situated along the coast, c. 170 m from the church, a cemetery defined by a rectangular enclosure wall included the remains of at least 134 children, women, and men ranging from the seventh to the thirteenth centuries (Scott 2006, 31–33, 63). This demography implies that laypeople worshipped and buried their dead on Omey for many centuries (Scott 2006, 109–10). Omey Island includes a number of undated hut sites and, like High Island, the remnants of a large stone wall, possibly related to livestock management, that divides the island in two. The people buried in Omey's cemetery may have been manaig tied to Féichín's communities on High and Omey Islands. Their labor would have fed the mill and the monks on High Island, and in return they might periodically have participated in pilgrimages to the monastery's saintly graves. They likely would have attended masses more regularly on Omey, where they would eventually be buried to await Judgment Day in the sandy ground sanctified by Féichín and his followers.

How does Inishark fit within this comparative context? Postmedieval occupation has largely obscured evidence for early medieval agriculture and domestic settlement on Inishark. However, CLIC's survey has identified some remnants of agropastoral infrastructure (fig. 4.12). As on High Island and Omey Island, a large (c. 380 m) stone wall runs the length of Inishark, dividing off the western half of the island (fig. 4.12). The wall is comprised of massive stones (much larger than those incorporated into nineteenth-century field walls) set atop an earthen embankment, likely cast up from a ditch running along its western side (Kuijt et al. 2010, 65–66). This last feature in particular suggests that the wall was built to keep livestock west of the wall, perhaps for summer pasture in areas away from arable crops. Indeed, the area west of the wall is among the more rugged terrain on the island and much better suited for pasture than arable.

The origin of the wall cannot be dated with precision. In recent years, survey work has shed light on the variety of early medieval field enclosures used to manage the interaction of livestock with arable agriculture (Harte and Ó Carragáin 2020; O'Sullivan et al. 2014, 183–94). These appear to have varied considerably according to specific conditions of environment, land use, and

Figure 4.12: The earth and stone wall that runs north to south for the length of Inishark. Traces of a ditch, likely a feature related to livestock management, are apparent on the western side. Photo by Ian Kuijt.

land management. The form and construction of the dividing wall on Inishark certainly does not correspond to any distinctive early medieval type known elsewhere in Ireland. Nevertheless, the presence of similar dividing walls on High Island and Omey Island points to a shared origin in the management of livestock for early medieval island monasteries. Indeed, even two of the smaller islands south of Inishark, Inishgort and Inishskinny More (*Inis Scine Mór*), include remnants of low stone walls running the length of the islands. Notably, early medieval farmers in Ireland did not customarily save hay for winter fodder but instead carefully managed livestock by moving them to areas of preserved grass (Kelly 1997, 45–46). As in the present, residents of the early medieval monastic settlement probably kept livestock on these islands in different parts of the year, with herdsmen and women using the low stone walls to manage animals' movements and their consumption of grass.

In addition to a low dividing wall, Inishgort includes the remnants of a cluster of stone structures. CLIC excavated two small test trenches in this area in 2012, revealing a substantial midden deposit of limpet and winkle shells, with small amounts of domestic and wild animal bone (Carden 2023). Five of the six faunal samples sent for radiocarbon dating analysis yielded calibrated median dates between the eleventh and thirteenth centuries (table 4.1). While the structures and middens almost certainly developed over a wider span of time, these dates provide clear evidence of activity in the medieval period. Monks or monastic tenants from Inishark likely traveled periodically to Inishgort to harvest marine life (fish, shellfish, seaweed, and seabirds), gather flagstones for cross-slabs, and tend to grazing livestock.

Medieval ecclesiastics had a genius for interweaving the practical and the symbolic, and the management of sheep on monastic islands would be no exception (Harney 2015–16; Holmes 2023). Pastoral imagery abounds in scripture and hagiography. Christ is both shepherd to the flock of humanity and the Agnus Dei—the spotless lamb of God—sacrificed for humanity's redemption. Saint Patrick's *Confessio* recalls the hardship of working as a shepherd during his captivity in ascetic terms, and early medieval Irish art, writings, and hagiography frequently invoke pastoral motifs to describe the missions of bishops (Stalley 2014; Verkerk 2014). The husbandry of sheep on the islands offered lambs for Easter meals, wool for monks' garments, and the embodiment of pastoral labor that could be associated with ascetic-like hardship, heroes of the Old Testament, and the benevolent rule of God and clerics over their flocks.

Lab ID Number	Species ID	Bone Element	Calibrated Date BP	Median Probability Date
UBA-51622	Sheep/Goat	1st phalanx	884 +/− 28	1174 CE
UBA-51623	Pig	Ulna fragment	888 +/− 36	1164 CE
UBA-51624	Cod Fish	Dentary	995 +/− 30*	1048 CE*
UBA-51625	Cattle	Radius fragment	776 +/− 35	1250 CE
UBA-51626	Cattle	Tibia fragment	730 +/− 43	1277 CE

* Dating has not been calibrated to account for marine reservoir effect.

Table 4.1: Radiocarbon dates of faunal samples from Inishgort. Each of the samples came from a midden deposit, primarily composed of marine shell, that covered the remnants of a stone structure and a simple hearth feature. The cattle tibia was chopped and split longitudinally for marrow extraction (Carden 2023).

Back on Inishark, at least one stone dwelling in the western prong of the island has yielded some evidence of medieval occupation. While many of the hut structures and field systems west of the dividing wall date to the Late Bronze Age, one of the excavated hut structures included a secondary hearth with charcoal dated to 1250–90 CE (UCIAMS-76146; 735 +/− 20 BP) (Quinn et al. 2018, 12). If not reoccupied as dwellings, some of the Bronze Age hut structures may have been periodically used by herders tending to livestock in this part of the island. Absence of evidence is not necessarily evidence of absence, and it is probable that remnants of medieval domestic settlement—the homes of manaig— have been obscured by the intensity of the later village settlement on the island. Most likely, medieval dwellings would have been unenclosed structures built of earth, stone, and possibly timber. Manaig may also have made more extensive use of the remnants of Bronze Age dwellings than is currently documented. Domestic structures, if present, were likely to have been located in areas peripheral to the main core of ritual monuments, perhaps to the west of Clochán Leo.

Figure 4.13: The remnants of an embankment for a former millpond on Inishark. The figure stands at the head of the likely raceway, where water continues to drain toward the eroding coastline. Photo by Ian Kuijt.

Survey of the island uncovered the remnants of another piece of infrastructure related to medieval subsistence activity—a possible millpond and raceway (Kuijt et al. 2010, 64–5). These are located roughly 400 m east of where the massive stone wall meets the southern coast of Inishark. While there is no natural lake on Inishark, a large drainage runs southwest from the elevated boggy ground beyond the hill Cnoc Leo. Near the coast, where this drainage runs to the sea, there are two large stone and soil embankments that appear to define the edge of a former millpond (fig. 4.13). The southern embankment, about 30 m long, is quite pronounced, with the pond side of the embankment standing up to 1.2 m in height. The two embankments come together close to the shoreline, creating a race. The millrace, formed by large stones on each side, drops approximately 2 m in elevation by the time it reaches the shore. The likely former location of the millhouse appears to have been destroyed by coastal erosion. Rubble cast up from the shore is scattered across the low-lying area, but some stones embedded in the soil near the northern embankment defined the outline of one or more rectangular buildings. Again, comparison with nearby ecclesiastical settlements suggest an early medieval origin for the mill. In addition to High Island, survey work on Inishbofin identified a possible millrace extending down from a lake adjacent to St. Colman's Abbey on Inishbofin (Kuijt et al. 2010, 65). Pollen cores taken from this lake suggest an upsurge in cereal agriculture contemporary with Colman's foundation in the seventh century (O'Connell and Ní Ghráinne 1994, 82–84). No such data exists for Inishark, yet the archaeological remains of the mill and the dividing wall suggest a great deal of agricultural labor undertaken by a mixed population of monks and manaig.

"DIFFERING IN STATUS, BUT ONE IN SPIRIT"— HIERARCHY AND COMMUNITAS

In the scene that started this chapter, I imagined how built settings and stone objects featured in practices that included monks and manaig in the mid-eleventh century. The Clochán Leo Complex served as both devotional and political infrastructure that reproduced the social and economic bases of the island's monastic community. In short, the configuration of bodies and materials in ritual gatherings cultivated experiences that legitimated monastic claims to manaig's labor. This was achieved, I suggest, through bodily movements and encounters that simultaneously emphasized inclusion and distinction, devotional affinity and sacred difference.

Textual and archaeological evidence demonstrates that ecclesiastical settlements accommodated social diversity but in ways that simultaneously underscored hierarchies of gender, class, and status. As outlined in the excerpt from the *Collectio Canonum Hibernensis*, boundary walls allowed monks to regulate the access of particular worshippers to sacred places. The criteria for access to the Clochán Leo Complex are unknown, but entry may have been offered exclusively to manaig and perhaps other laypeople offering alms, especially on particular feast days throughout the year. In making access to sacred places and objects contingent on one's economic contribution to the monastery, monks could leverage their claim to laypeople's labor and produce. The curation of occult objects—bells, shrines/cenotaphs, and cursing stones—was crucial to the operation of the legal and temporal powers claimed by monastic communities (Ó Carragáin 2003, 149–50).

Restrictive access to sacred places might also express other categories of social difference. While there is some limited hagiographical evidence that women were sometimes barred from monastic islands, historical and archaeological evidence suggests that churches and burials for religious women were established on the periphery of monastic islands (Ó Carragáin 2013, 26–27). Celibacy was more integral to women's than men's clerical status in the early medieval period, and the peripheral location of churches and cemeteries for religious women signaled a concern to demonstrate celibacy through gender separation (Collins 2019; 2021; Harrington 2002, 36–38). However, women's experience of and access to monasteries may well have varied considerably from foundation to foundation. Notably, the *Vita Columbae* describes the saint praying for a female relation while she suffered the pangs of childbirth (book II, chap. XLI) and later folklore surrounding turas traditions describes monuments or practices especially associated with pregnant women or couples hoping to conceive (Brenneman and Brenneman 1995, 54–59). The movements of lay women on Inishark, especially their interactions with celibate men, may or may not have been particularly regulated. The aspirations and uncertainty of the expectant mother in the scene above is meant to raise a question for which we have no clear answer. Such ambiguity may well have existed in the past. It is possible that a woman's gender and reproductive status would not have excluded her from entry to the Clochán Leo Complex, particularly if she had contributed labor to the monastery as a client. In fact, the remnants of two likely spindle whorls from excavations at the Clochán Leo Complex could hint at the presence of women within the enclosure (fig. 4.14). Women, both ecclesiastical and lay, are especially associated with textile production in Irish early medieval texts (Bitel 1996, 185). However, work by Bernadette McCarthy suggests that artifacts of textile production need not represent women's labor exclusively and, in some contexts, may shed light on alternative constructions of gender among celibate communities of monks (2013, 487–88). As such, spindle whorls alone cannot be taken as unambiguous indications of women's presence at ecclesiastical settlements.

Figure 4.14: Two soapstone artifacts recovered from excavations at the Clochán Leo Complex. (*Top*) Spindle whorl. (*Bottom*) Spindle whorl or loom weight, possibly broken during production. Photo by Meredith Chesson.

In the case of Inishark, there is good reason to imagine the presence of women, whether manaig or clerics, and to consider how the built-settings of devotion accommodated, elided, or emphasized differences in gender, lifestyle, and reproductive status.

Once within the Clochán Leo Complex, interactions with materials and bodies evoked not only the past and cosmological beliefs but also models of sacred and social hierarchy. How precisely pilgrims might have moved once within the complex is unclear, as are the specific arrangement of most of the stone crosses. We can theorize that access to the clochán, as an associative relic of the founder, was significantly restricted, perhaps only to monks and manaig undergoing some form of penance. I have depicted pilgrims moving from the entrance of the enclosure to kneel on the eastern side of the leacht. This reconstruction has much to suggest it. Kneeling on the eastern side of the leacht allowed pilgrims to see the incised face of Cross-slab D, to recognize the exposed edge-set stones of the chamber underlying the southern leacht, and to glimpse into the clochán to see a penitent at prayer. Monks addressing pilgrims from the western side of the leacht would face eastward, as appears to have been customary among priests delivering mass in early medieval Ireland (Ó Carragáin 2009, 129–30).

Different arrangements of actors and ritual choreography are of course also possible. We might, for example, imagine a priest delivering mass from the eastern side of the platforms while the congregation occupied the space between the platforms and the clochán. However, I have attempted in the imagined scene to reflect the tension between inclusion and exclusion apparent in textual descriptions of early medieval ritual practices and built settings. The monk Cogitosus, in his seventh-century *Vita Sanctae Brigidae*, includes a highly evocative description of worshippers in a church in Kildare (O'Keeffe 2023b, 165–75). He describes internal divisions within the church separating men and women and clerical and lay worshippers—"people of varying status, rank, sex and local origin, with partitions placed between them ... differing in status, but one in spirit" (Connolly and Picard 1987–88, 25–26). Although idealized, the text illustrates how at least one cleric imagined the choreography of devotion expressing both hierarchy of status and affinity of devotion.

Cogitosus's image of a diverse congregation united in spirit recalls the notion of *communitas*, first outlined by Victor and Edith Turner in their seminal study of Christian pilgrimage (Turner and Turner 2011). The Turners argued that pilgrimage events were liable to cultivate a particular social atmosphere characterized by the sublimation of everyday hierarchies and by heightened feelings of affinity and interconnection among participants. Although influential in cross-cultural analyses of pilgrimage, critics have argued that pilgrimages are often scenes of contestation that express the diverse and sometimes competing motives of participants with varying degrees of social power (Eade and Sallnow 1991; Lash et al. 2023). At least from the point of view of Cogitosus, the combination of spiritual affinity and sacred hierarchy need not constitute a contradiction. Indeed, expressions of communitas amid hierarchy may have been particularly prominent on Inishark. Unlike High Island, the most elaborated foci of pilgrimage on Inishark were not the relics of monks set within concentric boundaries but cenotaphs set within coastal complexes that also functioned as hermitages for ascetics. Hence, pilgrims granted access to the complex participated temporarily in an idealized form of devotion embodied by the ascetic devotee (and perhaps their own white stone offerings).

Instead of simply reiterating sacred hierarchy, ritual practices at the Clochán Leo Complex could highlight the similarity between lay pilgrimage and more permanent ascetic lifestyles as forms of peregrinatio. The possibility that pilgrims contributed to the formation of the complex by depositing quartz pebbles would have enhanced this sense of shared participation in ascetic devotion. Irish ecclesiastics, drawing on a metaphor well established in scripture and early church works, could envision the different stones within the fabric of church buildings as representative of the individuals that made up the living church: the congregation (Ó Carragáin 2005, 102–03). Monks and pilgrims may have similarly reflected on the gathered quartz stones as representative of an accumulated congregation of worshippers from different backgrounds that visited shrines on Inishark.

Allowing physical access to shrines may have been a useful strategy for attracting pilgrims and maintaining reciprocal relations with affiliated lay tenants. Crucially, monks could selectively restrict access to the complex and the occult objects curated within. Monks thereby maintained a privileged position as meditators of salvation, a role that could legitimate claims to the economic support of lay tenants and pilgrims. This tension between hierarchy and affinity resonates with cross-cultural analyses of pilgrimage and suggests how temporary experiences of equality in ritual can often sustain more durable, hierarchical social relations (Coleman 2002).

CONCLUSION—CULTIVATING ENDURANCE

There is good evidence that the endurance of ecclesiastical settlement on Inishark in the twelfth and thirteenth centuries relied, at least in part, on catering to lay worshippers. Taking its shape in the twelfth or thirteenth century, Teampaill Leo's dimensions (11.8 × 6 m, external) are comparable with Omey's church and could have accommodated a large congregation of laypeople. Likewise, Inishark's coastal cemetery is reminiscent of the lay cemetery excavated on

Omey Island. The origins of the coastal cemetery on Inishark remain uncertain, but its peripheral location and inclusion of carved crosses are suggestive of (perhaps late) medieval origins. Oak charcoal from the burnt feature visible in the eroding cliff edge does suggest a *terminus post quem* of the mid-twelfth century for the cemetery's foundation. As such, the construction of Teampaill Leo and the foundation of the cemetery might reflect attempts by members of an ecclesiastical community to remain viable by enhancing their accommodation of lay worshippers.

In contrast, evidence for activity at the monastery on High Island after the twelfth century is limited and sporadic, suggesting the gradual abandonment of the monastic settlement with some continued periodic pilgrimage (Scally 2014, 316–17). Scally (2014, 316) suggests that the religious community on High Island eventually returned to the affiliated establishment on Omey Island, which remained a center of lay worship and burial into the fourteenth and fifteenth centuries. Throughout the twelfth century, Gregorian ecclesiastical reforms (named after Pope Gregory VII) on the Continent inspired a series of transformations in the Irish church, particularly the formalization of a diocesan territorial structure (Flanagan 2010). This process of reform was accompanied by the incorporation of new architectural styles from abroad, an enhanced focus on lay devotion, and, in some cases, the stripping of land assets from indigenous monasteries (Ó Corráin 2001, 40; O'Keeffe 2003). By one estimate, as the twelfth century ended, most traditional monasteries in Ireland, if not abandoned, had become episcopal or pastoral centers or had adopted a reformed monastic rule (Flanagan 2010, 162). Across the west of Ireland, parish formation led to the construction of new church buildings or the renovation of older structures into buildings with longer dimensions and sometimes nave-and-chancel divides better suited to larger congregations of priests and laypeople (Fitzpatrick 2006; Ní Ghabhláin 2006; Nugent 2006; O'Keeffe 2006).

During the twelfth century on Inishark, a monastic establishment that included a group of monks supported by lay manaig appears to have transitioned to something more akin to a pastoral church. In the twelfth and thirteenth centuries, laypeople likely continued to support a smaller group of clerics whose primary focus was now pastoral care rather than ascetic devotion. This transition developed out of a deep history of ritual and economic interactions between clerics and lay groups. Indeed, affiliation with a papal Saint Leo would have held considerable discursive weight in the context of Gregorian reforms, which were instigated by papal figures and instituted to bring the Irish church in conformity with standards administered from Rome (Lash 2020). Thus, even if Clochán Leo ceased to function as a regular setting of asceticism in the twelfth century, its presence in the landscape could still evoke a heritage that resonated with the times and located worshippers in relation to contemporary debates over ecclesiastical authority.

In sum, the sustainability of settlement on Inishark from the seventh to thirteenth centuries relied on articulations of ritual experiences, political economic relations, and agricultural practices. Ritual infrastructure—churches, leachta, clocháns, cursing stones, and cross-slabs—generated experiences that situated worshippers in relation to the past, each other, and the divine agency animating the world. Tasks of devotion engaged worshippers with other-than-human forces and reaffirmed the social and economic relations on which the island's dwelling taskscape relied. Examining links between devotion and dwelling, between cult and cultivation, will provide a valuable framework for examining the subsequent history of heritage and ritual on Inishark.

FIVE

CULT, COMMEMORATION, AND COOPERATION

Heritage in Inishark's Modern Taskscape (c. 1600–1960)

FIVE DAYS ON INISHARK

Leo's monuments continued to figure in the lives and livelihoods of Inishark islanders in the postmedieval and modern periods. Five imagined scenes from five different eras on Inishark will provide a structure to the analysis that follows. I have grounded each scene with reference to material things known to have been present at the time depicted, either through excavation data or near contemporary accounts. The juxtaposition of these moments highlights once again a recurrent theme of this book: that encounters with bodies, objects, monuments, and elements of the landscape place people within temporal and social contexts. The goal of this chapter is twofold: (i) to examine how interactions with Leo's monuments situated people in relation to the past and to different communal formations across time and (ii) to assess if and how ritual monuments—as infrastructure for devotion, commemoration, and community reproduction—supported different regimes of dwelling in the historic village (c. 1750–1960).

As discussed in chapter 2, some traditional accounts of rural western Ireland depicted cultural continuity as the product of racial or environmental determinism (Evans 2000 [1957]; Gardiner 2011). More recent attempts to assess the development of Irish pilgrimage traditions rely predominately on textual or oral sources related to turas traditions scattered across the island of Ireland or within particular regional contexts (Brenneman and Brenneman 1995; Carroll 1999; Taylor 1995). A taskscape approach to re-engagements with medieval monuments on Inishark paints a more nuanced picture, better grounded in archaeological evidence and better attuned to local dynamics. Archaeological, folkloric, antiquarian, and cartographic evidence demonstrates the maintenance and refurbishment of ritual monuments as well as their neglect and destruction. These patterns of change and continuity become more intelligible when we attend to the sensory and commemorative affordances of monuments and consider devotional practices within the context of local dwelling tasks.

Despite the disintegration of Inishark's ecclesiastical community, Clochán Leo endured as a reminder of Catholic heritage and a periodic focus of devotion during the upheaval of the seventeenth and eighteenth centuries. The turas tradition as we know it from folklore and antiquarian accounts developed alongside the historic village settlement on Inishark (c. 1750–1960). The livelihood of this village relied to a great extent on transcontinental connections—the introduction of the potato from the Americas, national and international markets for fishing and other marine products, and remittances from migrant labor. Major political, economic, and religious developments noted across Ireland had distinctive local consequences on villagers' interactions with one another, the island landscape, and its early medieval heritage. Below, I will argue that developments in the turas tradition in the historic period reflect islanders' efforts to maintain cooperative relationships among themselves as well as to negotiate the absences, influences, and interferences of external authorities. Specifically, changing engagements with turas monuments represent islanders' reaction to the increased prominence of clergy and to different landholding regimes shaped by landlords and government agencies. As mediums for creating and contesting notions of local heritage, community, and spiritual authority, Leo's monuments factored significantly in islanders' struggle to sustain the livelihood of the village on Inishark.

TRAUMA, HIATUS, AND RESILIENT MEMORY C. 1650–1750

Inishark, 1700. Traces at Twilight.

A small group gathers in Clochán Leo in the twilight. They pass around a rectangular green glass bottle, manufactured to ship gin but now filled with whiskey. Smoke from a small fire built against the clochán's western wall escapes through gaps in the derelict roof. They have tidied up the collapsed stones, moving some outside the entrance, arranging others into a rough surface within. A few elders remember the days before a Dutchman occupied the English throne and gin was scarcely known. They recount stories they heard when young about the time before Cromwell's conquest and the distant days of Saint Leo, who dwelt in this very spot. They remember once seeing the fragment of an ancient cross-slab kept here—perhaps still underfoot now, lost in the collapse—but its design is vague in their memories. From talk of Leo, they move seamlessly to reflect on the quality of this year's whiskey compared to previous

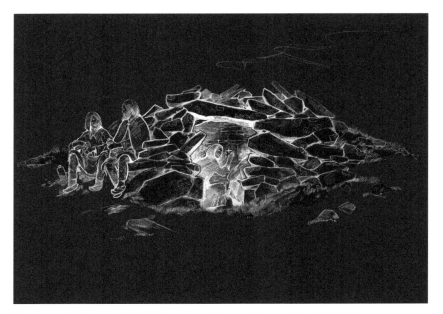

Figure 5.1: Visitors to Clochán Leo around 1700. Illustrated by Eric Carlson.

batches. This one has quite a bite and spurs once again an old argument on the ideal relative proportion of oats and barley in the formula. A young woman, already familiar with the contours of this debate, throws more driftwood on the fire, and the dance of the invigorated flames casts a low light, outlining the edges of a small cross incised on the clochán's western wall. She reaches out and traces its lines with her finger.

The nature of settlement on Inishark between c. 1300 and c. 1750 is unclear. The earliest phases of Teampaill Leo could offer accommodation to a sizable congregation dwelling on the island in the twelfth and thirteenth centuries. The church certainly remained a focus of burial in subsequent centuries, but radiocarbon analysis of skeletal material collected here yielded particularly broad ranges spanning the fifteenth to early seventeenth centuries (see chap. 3). Substantial settlement, perhaps with an ecclesiastical component, may have endured as late as the seventeenth century.

Ceramic and glass finds from within Clochán Leo provide the only datable artifactual evidence of activity on the island in the seventeenth century. Notably, CLIC excavations focused on the ruins of houses occupied in the nineteenth and twentieth centuries have never uncovered any seventeenth-century ceramics. Of course, absence of evidence is not necessarily evidence of absence. With the exception of the mid-seventeenth-century barracks, there are almost no visible traces of seventeenth-century settlement elsewhere on Inishbofin. The Old Barracks stands as testimony to the consequences that the Cromwellian regime must have had on the devotional and dwelling practices of islanders.

It is difficult to quantify the scale of devastation wrought by war, famine, disease, and persecution in Ireland during Cromwell's conquest (1649–53) and during the subsequent Commonwealth period (1653–59). Inishbofin was among the last Royalist outposts to surrender to Cromwell's forces in 1653. By 1657, the Commonwealth regime had constructed the fortification on Inishbofin to garrison troops and control the harbor (Walsh 1989, 36–45). Aside from protecting against foreign invaders and monitoring smuggling, the garrison also facilitated the surveillance of local Irish Catholics and may even have led to the expulsion of islanders. In June 1655, the Commonwealth Council listed Inishbofin among the garrisons "within which, or within one English mile therof, no Popish recusant" was allowed to reside or have lands allotted to them (Dunlop 1913, 163). A year later, the Commonwealth Council instructed the governor of Inishbofin, Colonel John Honnor, to "suffer no Irish to keep any boats upon any parte of that coast of Ir-conaght, the Co. of Mayo, or adjacent islands; also to exclude all ill-affected Irish out of that island" (Seymour 1921, 213). Enforcing this order almost certainly meant suppressing any remaining ecclesiastical establishment on Inishark.

In addition to stripping Catholics of land and rights, the Commonwealth regime applied legislation labeling Catholic clergy guilty of high treason and making it a felony to harbor them. At least many hundreds of Catholic clergy went into exile while others were imprisoned. Some clergy, along with other convicts, were eventually sent as indentured servants to the Caribbean (Handler and Reilly 2017; Hogan et al. 2016). Contemporary documentation indicates that the garrison on Inishbofin served as a prison for clergy between c. 1657 and c. 1662 (Walsh 1989, 39). Accounts by exiled Catholic clergy level charges that the priests imprisoned on Bofin were malnourished and tortured (Moran 1907, 306). Folklore on Inishbofin paints a similar portrait, though in even more dramatic style. Islanders refer to a rock in the mouth of Bofin harbor, visible only at extremely low tides, as Bishop's Rock. The place-name apparently commemorates a bishop who was chained there by Cromwellian forces and left to drown in the flowing tide.

Despite some respite from anti-Catholic suppression during the Restoration (1660–88), dynastic and religious conflict once again entangled Inishbofin during the Williamite War (1688–91). A Jacobite garrison was installed in the barracks on Inishbofin in 1690, but they surrendered to Williamite forces soon after the decisive Jacobite defeat at the Battle of Aughrim in 1691 (Walsh 1989, 44). A series of penal laws passed in the wake of William's victory sought to solidify the Protestant ascendancy, in which the vast majority of land and political power rested with English or Anglo-Irish elites. This legislation renewed the disenfranchisement of Catholics and discouraged Catholics from practicing openly. On Inishbofin, there is some documentary evidence that the barracks was intermittently reoccupied during the early eighteenth century to protect English interests (Walsh 1989, 45–46).

The traumas of the seventeenth and eighteenth centuries are essential context for any analysis of the development of turas traditions from their medieval precursors. With Catholic churches destroyed, monitored, or appropriated for Protestant worship, alternative settings of devotion became essential for the expression of Catholic devotion, including private homes, barns, and especially open-air sites. Archaeological and folklore surveys in Ireland record a number of mass rocks, outdoor landmarks, usually in secluded places, where Catholics could gather in secret to hear mass from outlawed priests in the seventeenth century (Bishop 2016). Other outdoor foci of devotion, such as holy wells, were attractive for the same reasons. Carroll (1999) argued that clergy played a major role in legitimating, overseeing, and developing turas traditions during the seventeenth and eighteenth centuries. The intermittent presence of colonial government authority on Inishbofin during the seventeenth and eighteenth centuries likely discouraged open displays of Catholic ritual, particularly the ministration of clergy. In one form or another, it is likely that laypeople now took a leading role in the maintenance of Inishark's devotional heritage.

Roderic O'Flaherty's reference to the veneration of St. Leo's relics on Inishark in 1684 need not imply the presence of a resident ecclesiastical community, nor indeed of any permanent settlement on the island at all. Perhaps engagement with the remnants of St. Leo's cult consisted of only periodic visits, potentially by people who settled on Inishark only seasonally. Seasonal transhumant pastoralism in upland environment—booleying—was common in western Ireland between the mid-eighteenth and twentieth centuries, and likely even earlier (Costello 2017, 198; Costello 2020; Horning 2007, 368–69). Booleying provided an important opportunity for semi-independence and social learning for adolescent women and men, who were commonly sent to look after livestock in summer pastures with adults checking in periodically (Costello 2017). This system of seasonal mobility could have been adapted to a maritime context, with some inhabitants of Inishbofin relocating to Inishark periodically to exploit the potential of summer grazing, prime agricultural land, and marine resources.

The disbanding of an ecclesiastical community, the suppression of Catholic devotion, and perhaps even a hiatus in permanent settlement in the late seventeenth / early eighteenth century may account for the apparent break in the material and folklore record relating to St. Leo's monuments. The memory of some monuments as scenes of medieval devotion appears not to have passed down through oral tradition, continued ritual circuits, or inference from their presence in the landscape. Both the Western Enclosure and the Clochán Congleo Complex, despite their affinity with the Clochán Leo Complex, fell into disuse and do not figure in nineteenth- and twentieth-century folklore accounts as monuments associated with Leo or the island's ecclesiastical past.

Archaeological evidence from Clochán Leo suggests that irregular but recurring visits to the monument did pass on some memory of its role in medieval devotions. Excavation results from Period IV (1600–1750) in Clochán Leo suggest a hiatus in permanent occupation punctuated by recurring episodes of collapse, renewed engagement, and minor renovations. Ceramic finds from the compacted floor surface of Clochán suggest that the structure remained largely intact at the beginning of the 1600s and began to collapse only subsequently. The vessels, albeit difficult to identify with certainty, likely represent the drinking of alcoholic and medicinal substances. These consumptive practices likely mark the transition from liturgies overseen by ecclesiastical officials to a turas tradition primarily undertaken by laypeople in a context of Catholic suppression. The medieval cross-slab fragments found within the clochán might attest to efforts to preserve artifacts at risk of being destroyed or forgotten.

Indeed, activities within Clochán Leo in the late 1600s and early 1700s may constitute deliberate efforts to gather ensembles of people, materials, and substances that commemorated a disappearing past while forging memorable new experiences that left material cues for future visitors. In the decades following the curation of cross-slab fragments within the clochán, these objects were again lost as the collapsing roof buried them amid anonymous stones. Subsequent visitors intermittently rearranged fallen stones into irregular floor surfaces. Discarded amid these stones were new signs of alcohol and tobacco use—a pipe stem, a Westerwald Stoneware sherd, and the fragments of olive green case bottles designed for the transport of gin (Munsey 1970, 84–86). Alcohol consumption should not be taken as inconsistent with devotional practices. Later accounts, albeit often scornful, depict drinking and conviviality as essential components of turas celebrations, usually following physically demanding penances earlier in the day (Carleton 1862, 194–95; Croker 1824, 280–1; Hardy 1840, 39). In addition to their physiological effects, both alcohol and tobacco could evoke political associations and discourses (Agbe-Davies 2015; Hartnett

2004). The promotion of gin in Britain and Ireland in the seventeenth century followed the ascent of Dutch William of Orange to the English throne in 1688. In England, gin consumption could signal patriotic devotion to the new Protestant ruler (Dillon 2003, 6). Sea traffic related to the garrison on Inishbofin may have made gin a fairly accessible commodity, suitable for marking a special occasion. Or, islanders could have repurposed the bottles for homemade whiskey, *poitín*. In either case, the use of these distinctive bottles by Irish Catholics would have inverted—perhaps with mocking intent—the association of the gin economy with Protestant ascendancy. Whatever more conventional forms of Christian devotion took place, people ingested pleasurable and perception-altering substances at the clochán, enjoyed themselves, and perhaps reiterated their own previous experiences and those of their predecessors.

A series of burnt deposits in the hut's southwestern corner testify to one type of reiterative practice. Perhaps these fires provided light and heat to visitors who, like later pilgrims, spent the night within the clochán periodically, perhaps on annual feast days. At one stage, thin flagstones edge-set against the western wall created a simple hearth below an incised cross on a wall stone. As mentioned in chapter 3, the four small crosses incised on the clochán's western and eastern walls cannot be dated with certainty, though subtle variations in their designs and tooling suggest that they were created on an ad hoc basis rather than as part of a single event. One or all may date from the medieval period or early modern period, and stratigraphic evidence demonstrates that the lowest three crosses certainly predate the nineteenth century. These crosses might represent a kind of devotional graffiti carved by different pilgrims over time, with later visitors' mimicking their predecessors' inscriptions of presence.

The precise social and settlement context of activity within Clochán Leo between 1650 and 1750 remains obscure. Nevertheless, the assemblage of artifacts in their stratigraphic contexts reveals how visitors gathered materials and substances that afforded *memorable* and *commemorative* experiences. The consumption of medicine, alcohol, and tobacco was liable to heighten the sensorial imprint of visits to Clochán Leo, particularly if undertaken at regular annual intervals. The dilapidating clochán, the curation of medieval stonework, and the traces of hearths and vessel fragments evoked multiple pasts within and beyond living memory. Engaging and adding to the material leftovers of activity within the clochán, visitors could reflect on the heritage of medieval asceticism and the endurance of local Catholic devotion despite its legal suppression. Indeed, by leaving behind the residue of fires and tidying up collapsed stone, visitors fostered subsequent commemorations that would engage the traces of earlier gatherings. Local devotions and commemorations contested with the adversarial forces of colonialism but also the ravages of time and gravity. Visitors left traces of their visits, and the objects they encountered left traces on them—stories and memories, however partial and fragmentary, to pass on to the next generation. This continuation of memory, despite the trauma of the seventeenth century, set the stage for reengagements with early medieval monuments during the occupation of the historic village.

DEVOTION AND DWELLING C. 1750–1880

The Development of the Historic Village

Perhaps more than any other factor, the introduction of potato cultivation afforded a renewed intensity of settlement on Inishark. First introduced in the sixteenth century, the potato began to transform settlement patterns in the west of Ireland in the eighteenth century. Landowners in Ireland (typically the Protestant English beneficiaries of colonial dispossession) reserved quality land for commercial agriculture. Landless tenant farmers (typically Irish Catholics) used the potato to sustain their families on the scarce land available for rent. Nutrient rich and with the capacity to grow on damp, acidic soils, the potato—particularly the lumper variety—enabled unprecedented population densities in traditionally marginal environments (Aalen et al. 2011, 85–86; Feehan 2012). In the eighteenth and nineteenth centuries, villages of small tenant farmers proliferated along the western crescent of marginal upland running from County Cork to County Donegal (Whelan 2012). Although circumstances of agricultural and landholding varied in subtle ways across time and space, the term *rundale* refers to a system of collective agriculture that appeared in this area at the time. In rundale, tenants held land jointly from a landlord and undertook a mixed agropastoral regime though collective governance of commonage resources (Aalen et al. 2011, 79–82; Bell and Watson 2008, 24–7; Flaherty 2015; Gardiner et al. 2020; Slater and Flaherty 2009). Flaherty (2015, 25–26) has outlined a number of features related to settlement location and morphology, land tenancy, demographics, local governance, and agricultural practice that are, when co-present, diagnostic of rundale. Analysis of Inishark's landscape, documentary evidence, and folklore suggest the presence of such a system on the island in the first half of the nineteenth century. Combining this data with archaeological evidence and landscape analysis allows one to reconstruct the material, demographic, and political economic context of devotional and dwelling tasks on the island.

Around 1776, the Orcadian cartographer Murdoch MacKenzie produced navigation charts for the west coast of Ireland (fig. 5.2). His depiction of Inishbofin and Inishark is the earliest extant map of the islands to include any details of settlement. His generic house figures seem to represent not individual houses but clusters of settlement. As such, his depiction of three houses on Inishark affords no estimate of population. It does, however, indicate the early development of the historic village by the third quarter of the eighteenth century. William Bald's map, published in 1816, offers greater detail, showing thirteen structures in the village (fig. 3.2). The first edition, six-inch Ordnance Survey (OS) map, produced in 1838, shows thirty-three houses and outbuildings in the village (fig. 3.3, fig. 5.3). The nearest contemporary census, 1841, records 208 islanders on the island. Predictably, following the potato blights of 1845–49, the population dropped by 34 percent down to 138 by the time of the next census in 1851. Subsequent records indicate a resurgence to pre-Famine levels by 1871. After 1881, emigration began to have a marked impact, and population again declined (Browne 1893, 338) (table 5.1). The twenty-five-inch OS map, produced in 1898, shows forty roofed structures plus the renovated Teampaill Leo (1881–84) and the recently built National School (1898). Population at the time of this mapping likely stood around 125 (fig. 5.4).

Characteristic of rundale landscapes, settlement on Inishark developed as a cluster of houses (*clachán*) with adjacent garden plots, surrounded by an infield of arable land and, at a greater distance from settlement, a more rugged outfield used for pasture (Whelan 2012). The amazing preservation of settlement

Year	Pop.	% Change
1820	100*	–
1841	208	–
1851	138	−33.70%
1861	181	+31.20%
1871	208	+13.00%
1881	207	+0.90%
1891	123	−40.60%
1901	129	+4.90%
1911	110	−14.70%
1926	72	−34.50%
1936	68	−5.60%
1946	67	−1.50%
1951	50	−25.40%
1960	25	−50.00%

Table 5.1: Population data for Inishark generated from census data (retrieved from the Central Statistics Office, CSO.ie) and an estimate of population in 1820 based on the Bald Map of Mayo. The symbol * indicates an estimate. The symbol – indicates no data.

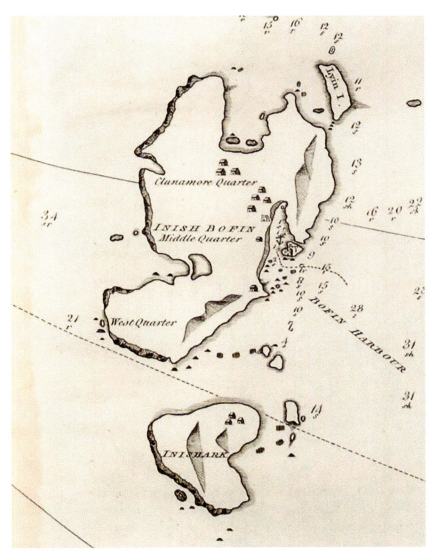

Figure 5.2: The depiction of Inishark and Inishbofin on the Murdoch Mackenzie maritime survey of Ireland (Volume 1, Chart 14), published in 1776. Courtesy of the Placenames Branch, the Department of Tourism, Culture, Arts, Gaeltacht, Sport and Media, and the website logainm.ie.

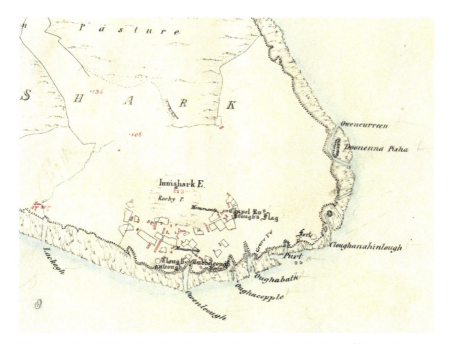

Figure 5.3: First Edition Fair Plan Ordnance Survey Map of Inishark (National Archives OS/105B/249/1). Based on a survey in 1838, the map shows approximately thirty-three structures in the village. While household garden plots are indicated adjacent to many buildings, there are no boundary features shown dividing up the infield area of cultivation surrounding the village. Reproduced with the kind permission of the director of the National Archives.

infrastructure on Inishark facilitates a basic understanding of the interdependence of the village's productive tasks. Comparative ethnohistoric data from nineteenth-century Ireland and Browne's observations in 1893 further refine this understanding.

The most obvious evidence of cultivation is the scars of spade-dug ridges used for planting potatoes in garden plots and within the strips of the village's infield. Though labor intensive, this method modulated soil temperature and facilitated drainage in a rainy climate (Bell and Watson 2008, 138–40). Animal dung, rotten thatch from houses, and seaweed, often gathered by women, acted as fertilizer (Bell and Watson 2008, 75–77; Browne 1893, 348). The primary crops grown were potatoes, grain (barley, oats, rye), and turnips. Farmers in nineteenth-century Ireland commonly rotated their potato and grain crops

Figure 5.4: The twenty-five-inch Ordnance Survey map of Inishark, surveyed in 1898. The map shows forty roofed structures in addition to the newly renovated Teampaill Leo and the National School at the northeastern tip of the village. Note two developments that have emerged since the 1838 mapping: greater division of the village area by enclosed household garden plots and the emergence of field divisions within the infield surrounding the village. © Tailte Éireann. Copyright Permit No. MP 000424.

within the same fields over the course of different growing seasons. Potatoes planted in soil diminished of nutrients by the last cycle of grain crops could still flourish while allowing nutrients to replenish for the next cycle of grain production (Yager 2002, 155). During the height of the growing season in summer, islanders herded livestock into the common pasture in the outfield. After the harvest, the infield reverted to commonage, and animals could graze the stubble and refertilize the soil with their droppings. In 1893, Browne observed that households on Shark and Bofin generally kept a couple of pigs and cattle, some sheep, and ducks and geese, though some of the poorer families had no cattle (Browne 1893, 348).

In addition to agriculture, islanders participated in commercial kelp production and fishing. As a means of extracting profit from marginal maritime environments, these industries provided an incentive for landlords to draw tenants to Inishark and Inishbofin in the late 1700s and early 1800s. However, the profitability of these industries fluctuated considerably across time. Burning kelp (a form of seaweed) produced an alkali ash that was manufactured into bricks and sold for use in various industries including soap, glass, and linen manufacture (Forsythe 2006, 219–20). Ash mounds and kelp drying racks in the village attest to islanders' participation in this industry. First incentivized by a blockade on the import of manufactured kelp from the Americas during the American Revolution, the industry had declined in Connacht by the 1830s but received a boost again in the 1840s when it was discovered that iodine, used in photography, could be refined from kelp. Nevertheless, Browne reported that kelp production had declined considerably on the islands by the late nineteenth century (Browne 1893, 349).

In addition to agriculture, fishing—primarily for mackerel, turbot, plaice, cod, and ling—provided an important source of subsistence and income. Teams of islanders sometimes hunted basking sharks (sunfish) with harpoons in order to sell oil extracted from their livers. This industry had declined by the late 1800s, owing to the decline in oil prices and the considerable danger it entailed (Browne 1893, 349). An 1873 report by Thomas Brady, inspector of Irish fisheries, includes a chilling report of the perils of hunting sunfish with defective gear. In one instance, as men were fastening a speared fish to the gunwale of their boat, the coil of the spear broke, and the flailing of the animal capsized a boat of nine men, five of whom drowned (Brady 1873, 7).

Islander households had to divide their time between agriculture, pastoralism, fishing, and industry to strike a balance that would ensure sufficient produce to feed their families and money to pay rent. This was a precarious balance at the best of times. The integration and functional articulation of different dwelling tasks meant that failures in one domain echoed and expanded in others. This rippling effect is documented starkly in a constabulary report of conditions on Inishark and Inishbofin in 1873. A series of bad harvests left islanders desperate and destitute. Few had any potatoes remaining to feed themselves or their animals, and foul weather prevented the import of Indian meal (maize meal) for relief.

> The islanders in winter slice up potatoes and carry them to the sheep on the hills, but as the potato crop of last year was so bad most of the potatoes were used by September, and nearly all were gone by December; therefore there was nothing to give the sheep during the hard weather of January and February, and numbers died.... Those of the islanders who have a beast [i.e., cow] are obliged to feed it on Indian meal, for if they lost the beast they would be ruined.... I visited a great many houses in Boffin and Shark, and I certainly

found great distress and dire poverty. In one house I found them eating their dinner, which consisted of boiled seaweed, with limpets in it.... In some houses in Shark I found there was only a quart of meal, and that too, borrowed from the last neighbor who had got a bag. Only three men in Shark have any potatoes. No potatoes were eaten since before Christmas. There is no seed there, except with one man. Many of the people in Boffin, very many of them, have nothing to put in the ground.... Dysentary has made its appearance, and I fear it is owing to want of proper nourishment. (Horne 1873, 52–53)

The precarity of islanders' livelihoods throughout the nineteenth century fluctuated with whims of weather, crops, and markets but also according to the character of the islands' landlords, estate agents, and tenancy agreements. Contemporary estate records and other tax assessments shed some light on the nature of land tenure on Inishbofin and Inishark. In the summary that follows, I draw partly from a master's thesis in which Lauren Marie Couey (2018) synthesizes census and valuation records to reconstruct developments in the landholding regime on Inishark.

In the 1820s, ownership of Inishbofin and Inishark passed from the Clanricarde Burkes to the Marquess of Sligo, Howe Peter Browne. Ownership of the islands would remain with the Browne family until the 1850s, when it was purchased by Henry William Wilberforce (National Library, MS 41,023/12). After Wilberforce's death in 1866, the islands passed among a series of men who had lent Wilberforce money for his initial purchase: Sir William Palmer (1866–69) followed by Rev. Edward Coleridge and Rev. Thomas Harding Newman (1869–76) (Horne 1873, 52–53). Thomas Allies purchased the island in 1876 and later passed it on to his son Cyril Allies, who was the landlord at the time of the island's purchase by the British Government's Congested Districts Board in the early twentieth century.

Before the Allies family, landlords rarely visited the islands. The Brownes never resided on the island, relying instead on an estate agent, Henry Hildebrand, who looms large in the documentary record for the islands. Hildebrand remained in place under Wilberforce until at least the early 1850s. The Tithe Applotment Books, compiled in the 1820s–30s, are the product of a survey to determine the amount due in tithes to the Church of Ireland from households occupying more than one acre. The records for Inishark and Inishbofin do not list individual heads of household. The occupants of Inishbofin are listed simply as "Mr. Henry Hildebrand and several others." As the estate agent and largest land tenant on Inishbofin, Hildebrand would have been responsible for collecting rent. Island tenants were less precisely documented than tenants living on other lands owned by the Brownes. An extant account book from the Browne estate held in the National Library generally lists the heads of household for each mainland property as well as the rent they owed and paid between 1842 and 1845 (MS 40,924/15-16). In contrast, rent collections and arrears of rent for Inishark and Inishbofin are recorded as just two totals on a loose-leaf sheet of paper, signed by Hildebrand and incorporated into the more detailed account book. Contemporary accounts suggest that Hildebrand promoted Protestant proselytization and monopolized the islands' fishing industry by threatening eviction to islanders who bought equipment from or sold their fish to anyone but him (Robinson 2008, 167–69). He is still remembered on Inishbofin as an exploitive middleman who enriched himself at the expense of islanders.

The lack of detailed recording of islander tenants and holdings before the mid-nineteenth century indicates the management strategy of Hildebrand, who evidently focused on regulating fishing rather than farming. The lack of specific lease agreements with particular households may have allowed Hildebrand to evict with impunity. This resulted in considerable precarity for islanders but perhaps also a greater degree of autonomy on how tenants organized agriculture and land use among themselves. There is good reason to believe that islanders on Inishark in particular, with no resident representative of the landlord on island, organized their farm work collectively under a joint tenancy agreement in the first half of the nineteenth century.

On other islands and inland areas under rundale, villagers held their land in joint tenancy—that is, land was not rented to particular households but to the village as a collective. In many cases, villagers redistributed parcels of arable land among themselves at regular intervals (Yager 2002, 156–57). This rotation distributed different kinds and quality of land (and therefore risk) among villagers. In the absence of estate agents, villages under joint tenancy typically had a local leader—often known as *an rí*, "the king"—charged with organizing the redistribution of land, gathering rent, and mediating with outside authorities (Dornan 2000, 157; Hayes and Kane 2015; Ó Danachair 1981, 24–25; Yager 2002, 158). Antiquarian and oral historic accounts suggest that villagers bestowed the title on a member of their community who embodied particular qualities or abilities including physical prowess and charisma, sound judgment, better than average education, and fluency in English and Irish. The title appears to have been commonly but not inevitably passed down within particular families. Kings were particularly common on islands along the west coast, appearing in folklore or antiquarian accounts relating to eighteenth- to twentieth-century communities on Cape Clear Island (Co. Cork), Great Blasket Island (Co. Kerry), the Inishkeas (Co. Mayo), Inishmurray (Co. Sligo), Tory Island and Inishtrahull (Co. Donegal), and Inishmore (Co. Galway) (Ó Danachair 1981, 20–25). Only one named king is known from Inishark: Michael Halloran, who was the king at the time of Browne's expedition in 1893. Myles Joyce, the

National School Teacher on Inishbofin, provided Browne with the following explanation: "The title of king is not hereditary in the island. There is at present a man removed something beyond his neighbours in the way of education and position, who is, *par excellence*, the king; and to whom all persons who want any information about the island or its history must apply" (Browne 1893, 350).

Michael Halloran was most renowned as a veteran harpooner of basking sharks (Gore-Booth 1891, 61). However, the title itself may have originated in the context of a rundale system of collective agriculture and joint tenancy on Inishark earlier in the nineteenth century. Indeed, in the 1820s Tithe Applotment assessment in which Hildebrand is listed as the representative occupant of Inishbofin, the occupants of Inishark are listed as "John Holleran & Co." Perhaps this John Holleran, like the later Michael Halloran, served as king. At the very least, the document suggests a joint tenancy agreement where John Holleran served as a representative for the village as a whole.

Documentation and ethnohistoric data from the later nineteenth and twentieth centuries may offer additional echoes of former joint tenancy regimes on Inishark and Inishbofin. Richard John Griffith's valuation of the islands, completed in 1855, is the first to include a detailed list of the heads of household dwelling on Inishark and Inishbofin. By 1855, the island had been purchased by Wilberforce, and the valuation indicates that tenants now rented particular holdings of arable land valuated individually. In the map adjoining the valuation, the infield area of Inishark is shown divided into a series of numbered holdings that did not figure on the 1838 OS map. Current and former field systems visible on aerial imagery of Inishark do not reflect the elaborate stripping depicted on Griffith's map. Perhaps divisions between strips were marked by less substantial and more easily adjustable boundaries such as low embankments or simple alignments of stone. As late as 1893, Browne remarked that holdings on the islands were insufficiently fenced (1893, 347–48), and the 1898 OS map shows many fewer divisions than on the Griffith valuation map. Couey's (2018, 96–100) analysis suggests that the field stripping apparent in the landscape today largely reflects developments of the early twentieth century (see the discussion of the Congested Districts Board below). As such, the boundaries of the Griffith valuation may represent an effort to impose a simplified order of direct tenancy on what was, on the ground, a more complicated arrangement of landholding and land use. Interestingly, in the twentieth century it was common for islanders on Inishbofin to refer to the land they owned as their *share*, perhaps a linguistic echo of a past system of collective tenancy and agriculture.

The balance of the evidence suggests that a rundale system of collective agriculture and joint tenancy existed on Inishark in the early nineteenth century. By 1855, the landlord or his agent had devised a system of direct tenancy. Bulk rent payments, as well as documented and undocumented subdivision and collective holding, likely endured to some extent. The taskscape of dwelling throughout the history of the village required a significant degree of collective action and cooperation but especially so in the first half of the nineteenth century. In the next subsection, I will examine the idea that Leo's monuments, with their associated traditions and prohibitions, acted as a kind of ritual commonage that could foster cooperation and discourage conflict.

CULTIVATING COLLECTIVITY? RITUAL IN THE RUNDALE

Inishark, April 11, 1840. A St. Leo's Morning.

Leo's Day is a holy day, and there are expectations to keep it so. Failing to observe might risk the wrong kind of attention. Those who are able abstain from work in the fields or on the sea. But some essential work—particularly women's domestic labor—must go on, and many have spent the early morning preparing what food is available for the day's meal. The previous weeks have seen all the potatoes and oats and barley sown in recently redistributed plots in the infield.

There's no priest for miles. Easter is eight days away, but there's no assurance that any priest would be on Bofin to deliver mass, even if the sea is calm enough for Shark people to attend. There's no ordained master of ceremonies for the feast day celebration, just elders who know how things ought to be done. The islanders informally split themselves into a series of groups, based on kinship and household, and each begins the turas circuit at a different time to avoid crowding at any one station. As they process from one station to the next, they walk past the drystone houses, garden plots, and livestock of their neighbors and relations. The groups pass each other with more or less solemnity, some greeting with smiles and jokes and others sufficing with silent nods. One group takes to laughing as their circuit encounters a line of ducks waddling along their way as if on their own pilgrimage. It's a foggy morning, with the haze enhanced by the smoke of hearth fires that breathes through the thatched roofs and hangs heavy in the damp air.

Villagers live in the smoke, scent, and sound of their neighbors' hearths. There's more than two hundred people living on the island in less than forty houses, many shared with milk cows and pigs who stay indoors overnight. Within dwellings and without, space is at a premium. Over the years, villagers have developed the configuration of houses and household plots not only to make use of the best draining land but also to avoid interference with Leo's monuments. Today, the turas draws islanders through the everyday landscape of the village in a circuit very different from their daily movements along familiar pathways. One group trudges up the slope of Cnoc Leo to visit the station there, a spot visited but once a year. Another group weaves around enclosed gardens to visit a leacht and bullaun, its basin full to the brim.

Whether by rain or periodic re-filling by those living nearby, the bullaun is scarcely ever short of water. Groups linger longest at St. Leo's Well, where the choreography of the station is most elaborate. The ruined church, more commonly used for a cattle barn, has been shoveled clean of manure, and some enter to look at the cross-slab fragments kept there. To the east of the church, a family completes a station by praying and circling a set number of times around a mound topped by a standing cross a little over a meter tall. One of the children in the back of the procession, distracted by a cramp of hunger in his belly, has lost track of the count but completes the steps and mouths the words under his mother's watchful eye.

—⚏—

To some nineteenth-century observers of rundale, collectivity was a flaw inherent in the system. Patrick Knight, an engineer hired to design and supervise the town of Belmullet, Co. Mayo, published an account of rundale settlements he observed in the barony of Erris, Co. Mayo, in 1836. He speculated that the periodic redistribution of landholdings disincentivized householders from investing time and labor to improve a holding that someone else might benefit from after the next cycle of redistribution: "No man has an individual interest in the improving or ameliorating the land" beyond his rotation. After redistribution, "his neighbours would, by *chance* have the benefits of his labors, and hence individual industry ceases to be applied for these purposes and all that can be done to extract the most from the soil, and from one another, is practiced for the current year" (Knight 1836, 59). In his opinion, the dissolution of the collective system, capital investment, and new agricultural techniques would increase productivity for tenants and profits for landlords and middlemen (Knight 1836, 93).

Knight's reckoning appears to emanate from a kind of rational choice theory rather than ethnographic observation of peoples' behavior. Cross-cultural anthropological research cautions against assumptions that the individual or individual household (as distinct from a wider community) represents the operative scale of affiliation that dictates behavior (Appuhamilage 2017). Likewise, Ostrom's (1990) analysis of regimes of collective resource management in various geographic contexts indicates their capacity to sustain over long time scales, given suitable political and cultural conditions (see Acheson 2011; Rabinowitz 2010; Yelling 1977). There is no doubt that the livelihoods of villages under rundale were precarious. Flaherty's (2014) statistical analysis indicates that areas under rundale were among the most devastated by famines in the mid- to late nineteenth century. This vulnerability, however, emanated not from the collective social organization of agriculture but from its political economic and ecological context. The rundale system of the eighteenth and nineteenth centuries developed in the wake of colonial dispossession that left a class of landless tenant farmers pushed to marginal land and heavily dependent on a single crop. Hence, the potato blights that devastated Ireland from 1845 to 1849 left tenant farmers in the west with little recourse to seek alternative food sources or to petition authorities with the capacity or incentive to provide relief (Fraser 2003). Between famine, disease, and emigration, the population of Inishark declined 33 percent between 1841 and 1851. The vulnerability of rundale villages like Inishark emanated from conditions initiated and perpetuated by a colonial regime. Colonialism made rundale necessary and necessarily vulnerable. Collectivity made rundale feasible.

What, then, fostered collectivity among the people dwelling in rundale and on Inishark in particular? Some analyses of rundale account for collectivity in essentialist, ethnohistoric terms. Connolly (1917, 3–4) depicted rundale as a relic of communal property relations and collective mentality characteristic of precolonial Gaelic society in Ireland. Evans believed communalism apparent in early modern Ireland reflected prehistoric property relations common across the western fringe of Europe (Evans 1939, 24). In addition to seeking historic antecedents, it is important to question how collectivity and cooperation were enacted, maintained, and reproduced in the specific context of nineteenth-century Ireland. Ethnographic research from subsequent periods provides clues. Arensberg and Kimball's (2001 [1940]) now canonical ethnography of 1930s rural life in Co. Clare emphasized the crucial role of kinship in fostering cooperation in agricultural labor and structuring social life more generally. They highlighted the degree of mutual loyalty among immediate family members and wider kinship networks that extended within local communities (Byrne et al. 2001, 70–71). From an archaeological perspective, Henry Glassie's observations on the relationship between kinship / community ties and material culture in twentieth-century Co. Fermanagh proves most instructive for examining collectivity on Inishark.

Glassie's folklore and ethnographic research in Ballymenone emphasized the role of vernacular architecture and material culture in mediating and reiterating bonds between neighbors and relations (1995; 1999). Although his research was undertaken in the 1970s, many of the houses his informants dwelt in were initially constructed in the nineteenth century. To Glassie, the common spatial template of traditional houses in Ballymenone—despite variations in size and quality—manifested neighbors' mutual inclusion in a single community (1995, 327–42). From outside, visitors would know the central door would lead to the kitchen, where most social activities, like cooking, eating, storytelling, and welcoming guests, were focused around the hearth. Glassie describes the hearth as the "crucible of continuity... keeping a fire alight that consumes the intervals between generations, between the Great Days and the every day and night" (Glassie 1995, 354). It was at once the center of the home and the nexus point linking community members (1995, 342, 351–56). By affording comfort, conviviality, and commemoration, the hearths of homes provided venues for people to enact and reenact binds of kinship, neighborliness, and reciprocal hospitality.

In addition to the arrangement of space within, the material composition of houses also configured social relations. Glassie remarks on the transition from thatch to metal roofs in Ballymenone as the disarticulation of household infrastructure from local social relations. Produced from locally sourced material, thatch decayed and required periodic replacement, a task formerly negotiated as part of reciprocal exchanges of aid with local craftspeople (1999, 234–37). Hence, the maintenance demands of thatch established a rhythm for periodically reactivating networks of mutual obligation—networks obviated by more permanent metal roofs.

The vernacular architecture of Inishark in the early 1800s shared important aspects with the houses analyzed by Glassie. Some of the houses that appear on the 1838 OS map are still standing on Inishark today. Despite some outliers, these houses shared many common characteristics when occupied. Most are oriented roughly north–south parallel to the direction of slope in order to facilitate drainage. The houses were drystone constructions fitted with thatched roofs. They also share a common spatial template, very similar to that observed by Glassie. Opposing entranceways led into the central kitchen and living space focused around the hearth with one or more additional rooms adjoined to either side of the kitchen (Kuijt et al. 2015, 140–41) (figs. 5.5, 5.6). Glassie's view that Irish vernacular architecture acted simultaneously as infrastructure for household dwelling and for fostering communal relations beyond the household likely apply to Inishark as well. Antiquarian accounts from the late 1800s and oral accounts from former Inishark islanders depict a close-knit community reliant on mutual aid, though of course not without disputes (Browne 1893, 345; Concannon 2007; MacLoughlin 1942). Archaeological and folklore evidence suggests that ritual gatherings on Inishark also generated movements, interactions, and commemorations that could activate community connections and tensions.

The cult of St. Leo could reiterate shared experiences and reinforce shared identities in various ways. In chapter 3, I discussed the story of St. Leo's Bell, the ill-fated attempt of foreigners to steal it, and the distribution of its fragments to America-bound emigrants as good luck talismans. The story creates a clear distinction between outsiders—who neither understand nor respect Leo's cult—from insiders, who can benefit from the sanctity of the bell, even by continuing its destruction and dispersal away from the island. For inhabitants remaining on

Figure 5.5: Building 6 on Inishark, a drystone house constructed in the early nineteenth century. Photo by Ian Kuijt.

the island, annual performances of the turas acted as expressions of collective devotion to Leo. Browne's description of St. Leo's Day celebrations, recorded in 1893, indicates that Inishark islanders observed the day by refraining from work, akin to a sabbath day. Former islander George Murray, when interviewed for the documentary *Inis Airc - Bás Oileáin (Inishark: Death of an Island)* (Concannon 2007), described Leo's Day as marking transition in dwelling tasks—from sowing crops to fishing. This almost certainly applied in the early nineteenth century as well. Refraining from work also distinguished Shark islanders from Bofin islanders, who did not observe the day (Browne 1893, 359). Taboos and the threat of social censure are likely to have upheld this observance. As a possible parallel, MacLoughlin mentions that any islanders who refused to sacrifice their work in order to participate in cake dance competitions "held himself, or herself up to the opprobrium and contempt of his or her neighbours" (1942, NFC 839, 2). Thus, the collective performance of the turas circuit on Leo's Day, by directing islanders' attention and movements around medieval monuments, served to place participants in relation to the annual cycle of collective agricultural labor and within a community bound by shared heritage and convention.

The locations of houses, field plots, and ritual monuments in the village suggest that monument curation relied on collective assent. The first edition OS map, documenting the village as it existed in 1838, indicates that houses and garden walls stood in the vicinity of monuments. But notably, the household garden

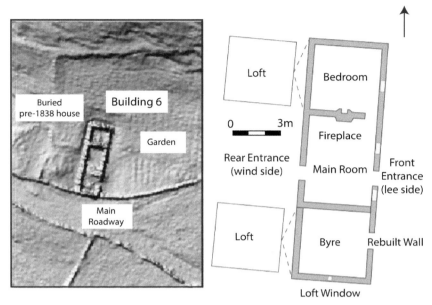

Figure 5.6: LiDAR image and reconstructed layout of Building 6 (adapted from Kuijt et al. 2015, 140). Although its plan is characteristic of early nineteenth-century houses on the island, it is particularly well built and is the only extant pre-Congested Districts Board house to include a chimney built into the internal gable wall. The descendants of Michael Halloran, king of Inishark in the 1890s, recall this as his home. If the common organization of domestic space facilitated hospitality and embodied shared identity, differences in the quality of construction and amenities also embodied distinctions of status or wealth.

plots do not enclose areas that include ritual monuments (see chap. 3, fig 3.3). Of course, we cannot know precisely how many ritual monuments stood in this area of the island prior to the development of the village. Perhaps by 1838, some monuments had already been recycled into houses. Regardless, all of the monuments still preserved by 1838 stood in areas that were easily accessible without crossing field boundaries associated with particular households. Humans and free-grazing animals in the village could walk directly up to monuments without entering land under cultivation or claimed by particular households. Leo's monuments appear to have been commonly accessible and under collective stewardship. Visible to islanders in the midst of their daily labor in the village, monuments were ever-present reminders of a shared devotional heritage reliant on collective curation. During annual St. Leo's Day celebrations, that shared heritage was enacted and performed as islanders—likely under threat of social censure—completed the circuit.

Relative to later periods, visits of a priest to the island must have been rather rare in the first half of the nineteenth century. There was no permanently stationed priest on Inishbofin until the late 1850s, and hence, priests would have had a limited capacity to attend or regulate devotions on Inishark. In the absence of priests, turas monuments offered opportunities for unmediated engagement with sacred objects that might ensure the spiritual and physical well-being of islanders. It is important to realize the considerable dangers that islanders faced while making their living on the sea. If weather-bound, islanders could succumb to treatable diseases without the aid of a doctor or the last rites of a priest. Islanders put their souls at hazard every time they put a boat in the water. The presence of sacred monuments likely provided encouragement to face these physical and spiritual risks on a daily basis. Twentieth-century accounts of fishermen's invocations of Leo for protection likely reflect a deeper history. "The Inishark men reverentially salute the Saint's reliques whenever they launch into the deep, and it is a pious custom to show a similar religious reverence to St. Festy and other saints when passing by their islands" (Neary 1920, 221). Islanders may also have turned to monuments to fulfill other functions priests might serve or oversee, such as the adjudication of disputes or swearing of oaths (see discussion of Leac Leo, chap. 3, p. 115). Islanders had grounds to perceive St. Leo's cult as a heritage distinctive to their village and for which they were collectively responsible. Hence, daily and periodic encounters with monuments emplaced islanders in relation to an illustrious, sacred past that they, their neighbors, and their ancestors had preserved.

I suggest that St. Leo's monuments constituted a kind of ritual commonage that ran parallel to and helped to maintain villagers' management of collective farming and agricultural commonage. Like other commonage resources, St. Leo's monuments could render apparent benefit to all villagers, but this relied on collective stewardship and observation of conventions of use. Stories collected in the later 1800s and early 1900s demonstrate how improper interactions with turas monuments risked supernatural or social censure.

As teased in chapter 3, Lady Francesca Wilde's collection of Irish folklore, published in 1888, includes the story of a woman from Inishark conducting an inversion of the turas in order to curse a man who called her a wicked name (see chap. 3, p. 105). Although the woman's curse is effective and the man drowns in a storm at sea, her vengeance recoils against her.

When the woman heard of the fate that had befallen her enemy, she ran to the beach and clapped her hands with joy and exulted. And as she stood there laughing with strange and horrid mirth, the corpse of the man she had cursed slowly rose up from the sea, and came drifting towards her till it lay almost at her very feet. On this she stooped down to feast her eyes on the sight of the dead man, when suddenly a storm of wind screamed past her, and hurled her from the point of rock where she stood. And when the people ran in all haste to help, no trace of her body could be seen. The woman and the corpse of the man she had cursed disappeared together under the waves, and were never seen again from that time forth. (Wilde 1888, 71)

This story, like the parallel anecdote recorded by MacLoughlin in 1942 (chap. 3, p. 104) is a cautionary tale about weaponizing turas monuments to pursue feuds within the village. Even without this narrative framing, belief in the power of cursing would have shaped the complexion of local relations. Indeed, the potential to settle scores through the harnessing of supernatural power might have provided a deterrent to mistreating one's neighbors or transgressing the rules implicit in rundale.

The risks entailed in the misuse of turas monuments are highlighted in two other stories collected by MacLoughlin and related in chapter 3. The first simply relates how a visitor to the island was surprised to find that water mistakenly gathered from St. Leo's Well (rather than the adjacent spring) refuses to boil when gathered for "domestic or cooking purposes." The more ominous second tale regards the destruction of a turas monument, purportedly in the 1860s (see figs. 3.1, 3.49). A family who removed stones from this monument to build a pathway from an old house to a new one was said to be punished with ill luck, misfortune, and otherworldly hauntings in their new home (MacLoughlin 1942, NFC 839, 12).

It is remarkable that three recorded narratives about turas monuments on Inishark—the woman's recoiling curse, the never-boiling water of Leo's Well, and the haunted family—all involve the improper use of common ritual resources, either by deploying monuments to meet the mundane needs of individual households or to pursue individual vendetta. Rather than propagating rigid oppositions between sacred and profane realms, these stories arguably reveal concerns about the proper relationship of individuals to the wider collective. Supernatural agency operates in each story to thwart the intentions or ruthlessly punish those who misuse the island's ritual commonage to pursue malevolent or simply mundane interests on behalf of individuals or households.

Such stories may have been preserved precisely because they were exceptional and instructive. Other monuments remained free of interference throughout the nineteenth century. Evidence from Leaba Leo demonstrates a significant effort to accommodate household infrastructure and collective heritage cheek by jowl. Sometime after 1838, a two-room house was built less than 2 m to the northeast of Leaba Leo (see chap. 3, fig. 3.44, fig. 5.4). The 1898 OS map shows the building as already partially deconstructed, with only one room still roofed, and indicates that Leaba Leo and a nearby monument had both been enclosed within a stone field wall. The lack of visible potato ridges suggests that this area was used for grazing livestock. Indeed, the flagstone pavement of the western room of the house and its lack of hearth likely indicate a byre for holding animals. Despite its proximity, Leaba Leo was not ransacked for the construction of these newer features and likely remained a focus of devotion, as it is one of the few monuments listed on both the 1838 and 1898 OS maps and identifiably referenced by Browne in 1893 and MacLoughlin in 1942. The house was dismantled to its foundations sometime in the twentieth century. Yet, during the house's brief occupation history in the mid- to late nineteenth century, household dwelling and community ritual were accommodated in the same area.

In sum, the monuments and practices of St. Leo's cult afforded experiences that could remind islanders of their shared participation in the stewardship of a distinctive sacred heritage. Taboos against the destruction of monuments—or their weaponization to pursue discord—may also have reinforced villagers' commitment to cooperation. St. Leo's Day was simultaneously set apart from the everyday and yet also the essential template for day-to-day encounters in the village. It was a collective undertaking that embodied the more general collectivity required by the rundale system. By affording commemoration and devotion, ritual monuments may also have formed infrastructure for the production and reiteration of communal relations. The tasks of devotion may have figured significantly in a village dwelling taskscape that required a great deal of collective action and cooperation. However, the presence of turas monuments in the landscape and the traditions of Saint Leo's cult could not simply enforce conformity or continuity of practice. Instead, the conventions of tradition provided a framework for reiterating, undermining, or reassembling perceptions of heritage and collective relations within the village. Opportunities for correspondence in convention are also opportunities for discord and deviation. By choosing to abide, ignore, or adapt the prescriptions of convention and taboo, islanders could act to maintain or transform their social worlds in accord with changing circumstances.

Indeed, narrative and archaeological evidence for the destruction of turas monuments might show the birth pangs of new conventions of heritage maintenance and household autonomy. Although dating is imprecise, the ill-fated destruction of a monument mentioned by MacLoughlin and the enclosure of Leaba Leo within a household plot occurred in the middle decades of the nineteenth century—just when a new system of direct household tenancy was taking shape. Perhaps these events reflect, in part, new attitudes to household autonomy influenced by new landholding relations. Tracing the subsequent history of the village indicates how islanders' engagements with monuments again changed in accord with the increased presence of clergy in the latter half of the 1800s and a further shift in landholding in the beginning of the 1900s.

DEVOTION AND DWELLING C. 1880–1960

Inishark, 1883. A Church Refounded.

Restoration work on Teampaill Leo is nearing completion. The priest resident on Inishbofin, Father James Rabbitte, has overseen the work of converting the ruined edifice, used in recent years as a cattle pen, into a functional church. Once the church is roofed and consecrated, he will travel periodically to Inishark to deliver mass to the villagers. Since his arrival in the parish, he has learned of the Shark people's celebrations of Leo's Day: how they gather water from Leo's Well, use water collected in a stone font to cure warts and sometimes pass the night or have picnics in Clochán Leo. Such devotions, however unorthodox, he chooses to see as a testament to the islanders' stubborn faith despite generations that suffered famines, sickness, migration, and exploitive landlords and estate agents, all endured without consistent pastoral guidance. The last, at least, has begun to change. Rabbitte looks on with pride and a quiet command as a group of men, under his direction, raise up an ancient stone cross taken from the vicinity of the church and install it atop the eastern gable of the old building made new.

—∞—

Clerical Accommodation and Appropriation

The development of St. Leo's cult on Inishark, particularly in the later nineteenth century, must also be understood in terms of islanders' interactions with clergy. Following years of protest and threats of insurrection, in 1829 Parliament passed the Roman Catholic Relief Act, which repealed many of the penal laws that had disenfranchised Catholics since the seventeenth century. Irish Catholics could now practice their faith more openly and began to construct a new generation of church buildings. On Inishbofin, the 1838 map shows a new Roman Catholic chapel set in the inner harbor. There was no parish priest permanently stationed on Inishbofin at this time, but clergy did periodically visit and administer on the islands. During the 1830s, Fr. Redmund Martin Fadden continued to administer to the sick and bury the dead during a cholera outbreak. He eventually succumbed to the disease himself, and a limestone slab set in the ruins of St. Colman's Abby on Inishbofin commemorates his service (Neary 1920, 228–29).

At least until the late 1850s, visiting priests had to contend with the estate agent Henry Hildebrand, praised and reviled by contemporary observers and in later accounts as ardently anti-Catholic and a promoter of the Protestant proselytization (Robinson 2008, 167–69). Father John Neary, a priest stationed on Inishbofin who wrote a history of the islands in 1920, boasted that Hildebrand's efforts only crystalized islanders' faith: "The unwarranted intrusion was so fiercely and so to say valorously resented, that, in after years, souperism looked in vain at the islands from the opposite shores of the mainland, and never succeeded in planting one blade of heretical-cockle in St Colman's or St Leo's patrimony" (Neary 1920, 224). The failure of "souperism" (Protestant proselytization that offered soup as famine relief contingent on renouncing Catholicism) likely also resulted from a shift in landlord. Henry William Wilberforce, who took over in the early 1850s and finalized purchase of the islands by 1858, was a former Anglican clergyman who converted to Catholicism. The biography of his son, Father Bertrand Arthur Henry Wilberforce, includes an account of the Wilberforces' visit to Inishbofin in 1857–58. The following story appears to have been compiled from contemporary memoirs of Father Bertrand.

> The chapel at Inishbofin was little more than a stable, with an earthen floor; there was no altar, only a wooden chest, in which the vestments—such as they were—were kept, and on this chest Mass was said. The candles were tallow dips stuck in bottles, and there were no pictures or statues of any kind. Inishbofin had no resident priest, the mission being served once a month from the mainland, when a sermon was preached in Irish, accompanied by groans and ejaculations of the congregation, who were extremely devout. Many came from the neighbouring island and spent the whole day in the church.
> (Capes 1912, 10)

This account suggests that Inishark islanders were effusively pious but could hear mass only by traveling to Bofin for the priest's monthly visits. The presence of priests on Shark must have been exceptional at this time. Later in the account, Henry Wilberforce is credited with obtaining a resident priest for the island and statues and stations of the cross for the simple chapel (Capes 1912, 11). This first resident priest was Father Tom McDonough, who lived in a newly built presbytery near the chapel (Neary 1920, 223–24). From this point onward, Shark islanders could row over to mass every Sunday so long as the weather permitted. Concomitantly, priests now could take a more active role in supervising and monitoring islanders' lives and devotions. Notably, none of the priests stationed in the parish had come from the islands. Purchase of the island in 1876 by the Allies family (also Catholic) enhanced the capacity of priests to campaign on behalf on islanders. Contemporary commentators and later accounts depict Cyril Allies as a sympathetic landlord who was the first to reside on Inishbofin and endeavored alongside local priests to improve the lives of islanders (Neary 1920, 224; Concannon 1997).

Comments by Browne (1893) depict islanders as pious and rather deferential to priests: "They [islanders] are very conscientious in their religious observances, and depend greatly on the advice and control of their clergy, with regard to temporal as well as spiritual affairs" (Browne 1893, 345). Of formerly raucous wakes for the dead, Browne comments, "Owing to the influence brought to bear on the people by the clergy in this matter, it is now only attended by relatives of the deceased, and the character of the ceremony is much altered, most of the old games, the mock marriage, &c., being altogether obsolete, while the insobriety, formerly common, is now a thing of the past" (Browne 1893, 352).

On Inishark, the most significant evidence of increased clerical influence is the renovation of Teampaill Leo, overseen by Father James Rabbitte sometime between 1881 and 1884. Prior to this renovation, the church had been in use as a cattle pen, and at least one stone cross was set inside the building to form part of a trough (Browne 1893, 365). Renovation of the church into a functioning building allowed Rabbitte and his successors as parish priest to travel to Inishark intermittently (about once a month) to deliver mass. Islanders now had a venue for communal ritual that was officially sanctioned by clergy. In these circumstances, the lesser revered turas monuments became increasingly obsolete as places of devotion, commemoration, and collective heritage. Organizing the priests' visit itself became a new collective effort. In the twentieth century, families took turns rowing the priest back and forth and supplying his breakfast. If weather prevented a journey to Inishbofin, islanders conducted the stations of the cross within the church.

Priests may also have been inclined to look at islanders' turas tradition with a certain degree of skepticism. Details of the church renovation and subsequent folklore records suggest that Rabbitte and successive parish priests acknowledged islanders' veneration of turas monuments but also sought to reframe the context of those venerations. This effort is demonstrated most clearly in the mounting of a stone cross atop the eastern gable of the renovated church. Folklore and antiquarian accounts disagree on whether this stone represents the Leac Leo documented by the 1838 Ordnance Survey as standing east of the ruined church (see chap. 3, p. 113). Yet, both Browne's and MacLoughlin's accounts describe the cross as having been taken from a former location in the vicinity of the church. Rabbitte is credited with organizing the renovation of the church, likely with some material support from Allies and with islanders providing the labor. Although Rabbitte may not have ordered the installation, he almost certainly approved of it. Whether islanders approved or objected to the installation, the movement of the cross had one unambiguous consequence: islanders could no longer physically interact with the cross as they once had. If the cross had been a station perambulated in the turas circuit or an object on which islanders laid their hands to swear oaths, neither action was possible any longer.

Folklore collected by MacLoughlin indicates that other objects once located at turas stations were brought into the restored church, including a stone font from the cluster of monuments west of the church and cross-slabs found at Clochán Leo. One of the cross-slabs, which was illustrated by MacLoughlin, features in home-video footage from the 1940s. The film shows a Shark man standing outside Teampaill Leo, holding the cross-slab toward the camera while a priest looks on (Higgins and Gibbons 2017). Thus, islanders' intimate access to sacred objects and materials remained, but the church provided a new, officially sanctioned venue for these interactions.

This recontextualization of sacred objects had important ideological implications. Crucially, the devotional tasks and landscape settings of turas practices did not require nor facilitate clerical administration or surveillance. Pilgrims could theoretically absolve their sins, curse their neighbors, and pray for health, fortune at sea, and a good harvest—all without clerical intervention. As Taylor argues, beginning in the early nineteenth century, Catholic bishops endeavored to reorder the geography of sanctity, supplanting outdoor holy wells and stones with masses administered by clergy within consecrated chapels (Taylor 1995, 53–58). Folklore and antiquarian accounts from Connemara record priestly efforts to prevent improper or unmediated veneration. Hardiman refers to a cursing stone formerly located at a church in Renvyle that was "taken away and buried by the parish priest, at which the people were much dissatisfied" (1846, 120). On Inishark, clergy appear to have adopted a strategy that combined accommodation and appropriation. Priests asserted their role as mediators of sanctity, not by destroying or removing objects but by encouraging continued veneration in a spatial context they had officially sanctioned.

In an oral history interview with my CLIC colleagues in 2009, former islander Martin Murray mentioned that in the early twentieth century, islanders would bring buckets of water from Tobar Leo for the priest to bless. Rather than simply approving the veneration of the well, by blessing the water within the church, priests redefined the source of the water's sanctity as their own benedictions. Similar to the mounting of Leac Leo on the eastern gable of the church, blessing the water of Leo's Well brought the substance of islanders' veneration into a space sanctioned and monitored by representatives of the church.

Priests' accommodation of islanders' traditions could be at once sympathetic and ideologically motivated. Islanders too had both religious and political incentives to maintain positive relationships with priests and their Catholic landlords. Catholicism offered a shared identity under which priests, islanders, and even Wilberforce and Allies might find common cause. However, this shared identity was crosscut by differences of class and education, which likely left priests and the landlords with different expectations of acceptable beliefs and devotions. Browne reports that islanders believe ardently in fairies, and Allies offered fifty pounds sterling to anyone who could show him one (1893, 358–59). Whether Allies hoped to prove or disprove this superstition is unclear, but it suggests a disjuncture in their presumptions about the supernatural. For islanders, deference to the authority of priests and landlords could be more than a matter of life and death. In Inishbofin filmmaker Kieran Concannon's 2007 documentary *Inis Airc - Bás Oileáin*, former islanders convey the fear that they, and especially their elders, felt at the prospect of dying without the last rites administered by a priest. Not only could priests administer the sacrament necessary for spiritual well-being but they also possessed the linguistic capacity, educational background, and social standing to negotiate with external authorities on behalf of islanders.

Contemporary accounts feature local priests working with or against British government agencies for the sake of islanders. Around 1844, a Father William Flannelly complained of Hildebrand's attempts to monopolize fishing to the Devon Commission, established by the British government to investigate problems with land leasing in Ireland. Flannelly says of the islanders, "They have told me repeatedly they would have come here; but holding no leases, they were afraid of exposing themselves to the consequences" (Kennedy 1847, 211–12). An article in the *Irish Times*, printed on November 14, 1887, describes the ill-fated attempt of cess (tax) collectors on Inishark. The local priest, Father Corcoran, aided by the landlord, Cyril Allies, is suspected to have warned islanders of the collectors' impending visit and conspired to have hidden all livestock to prevent their confiscation. In short, islanders' reliance on local Catholic authorities to stand up for them provided significant incentive for Inishark islanders to adapt their devotions to the expectations of priests and their Catholic landlords. While these circumstances may have contributed to the decline of certain aspects of the turas tradition, other elements endured, likely beyond the supervision or intervention of outside elites. Ceramic and glass artifacts from the uppermost deposits of Clochán Leo illuminate an unexpected mode of engaging with ritual heritage—picnicking.

PICNICS AND PILGRIMAGE

Inishark, April 11, 1890. A St. Leo's Evening.

Dressed in their finest freshly laundered clothes, islanders walk around the island in family groups, visiting monuments to mark Leo's Day. By late afternoon, the weather settles from overcast skies, and the sun, now dipping beneath the clouds, paints the village in golden light. Most villagers have completed their turas circuit, and some gather around Clochán Leo to pass the time. A group of men who have a share in a boat chew on their pipes, stand on the northern edge of the enclosure, and look out over the water. Through shortages and market fluctuations, the fishing industry has crashed in recent years, and those who remain on the island have endured considerable destitution. They try to reckon the fortune of the coming season from the play of light and shadow on the horizon and imagine their nets, stored all winter at home in their lofts, soon to be heavy with fish.

Near the base of the knoll on which the enclosure is set, a group of barefoot boys and girls push and shove and giggle, competing for their turn to set their foot in a track in the bedrock, supposedly the heel print of the great saint himself.

A woman and her daughter approach from the village, carrying a platter and a wicker basket with a teapot, a milk jug, mugs, bread, and marmalade. The woman cautions the children, reminding them that they accidently knocked over a full teapot last year, breaking the vessel and scalding themselves. Continuing into the clochán,

Figure 5.7: Picnicking and pilgrimage at the Clochán Leo Complex around 1890. Illustrated by Eric Carlson.

she serves the offerings to neighbors who have just finished the rosary, the beads still draped from their wrists. A good friend recognizes one particularly beautiful vessel usually displayed on her dresser. It was a gift from a relation who had spent harvest times in Scotland digging potatoes.

The soft evening breeze carries a chill that the roofless walls of the clochán can only partially obstruct. One woman plans to spend all night in the clochán. She nurses a limp and worries for her children, who, like so many in recent years, have emigrated to work in factories and mills in America. They send letters and remittances when they can, but she'll not see them again, nor hear their voices, nor take tea in their company. As the pot tips to fill her mug, steam wafts lazily in the air, and she smiles sadly at the familiar sensation of ceramic warmed with tea.

—⁂—

As described in chapter 3, Period V (1750–1960) artifacts excavated from Clochán Leo include items likely related to devotional practice (rosary beads) and votive deposition (buttons, notched stones) alongside the debris of material culture related to the consumption of alcohol, medicine, food, tobacco, and tea. Most of the glass shards are unidentifiable, with the exception of cobalt blue glass, typically used for commercial medicinal products, and fragments of a bottle of Bovril (a meat extract paste used as a spread or diluted with water to season soup). A more detailed look at the ceramic assemblage from Clochán Leo suggests how familiar household foodways shaped the sensory and commemorative dynamics of picnicking and pilgrimage. In the following analysis, I am indebted to conversations with Meredith Chesson and her work on the CLIC project's ceramic artifact database.

Excavations within the Clochán Leo Complex produced 170 post-1800 ceramic sherds, with the majority (131 sherds, 77 percent) uncovered within the clochán (fig. 5.8). The assemblage includes most nineteenth- and twentieth-century serving vessel forms and represents at least 37 distinct vessels. This minimum number of vessels (MNV) calculation is based on the identification of individual vessels within the assemblage. A number of criteria can distinguish individual vessels, including sherds or joinable sherds producing a complete profile of base, body, and rim; rim sherds with 20 percent or greater diameter present; and base sherds with a maker's mark or with a fabric and surface treatments not matching any rim or joinable body sherds from the same form category (Orton et al. 1993; Voss and Allen 2010).

The only maker's mark represented in the Clochán Leo assemblage comes from a molded and clear-glazed saucer produced by Charles Meakin, Eastwood Pottery, Hanley, England (c.1883–89; Kowalksy and Kowalksy 1999, 277, mark B1631) (fig. 5.8A). Decorated sherds in the assemblage include both

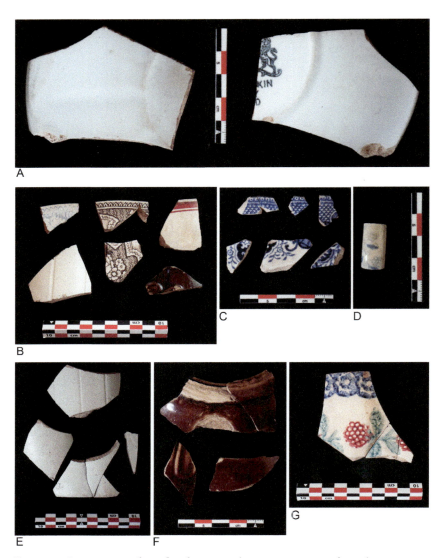

Figure 5.8: Late nineteenth- and early twentieth-century ceramics from the interior and exterior excavated areas of Clochán Leo. A: Saucer rim and base with mark from Charles Meakin's Eastwood Pottery in Burslem, Staffordshire; B: Variety of ceramic sherds, including blue transfer-printed plate rim (*top left*), brown transfer-printed rim and sherd from a plate (*middle top and bottom*), a plate rim with red bands around interior rim (*top right*), and a Rockingham Ware teapot body sherd (*bottom left*); C: Variety of ceramic rim (*top row*) and body (*bottom row*) sherds from plates and platters with blue Chinoiserie transfer-printed decoration; D: Fragment of a teacup handle with blue transfer-printed floral decoration; E: Sherds from two stoneware marmalade jars; F: Teapot rim (*top*) and body (*bottom*) sherds; G: Rim with mendable body sherds from a Spongeware mug. Photos by Meredith Chesson.

sponge-painted and transfer-printed ceramics that compare well with the ceramic assemblages from house sites excavated by CLIC on Inishark as well as heirloom collections still curated on Inishbofin. The Spongeware vessels, dated between 1835 and 1935 (Kelly et al. 2001), include a variety of colorful floral and geometric motifs. Brown and blue transfer-printed designs from Clochán Leo include the Blue Willow, Asiatic Pheasant, and Damascus patterns still familiar in Irish households today. Stoneware vessels are also represented, particularly by marmalade jars.

A comparison of the ceramic assemblages from Clochán Leo and three excavated houses on Inishark yields some notable similarities and differences (table 5.2). The three house sites compared in table 5.2 were fully excavated. Some sherds from each house no doubt represent vessels used by the household and deposited in adjacent middens. In other cases, abandoned houses became convenient dumps for midden material from neighboring households. In either case, these assemblages will represent the leftovers of household consumption. Comparison of the relative frequencies of different vessel forms from the houses and Clochán Leo reveals a few suggestive patterns (Brighton and Levon White 2006; Franklin 2020; Orser 2006).

Most significant is the contrast in the relative frequency of teapots: 13.5 percent of distinguishable vessels at Clochán Leo compared to an average among houses of 3.2 percent. Teacups (2.7 percent) are underrepresented at Clochán Leo relative to the average at house sites (15.1 percent). Mugs occur at a higher

Vessel Form	Clochán Leo MNV	%	Building 8 MNV	%	Building 57 MNV	%	Building 78 MNV	%
Bowls	6	16.2%	28	17.4%	17	16.2%	16	22.5%
Plates	9	24.3%	56	34.8%	15	14.3%	19	26.8%
Platters	1	2.7%	8	5.0%	8	7.6%	5	7.0%
Saucers	6	16.2%	11	6.8%	11	10.5%	12	16.9%
Teacups	1	2.7%	28	17.4%	19	18.1%	7	9.9%
Mugs	5	13.5%	11	6.8%	15	14.3%	6	8.5%
Marmalade Jars	3	8.1%	13	8.1%	8	7.6%	3	4.2%
Jugs or Creamers	1	2.7%	4	2.5%	6	5.7%	1	1.4%
Teapots	5	13.5%	2	1.2%	6	5.7%	2	2.8%
Total MNVs	**37**		**161**		**105**		**71**	

Table 5.2: Nineteenth- and twentieth-century ceramic Minimum Number of Vessel (MNV) estimates from the Clochán Leo Complex and three excavated houses on Inishark.

rate at Clochán Leo (13.5 percent) than in residences (9.9 percent). Saucers are only slightly overrepresented at Clochán Leo (16.2 percent; 11.4 percent among houses). These patterns are consistent with a preference for vessels and food items most suitable for picnicking events or overnight vigils at Clochán Leo. Teapots would have been essential for sharing hospitality away from the hearths of houses. The dearth of teacups may represent a preference for sturdier vessels, particularly mugs, to drink outdoors. Given the scarcity of teacups, saucers perhaps held small portions of food, such as individual slices of bread or scones. Indeed, the marmalade jars and a Bovril bottle fragment suggest the consumption of baked goods garnished with spreads. Fragments of plates, bowls, and platters likewise suggest food consumption, potentially by small groups sharing hospitality. Hypothetically, pilgrims may have brought sherds to Clochán Leo to leave as offerings within choreographies of devotion, but MacLoughlin's accounts suggest that small personal items or dress accessories were more likely to have served as votive deposits.

Whether on pattern days, vigils, or ad hoc visits throughout the year, the evidence suggests that small groups gathered near Clochán Leo to share food and company. As many scholars have demonstrated, foodways and hospitality offer opportunities for negotiating a variety of social identities and conventions (Atalay and Hastorf 2006; Franklin and Lee 2019; Hayes 2011; Seifert et al. 2000; Twiss 2012; Woods 2019). Just as the ceramic assemblages from houses provide context for assemblages at Clochán Leo, mundane household food practices would have served as essential reference points for picnics at Clochán Leo (Beaudry 2010; Symonds 2010). Picnics were primed to activate the sensory and emotional resonances of household meals that made use of the very same ceramic material culture.

As mentioned above, ethnographic and ethnohistoric research attests to the crucial role of household hospitality in cultivating communal affiliation in rural Ireland (Glassie 1995). Ceramic vessels, often curated by women on shelves, presses, and dressers near the hearth, were essential infrastructure for these activities. Often passed as heirlooms or gifted by friends or relations who had migrated abroad, ceramic collections acted as catalogs of memories evoking relations with people, places, and past events (cf., Hull 2006; Kinmonth 1995; Kirshenblatt-Gimlet 1989; Mytum 2010; Webster 1999). Welcoming friends, kin, and neighbors around the hearth with tea and food furnished opportunities for reiterating reciprocal bonds of hospitality and recalling how hosts and guests fit within wider networks of exchange, affiliation, and ancestry (fig. 5.9).

The sensory and commemorative power of picnicking at Clochán Leo emerged as participants reactivated familiar elements of mundane practices in a new spatial, atmospheric, social, and temporal context. If hospitality in the

Figure 5.9: Photographs of islanders taken during Browne's 1893 expedition. *Left*: a group of men from Inishbofin and Inishark, including Michael Halloran, king of Inishark (*back row, second from left*). *Right*: Women of Inishbofin. TCD MS 10961/4, Fol. 6r. Courtesy Trinity College Library Digital Collections Department.

house could create shared experiences of commensal comfort that reknit bonds of reciprocity and kinship, then picnicking at Clochán Leo could recontextualize these familiar sensations within broader frames of identity and heritage. Picnics, like pilgrimages, can raise tensions as well as harmonies and act to sublimate or accentuate particular aspects of social relations. Opportunities to cohere in conventional commensality also risked discord, perhaps through exclusion, refusal, and varying capacities to offer hospitality. Yet, picnics offered another gambit for harmonious social resonance in a celebration of devotional heritage that did not require the presence of clergy.

Indeed, Leo's Day picnics may have enhanced women's roles as orchestrators of commensal sociality by transplanting their customary authority within households into a setting of communal devotion. Tradition forbade servile work on Leo's Day, but women likely spent hours preparing food and laundering clothing for the celebration. These circumstances suggest an important contrast with institutionally sanctioned forms of Catholic devotion. At masses, male priests and younger male altar servers played leading roles in the choreography of devotion. Women were excluded from these roles, and their participation in the mass was regulated by conventions like the rite of churching, common in Ireland until the mid-twentieth century. Following childbirth, women could not go to mass until they received a blessing given by a priest (for a fee) to give thanksgiving for a safe delivery and purge them of the supposed uncleanliness of childbirth and the underlying sexual sin (Delay 2023). Though viewed alternatively and even positively by some women, the rite afforded priests leverage over women's behavior through the promise of inclusion or threat of ostracization. In stark contrast, picnics at Clochán Leo are likely to have been orchestrated by women and reliant on their labor. Prior to Catholic Emancipation, the absence of priests in more remote areas of rural Ireland may have carved out a larger space for women as practitioners of healing and cursing and curators of ritual heritage (Ó Crualaoich 2003; Whelan 2018, 107–08, 119–21). Evidence of picnicking at Clochán Leo suggests women could retain an important role in shaping interactions with sacred places, even after priests began to reassert their authority. Folklore accounts associating women with cursing at Leo's Well might reflect a fear of female agency inherent to a society fundamentally shaped by the patriarchy of the Catholic church. Yet, the perception of women's ability to harness supernatural power might also have proved useful for women who could not rely on other forms of social power to advance their goals or protect themselves from harm. Whether in pouring tea or draining wells, women could make use of the island's ritual heritage to assert their agency in the village.

If the renovated church required the presence and consecration of priests for mass, Clochán Leo required no priests to gather memorable and commemorative gatherings. Indeed, the reemergence of an official venue for mass may have altered the character of turas practices, possibly loosening prescriptions. Though not explicitly attested to in the folklore record, the material evidence suggests that picnics were sometimes staged at Clochán Leo, whether on St. Leo's Day or periodically throughout the year. These events provided opportunities for islanders, and perhaps especially women, to reknit community bonds and reassert their role as stewards of heritage that clergy could not wholly control.

RELIEF SCHEMES AND EVACUATION

Inishark, April 1942. MacLoughlin's Collection.

Brían MacLoughlin walks through the village on Inishark, his notebook in hand, taking a careful record of place-names and antiquities. Around their houses, islanders point out the remnants of monuments formerly visited as places of pilgrimage. Some have been simply left alone to decay; others have been partially stripped for building material. He is told that some ninety years ago the destruction of a pilgrimage monument brought down ill luck on a family. And yet, since islanders took possession of their holdings from the last landowner at the beginning of the twentieth century, stones from other pilgrimage monuments have been incorporated into new houses and field walls. Other traces of the past, the islanders will neither disturb nor question. Outside Clochán Leo, MacLoughlin looks on skeptically as an island man lifts the heel of his boot into an impression in the bedrock. This, the track of Leo miraculously imprinted in stone, the man claims is a sure proof of the great saint's presence on their island.

—⚜—

Even with Catholic authorities in place at the local scale, islanders' livelihood was still extremely precarious. Inishark's population had rebounded to pre-famine levels by the 1870s. But, as elsewhere in western Ireland, repeated blights, fishing failures, and the collapse of the kelp industry enhanced hardship and drove many to emigrate (Moran 1997). A report from the *Irish Times* in 1886 describes the conditions on Inishark: "About twenty families dwell on the island, the population having since 1880 been considerably reduced by emigration. The condition of these people is one of great poverty, and in the case of the vast majority it is one of downright misery."

The Allies family, as mentioned above, did attempt to improve islanders' lives. Sometime between the 1870s and the 1890s, Cyril Allies built two fish curing stations on Inishbofin, where ling and cod could be salted, barreled, and shipped to the mainland or abroad (Browne 1893, 350). The stations effectively cut out middlemen sellers, and when fishing was good, the industry kept almost everyone busy with some stage of the process. In the late nineteenth and early twentieth centuries, Allies collaborated with a new British government agency, the Congested Districts Board (hereafter, CDB), to ameliorate conditions. By the early twentieth century, islanders would have the opportunity to own their land and homes for the first time. The transformations in landholding and housing brought on by the CDB would shape the subsequent history of the village on Inishark and may also have contributed to the further decline of the turas tradition.

The CDB was established by Arthur Balfour, the chief secretary of Ireland, in 1891. From a political standpoint, the raison d'être of the CDB was to quell Irish political demands for home rule—that is, self-government for the island of Ireland within the United Kingdom (Guinnane and Miller 1997, 591). Rather than immediate subsistence relief, the CDB focused on providing funding for improved housing, better infrastructure for fishing and agriculture, and landholding reform. My CLIC colleagues have previously published an account of the material impact of CDB initiatives on Inishark and on islanders' lives (Kuijt et al. 2015). Here, I will only comment on the consequences of the CDB's initiatives on the village community and the cult of St. Leo.

Materially, the CDB altered Inishark's landscape in a number of ways. Public work schemes generated temporary local employment in construction and also improved local infrastructure. Projects initiated under the CDB include the construction of stone roadways along preexisting pathways in the village, a breakwater near the island's landing place (finalized, along with a renovated pier, in 1932), a new national school in 1898, and field enclosures surrounding holdings (Kuijt et al. 2015, 135–36). While the striping of the infield into individual holdings began much earlier, Couey's analysis of the valuation data suggests that the larger field walls present in the landscape today represent holdings as drawn in early twentieth-century valuations (2018, 96–100). The construction of more pronounced and durable field divisions was part of a larger reform of landholding in which the CDB consolidated holdings and provided loans for tenants to purchase their holdings. The CDB purchased the island from Allies c. 1905, and notably, the valuation of the previous year dissolved any remaining collective holdings, splitting them into separate single holdings (Couey 2018, 90).

Perhaps the most consequential infrastructural development initiated by the CDB was the construction of a new standard of houses for islanders (figs. 5.10, 5.11). When tenants, any improvements to islanders' homes might result in higher tax valuations. That changed as islanders became smallholders. New houses built by the CDB (and its successor agencies under the Irish Free State) after 1907 differed from earlier vernacular architecture in numerous ways. New houses tended to be oriented east–west rather than north–south; had fireplaces and chimneys rather than open hearths, concrete rather than dirt floors, and roofs not of thatch but of imported materials such as corrugated metal and, later, asbestos and slate (Kuijt et al. 2015, 142–44). The creation of these new houses, accompanied by decreased population, meant that inhabited homes were less clustered and more dispersed than in previous decades. Many older homes were left to dilapidate or converted to barns for storage or keeping animals. Removal of animals from the house and the introduction of closed hearths and chimneys vastly improved domestic sanitation and air quality.

The landholding reform and new domestic architecture generated by the CDB likely contributed to the continued disuse and destruction of turas monuments. Browne's informant in 1893 referred to fourteen stations visited by islanders. MacLoughlin's account in 1942 mentions only ten monuments formerly visited as places of pilgrimage, with three of those partially or comprehensively destroyed through recycling of their stone for building material. One of these monuments was said to have been destroyed in the 1860s. The disuse and destruction of other monuments may likewise date to the later nineteenth or early twentieth centuries, perhaps even in the midst of CDB works. It is likely that material removed from the two ruined monuments observed by MacLoughlin immediately west of the church (fig. 3.42) went into new field enclosures and perhaps even the new house built there in the early twentieth century.

Figure 5.10: Building 4 on Inishark, a Congested Districts Board house constructed c. 1910. It was occupied by the Gavin family at the time of evacuation in 1960. Photo by Ian Kuijt.

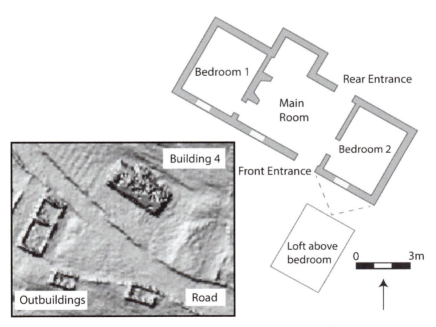

Figure 5.11: LiDAR image and reconstructed layout of Building 4 (adapted from Kuijt et al. 2015, 140).

205

Landholding and infrastructural changes in the early 1900s, like earlier landholding reforms, likely encouraged households to claim greater autonomy over the land immediately surrounding their homes. Indeed, Couey's research indicates that the valuation conducted in 1910 is the first to formerly divide and value the garden plots surrounding houses in the village (Couey 2018, 97–99). As Teampaill Leo now offered a venue of communal ritual collectively organized, turas monuments were becoming obsolete as places of devotion and commemoration. As such, monuments in the immediate vicinity of houses became particularly susceptible to disuse and destruction. Notably, the accounts of MacLoughlin and former islanders indicate that monuments most venerated in the twentieth century were located in the periphery of the village (Tobar Leo, Leata Mór, Clochán Leo) or away from an occupied house (Leaba Leo). Some islanders, at least, continued to devoutly believe in the power of Leo and his monuments, but the spatial context of islanders' devotions adapted to new social dynamics in the village.

However much the CDB's efforts may have ameliorated conditions, it did not halt the steady pace of migration that bled the island of young people who sought better economic opportunities in factories and building sites in England and America. The Irish Free State that eventually formed in the wake of the Irish War of Independence (1919–21) and the Irish Civil War (1922–23) unfortunately suffered under a stagnant economy. The governing party, Éamon de Valera's Fianna Fáil, entered a trade war with Britain in the 1930s. Protectionist policies combined with the Great Depression, which weakened demand for Irish produce abroad, hit rural Ireland hard. The Free State government ceased paying land annuities to Britain (i.e., repayment from loans offered by the CDB to tenant farmers), using the money instead to fund some rural assistance and infrastructure programs. On Inishark in the 1930s, government funding finalized construction of a pier and slipway as well as a winch to aid hauling up boats. These infrastructural developments could do little to slow emigration or mitigate the danger of landing or launching in foul weather.

The documentary *Inis Airc - Bás Oileáin* (Concannon 2007) highlights two tragedies in the mid-twentieth century that compelled islanders to seek a resettlement agreement from the Irish Land Commission. The first occurred on April 17, Easter Sunday 1949. Two brothers, Michael and Martin Lacey, and their cousin Peter Lacey had rowed from Inishark over to Inishbofin to attend Easter mass. Because of strong southeasterly winds, they had not landed in Bofin harbor. Instead, against custom, they put down on Trá Gheal, a sandy beach amid treacherous water on the southwest side of Bofin. After mass, they attempted to row home despite pleas from Bofin islanders to wait out the weather. Their currach capsized as they left the strand. Only Peter's body was recovered. The loss of three young, unmarried men in their prime had a devastating impact on the small community. In *Bás Oileáin*, Shark islander George Murray reflected on the event as the beginning of the end of Shark: "Shark died after that. The courage left the people, they hadn't the courage for the sea anymore."

The sea had always posed risks, but the threat became too much to bear in the wake of the Lacey men's drownings and with fewer and fewer able-bodied young people around to help launch or pull up boats. Likewise, the terror of weather-bound isolation, which had always troubled the village, became increasingly intolerable as services became more widely available along the coast. By the mid-twentieth century, Inishbofin had a priest and a doctor. Inishark had neither. In February 1957, an Inishark man died after suffering three days with appendicitis while the seas raged too rough to put down a boat. In *Bás Oileáin*, another Shark islander, Noel Gavin, became emotional recalling what little recourse islanders had when weather-bound. "The only thing really that we had at the time of an emergency was to go up the side of a mountain and light a bonfire. That was pathetic really." In the wake of this death, islanders once again pressed the Land Commission for aid. In 1960, islanders reluctantly accepted the Land Commission's offer of cottages and small holdings in the townland of Fountain Hill in Claddaghduff, on the mainland opposite their island. In *Bás Oileáin*, the last priest to serve Inishark, Father Flannery, characterized the islanders' decision: "They had mixed feelings. Definitely their heart was in Shark. They didn't want to leave it. But necessity was forcing them to go." Necessity and the promise of better living conditions for the elderly and for their children compelled islanders to leave their home. On October 20, 1960, the seas calmed after weeks of foul weather, and islanders evacuated the island along with their belongings. Thomas Lacey, whose sons had died in 1949, refused to leave that day and remained one night on the island on his own, hoping to make peace with his sons' deaths and the loss of his home. He left the following day when islanders came from their new home on the mainland to retrieve him. A few years later, Father Flannery instructed some men from Inishbofin to remove the roof from Teampaill Leo, officially decommissioning the church and dissuading islanders from thoughts of return. Flannery distributed the stations of the cross to the last families that had lived on Shark.

HERITAGE, RITUAL, AND THE LIMITS OF SUSTAINABILITY

The history of the village of Inishark demonstrates incredible endurance in the face of political, economic, and environmental precarity. The village survived absentee landlords and exploitive middlemen, the famines of the mid- to late nineteenth century, the rise and fall of the kelp industry, and periodic fishing failures. In the end, it was the lack of government investment in the island and the possibility of alternatives to continued hardship and precarity that compelled islanders to leave. What does the history of the village on Inishark tell us about the capacity of heritage and ritual to contribute to community endurance?

Synthesizing documentary, cartographic, folkloric, and archaeological evidence, I have demonstrated how engagements with turas monuments changed across time in accord with transformations in landholding and the increased influence of Catholic authorities on the islands. In analyzing these patterns, I have suggested some functional articulations between tasks of devotion and dwelling. In the early nineteenth century, I have argued that the collective stewardship of turas monuments was part and parcel of a dwelling taskscape that relied to a great extent on collective action and cooperation in the midst of adverse political, economic, and environmental conditions. Visible from day to day and visited in annual Leo's day celebrations, turas monuments reminded islanders of their participation in a shared heritage of devotion. Communal observance of St. Leo's Day and taboos against the destruction of monuments and their misuse to pursue strife reinforced ties of kinship and reciprocal aid that made rundale agriculture possible. By providing a means for islanders to engage the sacred and look after their spiritual well-being, turas monuments also helped islanders face down the considerable danger and hardship entailed in island life.

Changes to landholding, imposed by landlords and government agencies, dissuaded certain forms of collective land management and possibly altered ideas about the stewardship of turas monuments. More importantly, in the second half of the nineteenth century, a sequence of Catholic landlords and the emergence of parish priests altered the articulation between devotion and dwelling. The renovation of Teampaill Leo provided a new venue for communal memory and devotion that was officially sanctioned by the church. Devotional tasks, including the organization of priests' visits to the island and picnicking events at Clochán Leo, continued to foster collective action. Clergy sought to alter the ideological and architectural context of islanders' engagements with certain objects. Islanders themselves had great incentive to conform to priests' expectations of devotion. Priests were one of the few figures that could campaign on islanders' behalf to external authorities. Yet, islanders—and particularly women—could suffer great ostracization as a result of clerical condemnation.

In the twentieth century, the CDB and the Land Commission of the new independent Irish government provided some relief to islanders through land reform and infrastructural investment. Household ownership of land may have further eroded the sense that turas monuments were subject to collective stewardship, and some may have been partially recycled during the construction of new CDB houses. The figure of Leo continued to loom in the landscape; the few monuments that remained in active use were located near the village but not adjacent to particular houses or household plots. Leo's cult was one aspect of island life that bound them to their home and made it so painful to leave. But it could not keep them there.

These patterns of change suggest that embodied experiences of devotion, communal dispositions, and the labor and logistical requirements of dwelling taskscapes were all mutually constituted. This circumstance makes it difficult to assign priority to any one factor. However, it is possible to delineate something of the power and limitations of heritage. Political economic inequality originating in a history of colonial dispossession established precarity and collective action as necessary dimensions of life on Inishark. Maintaining Leo's cult clearly could not reverse or counteract this inequality. Nevertheless, I argue that islanders' creative curation of Leo's cult did help to make collective action and endurance of hardship socially feasible. Cultivating heritage could promote sustainability within political economic and ecological constraints, but it could not effectively alter those constraints. The scale at which St. Leo's cult could forge social bonds was limited. St. Leo's cult could promote collectivity and mutual aid on a local scale among closely related households, but it could not compel aid on the larger governmental scale that islanders desired. Heritage is limited in its capacity to contribute to sustainability when the scale of belonging it creates does not match the scale of networks of need and interdependence. In the next chapter, I will suggest that heritage tourism on Inishbofin today works toward the matching of these scales by forging durable social and economic relations that extend beyond the shores of the island.

SIX

TOURISTS, CORNCRAKES, CATTLE, AND CRAIC

Heritage in Inishbofin's Contemporary Taskscape (c. 1960–2019)

INISHBOFIN, AUGUST 15, 2016. AN ASSUMPTION MASS.

The Feast of the Assumption fell on a sunny but blustery Monday. By early evening, the wind settled, and Tommy Burke and I drove over to the ruins of St. Colman's Abbey to participate in a rare outdoor mass. The ceremony made a fresh memory in a long history of devotion in this sheltered valley on Inishbofin.

St. Colman established a community of monks on Inishbofin around the year 668. The remnants of a circular stone enclosure wall, pebble-strewn platform graves, and carved stone crosses are the last traces of the early medieval foundation. Time is biased toward stone. The solemn gray schist and sun-bleached quartz of these monuments are remnants of a stage setting for devotional practice but not the full ensemble. The Triads of Ireland, a ninth-century collection of wisdom organized around sets of three, tells us what once was expected as mainstays of a holy site: a bell, a psalm, a synod (Meyer 1906, 19). Early medieval devotion meant creating kinds of resonance that stones alone cannot echo: bells ringing the divisions of the daily monastic office and monks gathering their voices to recite the psalms.

Today, the shell of the late medieval parish church looms most over the site. As a regular setting for mass, the structure was long ago replaced by a newer church building near the harbor. Yet, the location of Colman's foundation has never been abandoned as a cemetery for islanders of Inishbofin. Browne's report offers a glimpse of the choreography of mourning practices at the end of the nineteenth century. "On reaching the graveyard [the coffin] is carried thrice round the church in the direction of the sun, and as soon as the grave is reached all those attending the funeral scatter and go to pray at the graves of their own relatives, which, having done, they raise the keen, beginning at the person farthest from the open grave" (Browne 1893, 352). By the rounding, mourners performed a final pilgrimage on behalf of the departed. By the keening, they created a new ensemble: a vocal harmony, raised in a moment of rupture, to make palpable the endurance of a community, the living and the dead, bound by kinship, custom, and memory.

The enduring presence of the dead is more than metaphor. Islanders typically maintained family plots that could be reopened and reused after nine years. Nevertheless, digging in a cemetery used for many centuries meant inevitably encountering the remnants of earlier burials. According to local oral history, before the mid-twentieth century, any skeletal material encountered by digging a grave could be gathered and reburied at the base of the new grave cut—all except crania. Instead, these were brought inside the ruins of St. Colman's Church and left in one of two niches in the southeast corner. This custom appears to explain why there was a collection of bones here in 1890, when Alfred Cort Haddon and Andrew Dixon were able to steal thirteen crania and four other skull fragments.

In the late 1950s, an extension was established to the west of the old graveyard. Family plots remain in use in both the old and new wings of the cemetery. As such, the graves of the recently deceased intermingle with those of more distant memory and those ancient enough to be anonymous. The area is no longer regularly grazed, and so in the summer months the grounds, particularly south and east of the church, can become overwhelmed with thorns, hogweed, and nettles. The last in particular offers ideal shelter for nesting corncrakes, a protected bird species and annual pilgrims to the island. The compilers of the Triads might well see the irony in this. In opposition to a blessed place known by bells, psalms, and synods, the Triads list nettles, corncrakes, and elder trees as three tokens of a cursed place, one perhaps showing signs of reclamation by plant and animal life following human abandonment (Meyer 1906, 19). Time is biased against aphorism. Some wisdom tends to expire, and islanders in recent times seek a new balance between use, commemoration, and biodiversity. Today, there are new players in the ensembles, and corncrakes sing in the synods.

Approaching from the west, Tommy and I parked at the end of a long line of cars on the low road. The mass already in motion, we joined a congregation of about thirty, mostly islanders and a few familiar visitors who, like the corncrakes, return every summer. With the exception of funerals, so many gathered here is extremely rare. Faced with an unusual event in a setting with clear spatial restrictions, islanders had improvised creatively to juggle the demands of the liturgy, feasibility of access for the congregation, and the reality of constant tourist traffic. Instead of an altar, the priest stood behind a small table set at the base of the cement steps that led down from the road into the cemetery (fig. 6.1). On his left side, he was attended by Gerry Moran, the Inishbofin sacristan. Contrary to the usual east–west orientation of the mass, the priest faced north and uphill toward the congregation, who situated themselves much as they would have in the new St. Colman's Church. The densest cluster used

Figure 6.1: Keeping to the side during the mass, five Bofin men and one visitor (note the backpack leaned against the headstone) stand amid graves in the modern wing of St. Colman's Abbey and cemetery. Repurposing the concrete steps as pews realigned the mass on a north–south access. This not only facilitated the participation of elder attendants confined to the roadway but positioned the ruined church and community cemetery as a visual backdrop and reminder of the island's deep devotional heritage.

the especially long steps as seats in place of pews. By a slight margin, the majority of those seated here were adult women. Five adult men stood among the graves to the west of the priest. At a typical Saturday mass in the new St. Colman's Church, these men would stand outside the nave or in the gallery during mass. In the early twentieth century on Inishark, men stood along the walls of the church while women and children sat on stools in the nave. On this day, a traditional pattern of gendered participation in mass played out in new circumstances.

Other attendants stood along the road, leaning on the stone wall enclosing the cemetery or against their cars. Margaret Day, a woman instrumental in developing tourism to Inishbofin, then in her nineties, sat in her wheelchair in the back of a van, the sliding door open for her to look down from the road onto the mass below. Others remained yet farther back where they could observe without feeling observed. A man in his twenties, home from his work in Wales to visit his family, had driven his grandmother down to mass but remained in his car, patiently browsing his mobile phone.

The line of cars and of people along the road left only a narrow space that prevented cars from passing by, forcing any approaching vehicles to reverse and find an alternative route. Through the duration of the mass, a number of sheepish looking tourists passed by on foot or bikes, uncertain of whether respect for the ceremony demanded turning back, staying still, or dismounting and passing on with as little disruption as possible. One group passing through caused a minor commotion as the man in the front wended through with his bicycle while a woman and children lingered behind, calling after him. At least two groups of tourists decided to remain and watch the rest of the mass from the road.

The priest was an Irish American with a New York accent. I would learn after the mass that he had first come to Bofin after reading the book The Islands of Ireland. He had no way of tracing his ancestors beyond their point of departure from Cobh in the overloaded and disease-ridden coffin ships that ferried so many Irish fleeing famine in the nineteenth century. He took great pride in the hardship his ancestors had endured and overcome. He wanted to deliver mass in Ireland and chose English-speaking Inishbofin in part because of his language restriction. "I have only two words of Gaelic, and you can't say either in a church." After getting the local priest's blessing to say mass during his stay, it was islanders who had suggested this Assumption Mass in the cemetery.

The content of his mass paid tribute to both the festival at hand and his own particular fascination with Ireland's Catholic heritage. His homily focused on the special role of Mary. Imagine how fully Mary trusted in God that she could watch her son endure torture and the foulest abuse shouted at him during the Passion. Considering how much Christ and his mother suffered for our sins, it is a "tragedy," he said, that so many go to church only on Christmas and Easter and cannot remember their last confession. While the souls of Saint Patrick and Saint Colman of Inishbofin exist in heaven, their bodies remain on earth in Ireland. The body of Saint Peter lies in Rome and his soul in heaven, but Mary alone was assumed into heaven body and soul.

After the sermon, the priest began the recitation of the creed, and the congregation followed along as if by reflex. In the open air, voices did not carry as well as in a church. Some voices faded as the creed went on beyond the initial lines that most *remember from their youth. The elder women along the road recited at unmatchable speed, and occasionally the priest had to raise his voice above the others in an effort to synchronize the crowd. With the dish and chalice for the Eucharist clustered precariously with other liturgical objects on a small table used in place of an altar, the priest took some time retrieving the large host to hold aloft for the re-creation of the Last Supper. When the time came, he asked those wishing to accept the Eucharist to stand. He then walked about the crowd accompanied by the sacristan to offer the Eucharist and wine. Unfamiliar with the faces in the crowd, he doubled back at one point, uncertain whether he had already served some members of the congregation. He eventually made his way to the road to serve Margaret in the van. I remained back on the road with my head down, and wordlessly the priest—perhaps all too familiar with the abashed look of a lapsed Catholic on a feast day mass—understood that I did not wish to receive the Eucharist.*

In his closing remarks, the priest conveyed what a pleasure it was to give mass on a beautiful sunny day in the midst of a place sanctified by Christian worship for more than a thousand years. He invited the congregation to recall and cherish the island's religious heritage. He said he was amazed to think that Colman and his monks held mass in this place long before Columbus came to America. That faith tradition endured despite the oppression of Catholics, not least of which, he was quick to note, was the imprisonment of priests and bishops in the Cromwellian-era fortress in Bofin's harbor. He closed by thanking the congregation for coming as well as all those who helped set up the mass. He declared his hope to be back again to deliver mass on another sunny Feast of the Assumption.

As the mass finished, the congregation dispersed, many going to visit their family plots in the graveyard as they would after a funeral. Tommy and I got back into the car and drove out to the north side of the island to see if we could spot some sheep that went astray during gathering some days before.

—⚏—

Although an ad hoc one-off event, the mass described above was remarkable in illustrating how islanders' archaeological and devotional heritage interacts with the tourist economy. The material traces of medieval ritual functioned not so much as the stage setting for liturgy but as its backdrop. With very little physical encounter between participants and ecclesiastical remains, the ruins nonetheless gathered attendants to view them and to recall their pasts. For the visiting priest, a proud Irish American, to place these ruins in a grand transnational narrative of Catholic resilience was to express his own identity as a product of that same heritage. For islanders, the cemetery backdrop recalled more intimate histories of ancestors buried on this small patch of ground for generations. For day-trippers and other visitors, the mass presented a latent offer to pass through or to participate—to find some space for themselves in this event and, if they could or cared to, in the pasts it evoked. Heritage tourism, as a subgenre of cultural tourism, has emerged in recent years as a subject of significant academic inquiry. As scholars have argued, the commercial transactions and social encounters involved with heritage tourism can often rely on or reinvigorate colonial stereotypes, Romantic or sentimentalized notions of authenticity, and other ideological framings of history and identity (Belliggiano et al. 2021; Bindi 2022; Cheer and Reeves 2013; Johnson 1999; Timothy and Boyd 2006; Waters 2006). Yet, heritage tourism may also provide an avenue for sustainable development in rural communities and a venue of cultural and economic exchange between visitors and local stakeholders (Li and Hunter 2015; Zhang and Smith 2019). On Inishbofin, heritage—as material things in the landscape, as traditions that engage those things, and as the collective experience thereby generated—plays a vital role in generating perceptions of belonging that encourage islanders to remain and visitors to return.

Since the evacuation of Inishark in 1960, the sister community on Inishbofin has endured while undergoing major economic and social developments that have transformed much of rural Ireland. Among the most significant changes has been the growth of a tourist industry in which nearly every island family has some part and on which the island's economy fundamentally relies. For good or ill, formerly dominant fishing, farming, and domestic production must now work around the tourist trade and the constraints and affordances of national and international legislation. Many small farmers rely on Irish and EU subsidies to support their living, but regulations and funding schemes can cause nuisance as well as more significant problems. The opening of Ireland's territorial waters to massive super-trawler fishing vessels has devastated small-scale Irish fishing and urgently threatens Atlantic fishing stocks (Donkersloot and Menzie 2015; Guyader et al. 2013). On Inishbofin, people have resourcefully adapted cycles of labor and custom to accommodate the particular opportunities and demands of a sharply seasonal tourist economy. Traditional festivities now overlap—sometimes in tension and sometimes in correspondence—with the tourist trade. Traditions that once gathered islanders from different villages on the islands now often act as scenes of interface between locals and tourists. Tourism inevitably alters the resources that drive it. This penultimate chapter will consider how the growth of tourism has altered how people on Inishbofin engage with and relate to the environmental forces and cultural heritage that animates their landscape. I suggest that islanders' curation and sharing of their heritage with visitors acts as a lynchpin for the contemporary tourist industry. While heritage tourism represents a growing aspect of the island's economy, it also affects islanders' engagement with their own heritage and complicates participation in traditional economies, particularly farming. Yet, islanders continue to negotiate these complications with creativity in hopes of sustaining the integrity of their heritage and their livelihoods.

HERITAGE AND HABITUAL TOURISM

The origins of the contemporary tourist economy on Inishbofin developed in the 1960s, when two Inishbofin families opened hotels. Margaret Day, who attended the Assumption Mass above and served for years as the island's nurse, began offering B and B accommodations with her husband, Miko Day, out of the old landlord's house in the 1950s, eventually converting it to Day's Hotel. Margaret Murray, formerly the schoolteacher on Inishark, began running a B and B with her husband, Paddy, out of the family home in the early '60s. Soon after, they established the Doonmore Hotel, the first purpose-built hotel on the island. The legacy of both family operations continues. Margaret and Miko's relations continue to manage the Beach Bar and B and B. More commonly known simply as Day's, the bar is a vital community hub and employer, the only pub and restaurant open year-round on the island. Margaret and Paddy's children have developed and extended the Doonmore (Murray's) over the years. Ireland's most westerly island hotel, Murray's is a renowned venue for traditional music and has been an exceptional host to CLIC project teams during our field seasons.

Since the 1960s, families and individuals have opened new businesses to capitalize on the increasing flow of visitors. This has included the Inishbofin Ferry, many B and Bs and self-catering cottages, a grocery, craft shops, a bakery and coffeehouse, walking tours and chartered boat trips, Inishbofin Equestrian Centre, King's Bike Hire, the Harbour Lights Bookshop, the Inishbofin Heritage Museum, the Inishbofin Island Hostel, the Dolphin Hotel and Restaurant, and the Galley Restaurant. Three recent additions by younger generations of islanders are particularly innovative. Inishwalla, a red double-decker bus converted into a food truck with South and East Asian–inspired cuisine using local produce, has become a pilgrimage destination in its own right for Irish gourmets. The Salt Box is a food truck by the harbor that serves fresh seafood caught locally by the Lavelle family's boat, the *Ceol na Mara*, "Music of the Sea." Finally, a microbrewery using local spring water, Bofin Brewing, launched its first beer, White Cow Pale Ale, in 2021. Today, most islander households make at least part of their living from the tourist trade in one way or another, even as many continue to have some involvement in animal farming and even fewer in commercial fishing.

The Inishbofin Development Company (IDC) is the local community organization which works to improve islanders' quality of life through the establishment, development, and provision of support and services through the Community Development Office. In addition to securing the socio-economic, educational, infrastructural, environmental, arts, cultural, and administrative requirements of the island, the IDC seeks to address disadvantage, social exclusion, and isolation by providing information, advice, and facilities. The IDC is headquartered in the Inishbofin Community Centre, a large building centrally and prominently located above the main pier. As essential infrastructure, the building houses a tourist center, a library, office space and meeting rooms, playgroup and afterschool activities, radio studio, and a large multifunctional gymnasium often fitted as a concert hall. It also includes a shop with locally produced crafts including knitted garments, jewelry, photography, and stunning felt art depicting landscapes and wildlife from Inishbofin. As a ticket office, exhibition space, or auditorium, the Community Centre is the base of operations for a regular cycle of events held throughout the summer tourist season. Beginning slowly around Easter, the tourist season booms by late June, begins to trail off from the end of August, and drops almost entirely by late October. The summer seasons of 2016–18 were punctured by a more or less regular sequence of annual festivals and events: Inishbofin Walking Festival (April); Inishbofin Arts Festival and Inishbofin Darkness to Light (early May); Inishbofin Half-Marathon and 5K (mid-May); INISH Island Conversations (early June); Inishbofin Yoga Retreat (late June); Summer School Inishbofin (July); Inishbofin Maritime Festival (mid-August); Inishbofin Set Dancing and Trad Weekend (September); Bia Bó Finne Food Festival (October).

For islanders, this sequence of events charts the progression of the tourist season. For visitors, individual events can become the focal point for annual visits to the island. Although systematic statistics are not available, a significant proportion of visitors to Inishbofin are repeat customers who live within Ireland and travel to Bofin every summer. Maintaining and cultivating returning visitors is certainly a primary objective of islanders involved in tourism. As Simon Murray, then manager of the IDC, mentioned in a 2016 interview for the RTE program Nationwide, "We've had generations of the same families, some families in their fourth generation, coming back to the island. A huge percentage of Irish people come to the island. That's a very strong backbone to the tourism sector here on Inishbofin." The economic advantage of this backbone is significant. Day-trippers purchase ferry tickets from the locally managed Inishbofin Ferry Company but may otherwise spend little money on the island itself—perhaps only for lunch, pints, and a postcard. Visitors who stay overnight pay for accommodation in the hotels, hostel, rental cottages or B and Bs; maybe rent a bike or go for guided walk; and purchase more than one meal and, chances are, more than a few drinks. Not only is more money spent on the island but it is also liable to be distributed more widely across the various businesses run by different families on the island. Additionally, annual bookings, often reconfirmed at the end of each stay, create an assurance of stability in an industry so contingent on weather and broader economic trends.

As illustrated by Diarmuid Ó Conghaile in his presentation at the Inishbofin INISH Festival in 2015, this model of stable, repeat domestic visitors distinguishes Inishbofin's tourism from other Irish islands such as Inishmore (*Árainn*). The largest of the Aran Islands (*Oileáin Árann*), Inishmore receives tens of thousands more tourists than Inishbofin per year, but the great majority are day-trippers who spend only a few hours on the island. Ó Conghaile, born and raised on Inishmore, highlighted the limitations of this high volume of day-trippers and the additional economic value of overnight visitors (Ó Conghaile 2013). Interestingly, these opposing patterns of tourism—high volume of day-trippers vs. low volume of extended stays by repeat visitors—exist on islands with relatively similar heritage resources.

In the west of Ireland and on western islands in particular, rural tourism is still often promoted as an opportunity to return to unspoiled landscapes that embody sentimentalized views of Ireland in the past (Clancy 2011). Such a strategy evokes the nineteenth- and twentieth-century discourses that depicted the rural west of Ireland as a timeless landscape preserving precolonial linguistic, racial, and technological forms, not to mention dramatic scenery (see chap. 2). Ironically, the growth of rural tourism in Ireland, left unmanaged, threatens to cannibalize the resources that drive it (Anderson et al. 2015; Royle 2003). You cannot eat scenery, but it is undeniably tourist infrastructure. The landscape of Inishbofin, like Inishmore, exudes a depth of history and environmental diversity disappearing in other parts of Ireland: the ruins of a medieval church, a seventeenth-century barracks, dozens of nineteenth-century cottages, sheep and cows grazing the fields and walking the roads, hills purpled by heather, secluded sandy beaches looking toward Inishark, or the cloud-cloaked peaks of the Connemara mountains. All of this is infrastructure as vital as a regular ferry service, paved roads, electricity, mobile coverage, and Wi-Fi access. Conservation of island habitats and cultural heritages represents a major premise of both government subsidies and tourist markets. Ireland's National Parks and Wildlife Service has designated under EU and national law the vast majority of Inishbofin and Inishark as Special Areas of Conservation (SAC) that harbor uncommon habitats for plant and animal species. Likewise, islanders' claims to government subsidies are based partly on their maintenance of unique cultural heritages. In this domain, the Irish-speaking islands can qualify for additional Irish and EU subsidies directed at preserving minority languages—an option unavailable to Inishbofin islanders.

Given the constraints and affordances of heritage-based tourism and government subsidies, how have islanders of Inishbofin been able to create and sustain the model of habitual tourism? I suggest it relies in part on islanders' capacity to share their heritage and to make visitors feel that they too have a share in that heritage. This perception of belonging need not be founded in shared ancestry or ethnicity. It can emerge rather by participating in a shared repertoire of experience and knowledge about the island's history, landscape, and customary modes of social interaction. The role of heritage in cultivating perceptions of belonging amid islanders and visitors emerges from a deep history of outsiders visiting the island for purposes of research, leisure, and inspiration.

SHARING HERITAGE AND GENERATING BELONGING

Whether scholars, adventurers, or artists, visitors to Inishbofin have been studying, partaking in, or dramatizing island heritage and lifeways since at least the late nineteenth century. Charles Browne and Brían MacLoughlin, whose work we drew from in previous chapters, came to the islands explicitly to record what they considered a distinctive heritage. The writings of both men reveal a certain admiration for islanders but also an implicit sense of distance, if not superiority. MacLoughlin, although from the nearby mainland and working for the Department of Irish Folklore, treats some islander lore with a degree of skepticism that can cross into condescension. As we have seen, he scoffed at the legend of the white cow and even questioned islanders' own interpretation of the place-name Inishbofin as "Island of the White Cow" (MacLoughlin 1942, NFC 838, 426–7). Yet, in doubting the place-name meaning, MacLoughlin unknowingly repudiated the account of the Anglo-Saxon historian Bede "The Venerable," who recorded that same translation in the early eighth century.

Around 1890, sports fisherman H. W. Gore-Booth ventured to Inishbofin with a harpoon gun and accompanied the king of Inishark, Michael Halloran, and a crew of Shark men in hunting basking sharks along the coast. Hunting these massive fish (6–8 m; 4,900 lb.) to extract oil from their livers was a valuable if dangerous industry for islanders in the nineteenth century. Gore-Booth's account suggests the practice had grown scarce of late: "The king is an old harpooner, this making his nineteenth fish, but he informed me it was eighteen years since he had killed a fish until this season" (Gore-Booth 1891, 61).

Gore-Booth's incidental collaboration with islanders in a disappearing maritime task reads as an early episode of heritage tourism and a prefiguration of later visitors' fascination with seafaring traditions and lore.

The most famous case of the latter was the Anglo-Irish poet Richard Murphy. As dramatized in his poem "Sailing to an Island," Murphy first visited Inishbofin by accident during an ill-fated voyage aimed for Clare Island in the 1960s. Murphy began visiting regularly and promoting the island, ferrying Sylvia Plath and Ted Hughes, among others, to Bofin in his boat the *Ave Maria*. Captivated by islanders and their oral histories, Murphy became a kind of poetic folklorists for Inishbofin. "Pat Cloherty's Version of the Maisie" and "The Cleggan Disaster" convert individual islanders' accounts of seafaring tragedies into epic verse. Of course, not every visitor to Inishbofin becomes the island's unofficial poet laureate. Nevertheless, as a habitual visitor drawn into the island by the allure of its people and their heritage, he is an early and extreme instance of a wider pattern. The experiences of two of my close friends and collaborators on Inishbofin help to illustrate the ongoing role that heritage plays in generating belonging and sustaining tourism on the island today.

Tommy

We have already encountered Tommy a few times in this book. He was born and raised on Inishbofin and, after completing secondary school, settled on the island to look after his family farm (fig. 6.2). Yet, he has traveled when able, having walked the Camino de Santiago multiple times and spent time in Mexico and Turkey. I first met Tommy around 2010, when he was working as a crew member on the Inishbofin Ferry. Over the years, he has become more actively involved in our team's research. Recall his was the hand that exposed the first of the cross-slabs at Clochán Leo in 2012. As a collaborator he is invaluable, not only for his command of oral history but for the speed at which he can draw connections between new findings and existing knowledge to raise new interpretations and new questions.

During the 2014 summer field season, at Tommy's invitation, I first went to Inishark to help with the gathering and shearing, and subsequently spent many years working alongside Tommy and his late brother John. Throughout the course of my research, and especially during the winter of 2016, Tommy has been a vital source of insider information, practical guidance, encouragement, and friendship. He also contrived to win me the role of playing Father Christmas at the 2016 Inishbofin Christmas Market, to his great amusement and the puzzlement of many Bofin children, who had to offer their gift requests to a thin-limbed Yankee Santa Claus.

Figure 6.2: Tommy with triplet lambs born from one of his blackface ewes in 2022.

Figure 6.3: Tommy Burke guiding attendants of the 2015 INISH Festival (see below) on a heritage walk.

Among islanders and visitors, Tommy is known for his capacity for recollection and recounting. Tommy has been offering occasional guided walks on Inishbofin for more than a decade (fig. 6.3). After completing a diploma in archaeology at the National University of Ireland Galway in 2015, he began offering tours throughout the summer, including walks around Inishbofin and trips to Inishark. Word of mouth is the base of the craft, and it is through word of mouth that the venture has grown.

Some tasks prime a mind to map networks of connection and analogy. Tommy's mother, Ann Marie, was a famous knitter whom others would seek out to consult when navigating complex patterns of stitching. Something of that genius for tracing entwinings passed to Tommy but exercised in the domains of oral history and genealogy. Over the years, he has collected a trove of stories and family histories from older islanders. These are treasures predominately transmitted through voice rather than text, and their curation relies on continual use rather than a frozen codification. They require curators able both to carry the stories and to recognize when the moment is ripe for their summoning. Tommy is seemingly capable, when pressed, of squinting, tilting his gaze upward to the right, and then turning his head sharply to the left before describing with luxuriant detail the kinship connection between any two islanders selected at random. And yet his depth of local knowledge comes with an expansive curiosity that has led him to explore widely across an eccentric assortment of topics. He will as soon and as well recite the story of a ruined house in Westquarter as recall the personalities at play in the fall of the Roman Republic, the racial politics of the Mexican American War, or Jimmy Hoffa's rule of the teamsters union (and perhaps all in the course of the same conversation). I have watched him calmly seize the tether of a metric-ton limousine bull and lead him to a field of cows and just as easily lead enraptured groups of tourists, who lean in to hear the soft currents of his voice. On an island rightfully renowned for storytelling, Tommy stands out in his capacity to relate the threads of local memory to wider patterns of history.

Tommy's style of tour-guiding draws from more common patterns of anecdote sharing on Inishbofin. In my experience, a common style of Bofin anecdote—whatever its emotional resonance—is pitched with the structure of a joke. Conventionally, a storyteller, recognizing some connection between the present course of events and a story in their repertoire, will first establish the analogous past context, and then, with careful control of tempo and inflection suitable to the tone of the narrative, lead into the punch line: most often, a memorable turn of phrase whose old wit sheds new light on the present moment.

One characteristic anecdote is often recalled by Tommy when he encounters "new knitters" who celebrate their first finished items, typically a basic cap. The story begins years ago when Tommy's mother Ann Marie took commisions for knitwear:

> My mother said to me: "I wish our Ann [i.e her daughter] was here. I have a big order for caps from a diving club, and I won't have them finished in time. They're leaving Saturday." I said, "you should ask Ann Day." So Ann came to our house and she and my mother were in the sitting room, knitting away one cap after the other while watching TV. I brought in the tea and mentioned how they could follow the pattern and the TV at the same time. Ann replied, "Anyone who couldn't knit a cap . . ."

The implication of Ann's response is that for two women who had been knitting since they were small girls, to knit was second nature and to knit a cap was child's play. Ann Day remembers starting to knit with the quills of goose feathers when she was only six years old. She still knits, and like her friend Anne Marie, taught generously and encouraged many new knitters over the years, including visitors to the island. For Tommy the anecdote represents the distinction between the skills acquired by a hobbyist to pass the time vs. the skills passed down through generations to foster a livelihood. The latter enjoys an ease in basic work and a pride to strive for finer and more complicated works in their craft.

More than most storytellers, Tommy is able to weave in, out, and around the thread of an anecdote by following digressions—typically local or historical parallels and genealogical information—that make multiple contexts for a tale in the midst of its telling. In many cases, the sharing of an anecdote by one speaker will cue another speaker to offer a different anecdote, linked to the first by theme, content, or character. Tommy re-deploys this conversational style in his walking tours. These are not potted lectures, prepared and delivered every time with the same content, inflection, and pitch. (Tommy likes to parody these robotic spiels in the blaring monotone of an imagined AI docent: "In this spot in 1837, this structure was built in drystone.... You will notice there are no trees on the island, therefore driftwood was an important resource...."). Instead, his tours are open-ended exchanges between Tommy and the group, where local anecdote acts as premise for conversation and conversation acts as premise for anecdote. What stories are told and which monuments are visited depends on weather and visibility and the fitness and interests of the group. As such, each tour—even those that follow a common circuit—is a kind of one-off event shaped by the configuration and character of its participants. Tour-goers often ask Tommy if he'd consider writing a book to collect island stories in his style of narration. The problem, as Tommy and I have discussed, is that his style is not just in turns of phrase and patterns of speech. His style is in shaping the narration to the context of the telling. The order of facts, the elements accentuated and elided, the analogies and digressions followed all depend on the faces before him. This is precisely why tour-goers feel like they are participating in unique events impervious to replication.

As in the case of the Assumption Mass in 2016, Tommy's walking tours represent a forum wherein exposure, engagement, and participation with the island's heritage, whether archaeological, religious, or genealogical, are extended to visitors. I hinted in chapter 1 at the importance of the circulation and recirculation of commonly held narratives about the island's past—lore of places and place-names, perfectly delivered lines of wry wit, characters and the characteristics they embodied. In the case of the gathering group, the recitation of a cycle of well-known stories during lunch, I argued, acted as a timely reminder of the gatherers' shared experience in the midst of a highly collaborative task. Through my inclusion as a listener in the recitations, I too was becoming introduced, in some small way, into the community of those familiar with a repertoire of narratives. Indeed, my fieldwork on Inishbofin as a whole can be viewed in the framework of very partial incorporation into the realm of the islanders' shared experience. My experience, however, represents an extended form of what many visitors to the island experience. Those who go on Tommy's walking tours, even if first-time visitors, get exposed, however partially or briefly, to an insider's perspective on the island's history and its relation to the world beyond.

Most of Tommy's walkers are themselves Irish and often from the surrounding area of Connemara and the west of Ireland. While accompanying Tommy on his tours, I have often noted how participants relate specific aspects of Bofin's past to more general themes in Irish history that resonate with their own local lore from elsewhere in Ireland. Such themes include the veneration of early medieval saints, dubious folklore related to the deeds of the pirate queen Granuaile, the ruthlessness of the Cromwellian regime, the callousness of estate agents, and friendly intercounty rivalries. For example, reciting the story of Colman's exile to Inishbofin commonly leads to one or more of the tour participants sharing stories of traditions related to their own local saint and his miracles. Likewise, recounting Inishbofin's history of transfer from County Mayo to Galway in 1873 almost inevitably leads to an exchange of barbs on Mayo's recent misfortunes in All Ireland Gaelic football finals. By visiting specific monuments that relate to broader themes in Irish history, walking tours underscore heritage shared among the Irish, and residents of western Ireland in particular. In other words, Tommy's interactions with walking tour participants situate Bofin within wider currents of Irish history and simultaneously invite participants to situate themselves within these currents. His walking tours have also become a new focal point for returning visitors to the island. In the few seasons that I contributed to the Inishbofin Walking Festival (2021–23) with Tommy, the tickets sold out on the first day of availability, with many of the same participants returning from year to year.

Marie

In recent years, no islander has been more active and instrumental in the preservation and promotion of island heritage than Marie Coyne (fig. 6.4). Like Tommy, Marie has lived on Bofin all of her life. I rented the cottage adjacent to her home during the fall and winter of 2016. In subsequent years, I have often stayed in one of the spare bedrooms of her own house. She has been a generous and kind host, not least in sharing joint custody of a black cat (who, despite a contested history that spans human companions in three townlands, clearly favors us). Marie's demeanor can sometimes be quiet, gentle, and shy, but this belies her immense talent as an artist and the intensity of her compassion for friends, relatives, animals, and landscape. Whether poetry, photography of abandoned cottages or artifacts, hand-painted beach stones, or fragments of sea-glass and delph arranged into designs, her artistic output is premised on

Figure 6.4: Marie Coyne and a pet lamb, Shenanigans, in 2022.

Figure 6.5: A map of Inishbofin created by Marie Coyne with a collage of sea-delph—fragments of broken ceramic worn smooth by the ocean and collected from the island's shorelines.

recognizing beauty in those things that can endure, at least for a time, without our attention or admiration (fig. 6.5). Her dedication to the curation of Bofin's heritage is itself a kind of compassion for islanders in the past, whose lives, customs, creations, and especially hardships might be forgotten without our attention.

In 1998, Marie repurposed a small building that once held a shop adjacent to the old pier to create the Inishbofin Heritage Museum and Gift Shop (fig. 6.6). In 2016, the front of the shop displayed items for sale: knitwear, postcards, candy, jewelry, souvenirs handmade by Marie and other women from the island, hundreds of her photographs of scenic views on the island, and books on the island's natural and cultural history.

As many of the items for sale were set up on traditional dressers and furniture, the gift shop at the front of the building seemed to blend without seam with the museum area at the back. Marie carefully gathered and thoughtfully displayed nineteenth- and early twentieth-century artifacts relating to fishing, farming, traditional crafts, and everyday household living. In addition to a bed, mantelpiece, and dresser set up and furnished with ceramics and knickknacks as if in an occupied house, the walls were lined with hundreds of scanned and laminated reproductions of early twentieth-century photographs. Most were labeled with the identities and dates of those depicted, often including both

Figure 6.6: The Facebook banner for the Inishbofin Heritage Museum and Gift Shop, showing the interior of the museum and its displays. The page itself is a repository of community memory, as Marie commonly posts not only her own photography of recent events but archival photos and in memoriam commemorations on the anniversaries of deaths or tragedies.

maiden and married names. In addition to those displayed on the walls, Marie has collated a vast archive of photographs, census records, shop accounts, genealogical information, and newspaper clippings relevant to the island. Due to ongoing risks of flooding from extreme weather in the area around her shop, Marie has had to put much of the museum collection into storage while she raises funds for a new facility.

Marie's careful curation of island heritage is an ongoing labor of love that extends across multiple media. Among the books for sale in her shop are two Marie worked to produce. The first, *Inishbofin through Time and Tide*, edited by local documentary filmmaker Kieran Concannon, combines historical overviews drawing from archaeology and archival evidence, historic photographs, and oral history records (Concannon 1997). A second volume is *St Colman's Abbey and Cemetery Inishbofin*, which Marie compiled (Coyne 2008). For the book, Marie went around to the families on the island gathering names and photographs. In the end, she created a detailed map of the cemetery, assigning, when possible, the names of the deceased to individual graves. In addition to brief historical descriptions of the abbey ruins, the book includes a series of in memoriam tributes illustrated with photographs and produced in consultation with families of the deceased. The result is a repository of memory directed simultaneously inward toward the community of islanders and outward toward visitors.

Also in the shop are two more recent volumes, each produced by visitors in consultation with islanders and both catering to an islander and visitor audience. James Morrissey, a familiar visitor to Bofin originally from County Mayo, edited *Inishbofin and Inishark, Connemara* (Morrissey 2012). The book compiles a series of historical reports—including that of Charles Browne—alongside archival photography and more recent photographs taken by another familiar visitor, John Carlos, between the 1970s and 1990s. The book thus juxtaposes the ethnographic portraits of Charles Browne's craniometric research with images of islanders from the mid- to late twentieth century, some of whom still reside on the island. The result is an odd development of ethnographic photography, one latently endorsed by islanders as a valuable repository for their own memory and a means of appealing to visitors. Rather than presented as specimens of racial profiles, islanders are now presented in photographs as embodying a dwindling and romanticized lifestyle of traditional crafts and tasks, such as farming and fishing.

The second book is *Solas: Stories from Inishbofin* (https://solasinishbofin.wordpress.com). The book is the outcome of the Artist and School Residency program funded by Galway County Council. The artist in residence, Veronika Staberger, and the then principal of the Inishbofin National School, Cathy O'Halloran, developed the book to commemorate the 125th anniversary of the Inishbofin National School in 2014 and to mark UNESCO's International Year of Light in 2015. Accordingly, students in the school (ages five to ten) gathered stories from their parents, grandparents, and neighbors about Inishbofin before the arrival of electricity. The book collects the children's transcriptions and illustrations of the stories along with photographs of the storytellers and their demonstrations of traditional tasks (making butter, weaving rope, handwashing clothes). The whole project—from classroom to website to published book—simultaneously transmitted knowledge and experience from the past to young islanders and to the outside world.

The internet has provided a new means for islanders to promote their island and its heritage. In this regard, Marie is also at the forefront. Marie curates a Facebook page for her museum, which she regularly updates throughout the year with links to news relevant to the island, posts of archived photos newly scanned, and her own photography documenting community events and gatherings and a never-ending supply of beautiful landscapes. As of 2024, the page had more than eleven thousand followers and allows annual visitors and islanders living elsewhere to keep apace of news on the island throughout the course of the year. Two other Facebook groups join together islanders residing on Inishbofin, former islanders, familiar visitors, and people around the world. Inishbofin Local News is a forum for posting news items relevant to the island—events, births, deaths, lost and found items, accommodation availabilities, etc. The group is public but requires existing members to approve new members. As such, it operates as an information network linking islanders and familiar visitors. Similarly, the Inishbofin Descendants Facebook group provides a network for searching and exchanging genealogical research, family photographs, and archival documents among people around the world who can trace their ancestry through Inishbofin. Tommy and Marie are active on the page, themselves having gathered a great deal of the research that members draw on and enrich. Some members of the group eventually travel to Inishbofin.

Tommy's and Marie's work are forums for both preserving island heritage and sharing it beyond the community of islanders who live year-round on the island. I suggest that this work, alongside other recent projects, helps to generate a sense of participation in the local, regional, national, and transnational heritages that Inishbofin represents for visitors. In chapter 4, I made a parallel argument about the experience of early medieval pilgrimage on Inishark—namely, that the infrastructure of ritual could cultivate a sense of shared participation in penitential devotion among monks and lay pilgrims. On Inishbofin today, the cause of many visitors' annual journeys to the island is likewise a sense of partial incorporation within a small community.

Notably, the logistics of journeying to the island are akin to the classic structure of pilgrimage. Arriving in Cleggan pier by car or coach from various locations, visitors must coordinate their actions to the schedule of a set number of ferry departures. Boarding the ferry, they abandon more routine modes of transport over land for a vessel that navigates the constantly shifting complexion of weather and open water. As a liminal phase of transition, the ferry crossing begins the process of resituating visitors outside their daily routines and social circles and into what is sometimes affectionately referred to as "island time."

For return visitors, this transition may be an eagerly anticipated annual event, one that usually brings their first encounter with familiar faces in Cleggan or on board the ferry. For visitors who have come to the island as family groups over many generations, islanders are often the summertime friends and coworkers of their youth. Intermarriage between such visitors and islanders is not uncommon. I have noted how repeat visitors, sometimes unaware of my participation in an archaeological project, are eager to demonstrate their knowledge of the island's history, geography, and complex kinship connections to a perceived newcomer.

As other scholars have documented (Moyle et al. 2010), social exchange between tourists and small island communities has a variety of motivations, from financial gain to individual curiosity to cultural traditions of hospitality, and may take a variety of forms, from warmth and friendship to open hostility. Bofin, of course, sees a spectrum of such interactions, but the tourism model that has proved advantageous thus far is one of cultivating durable, hospitable relations with repeat visitors. This bulwark of dedicated visitors offers both dependable annual bookings and a degree of leverage when government funding for the maintenance of the islands is threatened. As remote, low population settlements that are incorporated into larger mainland council areas, island communities are at a disadvantage when it comes to competing for political attention to ensure adequate funding for essential services like healthcare, schooling, roads, waterworks, and telecommunications. As part of the austerity measures coming in the wake of the European financial crisis, the former Department of the Environment, Community and Local Government planned to terminate core funding to island Community Development Companies in 2014. Campaigning with other island representatives to restore core funding, Simon Murray's testimony to members of the Oireachtas (the Irish legislature) in 2014 emphasized the substantial contribution made to the Irish exchequer by the collective economy of offshore islands. The island Development Companies merely wanted their fair share of support to continue their work in advocating and providing essentials services for their communities. In the end, the islands convinced the government to mitigate the cuts, but the struggle to maintain adequate funding structures for the islands never ceases.

As I will discuss in the concluding chapter, the love that visitors have for Inishbofin proved consequential again when the Covid-19 pandemic and necessary travel restrictions nullified the tourist market in spring 2020.

METONYMIC, INTIMATE, AND EMBODIED HERITAGE

As we have seen in the investigation of early medieval and historic pilgrimage on Inishark, engagements with heritage are liable to promote perceptions of affinity as well as difference. Likewise, on Inishbofin in the early twenty-first century, tourism experiences can generate a sense of partial participation in island heritage without wholly dissolving distinctions between islanders and visitors. Unsurprisingly, islanders' engagements with heritage are often very different from visitors' and can be glossed with alternative political valences and more intimate local memories.

Heritage tourism incentivizes islanders' curation of certain kinds of material heritage, particularly the oldest, most spectacular remains, like the Old Barracks and St. Colman's Abbey. Such monuments are also best-suited to evoke major historical themes into which Irish domestic and diasporic visitors can situate themselves. The Irish American priest who delivered the Assumption Mass is paradigmatic of this engagement with heritage as material metonyms that stand for cherished historical narratives. His sermon, by referencing both Colman and Cromwell, positioned Bofin's history as an extraordinary manifestation of the antiquity of Catholicism and its persecution by Protestant authorities in Ireland

and elsewhere. As expressed that day, his perception of Irish heritage was linked to a history of Catholic resilience in the face of oppression. After the mass, he told me how strange it seemed as an Irish American to celebrate the history of Puritans in America on Thanksgiving, considering how members of that faith had treated his ancestors during the Cromwellian era.

At the time, the mention of Thanksgiving in this context startled me, as throughout the spring and summer of 2016, corporate and state-sponsored violence was unfolding against indigenous protesters of the Dakota Access Pipeline near the Standing Rock Reservation (Estes 2016). I knew nothing of the priest's political persuasion or sympathies. But, I had spent enough time in Ireland to recognize how the juxtaposition of Irish and other colonial histories often produces very different political standpoints on either side of the Atlantic. In our conversations about America, I have been impressed by Simon's and Tommy's depth of knowledge and indignation about histories of settler colonialism and slavery and their impact on indigenous peoples from around the world. Consider also the traditional support for Palestinian liberation in Ireland and especially within Irish Republicanism (Rolston 2009). Comparing histories of oppression can build solidarity with other marginalized groups—but also quite the opposite. Among the reactions to the Black Lives Matter movement was the resurgence of internet memes that inaccurately depicted the history of Irish indentured servants in the Caribbean as equivalent to the experiences and legacies of African American chattel slavery (Hogan et al. 2016; Zacek 2023). Such memes, often shared on social media explicitly to delegitimize BLM, commonly blend misinformation and misidentified imagery (Hogan 2015). The Old Barracks on Inishbofin evokes the real history of political imprisonment and indentured servitude distorted by the "Irish Slave" memes. Tommy is aware of this distortion and will address it on tours of the barracks. Suffice to say, the political valence of Irish history can be very different for islanders, Irish American visitors, and island descendants in America.

Tourists are drawn to Bofin as a landscape of leisure and evocative scenery, sometimes tied to cherished historical narratives. For islanders, the landscape can evoke more intimate stories that visitors do not recognize and may never be told. Those who grew up on the island, particularly before the installation of electricity and running water, develop a subtler understanding of the landscape and the ways it can be read, worked, and traversed. Think again of Béal Cam, the twisting shortcut through the chain of rocks on the east end of Inishbofin that appeared in chapter 2. That spot also features in a memorable anecdote, often invoked on Bofin as a humorous frame for drawing distinctions between islanders and outsiders. A Bofin man, Jim Tierney, had endured too much condescension in a conversation with a visitor to the island. Exasperated at last, he declared,

Figure 6.7: Three limestone blocks from the Old Barracks incorporated into a stone wall running along the main ring road of the island. On the gate is a sign directing passersby to the Inishbofin Heritage Museum and Gift Shop.

"You may travel the world and be a college educated man, but you know nothing of Béal Cam!" In Jim's reckoning, pride of place went to local knowledge of place—and, more specifically, the kind of practical cunning earned from the experiences of making a living on the island.

In addition to the grander archaeological monuments highlighted in promotional material and walking tours, there are countless other smaller, less conspicuous remnants of the past that can serve as points of pride. Repurposed building stone from the Old Barracks and other premodern remains are incorporated within the fabric of houses and field walls at different places across the island (fig. 6.7). While some stones evoke the fortresses associated with figures like Cromwell and Granuaile, others are simply remarkable for the feats of strength and will needed to set them in place. I have heard Tommy refer with admiration to a particularly large stone incorporated into the central room of a nineteenth-century house, comparing this former deed to him and his brother setting three massive stones above the door lintel of a ruined house that they restored as a barn for storing hay bales. Tommy's pride in seeing a link between his own building work and that of his forebears on Bofin is a distinctly private one embodied by anonymous stones. Had I not happened to be along with him and his brother to collect the hay, those stones would have been as invisible to me as any casual visitor to the island.

This quiet, more private pride in unobtrusive material heritage is not particular to Tommy. The abandoned cottages scattered around the island are, to many who pass by, part of the evocative scenery that summons an Irish landscape that once was. To islanders, they were houses where their relatives dwelt, people whose names, deeds, and tragedies can still be recalled.

A number of island households curate quern stones within their houses, yards, or garden walls. Although sometimes visible to those walking on the street, they are unobtrusive and easily missed by those not attuned to the varying textures of the island's stone walls. The querns, if not strictly heirlooms, have often been recovered from digging around family homes or fields, and pride is taken in those of the finest craftmanship. Likewise, some monuments are encountered or recognizable only by those familiar with or engaged in farming tasks on the island. For example, set along the mountain road in the townland of Fawnmore is a large boulder known as the Resting Stone (fig. 6.8). In the nineteenth and early twentieth centuries, islanders commonly used wicker baskets called cleaves for hauling fish, seaweed, manure, and turf. Rather than removing the basket from their back, carriers walking the mountain road could simply stand against the stone, allowing its top surface to take the weight of their burden. Similarly, one is unlikely to encounter the little-known medieval period mill stones along the drainage leading to Bunamullen Bay (*Bun an Mhuilin*— "The Foot of the Mill") unless they are collecting livestock from the mountain, repairing fences, or straying far off the loop walks. Monuments such as these can go unknown and unrecognized even to many islanders, leading to a few occasions in which they have been inadvertently damaged or displaced.

A memorable exchange in Day's Bar in mid-December 2016 demonstrated both islanders' pride in these lesser-known fragments of their island's archaeological heritage and their capacity to situate it within wider frames of

Figure 6.8: The Resting Stone, set along the main roadway running from the village of Fawnmore through its commonage toward the North Beach.

experience. Tommy and I had just returned from speaking for a few hours with Matty Concannon, then the oldest man on Bofin, aged one hundred years, still keen minded and capable of summoning otherwise forgotten genealogical details. We were reviewing some of the things we had learned alongside a group of Tommy's relatives who happened to be in the pub that night. After discussing a few cases of accidental or intentional interference with heritage monuments, one islander mentioned that she had not heard about many of these lesser-known landmarks and that it would be easy enough to disturb them inadvertently. Tommy suggested that, just as anywhere else on earth, these hidden landmarks and the stories behind them give Bofin's heritage its distinct identity. To lose those landmarks would be to lose that identity, to lose what makes Bofin Bofin. Agreeing, John replied, "That's just what they're up to in Syria"—a reference to the so-called Islamic State's attempt at obliterating the histories and identities it opposes through the destruction of archaeological heritage.

Islanders know the affordances of their archaeological heritage. They understand how the scenic, seemingly archaic landscape and monumental ruins draw in visitors, and they understand how rather ordinary objects keep alive more intimate family histories and echoes of local experience. In chapter 2, I outlined an expansive definition of heritage that includes old monuments, old traditions, and the living, practical knowledge that emerges from engaging those elements of the past. Heritage is also the tact to recite the right tale for the right moment, to knit a pattern from memory, to navigate an advantageous route through commonage while gathering sheep, to recognize instantly a field or house by the name of its owner three generations ago, to anticipate when to slow your vehicle when approaching blind intersections along the island's narrow roads, and to instinctually say "back" for west and "over" for east. In the course of interactions on the ground, it is often this kind of embodied know-how, rather than family or residential history, that highlights distinctions amid islanders, familiar visitors, and others. Among people with no kinship connections to the island, those who have worked multiple summers in hotels or pubs or on the ferry might develop as much or more of this islander embodied knowledge than others who have owned holiday homes on the island for years.

Heritage tourism, on Bofin and around the world, is built around monuments, material landmarks that can be visited and their histories conveyed. While the tourist market might thereby incentivize the maintenance of these places, it can also threaten the persistence of other forms of embodied heritage. This is particularly clear in relation to farming tasks that were once so essential to the dwelling taskscape of Inishbofin islanders. The tension between farmwork and the tourist trade is also prone to highlight key distinctions between locals, visitors, and others.

THE HEN, THE PIG, AND THE CORNCRAKE—TOURISM, CONSERVATION, AND THE FARMING TASKSCAPE

However long visitors may have been coming to the island, those with any self-awareness recognize they will never be considered in the same category as those raised on the island. The distinction is more than incommensurate experience and goes beyond kinship. Traveling to Irish islands, one often hears the term "blow-in" to refer to people who have settled on an island, but who grew up elsewhere without family links to the island. In the middle and late twentieth century, visitors and outsiders on Bofin were more commonly refered to as "strangers," a term not inherently pejorative, but connoting their unfamiliarity.

Nearly half a century of tourism and enhanced mobility and changing conventions have altered the picture, but distinctions remain.

Once invited to describe the difference between islanders and "blow-ins," Tommy borrowed an old figure of speech to describe the situation. "The difference is the difference between the hen and the pig in an Irish breakfast. The hen is involved, but the pig is committed." The hen has played her part by laying the eggs, but the pig quite literally has its flesh on the table. Even if taken along to the island by their parents years ago, habitual visitors have the privilege of means and of choice to return to the island and engage with the community as much as they wish. Acquiring property on the island, particularly housing, is a costly undertaking and increasingly more feasible to wealthy strangers than to locals. Islanders have inherited the opportunity to make a life on the island, with all the affordances and constraints such a life entails. The decision they make—whether to stay or seek a life elsewhere—fundamentally shifts their relationship to their heritage. And for those who make the decision to stay, Irish and EU policies, fluctuating funding schemes, increasingly erratic weather, rising tides, and the form and fortunes of the tourist economy impact their livelihoods, their way of life, and the opportunities their children can inherit.

The character and viability of small-scale farming is one aspect of Bofin's heritage profoundly impacted by the promotion of the island as a tourist destination and reservoir of biodiversity. With the exception of some hens raised for household supplies of eggs, some pet donkeys, one group of pigs, and Connemara ponies, the vast majority of livestock on the island are sheep and cattle raised for meat. Sheep are the most numerous, and tourists arriving in early spring will see young lambs gambling around fields and across the commonage. Lambing season, typically extending from February to April, is an exhausting time of irregular hours, in which farmers monitor the conditions of their breeding ewes and must be ready to intervene in the case of difficulty. This could mean adjusting ill-presented lambs, pulling lambs too large to be delivered naturally, and facilitating bonding between lambs and ewes. Lamb production and nursing entails significant nutrient costs, so supplemental feeding for ewes is common throughout winter to early spring.

Ireland's climate generally ensures grass growth throughout the late spring and summer. Yet, the availability of grazing in summer does not mean an end to work. For most farmers who supplement their farming income with work related to the tourist trade, the progress of summer brings more tourist traffic and new logistical challenges. The most labor-intensive and time-demanding summer task for farmers is shearing their sheep, a practice essential for animal welfare but ultimately economically unrewarding. Wool was a valuable product in the past, both for sale and for homespun clothing. However, across the

Figure 6.9: Simon Murray demonstrates a technique for introducing bottle-feeding to a young lamb whose mother could not provide milk (2022). The artificial teat of the bottle is inserted into the corner of the mouth and over the tongue to induce a swallowing reflex. As the lamb learns to initiate and control their swallowing, Simon will slowly move the bottle toward the front of the mouth to encourage sucking of the teat. Attentiveness and skills like this are essential for reducing losses during lambing season.

twentieth century, fine-quality Merino wool has become readily available on the international market from producers in Australia, China, and elsewhere. The costs entailed in shearing and shipping out wool now far outpaces the price, particularly for the rougher fibers of the hill breeds better adapted to conditions on Bofin. Farmers now in their fifties remember when wool meant more than worthlessness and waste and lament the lack of government support for developing Irish wool as an alternative to petroleum-based fibers and as a product with potential applications as fertilizer and insulation.

Figure 6.10: Simon Murray leads a group of relations, off-duty bar staff, and an archaeologist to encourage sheep to walk and, when necessary, swim across the narrow intertidal zone separating Inishlyon from Inishbofin (2019). Photo by Lesley O'Farrell.

Despite the costs and labor incurred, shearing is a necessity. Overgrowth can mean sheep are unbalanced, are unable to nurse, or become dirty and susceptible to topical parasites, particularly maggots. The burrowing larvae of green bottle flies in late summer can be particularly lethal if not treated within hours. "Dipping" sheep through emersion or spray with a chemical solution can treat and prevent topical parasites. In addition to regular welfare checks, sheep also need to be periodically vaccinated against bacterial infections and dosed with oral medication to prohibit internal parasites like intestinal worms and liver fluke. All of this work is necessary to have animals in top form to endure the energetic costs of the breeding season in late fall and the physical and immune-system stress of cold, damp winters.

Importing supplemental fodder, whether hay or enriched feeds, for winter provisioning is a major expenditure, particularly with the added transport fees necessary to get them to the island. As such, grass is at a premium. Many fields used for potato and grain crops in the nineteenth century are now intensively grazed. Farmers also have grazing rights in the commonage or mountain associated with the townlands in which their fields are located. Careful management is necessary to avoid exhaustion of resources. Ideally, periodic movement between fields and seasonal use of the commonage prevents overgrazing and allows vegetation time to replenish. As we have seen, outlying islands in the Inishbofin-Inishark archipelago offer a valuable additional source of pasture, particularly for weaned lambs. The low stocking densities and plentiful grass tend to produce exceptionally well-conditioned hoggets (sheep between one and two years old).

To transport livestock between islands can be tricky to say the least. In the case of Inishlyon, sheep can be encouraged to wade and swim across a narrow intertidal zone at extreme neap tides (fig. 6.10). In the case of Davillaun, Inishgort, Inishskinny More, Inishskinny Beg, and Shark, inter-island movement means the more challenging task of getting sheep on and off boats, primarily on islands without any harbor infrastructure. These journeys demand the application of a very particular set of skills, environmental knowledge, and coordinated action in what can be physically arduous undertakings. Maritime pastoralism requires cool and capable boat handlers and crew able to manage the interactions of coastlines, waves, craft, and living cargo that may shift their position and thus the distribution of weight during transport. The most difficult challenge—gathering sheep on uninhabited and unenclosed islands and getting them on the boat—requires a special sensitivity to the actions of human and animal collaborators. Working together with dogs on irregular terrain, gatherers need to encourage flocking toward the seashore—the exact opposite of sheep's natural inclination to seek high ground during a flight response. Managing the job safely demands a keen awareness of sheep body language, which can hint at imminent actions, whether efforts to split and break away from the gathering or to jump toward the awaiting boats. The knack of it is to imagine the world simultaneously from the perspective of the flock, your dogs, and your companions, each with their own capacities, tendencies, and motivations. Mastering those multiple perspectives allows a group to elicit desired behaviors through gestures, calls, and coordinated action.

Figure 6.11: John Burke and Marcais Lavelle begin the transfer of sheep from the rocky shore to their boats tied at the landing place on Davillaun (2019). The plastic mesh fencing allows Willie Lavelle and me to hold the gathered sheep in place while the boats are loaded.

Maritime pastoralism has a deep history on the islands, and even in the twentieth century, grazing rights to the islands and the management of stock numbers were meticulously guarded. The continuation of the practice across time has proved vital for the reproduction of local environmental and place-name knowledge and the maintenance of archaeological visibility. This is particularly true on Inishark, where grazing prevents vegetation from obscuring the

Figure 6.12: Willie Lavelle, with his son Marcais, transports a load of sheep from Davillaun towards *tráin*, a small strand in Cloonamore townland on Inishbofin (2019). Willie has run sheep on Davillaun for decades and continues to fish with his sons Oisín and Marcais on their boat the *Ceol na Mara*.

remnants of relict field systems from the twentieth century all the way to the Bronze Age. As of 2024, only a few families are still involved with the practice, and even during my years of research on Bofin I witnessed a decline in participation. More than most farming tasks, maritime pastoralism is facilitated by coordinated action between groups involved with the same livestock management system and reliant on one another for mutual aid. As the number of families involved become fewer, the boats fewer and crews smaller, so too the system becomes more difficult, more risky, and less feasible. The decline is due in part to the presence of alternative economic opportunities for young people offered by the tourist trade. Even the younger generations who have taken over family farms are hesitant to maintain the practice, not only because of the risk involved but also because of the behavior of the yearlings that return from the islands. Returning to Bofin after months of grazing, these hoggets may be in excellent condition, but they can also be extremely flighty, so unfamiliar with human proximity that they might not even accept feed during the winter.

Compared to sheep, raising cattle is less onerous during the summer season. Yet, recent developments in the island economy have impacted the relationships of farmers to cattle to a greater extent. Calving season can extend from late winter to summer and requires much of the same monitoring as lambing. While most cows deliver without issues, in the case of complications—failure to dilate sufficiently for an over-large calf, prolonged labor, or an unusually positioned calf—farmers can intervene to pull the calf or summon the local vet to consult. After delivery, farmers must ensure that the cow takes to the newborn calf. This sometimes requires physically positioning the calf under the head of its mother, where she can smell and lick her offspring. The stakes of "the take" are high. The colostrum, the thick and yellowy initial feed of milk (known locally as the beasting), contains essential antibodies and nutrients necessary for calves and lambs, like human infants, to develop a robust immune system. Failure to take can mean bottle-feeding the calf with powdered milk solution at considerable expense.

As with sheep, cattle are moved periodically throughout the summer to ensure sufficient grazing and must be gathered occasionally to administer medication, to apply ear tags to young animals that indicate their registration within the national herd, and to conduct government-mandated testing for certain contagious diseases. Whereas the presence of rams around ewes in fall will generally elicit estrus in the flock, cows come into heat more variably. Monitoring is necessary to recognize when a cow is "around," typically signaled by mounting behavior with fellow herdmates. If there is no bull in the field, one will have to be brought to her (or vice versa). Anyone who has stood close to a mature bull, heard the deep resonance of its lungs filling and emptying, or seen a trailer lurch under its shifting bulk will recognize that this is a delicate task that requires a degree of mutual trust between farmers and animals.

The generation of farmers now in their fifties have seen significant shifts in the taskscape of cattle rearing. Until the late twentieth century, many families kept cows to milk for household consumption as islanders did throughout the nineteenth century. Rather than facilitating the taking of cow to calf, people instead prevented this bond, separating calf from cow and bucket-feeding the newborn themselves. Calves thus raised became particularly bonded to their humans from their initial feedings to their own milking and calving experiences later in life. When a cow was accustomed to twice-daily milkings, one could simply approach her in the middle of a field knowing that she would stand peacefully and await the release of pressure from her teats. As milk became cheaper to import and the industry more heavily regulated, farmers transitioned to raising cattle exclusively for meat production. This led to significant shifts in the socialization of animals. Without the prolonged daily interaction of milking,

Figure 6.13: Livestock take right of way. John Burke moves a group of cows and calves along the road to a fresh field while an oncoming car reverses to give way. Luckily enough, the island's vet happened to be behind the wheel (2017).

it is almost unheard of for cows today to become as comfortable with human proximity and as responsive to human movement as the "pure pets" of the milk cows of the past. As John Concannon, then in his eighties, once said of the milk cows' familiarity with their owners, "They would do everything but talk to you."

In other words, shifts in the taskscape of cattle rearing have altered the complexion of farmers' relationships with their cattle, arguably making the work of gathering, calving, tagging, and dosing more difficult. Aiding the birth and the take means manipulating animals more than they are accustomed to just when the stakes of intervention are highest. Moreover, farmers today must also contend with new intersections between the farming taskscape and the tourist economy. The scheduling of animal markets and the necessity of fine weather for transporting stock between islands set limits on when farm work can take place. The physical presence of tourists walking and cycling along the roads and the taxiing of visitors between the ferry and the island hotels can complicate the movement of stock. Unsurprisingly, encounters between farmers and tourists can be fraught. As James Rebanks (2015) has illustrated from his perspective as a hill farmer in the Lake District of Northern England, tensions are liable to emerge where pastoral landscapes are romanticized as picturesque venues of touristic consumption rather than respected as sources of heritage and livelihood. When moving stock in the summer, encounters with cars, cyclists, or pedestrians are almost inevitable during daylight hours (fig. 6.13). Simon in particular would be known for moving sheep soon after dawn to avoid the traffic. Confrontations between tourists and cattle range from startled fascination to panic by both two- and four-legged creatures. Tommy recognizes two types of tourists in these encounters: "one thinks they're in a petting zoo; the other thinks it's the running of the bulls at Pamplona and jump over fences for fear of getting trampled, even though they are only slowly moving along." Most vexing of all, visitors to the island sometimes accidentally open or shut gates behind them when exploring the island. During one particularly difficult sheep gathering in the lashing rain, we had our work thwarted when a group of tourists shut a gate we had opened earlier, intending to drive the flock through it.

Managing animals in the bustle of tourist season can create complicated logistics and considerable frustration. Yet, I have heard the men I have worked with curse the work as much as they have remarked fondly on a job done finely and beasts raised well. Maintaining the skill and knowledge to raise animals today is heritage in action. As we saw in chapter 1, farming tasks also become the catalyst for reciting stories about islanders in the past, either from first-person experience or passed down by oral tradition. In providing opportunities to recite old narratives and enact bodily skills, the farming taskscape is not just an economic undertaking but also a means of reproducing identity. Structured by cyclical rhythms of labor, nearly every farming task is an opportunity to recall the past. These memories often tie the present moment to mundane or momentous occasions within family histories. Simon can lean on a gate next to his son, watching a flock of sheep settle in the field at *Fál Dubh* ("the black enclosure") in Middlequarter, and recall doing the same thing in the same spot thirty-five years earlier with his own father. Some kinds of continuity are cherished.

For an island that relies to a great extent on a seasonal economy, farming can also provide a basic source of income for year-round residents. The majority of Irish farmers receive subsidies of direct payments as part of the European Union's Common Agricultural Policy (CAP) or other EU or Irish government initiatives. Increasingly, new funding opportunities and, as of 2023, a reconfigured CAP seek to promote environmental health, emissions reduction, and biodiversity alongside rural development and food security. On Bofin, recent agro-environmental funding initiatives have focused on one particular species of annual visitor to the island, the corncrake. The fascination and frustration surrounding the bird illustrates well the interplay between heritage, conservation, agriculture, and tourism that characterizes Inishbofin's contemporary taskscape.

Corncrakes are elusive, ground-nesting birds that migrate from Southern Africa to Inishbofin and other coastal areas of Ireland and Scotland to breed between May and August. Hard to spot, they are harder not to hear. The species name, *crex crex*, imitates the ratcheting, rhyming couplets of the courting males' advertising calls. For the concealment of their nests from predators, the birds require vegetation coverage of at least twenty centimeters with an open structure that allows movement for the birds and chicks. In Ireland, this has often meant human-managed habitats where vegetation could not grow too thick due to periodic grazing or cutting. Prior to the second half of the twentieth century, hayfields and the mosaic of habitats created by mixed farming regimes provided ample shelter, and corncrakes were common across Ireland. From the late twentieth century, agricultural intensification, greater specialization, and the transition to silage harvesting of meadows (in spring) rather than haymaking (late summer) eroded corncrake habitats and devastated their numbers from an estimated four thousand breeding pairs in c. 1970 to 189 breeding males in 1993 (https://www.corncrakelife.ie/conservation-status).

Because of Inishark's evacuation and Inishbofin's retention of small farming, the islands are now among the last remaining Irish refuges for the birds. Their repetitive vocalizations, annoying to some, evoke for older visitors the lost sounds of summer from the Ireland of their youth. To bird-watchers, they are a siren call and the cause of annual voyages to the island. For farmers, the presence of these pilgrims, both human and avian, is the source of both challenge and opportunity.

Islanders with land within designated Corncrake Special Protection Areas (SPA) can find it difficult to receive planning permission for new buildings or restoration work. Under various grant schemes active in west Connacht from the mid-1990s farmers and landowners can receive payments for maintaining corncrake habitats. Most recently, the EU-funded Corncrake LIFE Project has endeavored to enhance cooperation with farmers and landowners to foster corncrake conservation. A results-based payment scheme supports farmers and landowners who volunteer to adopt corncrake-friendly practices, such as the sowing of suitable vegetation or the adoption of grazing or mowing regimes that maintain areas of adequate coverage during the breeding season. For some islanders, these adjustments can mean less grazing available in summer or less hay or silage laid by for winter, and thus greater investment in imported fodder. Such added cost can cut into profit margins for farmers who generally maintain small herds of fewer than a dozen heads of cattle and a few score of sheep. And yet, increasingly farmers find themselves compelled to "farm the grants." Whether in filing subsidies paperwork or selling food and lodging to bird-watchers, as was once remarked to me offhand, "There's more money in corncrakes than cattle."

Since the twentieth century, pastoral farming on Inishbofin has become increasingly disarticulated from local subsistence. Household dairying has disappeared. There are no licensed facilities for butchering on the island, and so animals must be transported off island before their meat can enter the market. The decline of subsistence arable farming has nearly nullified the former value of manure as fertilizer. Across Ireland as a whole, the majority of pastoral farming is directed toward the export market for meat and dairy products. Amid climate crisis and biodiversity collapse, the environmental impact of Ireland's agricultural sector, particularly pastoral farming, has come under enhanced scrutiny. Likewise, the prospects of so-called re-wilding to transform the appearance and biodiversity of intensively grazed, traditionally marginal Irish landscapes have captured public attention (Daltun 2022). And yet, for all this, subsidized small-scale farming provides an important lifeline for the maintenance of year-round residents on the island. The work of raising animals on the island is also a living heritage, a vital mode of engaging and reproducing the presence of the past in landscape. Farming also maintains connections with family plots of land and affords a degree of autonomous venture and ownership that was impossible for islanders' ancestors as tenant farmers in the nineteenth century. Should new regulations or cuts to funding structures make small farming increasingly infeasible, it is likely to contribute to the gentrification of the island, as land would become more valuable as a commodity to be sold for new summer homes rather than as a means of livelihood for local residents.

The concept of re-wilding, however well intended or nuanced, risks reviving that old division between human and nature that posthumanism rails against. Any conservation initiative inevitably puts a thousand human choices in play: choices about what areas to target, what kind of biodiversity to prioritize, and which communities will have their livelihoods and traditions affected. Who will be the pig, who the hen, who the corncrake? Imagine the frustration of a young island family, priced out of the market for turnkey houses by wealthy visitors seeking vacation homes, only to be denied planning permission to convert a ruined building on family land because of its proximity to designated corncrake habitat. Notably, while the Irish corncrake population has plummeted from historic numbers, the International Union for the Conservation of Nature lists its status as "least concern" due to large and stable populations observed in summer breeding grounds in Eastern Europe and Asia (https://www.iucnredlist.org/species/22692543/86147127). To be clear, such statistics do not invalidate conservation efforts in Ireland or elsewhere in Europe. Valued in part because of a nostalgic association with Ireland's rural past, corncrake conservation relies on habitats that require human stewardship rather than the hands-off approach evoked by re-wilding.

As people who engage daily with the landscape, carry its memories, and rely on its potential, farmers are best placed to act as stewards of heritage and biodiversity. Yet, as Crowley (2017) has shown in her analysis of the Rural Environment Protection Scheme (REPS) in West Cork, prioritizing scientific and technocratic knowledge within agri-environmental initiatives can sometimes suppress rather than articulate farmers' practical and embodied knowledge of the land. Before corncrake conservation projects existed, it was the knowledge and sensitivity of individual islanders that ensured the maintenance of corncrake habitats on Inishbofin. The livelihood of the corncrake is fundamentally entangled with the viability of traditional farming. For this reason, the Corncrake LIFE Project could offer an important model for developing new initiatives that enhance harmonies between tradition and conservation. To create a future that balances that value of rural livelihoods, tangible and intangible heritage, biodiversity, and animal and environmental welfare will require dependable, long-term funding structures and a recognition of islanders as stewards of the landscape with the knowledge essential to configure conservation schemes to specific local conditions. Other models for such locally led agri-environmental schemes (LLAES) exist elsewhere in Ireland, including those that focus on conservation of archaeology (Fitzgerald 2019; MacLoughlin et al. 2020). Failure to support this kind of collaboration, I fear, could contribute to conservation policies that abet the simultaneous depopulation and gentrification of islands.

THE LAST GENERATION AND THE NEXT

Islanders now in their fifties have lived through major transformations in the island dwelling taskscape. Their generation will one day be the last to have firsthand experience of older farming practices and of the daily cycle of household chores prior to the introduction of electricity and running water. I suspect fewer in the generation following them will take up farming as a primary means of livelihood. Young people, predominately young men in their teens and twenties, sometimes help out their relations or neighbors during gathering or shearing events. I have even seen whole families, parents and young children, out on the road corralling stray livestock who broke or jumped a fence. For young people,

I wonder how many of those experiences will become in years to come the basis for a future livelihood on the island and not just fond memories of an island upbringing.

The census of 1961, a year after Shark's evacuation, recorded 248 people on Inishbofin. Subsequent census records reveal fluctuations up and down but an overall downward trend culminating in the 160 people recorded in 2011. Yet the last two censuses have seen a slight upward trend with 175 in 2016 and 184 in 2022. The contrast between summer and winter activity on the island reflects the parallel rise in tourism since the mid-twentieth century and the decline in numbers of permanent residents. On a summer holiday weekend, extra ferry runs accommodate swarms of visitors. At night, crammed pubs are abuzz with multiple generations of locals and familiar visitors: divers, musicians, artists, walking groups, and families who have come to the islands for decades. On evenings in November and December 2016, I could walk into Day's Bar, the only pub open throughout the winter, and be surprised to see more than some combination of five people, mostly men in their late forties or older. Besides myself, inhabitants in winter 2016 in their twenties or thirties amounted to about a dozen, almost half of which had no kinship connection to the island. They worked at jobs available across the whole year—fishing, child minding, staffing Day's Bar and the Community Centre, working construction, and crewing the cargo ferry. Although few in number, this group of young people played a quiet but important role in staffing the essential services for islanders throughout the winter.

For many islanders in their twenties, a more common pattern of employment is to work on the ferry or in the island's pubs or hotels in the summers and to travel, attend university, or work a variety of other jobs on the mainland or abroad during the rest of the year. These young people participate in more traditional tasks in their own way, helping their relations or neighbors with farming on their days off or going fishing off the rocks between shifts at the pub. Since the establishment of the first family-run hotels in the 1960s, work in the tourist industry not only has structured participation in traditional activities but also has become a kind of heritage in its own right. I once noted a barman in his early twenties, observing a new batch of his teenage cousins and neighbors working as waiting staff in Murray's Bar, begin to lament the luxury of the youngsters. Adopting the cadence and inflection of an older generation's speech patterns, he recalled with mock nostalgia the days before the computerized cash register with its systematized table numbers and digitally recorded drink tabs.

As a new traditional task, work in the service industry has promoted the maintenance and development of another form of island heritage by young islanders: musical performance. As elsewhere in Ireland, on Inishbofin the setting of traditional music performance transitioned during the twentieth century. In the early twentieth century, most musical performances took place in the home or at dances or parties held at the National School, sometimes as going-away parties for emigrating islanders. Pub sessions became regular occurrences in the 1980s, and the island's reputation for excellence in traditional music has grown subsequently. An annual Inishbofin Step Dancing and Trad Festival, often organized by local fiddler Kevin Abeyta in late September, provides a venue for locals to perform with one another and with a rotating cohort of familiar musicians who visit year to year. With the exception of interuptions due to Covid regulations, Murray's hotel hosted live music sessions every night throughout the summer tourist season, with some of the younger bar staff—locals and longtime returners—proving some of the finest singers and performers.

The many performances I witnessed acted as more than simple fun of a local color. Scholar-performers, like Lillis Ó Laoire (2007) and Deirdre Ní Chonghaile (2021), have offered particularly sensitive analyses of island musical traditions as elements of heritage, malleable frameworks for memory and emotion, and scenes of interface and collaboration between islanders and outsiders. At a more general level, Ingold has noted that musical ensembles usefully epitomize how gatherings possess emergent properties that are at once physical, sensory, mnemonic, and emotive (Ingold 1993, 160–63). An ensemble of musicians applies bodily skills and mutual attention to synchronize their playing of instruments in particular atmospheric conditions, thereby generating an emergent property—musical resonance—that can elicit bodily movements, stir emotions, activate memories, and spur contemplation of relations among themselves and their audience. Indeed, the Irish themselves evoke this resonance with the concept of *craic*. The term generally refers to social buzz, happenings, or fun, particularly that generated by traditional music. According to Kaul (2012, 130), who studied traditional music in Doolin, County Clare, craic describes "particularly good sessions when the audience, the musicians, and the tunes all seem to come together in one harmonious 'flow.' It is a kind of enchantment, maybe the closest state of collective ecstasy that a group of people can achieve outside of religious rituals." Similarly, Ashwood and Bell (2017) suggest that folk music performance offers an opportunity for shared affect that can allow performers and listeners to transcend their differences.

Prior to Covid, the pubs were matchless as venues for ensembles that generated a shared resonance of being between locals and visitors of multiple generations. This is the mighty craic for which Bofin is famed. At Murray's, in particular, the shared resonance was quite literal, as the small, rectangular space ensured that everyone was immersed in the same field of interacting vibrations of sound. Every individual conversation was caught up in an atmosphere dominated by the drive of music. The performers themselves took turns to lead on jigs, reels, polkas, hornpipes, and slow ballads that shaped the current of the craic. Periodically, instrumental tune sets would give way to vocal performances by one of the musicians or by one of the audience members who volunteered—or found themselves irresistibly volunteered by their peers. A well-known singer or a voice of commanding quality could hush the crowd to attention. The performance of familiar Irish ballads and distinctive Bofin songs not only reiterated themes tied to national and local identity. The poetry of lyrics and the emotive energy of different musical modes common in Irish traditional music (i.e., major, minor, dorian, mixolydian, etc.) invited listeners to participate in shared embodiments of emotion, whether joyous laughter, nostalgia, or lamentation. For younger islanders, musical performance served as a way to partake in the crafting of shared experience that links islanders across generations and to the extended community of familiar returners. Of course, like all forums of ensembling, the craic can produce harmony or discord, inclusion as well as exclusion, *gas craic* (mighty fun) and *shit craic* (the opposite). Occasionally, groups of visitors with great welcome for themselves will cross a line in too often shushing the crowd to take turns in singing their party pieces, unaware of rolling eyes elsewhere in the bar. Yet, even this too may become a source of shared experience among the eye rollers.

Islanders in their twenties and thirties have great affection for the island and its traditions, but the prospect of settling permanently is not always feasible. The community on Inishark faced a similar challenge in the twentieth century—a scarcity of feasible or desirable livelihoods for young people compared to the opportunities abroad or on the mainland. The rate of emigration of people in their prime and an aging population were major factors in the final decision to evacuate the island. Demographic polarity split between old and young remains a concern. For some young Bofiners today, their university education has afforded them access to rewarding jobs that do not exist on the island. There is simply not enough year-round employment or housing available for many to settle permanently and raise families on the island at the moment. In some cases, as time goes on, younger islanders will be able to take the reins of family businesses that might allow them to settle permanently. Improved broadband connection on the island has allowed some residents to work remotely, and the future potential for virtual work on offshore islands is huge, particularly since Covid.

Young people with kinship connections to the island contribute immensely to the workforce that allows their older relations and neighbors to maintain livelihoods from managing businesses that make their profits almost entirely between May and October. As musicians and athletes, they participate in the heritage activities that draw visitors to the island. One man from the island developed an innovative new addition to the cycle of summer festivals, one that sought to build on the island's history as a scene of artistic output and inspiration. Peadar King conceived of INISH: Island Conversations in the wake of the 2014 storms that caused considerable damage on Inishbofin. Peadar is a producer and musician with a vast network of friends and collaborators that spans Ireland's arts, culture, and academic scene. Although Peadar settled in Galway to start a family, he wanted to create a multidisciplinary arts festival that would create revenue for the island while simultaneously echoing "the resourcefulness, ambition, pride, and inherent creativity of the local community" (http://inishfestival.com/about-inish). Fittingly, the first INISH Festival in 2015 paid tribute to Richard Murphy as an icon of the artistry and mutual exchange that can arise from islanders' interactions with visitors. In a sort of role reversal, the islander Peadar traveled to Murphy's home in Sri Lanka to record a series of discussions where Murphy recited his poetry and offered his best wishes to his islander friends, whom he had not seen for many years. The festival ran for four years (2015, 2016, 2017, 2018) with each day liable to include academic lectures, artistic exhibitions, poetry recitals, film screenings, and musical performances featuring locals and outsiders. Each festival has also included a heritage walking tour with Tommy guiding new and returning festival attendants and participants. INISH, in its time, became another annual pilgrimage that drew visitors back to the island to engage with, celebrate, and extend islanders' heritage of storytelling, performance, and artistic inspiration and collaboration. In subsequent years, Peadar, his brother Liam King, and fellow islander Eamonn Day Lavelle have given new life to the creative energy behind INISH in a production company, studio, and cultural centre in Galway City. Each venture goes by the name Black Gate, a reference to a disappeared landmark that served as a traditional meeting spot on Inishbofin.

In many ways, INISH epitomizes the argument I have put forward in this chapter. Inishbofin's contemporary dwelling taskscape is dominated by and reliant on the tourist trade. Within that taskscape, heritage—whether traditional practices, embodied knowledge, or archaeological remains—plays a vital role as infrastructure that helps to forge a sense of identity among islanders and a sense of belonging and fascination among habitual visitors. The INISH Festival, like the Feast of the Assumption Mass, was an event that activated heritage to create experiences and memories that foster particular social and economic relations. Heritage incentivizes tourism, and tourism incentivizes the maintenance or continued development of at least some aspects of heritage. At annual festivals, Tommy's storytelling or youngsters' participation in music or maritime sports reproduces the knowledge and skill necessary for aspects of heritage to remain available to the next generation. Of course, the recursive cycle linking the maintenance of heritage with the reproduction of the tourist trade favors some aspects of heritage over others. The selective maintenance of heritage in the face of new economic conditions is nothing new, as our survey of the selective maintenance of St. Leo's pilgrimage monuments on Inishark in the nineteenth and twentieth centuries illustrated. In recent years, a new addition to the cycle of summer festivals has begun to revitalize currach rowing and racing among young people on the island. To close this chapter, I recall my observations at the inaugural Inishbofin Maritime Festival in August 2016. The events of that day and subsequent developments reiterate the central themes of this chapter.

As a stimulus to tourism, the Maritime Festival was designed in part to promote a series of water-sport activities that were offered on the island for the first time in 2016, including stand-up paddleboarding and dinghy sailing. However, the weekend culminated on Sunday in a regatta of currach races, an event that islanders formerly held more regularly during the last decades of the twentieth century. Currachs are round-bottomed boats, traditionally made from tarred canvas and timber but now often coated in fiberglass. With the exception of a group from Carraroe, most of the competitors in the 2016 regatta were from Inishbofin. The especially light fiberglass racing currachs brought in for the occasion were rented out to a series of regattas throughout the summer, and it took a great feat of driving to collect the four scattered currachs and bring them to Bofin in time for the races. The regatta itself—carefully timed so as not to interfere with the ferry voyages—drew a fair crowd of a few dozen spectators. Mostly locals, but also longtime visitors, day-trippers, and summer workers gathered on the pier to watch the races, cheer on their friends or relations, and comment on the relative abilities, techniques, and tactics of the racers. A young couple, one partner a local, one American, sold commemorative T-shirts that had been printed and delivered in the nick of time. Locals also sold confectionary, fizzy drinks, and baked goods from two stands set up on the pier. Marie took photographs all the while, preserving a record that would soon be archived online on her Facebook page.

If designed in part as an attraction for visitors that might generate revenue for the community, the regatta acted de facto as a multigenerational gathering of people from Inishbofin that would not usually see each other all in one place in the course of a normal summer day. The event also presented an excuse for young people from Bofin now living elsewhere to return home and to celebrate a local tradition of seafaring. Old crews reunited, and new ones formed. A father rowed with his daughter, and one young Bofiner who lives in Galway returned to the island to race with his uncle (fig. 6.14). After the customary races of crews of three men, two men, and mixed doubles, the organizers managed to muster

Figure 6.14: Three currachs compete in the Inishbofin Regatta by racing through a course marked by buoys with the Old Barracks looming behind (August 2016).

enough young men from Bofin to do a final race of three men crews in an under-sixteen division. This final race was a highlight for the local spectators, who had made the effort to encourage the more uncertain boys and commended them for doing so well despite limited experience. The young men's female peers cheered, but at least one felt slighted that there was no matching enthusiasm to promote an under-sixteen women's division. As a revitalized event, there was no force of tradition cementing the regatta to a particular series of events or a time in the year. Even in 2016, there were some initial doubts that the boats could be gathered in time, the event sufficiently publicized, and the weather, community, and visitors sufficiently amenable. The regatta was a challenge of navigating complex logistics and social and weather contingency. Festivals, whether buttressed by tradition or not, are opportunities for correspondence and coherence. The capacity of such events to generate communal feeling is based in part on the contingency of those moments of coordination—the fact that they might go awry in so many ways for so many reasons.

The Maritime Festival was organized as an event weekend to attract visitors, but it also acted as an excuse for both resident and formerly resident islanders to gather together to celebrate and to reproduce pride and skill in traditional maritime practices among a younger generation of islanders. In both regards, the Maritime Festival was successful, and subsequent initiatives have enhanced participation and interest in traditional maritime skills. In 2017, the Inishbofin Community Services Programme won a grant from the Coca-Cola Thank You Fund to pay for the construction of four community currachs to be used in future regattas. A group of local teenagers participated in the construction of one of the currachs, including the young men who rowed in the under-sixteen division in the 2016 regatta. The field of competitors grew in the 2017 regatta, and young Bofiners have gone on to compete successfully at regattas along the coast.

Like the ruined field walls and shearing cottage reclaimed by the sheep-gathering expedition that introduced this book, the oar-propelled currach is infrastructure that has outlasted one taskscape to be incorporated into another. Rowing now is not about fishing or traveling; it is a practice of identity that maintains a link of embodied skill and knowledge connecting young islanders to their predecessors. Sustaining a dwelling taskscape on Inishbofin in the future will mean developing the infrastructure to allow greater year-round employment opportunities, whether that means working remotely or developing attractions to extend the tourist season. Sustainability will also mean finding ways to make heritage relevant, as a source of pride, belonging, and attraction for islanders and visitors. As in the past, the future is made from infrastructure new and old.

SEVEN

THE ENDURING CHALLENGE

INISHARK, AUGUST 26, 2021. GRASS BALL.

This was the largest group I had ever seen going back to Shark to gather sheep. Because of Covid travel restrictions, I did not return to Inishbofin until the end of July 2021, about a month after my friends had gone to Shark to gather and shear the sheep. But a new strategy for managing sheep on the islands meant another trip to Shark had to be organized. When I first started working with Simon, Tommy, and John, they kept breeding ewes on Shark to raise lambs for the market or to replenish their own breeding stock. In subsequent years, they shifted to an alternative strategy: putting only weaned ewe lambs and castrated wethers back to Shark to keep for hoggets. In August 2021, this new strategy required taking every sheep off the island and replacing them with a fresh stock of lambs born the previous spring. This was a major undertaking that required coordinating all the Bofin farmers with sheep on Shark and booking the cargo ferry (typically used to bring freight and livestock between Bofin and the mainland) to sail into Shark's unpredictable landing place.

Unusually, more people were available for the gather than were actually required. Travel restrictions for Covid in 2020–21 actually created circumstances that encouraged some islanders who might otherwise live in Dublin or Galway to return to the island, wait out lockdowns, and work remotely. Tommy and John's niece, Emer, and young nephews, Sean and Dafe, became common fixtures for farmwork in summer 2021. On the day of the gather, I even managed to convince Marie to close the museum shop in the afternoon to come back to Shark with us.

Even with eleven people and four dogs, things could still have gone wrong. A surplus of people can be worse than not enough if we fail to coordinate and communicate. But with our numbers, the younger and less-experienced could take a larger role. A teenage islander, Ryan Coyne, boisterous with energy, took the lead in walking the coastal perimeter of the island.

My two years away from Shark had made slow-rolling changes appear sudden. There were fewer sheep than in previous years, and it was clear in how the grass had encroached on the ruins, swallowing up the traces of those features formerly shrouded in only a thin layer of sod.

The gather was clean enough—just one attempted breakaway was forestalled as the flock neared Shark head. As we funneled the last of the flock through the old break in the wire fencing, a hardy little blackface wether turned and bolted for a gap between the gatherers. We gave ground as he zigged and zagged until he was forced to chance a dash at a losing angle, and I dove and caught him by the fleece of his rump. Even after I carried him through the entrance of the pen, he tried again to break away. We laughed and admired his spirit.

But the entrance to the pen was a problem. The wire fence, bent back and interlaced through itself to stay open, had gone to rust and could not be unwound to close the gap. The cargo ferry had to await high tide to feasibly enter Shark's landing place. Meanwhile, Simon, Tommy, and Marie's brother Pat had to return to Bofin to prepare the lambs that would replace the stock on Shark. So, the younger among us, with some older trusty hands to oversee, were deputized to watch over the flock and mind the gap for the next three hours.

We were an unlikely ensemble. There was Ryan Coyne, then fifteen, grandson to the oldest man on Inishbofin and of his generation among the most eager and able for farm work. (I heard once that as a child, Ryan was asked by a patronizing adult whether he too worked with sheep. His response: "Do you know who I am?") I knew from his participation in our project's community excavations years before that he had a curious and lively mind, and I was impressed in 2021 by his confidence and initiative in working with sheep. Next was Dafe, then twelve, the youngest son of Tommy's sister Ann, who worked remotely with her family on Bofin for the summer. In those months, Dafe became the familiar of his uncles. Whether gathering sheep, dosing cows, giving tours with Tommy, or fishing with John, I'd be sure to find him in the midst of things. Like John, he'd always keep an eye on whether the sea was suitable for fishing and always game. Like Tommy, he'd as soon speak insightfully about Bofin's landscape as analyze a work of nineteenth-century Russian realist painting. And finally there was Zach, twenty-two, Simon's nephew, who grew up on the Swiss/French border and in the years before Covid would return annually to work at his family hotel, Murray's, on Inishbofin. His English accent and facility for French and German caused confusion for visitors to the island, who were unaware of his family links. His eccentric charm and warm energy are legend. He helps out with farming when needed, but his deepest passion and skill are in food culture, from sourcing to preparation to hospitality.

Figure 7.1: Grass ball on Inishark (2021).

We spread ourselves out to surround the sheep and keep them from wandering or splitting. If this had been years ago, the sheep might have strayed into the old Lacey House, where we used to pen them for shearing. But in recent years, that house had finally begun to give way. Only a few weeks earlier, the stubborn roof saw a final storm it could not master and collapsed entirely. For the first hour and more, the sheep were restless and watchful, unnerved by our proximity, their heads up, measuring distances and calculating our attention. At first our group spoke very little as we gathered our strength, grabbed some snacks, checked our phones. I've known each of the lads to a greater or lesser degree for years, but they knew each other only a little. We paced around, trading positions, and by an unspoken mutual consent rotated in and out to mind the gap in the fence. As time wore on, the sheep began to settle and graze. We loosened too and began to chat and joke and tried to reckon the wait ahead of us. It was golden light and clear skies. We could see the passenger ferry hadn't even come in from Cleggan yet, and the cargo ferry was still docked at the old pier on Bofin. With at least an hour to go, a muse struck Ryan with the ingenuity of boredom. As we lamented the lack of a ball, Ryan started pulling handfuls of the dried high grass, curling them around themselves and then tying a knot. If made dense enough, the grass ball flew surprisingly well, though the early prototypes tended to fall apart after a few throws. The final model was like a grass brick, dense and fastened by some twine that Ryan managed to scrounge up. Amazed at its durability and absurdity, we tossed it between us, laughing at what the sheep must be thinking and how Simon would give out if he saw us goofing around. I stopped to take a video to give Simon a laugh later. Zach narrated for him:

"The new generation on Shark here, Uncle Simon, making do with what we have!"

He was joking, but I prayed he hit on some truth. *The four of us had been joined in this spot, brought by the work from our different paths, to find a bit of craic among the ruins and the wait. Zach's comment, even in jest, was an acknowledgment of the group's relationship to each other, the past, and a possible future: a future when "that time with the grass ball back on Shark" might be recited as one in a string of tales and when young people can still imagine Shark, sheep, and craic living in the same sentence. Our shared experience of boredom had become, with a little improvisation with materials at hand, the basis for a sense of belonging that matched the scale of our interdependence in those hours.*

This challenge—to match scopes of belonging to scales of interdependence—is precisely the enduring challenge of community vitality.

―᭓―

ISLAND ENDURANCE

The main aim of this book has been to confront primitivist tropes and to formulate more nuanced analyses of endurance. To pursue this goal, I have adopted a taskscape approach that attends to both logistics and lived experience, both the ecological and phenomenological dynamics of landscapes. Human participation in taskscapes offers opportunities for the perception of temporality and relationality, for the sensing of one's place in the swirl of time, tide, cosmos, and community. Thinking with taskscapes, I have defined heritage expansively to include material things in the landscape, actions that engage those things, and the knowledge and experiences that emerge from those engagements. My archaeological and ethnographic research suggests that heritage in all these forms has fostered articulations between notions of identity, perceptions of belonging, social and political structures, and patterns of subsistence and economy. In short, islanders' creative cultivation, maintenance, and adaptation of heritage has contributed to the vitality and resilience of communities across time. It is precisely the creativity of heritage, its capacity to articulate and resonate with new circumstances, that creates the illusion of timelessness.

Our archaeological analysis focused on the development of the turas associated with St. Leo on Inishark. In the early medieval period, monks designed ritual infrastructure to facilitate certain devotional practices and to buttress their claims to spiritual authority and to laypeople's economic support. As monuments of commemoration, stone huts, cenotaphs, and leachta cultivated a venerable heritage of ascetic devotion, possibly linked St. Leo the Great. A saint cult imbued with papal authority would have afforded Inishark's monastic community a distinct identity within the region. However fanciful, claiming such a heritage may have advantageously positioned the monastery for attracting pilgrims, particularly in the midst of ecclesiastical controversies concerning the authority of Rome. For monks and pilgrims, the gathering, deposition, and manipulation of distinctive stone objects rendered by the action of water evoked the divine forces of creation that governed the natural world. Submission to divine force was essential to the theology of peregrinatio, and encounters with such objects may have highlighted the shared devotional aspiration of monks and pilgrims. Nevertheless, enclosures surrounding ritual complexes meant that monks could monitor and restrict access to pilgrims, likely according to their gender, lifestyle, and economic contribution to the monastery. Cultivating an illustrious heritage and curating occult objects thus allowed Inishark's monastic community to leverage their claim to the labor and produce of affiliated lay clients.

During the twelfth and thirteenth centuries, the construction of a new congregational church and the foundation of a coastal cemetery heightened focus on lay devotion and likely marked the decline of monasticism as the primary organizing principle of settlement on the island. In subsequent centuries, laypeople living on the island and in the surrounding seascape became the primary curators of the island's ecclesiastical heritage. Cromwellian forces may have suppressed or discouraged any residual ecclesiastical community on the island in the mid-seventeenth century. Some monuments may have been destroyed, and others would fall out of use and memory. Nevertheless, ceramic evidence from Clochán Leo and subsequent folklore accounts indicate the endurance of some memory of a saint cult and at least periodic reengagement with early medieval monuments during the seventeenth and eighteenth centuries.

By the end of the eighteenth century, a new village settlement developed on Inishark, whose inhabitants built their houses amid the remnants of the medieval monastery. For most of the nineteenth century, islanders were tenant farmers, left to the whims of a profiteering estate agent, rarely served by Catholic clergy, subject to a callously indifferent British regime, and vulnerable to the caprices of weather, fishing stocks, international trade markets, disease, tragedy, and potato blights. For islanders, visiting St. Leo's monuments for personal devotion or as part of collective rituals provided a means of ensuring spiritual well-being in the midst of dangerous dwelling tasks and in the absence of regular interaction with clergy. Folklore accounts and historic maps suggest that in the first half of the nineteenth century, islanders avoided enclosing turas monuments within household garden plots and maintained stigmas against the destruction of monuments or their misuse to pursue discord. The common accessibility and collective maintenance of turas monuments suggest that islanders perceived them as a kind of commonage of sacred resources from which all could benefit and for which all were responsible. Fear of supernatural punishment or social censure protected this commonage from violation while annual celebrations on St. Leo's Day reiterated villagers' shared devotional heritage. I suggest that the collective maintenance of this ritual commonage facilitated the village's rundale system of cooperative agro-pastoralism, joint tenancy, and common resource management.

Islanders' engagement with turas monuments changed in the late nineteenth and twentieth centuries in response to the enhanced influence of local Catholic authorities and transformations in landholding. Relative to the first century of village settlement, evidence for the destruction and disuse of turas monuments increases from c. 1860 onward. This timing accords with the increased presence of parish priests, resident on Bofin, from the late 1850s onward. The renovation of St. Leo's church in the 1880s introduced a new venue for communal devotion officially sanctioned and surveilled by priests who sought to reassert their role as mediators of the divine. Concurrently, reforms by Catholic landlords sought to dissolve collective holding from the mid-nineteenth century, and household autonomy increased. In the early twentieth century, the actions of the Congested Districts Board made islanders into smallholders and funded the construction of new houses and other infrastructure in the village, which required stone material that turas monuments could supply. In short, the increased presence of priests and the dissolution of rundale meant that the collective curation of turas monuments became less essential for ensuring access to spiritual well-being or reinforcing notions of collectivity within the village.

Nevertheless, reverence for Saint Leo and his feast day endured until the evacuation of the island. Venerations focused primarily on Clochán Leo and Tobar Leo, monuments set along the coast at a distance from houses. Picnics at Clochán Leo, perhaps undertaken alongside Leo's Day celebrations, redeployed the familiar elements of household hospitality in celebrations of collective heritage. Women likely played a leading role in orchestrating these events, which perhaps asserted their role as stewards of social memory, communal harmony, and a devotional heritage that priests could not wholly control.

Throughout the occupation of the modern village, St. Leo's cult and its monuments offered a framework for enacting social coherence. Yet, the process of reiterating communal bonds was neither automatic nor inevitable. The existence of heritage infrastructure alone does not guarantee the maintenance of collective action and shared identity. Opportunities for cohering in convention or collective undertaking are also opportunities for discord and exclusion. Surviving stories about the misuse or weaponization of turas monuments suggest that islanders were aware of these risks and circulated these cautionary tales to mitigate the possibility for divisiveness in this domain. Throughout the occupation of the modern village, maintenance and adaptation of ritual heritage helped Inishark islanders to sustain the village's social viability despite considerable political, economic, and ecological constraints. However, creative use of heritage could not alter those constraints. Lack of government investment and increased living standards and economic opportunities elsewhere in Ireland promoted emigration and eventual resettlement.

In the decades following the evacuation of Inishark, islanders of Inishbofin have developed a bustling, seasonal tourist economy based on extended stays by return visitors. The visibility of the past in the landscape and the continuation of traditional tasks (such as knitting, small farming, boat building, and rowing) provide significant appeal to visitors. Interactions with heritage play an important role in negotiating relationships amid islanders and visitors. For Irish domestic and diasporic visitors who partake in guided walking tours, monuments like St. Colman's Abbey, Cromwell's Barracks, and abandoned cottages stand as metonyms for broader themes in Irish history into which they can situate themselves. However, the local Heritage Museum, Facebook groups, a number of recent publications produced by or in collaboration with islanders, and a cycle of summer festivals provide additional forums for sharing more specific aspects of the islands' heritage with visitors. By fostering shared experience and a sense of belonging among familiar visitors, islanders' curation and presentation of heritage helps to sustain habitual tourism to the island. For islanders, the experience of having grown up, worked, and dwelt on the landscape affords access to more intimate knowledge and exclusive know-how that distinguishes them from even longtime visitors. While the tourist trade is instrumental to maintaining islanders' livelihoods, it also interferes with the logistics of traditional activities, particularly small-scale farming. Nevertheless, islanders' incorporation of heritage activities into primary education and summer festivals reproduces interest and knowledge of heritage among younger islanders, particularly traditional music and rowing. The seasonality and excitement of the tourist trade draws younger islanders back to the island for summer employment, but, with limited wintertime employment, settling on the island to raise a family remains difficult. Sustaining the community in the future will rely on continued creativity and innovation in the business sector; stable "lifeline" subsidies for transportation and community development; investment in healthcare, housing, telecommunications, and green energy infrastructure; and agri-environmental schemes that prioritize the lived experience, local knowledge, and livelihoods of year-round residents.

The years since the completion of my primary fieldwork in 2019 have seen significant developments on Bofin that reinforce and resonate with arguments set forth so far. Before reflecting on the broader implications of this study, I will consider two of these developments: the response to the Covid-19 pandemic and the campaign to return the human remains stolen by Haddon and Dixon from Bofin in 1890 and kept subsequently at Trinity College Dublin.

COVID-19: SOCIAL DISTANCE, SOCIAL INTIMACY, AND REMOTE COMMUNITIES

The onset of the Covid-19 pandemic in Ireland by early 2020 and the enforcement of travel restrictions until late summer obviously interrupted the annual cycle of tourist traffic. Islanders' responses to the pandemic reinforce an important component of my analysis—the role of social media in fostering visitors' bonds of affection for the island and their eagerness to contribute to the maintenance of island heritage.

In spring 2020, the spread of the Covid-19 pandemic in Ireland led to travel restrictions barring nonresidents from visiting Ireland's offshore islands during spring and early summer. While a necessary precaution for communities with many vulnerable elders, the restrictions essentially nullified the island tourist market at what is typically the high season. From March to July, the ferry service continued to run on the normal schedule, but often the crossings carried no more than the crew and occasionally only a handful or less of other locals for running approved errands on the mainland. I was at the time in the United States and relied on social media posts and contact with friends to glean circumstances on the island.

In some ways, the lockdown acted as an extension of the winter off-season in finer weather. Inishbofin Facebook pages—Inishbofin Local News; Inishbofin Island, Co. Galway; and Marie's Heritage Museum page—took on enhanced roles as channels of communication and commemoration for familiar visitors following online. In April, the Inishbofin Island, Co. Galway page began a Bofin Memories series in which they asked followers to submit photographs and short notes about fond memories of previous trips to the island. Almost daily throughout May, the page posted these submissions with the tags #bofinmemories and #lovebofin. Visitors reflected on memorable experiences and activities sometimes spanning decades of visits. They related initial encounters with islanders who became friends and often remarked on how previous visits corresponded with important life events such as pregnancies, wedding engagements, and anniversaries. Most expressed hopes of returning either later that summer or in years to come. The posts resonated with my own experience of reckoning with a year without a visit to Inishbofin and recognizing how annual trips have acted as markers of time, a steady reference point for reflecting on what had changed—with me and with the world—since my first and last visits. Without Bofin, the clock seemed to spin round and round endlessly but never strike midnight.

Meanwhile, islanders developed their own creative project for documenting their experiences of lockdown. Tara McMahon, then the community tourism and marketing officer for the Inishbofin Community Service Programme, coordinated the use of Galway County Art Office funds to commission local filmmaker Kieran Concannon to produce a video series called *Inishbofin in Lockdown*. Filmed in June 2020, the series featured interviews with islanders well known to familiar visitors, including Tommy Burke; Marie Coyne; James Coyne, at the time the island's eldest man; musician Kevin Abeyta; and the operators of the major hotels and services on the island. The ten-part video series, which premiered piecemeal online in late 2020 and early 2021, is an artifact addressed both inward and outward and forward and backward. The interviews document for islanders and for the outside world the experiences of a very particular moment in time, which the interviewees themselves consider retrospectively, in the broader history of what islanders have endured and, prospectively, in the hope of better days to come.

Of course, for islanders, travel restrictions meant not just sacrificing social interactions but also a significant cut in income. Islanders found themselves suddenly in fair weather with time on their hands to turn to tasks that lose priority in the bustle of the tourist season. In response to these conditions, Marie launched the Inishbofin Island Work Fund through GoFundMe (an online fundraising platform). Initially published on the Heritage Museum's Facebook page and shared by other Inishbofin pages, the fund swiftly raised more than ten thousand Euros toward public area projects on the island. A new Inishbofin Island Work Fund page then documented progress on work projects that the fund supported. Notably, some of the more visible and larger scale projects involved maintenance or renovation work focused on heritage monuments. This began with the repainting of one of the early nineteenth-century navigation towers used to orient the approach of ships into the harbor. A larger group of islanders joined in to reinforce an area of the inner harbor that includes the remnants of a barking pan. The monument, which typically features in walking tours destined for the Old Barracks, consists of a large iron pan encased within a brick kiln. In the late nineteenth and early twentieth centuries, islanders used the pan to heat a chemical solution derived in part from tree bark. Sails and fishing nets would be soaked in the solution to weatherproof them. The massive storms of 2014 had destabilized the brick work of the kiln and shattered the adjacent stone wall that lined the edge of the harbor. Islanders stabilized the enclosure wall, cleared residual debris, and laid a new brick-tiled pavement and drainage feature to mitigate further erosion. Islanders also used the time of the lockdown to tidy the older part of the cemetery around St. Colman's Church. This included refurbishing early twentieth-century graves of kin and neighbors. Cement grave platforms were cleared of vegetation and their fixtures repainted. In a nod to an older tradition, islanders have also taken to removing the mass-produced gravel that adorned twentieth-century graves and replacing it with freshly gathered beach pebbles.

The Inishbofin Island Work Fund, on a small scale, demonstrates the integration of heritage maintenance and the tourist economy. Funds from online donations, offered by visitors, supported small public work projects that became forums for islanders to collaborate in the maintenance of heritage monuments. Those monuments, experienced in the digital and physical landscape, evoke aspects of the past that center islanders' identities and buttress perceptions of Bofin as a refuge of traditional Irish culture. Ironically, but fittingly for the Covid era, these engagements with heritage have been generated and propagated through twenty-first-century social media. Heritage, as I have argued, can serve as an infrastructure for commemoration and the generation of belonging across the bounds of different social categories. As a medium for sharing and commemorating experience, the internet has facilitated the maintenance of bonds between islanders and visitors, a kind of remote community accustomed to extended periods of separation.

Covid did not wholly obliterate the 2020 season. Mitigation efforts had sufficiently reduced transmission rates nationally that the Irish government loosened travel restrictions sooner than planned, and Inishbofin opened to visitors in July. The tourist season, abbreviated and adapted to Covid mitigation policies, boomed with visitors from within Ireland. Return visitors rushed to get their dose of Bofin while many others, unable to travel abroad, found their way to the island for the first time. Covid restrictions meant masks, extra cleanings for service staff, extra turnover work for those letting self-service cottages, limited capacities, and, almost unfathomably, no traditional music sessions in the pubs.

By spring 2021, Ireland's mass vaccination program had picked up pace, and Inishbofin opened for a full tourist season, albeit with continued restrictions on indoor dining and enhanced public hygiene protocols in place. Outdoor seating in the pubs allowed for some glimmers of pre-Covid craic. Inishbofin's success in the tourist trade has relied in large part on islanders' capacity to foster social intimacy with outsiders. Infectious diseases taint with collective risk those gatherings where belonging is born. The craic that Bofin is so famous for relies on those extended sessions of physical proximity among familiars and strangers in the pub. The craic is in ordering a round of drinks for your comrades and carrying every glass back to your table all at once while contorting your body to navigate the nonexistent gaps in the crowd. It's cupping your hand and practically yelling into the ear of the person next to you to pass a punch line or the latest gossip through the roar of the chatter and the drive of the music. It's in cutting short a conversation by sudden mutual consent when a masterful voice hushes the pub to rapt attention with the opening lines of a song. It's in hearing an old local story you might never have heard if you hadn't lingered as the crowd dwindled and just happened to be with the right teller at the right time. And it's seeing someone the next morning, the next week, the next year, and remembering you had shared the experience together. The years ahead may see continued disruption from Covid's variants or other pandemics, but islanders have endured by creating new ways to find resonance.

The pandemic also heightened the prospect of remote working from the island as a feasible option. Travel restrictions and the growth of Zoom meant that many islanders, usually based in Galway or Dublin, could return to the island during 2020–21 for longer stretches than usual. Wi-Fi on the island remains variable and unpredictable, but some islanders have updated the capacity of their homes, and the Community Centre and National School have facilities for remote working. Should remote working become more accessible on the island and remain a normal practice, it would potentially allow islanders—particularly younger islanders—to resettle on the island throughout the year. However, this would also require greater accessibility to housing, particularly for young families. Planning permission for new constructions is difficult to obtain on the island, and houses that come up for sale most frequently go to wealthy outsiders who can afford island real estate prices. Remote working, therefore, is not a simple fix but a development that will rely on addressing other stumbling blocks that prevent islanders from remaining on the island. As we saw in chapter 6 and in the opening to this chapter, there is no shortage of young people who love the island and its heritage and might find a way, given support, to enhance the vibrancy and vitality of the community.

THE RETURN: ANCESTRY, HERITAGE, AND COMMUNITIES OF CARE

Another major development in the early 2020s put Inishbofin in the news and at the center of debate concerning the curation of human remains within museum and university contexts. I have alluded already in this book to the thirteen crania stolen from St. Colman's Abbey on Inishbofin by Haddon and Dixon in 1890. The story of the campaign to return the remains to Inishbofin is long and complex and deserves a more detailed account, particularly by others more instrumental in the process, than I could possibly muster here. This brief commentary will consider how the repatriation of the remains reflects the current contours of debate concerning the relationship of Ireland to indigeneity and decolonizing practice (Hussain et al. 2025). Such debates, however seemingly theoretical, have important implications for how heritage legislation reckons the rightful stewardship of human remains from anthropological and archaeological collections. In particular, the episode demonstrates the need for new discussions and new policies that reserve a role for local stakeholders in determining the curation of archaeological materials.

The research of Ciarán Walsh, a freelance writer and curator, was initially responsible for drawing renewed attention to the presence of the Inishbofin crania as well as the remains of eleven other individuals from St. Finian's Bay (Co. Kerry) and the Aran Islands (Co. Galway) within the Haddon-Dixon collection at the Old Anatomy Department at Trinity College Dublin (TCD). In 2012, Ciarán and Marie Coyne made contact online and began investigating the whereabouts of the crania and requesting their repatriation. The campaign grew over the years, with New York University anthropologist, filmmaker, and Inishbofin descendant Pegi Vail joining Coyne and Walsh to write the first official request to the Provost's Office of TCD for the return of the human remains in December 2020. Soon after, in February 2021, a follow-up letter to the Provost's Office from the newly formed Haddon Dixon Repatriation Project was signed by Coyne, Walsh, Vail, journalist and poet Cathy Galvin, and community representatives from Inishmore and St. Finian's / the Glenn. The campaign continued to grow in 2022 through the additional efforts of anthropologists Fiona Murphy and Ivana Ivasiuc. Walsh's blog (curator.ie) and accounts in the *Irish Examiner* (Walsh 2023b), the *Irish Echo* (Vail 2023), and the *Anthropological Journal of European Cultures* (Vail 2023a, Walsh 2023c) summarize the blow-by-blow of the campaign's interactions with representatives of various bodies within Trinity, procedural hurdles, and the final reinterment of the remains. Remarkably, efforts to return the skulls owe their success in part to the Black Lives Matter movement. Senior academics within TCD began to acknowledge the request for repatriation only in 2020, following in the wake of the murder of George Floyd and the massive public protests demanding a reckoning for institutions historically implicated in colonialism, slavery, and the perpetuation of racism. As Walsh saw it, "After that point, we became part of an international movement demanding that universities and museums deal with their colonial legacies" (Walsh 2023b).

Although TCD had repatriated *toi moko*, the preserved heads of Māori individuals, to Te Papa, the National Museum of New Zealand, in 2009, this did not act as precedent for decisive action in the case of the Inishbofin remains. The Old Anatomy Steering Committee, a sub-committee of the School of Medicine at TCD, manages the Old Anatomy Museum's collection of human remains. This collection, acquired between the eighteenth and twentieth centuries, comprises more than 484 human remains from around the world, including Burma, Nigeria, Thailand, New Zealand, South Africa, Australia, and numerous Pacific Islands (Hussain et al. 2022, 2). In August 2022, the Old Anatomy Steering Committee sent a letter to representatives of the Haddon Dixon Repatriation project that outlined their rationale for rejecting the return of the Inishbofin remains. Setting aside the ethical stance of retaining materials acquired through theft, the argument provided for the rejection was both methodologically and theoretically flawed. The letter cited the radiocarbon analysis of a single sample from the collection, which yielded a date range between 1509 and 1660 CE, with a median probability of 1563. This date, the letter implied, was sufficiently distant to nullify islanders' claim for repatriation. "The resulting findings do not indicate any genealogical link to living individuals or related peoples, hence the crania are from unknown individuals. Indeed, we cannot even assume they are of Irish origin" (Hennessy et al. 2022).

While there is no reason to doubt the validity of the radiocarbon result, there is likewise no reason to assume the date of a single sample would reflect the date of the collection as a whole. Oral history preserved on Bofin recalls that until the early twentieth century, skulls disturbed while grave digging in the crowded cemetery would be removed to St. Colman's Church to prevent their destruction during new inhumations (Walsh 2022). As such, the remains stolen by Haddon and Dixon are likely to have accumulated piecemeal from various different original burial locations throughout the cemetery. The unsampled cranial fragments within the collection were liable to have been either more ancient or more recent. If the latter, there might well have been discernible genealogical links with islanders today. However, this could have been ascertained only through DNA extraction (a destructive analysis that might fail to yield sufficient genetic material) and subsequent comparison with reference samples of contemporary islanders. The letter, in short, established impossible criteria for the crania's deaccession: the only valid basis for return would be to demonstrate genetic descent through a destructive analysis that the Steering Committee deemed likely to fail and unwilling to consider. This framing, in my opinion, poisoned the process to follow. It foreclosed the potential for a collaborative discussion, in which islanders would have had an opportunity to consider options for additional study prior to reburial. Instead, scientific analysis was presented solely as a means of contesting the community's claim.

Fortunately, the letter from the Old Anatomy Steering Committee would not be the final word on the matter. In November 2022, members of the newly minted Trinity Colonial Legacies Project, including Mobeen Hussain, Ciarán

O'Neill, and Patrick Walsh, held a public meeting on Inishbofin. They struck a very different tone from the letter and outlined a process that might eventually lead to the return of the remains. They presented a draft report that detailed the provenance of the crania as material taken without consent from Inishbofin and considered the comparative context of recent cases in which museums and universities had returned materials from their collections to communities of origin (Hussain et al. 2022). Unfortunately, the extraordinary and incontrovertible documentation of theft—essentially Haddon bragging to himself in his own diary—existed for the Inishbofin crania but not for other human remains collected by Haddon and Dixon. Given these circumstances, the Board of TCD—the de facto governing authority of the University—would first consider the fate of only the Inishbofin remains and leave the fate of the rest of the Haddon-Dixon collection for future consideration.

The meeting on Inishbofin elicited both renewed hope and frustration among islanders and representatives of the Haddon Dixon Repatriation Project. On the one hand, the Trinity Colonial Legacies Project had officially recognized the theft of the crania and were soliciting public input that might lead to their return. On the other hand, the process imposed a new hurdle and overturned initial optimism that the Board of TCD would consider the entire Haddon-Dixon collection for repatriation all at once. In the following weeks, a petition signed by nearly the entire population of Inishbofin demanded a return of the Bofin remains without further evidence. Marie Coyne, who led with characteristic passion and a hyperextended patience, promoted the campaign online and through the press. Pegi Vail set up a second petition on Change.org that circulated on the Inishbofin Heritage Museum and Inishbofin Descendants Facebook page and garnered 948 signatures, with members of the Inishbofin diaspora in America well represented. The American Anthropological Association and the European Association of Social Anthropologists likewise submitted letters in support of repatriation. In January 2023 the Board of TCD decided to return the remains and announced the decision in February. Members of Trinity Colonial Legacies remained in contact with islanders and the Haddon Dixon Repatriation Project to navigate the final legal hurdles and to facilitate the transfer of the remains.

On July 16, 2023, exactly 133 years after their theft from St. Colman's Church, the skulls were reburied on Inishbofin. The reburial ceremony, widely covered in the press, adapted and embellished the traditional choreography of Bofin funerals. A carpenter from the island, Christopher Day, built a traditional pinewood coffin with wood slats to hold the crania. The remains arrived by boat and remained in the new Saint Colman's Church overnight before a brief service on the day of reburial. As usual, the coffin was carried on the shoulders of teams of four that rotated in and out along the procession from the new church to the graveyard. For the first time in living memory, one of those teams of four consisted entirely of women: Marie Coyne, Bridget Cunnane, Veronica Cunnane, and Tuuli Rantala. The reburial location had been selected weeks earlier in the new wing of the graveyard to avoid disturbing earlier interments. By a gift of chance, the next available plot stood in perfect alignment with the medieval church. One standing at the head of the new grave can look directly east through gaps in the ruined walls of the church and see the niche from which the skulls were taken (fig. 7.2).

Lacking obvious precedent in the history of Ireland, the campaign for repatriation was long and trying. Although return and reburial has provided a degree of closure for some, the process has raised more questions than it could answer. Most obviously, the Old Anatomy Museum retains the remains of eleven other individuals in the Haddon-Dixon collection, taken from St. Finian's Bay and the Aran Islands, but without the contemporaneous diary entries explicitly documenting theft. This should not forestall ongoing discussions of repatriation. Haddon's diary entry for Inishbofin establishes a modus operandi of clandestine theft. Moreover, we must consider—as the Haddon Dixon Repatriation Project has argued all along (Walsh 2023c)—that definitive provenance of theft is not necessary for local communities to claim repatriation. The case of the Bofin crania raised a fundamental question that citizens of Ireland, archaeologists, anthropologists, and legislators must ask themselves: how do we reckon the weight of stakeholder claims to stewardship over human remains from archaeological or anthropological contexts?

A recurring element of the debate about the Bofin crania was determining which legal framework applied to them (Walsh 2023b). On what grounds could anyone claim stewardship of the remains? The Steering Committee's letter of August 2022 implied that demonstrable genealogical descent would be necessary for islanders to reclaim the crania. Alternatively, understanding islanders today and in 1890 as an indigenous community would confer a right to repatriation under the United Nations Declaration of the Rights of Indigenous Peoples. Because the Haddon-Dixon collection came to Trinity before the foundation of the Irish State, the crania did not fall under the remit of the National Museum of Ireland. Yet, in different situations—for example, a contemporary licensed excavation or a chance find—skeletal material from more than one hundred years ago could be claimed by the National Museum of Ireland as archaeological objects and retained in their collections on behalf of the state as part of a shared national patrimony.

How does one begin to adjudicate between these competing frameworks? From my perspective, demonstrating shared ancestry through genetic descent

Figure 7.2: The new grave for the returned remains on Inishbofin (2023). Topped by quartz pebbles, the grave points east toward the ruined medieval church and the niche from which they were stolen in 1890.

should not be necessary for local stakeholders to claim a say in the stewardship of human remains from archaeological or anthropological collections. Across human history, ancestry, kinship, and relatedness has been configured and understood in various ways that may or may not resonate with contemporary scientific understandings of genetics (Brück and Frieman 2021). Moreover, identifying direct ancestry through DNA analysis becomes increasingly problematic after six generations of separation from archaeological remains. In the case of islands specifically, the privileged focus on genetic descent risks reproducing the old trope that islanders represent an isolated population, if not atavistic race, genealogically distinct from the rest of Ireland.

In our own letter submitted during the public consultation process in December 2022, my colleagues and I argued in favor of repatriation, but not on the grounds of indigeneity or probable genealogical links. Instead, we argued that islanders today represented the living members of a community of care that had venerated and safeguarded the site of St. Colman's Abbey across more than one thousand years of history. Significantly, this is not a declaration of timeless tradition, genetic ancestry, or indigenous status. Although mortuary practices and religious beliefs no doubt changed throughout this time, there is good archaeological and historical evidence to demonstrate that people living on Inishbofin, across various phases of settlement and immigration, have revered the ruins of St. Colman's Abbey and developed their customs of burial and commemoration from the precedents of their forebears. This book has attempted to outline a path that wends between the twinned simplicities of timeless persistence and invented traditions. Forms of endurance are almost inevitably dynamic. But this observation does not nullify the possibility of identifying significant threads of continuity across time. The transmission of heritage and respect through reiterative engagements with the past are the threads of continuity that can stretch a community of care across centuries.

Debates over the stewardship of human and artifactual remains will only become more frequent in the years to come: not only as university and museum collections come under greater public scrutiny but also as the rate of coastal erosion threatens both known and unknown burial grounds along the Irish seaboard. New legal guidelines and theoretical frameworks are needed. On what grounds can legislation assess claims that certain stakeholders in Ireland—such as descendant communities or traditional communities of care—should have greater influence on the treatment of archaeological materials, human or otherwise? In what cases, if any, might the National Museum's authority to hold archaeological materials as national patrimony yield to the claims of a traditional community of care?

There are models from around the world for confronting these issues and decolonizing collections. These include repatriation processes that incorporate community-approved research activities conducted in advance of reburial (Gibbon et al. 2023). Recent Black feminist scholarship in bioarchaeology provides another guide, one that elevates the perspectives of stakeholders and researchers from within historically marginalized communities and questions the absolute hegemony of traditional frameworks of scientific knowledge, historically rooted in colonialism and racism (Lans 2021). To the extent it is possible, attempts to restore dignity and humanity to individuals kept as specimens can benefit from interventions that incorporate the interests, artwork, and other creative expressions of affiliated communities (McKittrick 2010; Lans 2021). Crucially, these interventions can supplement and enrich—rather than wholly supplant—scientific analyses.

As argued in chapter 2, the experiences and legacies of colonialism in Ireland are both similar to and notably different from other areas outside Europe. Models from other contexts will likely require adaptation in their application to Ireland. My only certainty is that navigating these challenges will require greater collaboration and transparency among stakeholders, anthropologists, archaeologists, institutions, and policymakers. In June 2023, the Department of Tourism, Culture, Arts, Gaeltacht, Sport and Media convened a committee to advise government on the restitution and repatriation of cultural heritage. Unfortunately, the first meeting of the committee in December 2023 failed to include a single representative of an Irish claimant community, as was initially promised in a press release for the committee's formation in June 2023. In a sad irony, the only members of the committee that could reflect on their experience of the return of the remains to Inishbofin were representatives of Trinity College Dublin.

I would hope that this book, if it shows nothing else, shows how community collaboration and engagement with local traditional knowledge can enhance interdisciplinary research. Collaboration ought not to be restricted to the investigation of heritage but should extend to the creation and revision of heritage policy. Otherwise, scholars, universities, and museums, no matter how well intended, will only ever offer partnerships and possibilities bound by frameworks that stakeholders and descendant communities had no hand in devising.

THREE THOUGHTS AT THE CLOSE

In this final section, I will highlight three ideas that emanate from the research in this book. Rather than conclusive statements, I offer these points as frameworks for posing additional questions or addressing new challenges: heritage is creative; posthumanist premises can address human problems through collaboration; community endurance relies on matching scopes of belonging to scales of interdependence.

HERITAGE IS CREATIVE

This is the most essential point I have sought to make. As discussed in chapter 2, primitivist tropes, emanating from a variety of intellectual traditions, have long informed scholarly and popular accounts of apparent long-term continuities of practice among indigenous or colonized groups. As Inishark and Inishbofin clearly illustrate, persistent traditions can look like primitive stasis only if they are viewed in isolation of the wider social, political, economic, and ecological contexts in which they have been enfolded. I have adopted a taskscape approach to reinstate those contexts and to explore how superficially similar interactions with monuments may afford very different patterns of lived experience and dwelling. It is precisely the creative flexibility of heritage that generates the illusion of timelessness. By tracing correlated variation in ritual and dwelling practices on Inishark, this study has demonstrated how different people created, developed, and adapted monuments to cultivate different perceptions of the past and of social affinity and hierarchy in different historical contexts. This analysis not only demonstrates the foolishness of primitivist tropes but also makes an essential point: engagements with heritage can foster social reproduction as well as innovation. That is, maintenance of heritage need not inevitably foster the preservation of a status quo. Instead, selective maintenance, creative adaptation, or recontextualization of heritage can actually enable social transformation. The creativity of heritage is particularly clear in how villagers on Inishark adapted a turas tradition with medieval antecedents to shifting community dynamics and landholding patterns in the nineteenth and twentieth centuries. It is also clear in how islanders of Inishbofin have developed heritage tourism and utilized social media to foster durable social relations and perceptions of belonging that extends beyond those living on the island.

POSTHUMANIST PREMISES, HUMAN PROBLEMS, AND THE NECESSITY OF COLLABORATION

In this study, I have followed the suggestions of Barad (2007) and Cipolla (2018) that posthumanist premises may have some pragmatic value in addressing human problems. Moreover, I have followed other scholars in recognizing that the central posthumanist premises of relationality and other-than-human agency are inherent to or latent in other intellectual traditions, particularly some indigenous perspectives and threads of ecological anthropology (Cajete 2000; Ingold 2012; Kelechi Ugwuanyi 2020, 266–67; Todd 2016). I suggest that the utility of taskscape lies in allowing analysts to shift focus between posthumanist relationality and humanistic empathy for individual lived experience. This shifting perspective, I contend, is necessary to avoid an intellectual pitfall of posthumanism: comprehensive big-picture analyses that risk downplaying structures of political inequality and erasing the experiences of marginalized people. This theoretical proposition comes with an obvious methodological implication: a dedication to multidisciplinary research and collaboration among a broad sweep of stakeholders.

In this study, I have sought to maintain a shifting focus by considering dwelling taskscapes (tasks of human dwelling) in relation to broader taskscapes of the "becoming of the world as a whole." The *task* in taskscape wavers analytical attention in useful ways. For one, it forces us to confront questions of logistics, labor, and experience: What work is necessary to maintain the livelihood of settlements? Who is doing that work, why, and what are its bodily consequences? How does such work generate or hinge on experiences of enchantment, commemoration, belonging, coercion, or conflict? Answering these questions means confronting how social formations and means of livelihood, whether premised on hierarchy or collectivity, might be experienced, upheld, and transformed. Meanwhile, when *task* is applied to the actions of other-than-human forces, materials, and life forms, it encourages us to view the becoming of the world from alternative positions that may be wholly foreign to or unmoved by human experience. Taskscape connotes a world constantly in motion, in growth, and in decay, a dynamic system of interactions that can be both recalcitrant and responsive to human action and intent.

Scholarship, policymaking, and planning could benefit from exploring the productive tension between posthumanist relationality and humanist attention to lived experience. Taskscape could serve as a useful framework for developing, assessing, and implementing agri-environmental schemes that seek to promote biodiversity, rural livelihoods, and heritage conservation on islands. As I have tried to demonstrate, the shifting perspective of taskscape can help to elucidate what is at stake—ecologically, politically, economically, and culturally—when charting the future of human-environment interactions. We must always ask: who is liable to be the hen, who the pig, and who the corncrake?

To answer those questions requires more than good theory. In the last chapter, I described a core skill in sheep gathering as the capacity to imagine the world from multiple perspectives simultaneously and to orchestrate human-animal-environment interactions with sensitivity and responsiveness. Scholars and policymakers should likewise strive for this capacity to move between multiple perspectives and coordinate with diverse partners. That skill can come only through practice and repeated, open-ended engagement among others with very different fields of experience and expertise. This not only includes researchers working across multiple disciplines in the humanities and sciences. Collaboration must also center the traditional knowledge and future aspirations of islanders as those with both the most intimate experience of island taskscapes and the most at stake in their continued vitality.

SCOPES OF BELONGING AND SCALES OF INTERDEPENDENCE

I have undertaken this study in the hope that some of its findings might have utility beyond the realm of individual academic disciplines. This hope was staked in the potential of long-term, local histories to shed light on fundamental human challenges. There is something to be learned from histories at once grand and granular, macro-scalar in time-depth and micro-scalar in geographic focus. To fulfill this promise requires interdisciplinary, collaborative research that can combine the material remnants of the past and the knowledge, perspectives, and concerns of people in the present. Echoes of the past and voices in the present can create quite a polyphony, and I have tried to listen for both harmonies and dissonances. The histories of Inishark and Inishbofin enrich the comparative context for understanding the prospects of heritage to foster sustainability among small, historically marginalized communities. In particular, the character of heritage tourism on Inishbofin may provide a model for other island or small rural communities. Locally curated engagements with tangible and intangible heritage provide a means of cultivating respect, shared experience, and belonging among visitors and can potentially foster patterns of habitual tourism that enliven local heritage and sustain local communities. Research that combines archaeology, participant observation, and community collaboration could play a role in enriching heritage tourism where it exists and developing its prospects elsewhere. Assessing the potential of this model in new settings would require attention to specific local conditions and necessarily lies beyond the compass of this book. As such, I will conclude by remarking on a more general observation: the importance of thinking about heritage and sustainability in terms of scopes of belonging and scales of interdependence.

This observation emerges from my analysis of the modern village settlement on Inishark and contemporary tourism on Inishbofin. In the case of the former, I suggested that the cultivation of the turas tradition as a kind of ritual commonage and shared heritage fostered collective action among islanders. Adaptation of that heritage in the later nineteenth century may have been influenced in part by a need to adjust to the expectations of a new Catholic landlord and local priests, authorities to whom islanders were subject. However successful the cultivation of heritage was in negotiating collaborative relationships on a local scale, it could not alter broader structural conditions and inequalities that marginalized islanders and that eventually compelled the evacuation of the island. The local scope of belonging and collective action fostered by heritage did not match the scale of islanders' need for investment from a national government. In contrast, in the case of Inishbofin today, I have argued that the pattern of habitual tourism is sustained in part because sharing heritage fosters a sense of belonging that extends to familiar visitors. In other words, the capacity of heritage to foster community sustainability relies in part on matching scopes of belonging to scales of political, economic, and logistical interdependence.

This observation points to a concept of sustainability that models the articulations between lived experience, political relations, and means of livelihood. As discussed in chapter 2, the notion of imagined communities and the invention of tradition have centered attention on how people cultivate heritage to define boundaries of shared identity and political integration, often opposed to some *other*. Heritage, for this reason, is notoriously susceptible to political opportunists who configure the past to constrict the scope of belonging, often sowing division, fear, and suspicion to enable their rise to power. The political, public health, and ecological challenges of the present era require almost the exact inversion of this process of cultivating heritage to divide, suppress, and rule. At the macro scale, catastrophic climate change demands a response unprecedented in terms of the global scale of cooperation and collective action. Theoretically, such a response might require a similarly unprecedented perception of shared heritage, vulnerability, and belonging, the scope of which includes fellow humans, animals, plants, and environments across the world. Indeed, some posthumanist theorists (e.g., Bennet 2010, vii–xiii) hope that notions of relationality and material vibrancy will foster less anthropocentric, more conservationist mentalities. Yet, among other factors, the unequal distribution of vulnerability to and perception of climate change and the entrenched political influence of those profiting from the fossil fuel industry has forestalled any substantial response (Klein 2015).

This juxtaposition of the great challenges of our time with the history of the islands is not, I hope, wholly ridiculous. Indeed, the juxtaposition reaffirms the necessity of forefronting lived experience and inequality alongside relationality when contemplating models of sustainability. On Inishark and Inishbofin, I have argued that perceptions of heritage emanate from engagement with landscapes and built environments, in the context of both daily and periodic activities. I have stressed islanders' creativity in configuring their heritage to make socially feasible—on a limited local scale—the interactions and economic exchanges necessary to maintain their livelihoods. The sustainability of social groups relies in part on matching scopes of belonging to scales of interdependence. This is the enduring challenge of sustainability. It is perhaps too obvious that it warrants to be repeated and said plain. Coordinated and collective action requires a matching framework of belonging. Yet, this study supports an equally essential corollary: structures of political economic inequality and ideology shape our capacities for imagining shared belonging. As we have seen on the islands, those who control access to and knowledge about heritage monuments—whether monks, laypeople, priests, tourists, or archaeologists—can shape narratives of the past and their ideological implications in the present. Any initiative that forefronts heritage as a means of cultivating more inclusive perceptions of belonging must recognize how fundamentally existing inequalities and old lies about human difference are bound to each other. The Irish, at one time, were among the victims of these lies, the fables about racial primitivism and innate incapacity that have served to justify so much colonial violence and its ongoing legacies around the world. Posthumanism attempts to erode another kind of deceit about human exceptionalism that pandemics and climate change reveal as folly. To create more just and sustainable futures means repudiating these deceptions and exploring alternative stories about our shared history, agency, and vulnerability, among many other life forms, elements, and forces that comprise the world. We need new kinds of ensembles, new ways of cultivating a shared resonance of being and belonging.

Bibliography

Aalen, F. H. A., K. Whelan, and Matthew Stout, eds. 2011. *Atlas of the Irish Rural Landscape*. Second edition. Cork: Cork University Press.

Agbe-Davies, A. S. 2015. *Tobacco, Pipes, and Race in Colonial Virginia: Little Tubes of Mighty Power*. New York: Routledge.

Anderson, E., A. Bakier, and E. Wickens. 2015. "Rural Tourism Development in Connemara, Ireland." *Tourism Planning & Development* 12 (1): 73–86.

Anderson, B. 2006 [1983]. *Imagined Communities: Reflections on the Origin and Spread of Nationalism*. Revised Edition. London: Verso.

Anderson, M. O., and A. O. Anderson, eds. 1991. *Adomnan's Life of Columba*. New edition. Oxford, UK; New York: Oxford University Press.

Antczak, K. A., and M. C. Beaudry. 2019. "Assemblages of Practice. A Conceptual Framework for Exploring Human–Thing Relations in Archaeology." *Archaeological Dialogues* 26 (2): 87–110.

Appadurai, A., ed. 1986. *The Social Life of Things: Commodities in Cultural Perspective*. Cambridge, UK: Cambridge University Press.

Appuhamilage, U. M. H. 2017. "A Fluid Ambiguity: Individual, Dividual and Personhood." *Asia Pacific Journal of Anthropology* 18 (1): 1–17.

Arensberg, C., and S. T. Kimball. 2001 [1940]. *Family and Community in Ireland* (3rd edition). Ennis, Ireland: Clasp.

Ashley, S. 2001. "The Poetics of Race in 1890s Ireland: An Ethnography of the Aran Islands." *Patterns of Prejudice* 35 (2): 5–18.

Ashwood, L., and M. M. Bell. 2017. "Affect and Taste: Bourdieu, Traditional Music, and the Performance of Possibilities." *Sociologia Ruralis* 57: 622–40.

Atalay, S., and C. A. Hastorf. 2006. "Food, Meals, and Daily Activities: Food Habitus at Neolithic Çatalhöyük." *American Antiquity* 71 (2): 283–319.

Barad, K. 2007. *Meeting the Universe Halfway: Quantum Physics and the Entanglement of Matter and Meaning*. Durham, NC: Duke University Press.

Basso, K. 1996. *Wisdom Sits in Places: Landscape and Language among the Western Apache*. Albuquerque: University of New Mexico Press.

Beaudry, M. C. 2010. "Privy to the Feast. Eighty to Supper Tonight." In *Table Settings. The Material Culture and Social Context of Dining, AD 1700–1900*, edited by J. Symonds, 62–79. Oxford, UK: Oxbow Books.

Beck, R. A., and J. A. Brown. 2011. "Political Economy and the Routinization of Religious Movements: A View from the Eastern Woodlands: Political Economy and Routinization." *Archeological Papers of the American Anthropological Association* 21 (1): 72–88.

Beck, R. A., L. A. Newsom, C. B. Rodning, and D. G. Moore. 2017. "Spaces of Entanglement: Labor and Construction Practice at Fort San Juan de Joara." *Historical Archaeology* 51 (2): 167–93.

Bell, J., and M. Watson. 2008. *A History of Irish Farming, 1750–1950*. Dublin: Four Courts.

Belliggiano, A., L. Bindi, and C. Ievoli. 2021. "Walking the Sheeptrack. Rural Tourism, Ecomuseums, and Bio-Cultural Heritage." *Sustainability* 13 (16): 8870.

Bindi, L. 2022. "Transhumance Is the New Black: Fragile Rangelands and Local Regeneration." In *Grazing Communities: Pastoralism on the Move and Biocultural Heritage Frictions*, edited by L. Bindi, 149–73. Studies in Environmental Anthropology and Ethnobiology 29. New York: Berghahn.

Bennett, J. 2001. *The Enchantment of Modern Life: Attachments, Crossings, and Ethics*. Princeton, NJ: Princeton University Press.

———. 2009. *Vibrant Matter: A Political Ecology of Things*. Durham, NC: Duke University Press.

Bhreathnach, E. 2014. *Ireland in the Medieval World, AD 400–1000: Landscape, Kingship and Religion*. Dublin: Four Courts.

Bishop, H. J. 2016. "Classifications of Sacred Space: A New Understanding of Mass Rock Sites in Ireland." *International Journal of Historical Archaeology* 20 (4): 828–72.

Bitel, L. M. 1996. *Land of Women: Tales of Sex and Gender from Early Ireland*. Ithaca, NY: Cornell University Press.

Blakey, M. L. 1987. "Skull Doctors: Intrinsic Social and Political Bias in the History of American Physical Anthropology; with Special Reference to the Work of Ales Hrdlicka." *Critique of Anthropology* 7: 7–35.

———. 2020. "Archaeology under the Blinding Light of Race." *Current Anthropology* 61 (S22): S183–S197.

Boas, F. 1912. "Changes in the Bodily Form of Descendants of Immigrants." *American Anthropologist* 14 (3): 530–62.

Bourke, C. 2020. *The Early Medieval Hand-Bells of Ireland and Britain*. Dublin: Wordwell.

Bourke, E., A. R. Hayden, and A. Lynch, eds. 2011. *Skellig Michael, Co. Kerry: The Monastery and South Peak: Archaeological Stratigraphic Report: Excavations 1986–2010*. Dublin: Department of Arts, Heritage and the Gaeltacht.

Bradley, R. 1987. "Time Regained: The Creation of Continuity." *Journal of the British Archaeological Association* 140 (1): 1–17.
Brady, T. F. 1873. *Boffin and Shark Islands, Distress, 1873*. Dublin: Alexander Thom.
Brenneman, W. L., and M. G. Brenneman. 1995. *Crossing the Circle at the Holy Wells of Ireland*. Charlottesville: University Press of Virginia.
Brighton, S. A., and J. M. Levon White. 2006. "Teacups, Saucers and Dinner Plates: English Ceramic Exports to Ballykilcline." *Unearthing Hidden Ireland: Historical Archaeology at Ballykilcline, County Roscommon*, edited by C. E. Orser Jr., 109–39. Bray, Ireland: Wordwell.
Browne, C. R. 1893. "The Ethnography of Inishbofin and Inishark, County Galway." *Proceedings of the Royal Irish Academy* (1889–1901) 3: 317–70.
Brück, J., and C. J. Frieman. 2021. "Making Kin: The Archaeology and Genetics of Human Relationships." *Journal for Technology Assessment in Theory and Practice* 30 (2): 47–52.
Butler, J. 2015. "Paganism in Ireland: Syncretic Processes, Identity, and a Sense of Place." In *Modern Pagan and Native Movements in Europe: Colonial and Nationalist Impulses*, edited by K. Rountree, 196–215. Oxford, UK: Berghahn.
Byrne, A., R. Edmonson, and T. Varley. 2001. "Arsenberg and Kimball and Anthropological Research in Ireland: Introduction to the Third Edition." In *Family and Community in Ireland*, 1–101. Ennis, Ireland: Clasp.
Cajete, G. 2000. *Native Science: Natural Laws of Interdependence*. Santa Fe, NM: Clear Light.
Campbell, E., and A. Maldonado. 2017. "New Discoveries from Iona." Keynote Lecture. Peopling Insular Art: Practice, Performance, Perception. 8th International Insular Art Conference. University of Glasgow. July 11, 2017.
Campbell, E., and A. Maldonado. 2020. "A New Jerusalem 'At the Ends of the Earth': Interpreting Charles Thomas's Excavations at Iona Abbey 1956–63." *Antiquaries Journal* 100: 33–85.
Canny, N. 1988. *Kingdom and Colony: Ireland in the Atlantic World*. Baltimore, MD: Johns Hopkins University Press.
Capes, H. M. 1912. *The Life and Letters of Father Bertrand Wilberforce of the Order of Preachers*. London: Sands.
Carden, R. 2023. "The Animal Bones: Inishgort, Co. Galway (10E0399 Ext.)." Unpublished Archaeological Report.
Carew, M. 2018. *The Quest for the Irish Celt: The Harvard Archaeological Mission to Ireland, 1932–1936*. Newbridge, Ireland: Irish Academic Press.
Carey, J. 1998. *King of Mysteries: Early Irish Religious Writings*. Dublin: Four Courts.
Carleton, W. 1862. *Traits and Stories of the Irish Peasantry*. Dublin: W. Curry, Jr. and Company.
Carrol, C. & P. King, eds. 2003. *Ireland and Postcolonial Theory*. South Bend, IN: Notre Dame University Press.
Carroll, M.P. 1999. *Irish Pilgrimage: Holy Wells and Popular Catholic Devotion*. Baltimore, MD: JHU Press.

Cashman, R., T. Mould, and P. Shukla. 2011. "Introduction: The Individual and Tradition." In *Individual and Tradition: Folkloristic Perspectives*, edited by R. Cashman, T. Mould, and P. Shukla, 1–26. Bloomington: Indiana University Press.

Catlin, K. A., and D. J. Bolender. 2018. "Were the Vikings Really Green? Environmental Degradation and Social Inequality in Iceland's *Second Nature* Landscape." In *Uneven Terrain: Archaeologies of Political Ecology*, edited by J. K. Millhauser, C. T. Morehart, and S. Juarez, 120–33. Archaeological Papers of the American Anthropological Association.

Charles-Edwards, T. 1976. "The Social Background to Irish Peregrinatio." *Celtica* 11: 43–59.

———. 1993. "Palladius, Prosper, and Leo the Great: Mission and Primatial Authority." In *Saint Patrick A.D. 493–1993. Studies in Celtic History 13*, edited by D. N. Dumville and L. Abrams, 1–12. Woodbridge, UK: Boydell.

———. 2000. *Early Christian Ireland*. Cambridge, UK: Cambridge University Press.

Chase, A. F., and V. Scarborough. 2014. "Diversity, Resiliency, and IHOPE-Maya: Using the Past to Inform the Present." *Archeological Papers of the American Anthropological Association* 24 (1): 1–10.

Cheer, J. M. and K. J. Reeves. 2015. "Colonial Heritage and Tourism: Ethnic Landscape Perspectives." *Journal of Heritage Tourism* 10 (2): 151–66.

Cipolla, C. N. 2018. "Earth Flows and Lively Stone. What Differences Does 'Vibrant' Matter Make?" *Archaeological Dialogues* 25 (01): 49–70.

Cipolla, C., R. J. Crellin, and O. J. T. Harris. 2022. "Posthuman Archaeologies, Archaeological Posthumanisms." *Journal of Posthumanism* 1 (1): 5–21.

Clancy, M. 2011. "Re-Presenting Ireland: Tourism, Branding and National Identity in Ireland." *Journal of International Relations and Development* 14 (3): 281–308.

Clark, B., and A. Horning. 2019. "Introduction to a Global Dialogue on Collaborative Archaeology." *Archaeologies: Journal of the World Archaeological Congress* 15 (3): 343–51.

Coleman, S. 2002. "Do You Believe in Pilgrimage?: Communitas, Contestation and Beyond." *Anthropological Theory* 2 (3): 355–68.

Collins, T. 2019. "Space and Place: Archaeologies of Female Monasticism in Later Medieval Ireland." In *Gender in Medieval Places, Spaces and Thresholds*, edited by Victoria Blud, Diane Heath, and Einat Klafter, 25–44. London: School of Advanced Study, University of London.

———. 2021. *Female Monasticism in Medieval Ireland: An Archaeology*. Cork, Ireland: Cork University Press.

Collis, J. R. 2017. "Celts Ancient and Modern: Recent Controversies in Celtic Studies." *Studia Celtica Fennica* 14: 58–71.

Colwell, C. 2016. "Collaborative Archaeologies and Descendant Communities." *Annual Review of Anthropology* 45 (1): 113–27.

Colwell-Chanthaphonh, C., T. J. Ferguson, D. Lippert, R. H. McGuire, G. P. Nicholas, J. E. Watkins, and L. J. Zimmerman. 2010. "The Premise and Promise of Indigenous Archaeology." *American Antiquity* 75 (2): 228–38.

Concannon, K. (ed.) 1997. *Inishbofin through Time and Tide*. Inishbofin, Ireland: Inishbofin Community Centre.

Concannon, K. (dir.) 2007. *Inis Airc - Bás Oileáin (Inishark - death of an island)*. Galway: C-Board Films.

Connerton, P. 1989. *How Societies Remember*. Cambridge, UK: Cambridge University Press.

Connolly, J. 1917. *Labour in Ireland: Labour in Irish History: The Re-Conquest of Ireland*. Dublin: Maunsel.

Connolly, S., and J.-M. Picard. 1987. "Cogitosus's 'Life of St Brigit' Content and Value." *Journal of the Royal Society of Antiquaries of Ireland* 117: 5–27.

Conway, M. 2019. "A Choice to Engage: Selective Marginality and Dynamic Households on the 18th-19th Century Irish Coast." Unpublished Doctoral Dissertation. University of South Carolina.

Coombe, R. J. 2009. "The Expanding Purview of Cultural Properties and Their Politics." *Annual Review of Law and Social Science* 5 (1): 393–412.

Corlett, C. 1998. "The Prehistoric Ritual Landscape of Croagh Patrick, Co. Mayo." *Journal of Irish Archaeology* 9: 9–26.

———. 2012. "Cursing Stones in Ireland." *Journal of the Galway Archaeological and Historical Society* 64: 1–20.

———. 2014. "The Early Church in Umhall, West Mayo." In *The Church in Early Medieval Ireland in Light of Recent Archaeological Excavations*, edited by C. Corlett and M. Potterton, 39–92. Dublin: Wordwell.

Corlett, C., and M. Potterton, eds. 2014. *The Church in Early Medieval Ireland in Light of Recent Archaeological Excavations*. Dublin: Wordwell.

Corning, C. 2016. "Columbanus and the Easter Controversy: Theological, Social and Political Contexts." In *The Irish in Early Medieval Europe: Identity, Culture and Religion*, edited by R. Flechner and S. Meeder, 101–15. London: Palgrave.

Costanza, R., L. Graumlich, and W. L. Steffen. 2007. *Sustainability or Collapse?: An Integrated History and Future of People on Earth*. Boston, MA: MIT Press.

Costello, E. 2017. "Liminal Learning: Social Practice in Seasonal Settlements of Western Ireland." *Journal of Social Archaeology* 17 (2): 188–209.

———. 2020. *Transhumance and the Making of Ireland's Uplands, 1550–1900*. Woodbridge, UK: Boydell.

Cotter, C. 2014. "The Finds." In *High Island (Ardoileán), Co. Galway. Excavation of an Early Medieval Monastery*, edited by G. Scally, 140–63. Dublin: Wordwell.

Couey, L. M. 2018. "A Shifting Island Landscape: Changes in Land Use and Daily Life in the 19th and 20th century Village of Inishark, Co. Galway, Ireland." Unpublished MA thesis. University of Denver.

Coyne, M., ed. 2008. *St Colman's Abbey and Cemetery Inishbofin*. Inishbofin, Ireland: Inishbofin Development Company, Limited.

Crellin, R. 2020. *Change and Archaeology*. London: Routledge.
Crellin, R. J., C. Cipolla, L. Montgomery, O. J. T. Harris, and S. Moore. 2021. *Archaeological Theory in Dialogue: Situating Relationality, Ontology, Posthumanism and Indigenous Paradigms*. London: Routledge.
Croker, T. C. 1824. *Researches in the South of Ireland, Illustrative of the Scenery, Architectural Remains, and the Manners and Superstitions of the Peasantry. With an Appendix, Containing a Private Narrative of the Rebellion of 1798*. Dublin: John Murray.
Crowley, E. 2017. "The Rural Environment Protection Scheme (REPS): The Site of a Symbolic Struggle over Knowledge." In *Irish Ethnologies*, edited by D. Ó Giolláin, 111–25. South Bend, IN: University of Notre Dame Press.
Cunningham, D. J., and A. C. Haddon. 1891. "The Anthropometric Laboratory of Ireland." *Journal of the Anthropological Institute* 21: 35–39.
Dailey, E. T. 2015. "To Choose One Easter from Three: Oswiu's Decision and the Northumbrian Synod of AD 664." *Peritia* 26: 47–64.
Daltun, E. 2022. *An Irish Atlantic Rainforest: A Personal Journey into the Magic of Rewilding*. Dublin: Hachette Books Ireland.
Davis, R. 2000. *The Book of Pontiffs (Liber Pontificalis): The Ancient Biographies of the First Ninety Roman Bishops to AD 715*. Liverpool, UK: Liverpool University Press.
Delanda, M. 2006. *A New Philosophy of Society: Assemblage Theory and Social Complexity*. New York: Continuum.
Delay, C. 2023. "Women, Childbirth Customs and Authority in Ireland, 1850–1930." *Lilith: A Feminist Journal* 21: 6–18.
Deleuze, G., and F. Guattari. 1987. *A Thousand Plateaus: Capitalism and Schizophrenia*. Brian Massumi, trans. 2nd edition. Minneapolis: University of Minnesota Press.
DeMarrais, E., L. J. Castillo, and T. Earle. 1996. "Ideology, Materialization, and Power Strategies." *Current Anthropology* 37 (1): 15–31.
Dillon, P. 2003. *The Much-Lamented Death of Madam Geneva: The Eighteenth-Century Gin Craze*. Boston, MA: Justin, Charles & Co.
Doherty, C. 1985. "The Monastic Town in Early Medieval Ireland." In *The Comparative History of Urban Origins in Non-Roman Europe* (British Archaeological Reports International series 255), edited by H. B. Clarke and A. Simms, 45–75. Oxford, UK: British Archaeological Reports.
Donkersloot, R., and C. Menzies. 2015. "Place-Based Fishing Livelihoods and the Global Ocean: The Irish Pelagic Fleet at Home and Abroad." *Maritime Studies* 14: 1–19.
Dornan, B. 2000. *Mayo's Lost Islands: The Inishkeas*. Dublin: Four Courts.
Douglass, F. 1854. "The Claims of the Negro Ethnographically Considered." [Rochester, NY: Lee, Mann & Co] Retrieved from the Library of Congress, October 4, 2021: https://www.loc.gov/item/a17001155/.

Dowd, M. 2018. "Saintly Associations with Caves in Ireland from the Early Medieval Period (AD 400–1169) through to Recent Times." In *Caves and Ritual in Medieval Europe, AD 500–1500*, edited by K. A. Bergsvik and M. Dowd, 116–32. Oxford, UK: Oxbow.

Draper, N. 2013. "'Dependent on Precarious Subsistences': Ireland's Slave-Owners at the Time of Emancipation." *Britain and the World* 6 (2): 220–42.

Dumville, D. N. 1976. "Echtrae and Immram: Some Problems of Definition." *Ériu* 27: 73–94.

Duncan, E. "The Irish and Their Books." In *The Irish in Early Medieval Europe: Identity, Culture and Religion*, edited by R. Flechner and S. Meeder, 214–30. London: Palgrave.

Dunlop, R. 1913. *Ireland under the Commonwealth: Being a Selection of Documents Relating to the Government of Ireland from 1651 to 1659*. Manchester, UK: Sherratt and Hughes.

Dwyer, E. 2009. "Peripheral People and Places: An Archaeology of Isolation." In *Ireland and Britain in the Atlantic World: Irish Post-Medieval Archaeology Group Proceedings 2*, edited by A. Horning and N. Brannon, 131–42. Dublin: Wordwell.

Eade, J., and M. J. Sallnow, eds. 1991. *Contesting the Sacred: The Anthropology of Christian Pilgrimage*. London: Routledge.

Egan, K. M., and F. E. Murphy. 2015. "Honored Ancestors, Difficult Legacies: The Stability, Decline, and Re-Emergence of Anthropologies in and of Ireland." *American Anthropologist* 117 (1): 134–42.

Estes, N. *Our History Is the Future: Standing Rock versus the Dakota Access Pipeline, and the Long Tradition of Indigenous Resistance*. London: Verso.

Etchingham, C. 1991. "The Early Irish Church: Some Observations on Pastoral Care and Dues." *Ériu* 42: 99–118.

———. 1993. "The Implications of Paruchia." *Ériu* 44: 139–62.

———. 1999. *Church Organisation in Ireland, A.D. 650 to 1000*. Maynooth, Ireland: Laigin Publications.

———. 2006. "Pastoral Provision in the First Millennium: A Two-tier Service?" In *The Parish in Medieval and Post-Medieval Ireland*, edited by E. Fitzpatrick and R. Gillespie, 79–80. Dublin: Fourt Courts.

Evans, E. E. 1939. "Some Survivals of the Irish Open Field System." *Geography* 24 (1): 24–36.

———. 1973. *The Personality of Ireland. Habitat, Heritage and History*. Cambridge, UK: Cambridge University Press.

———. 2000 [1957]. *Irish Folk Ways*. North Chelmsford, MA: Courier Corporation.

Evans, G. 1999. "Emyr Estyn Evans." Edited by M. Stout, J. A. Atkinson, I. Banks, and J. O'Sullivan. *Ulster Journal of Archaeology* 58: 134–42.

Fallon, B. 1999. *An Age of Innocence: Irish Culture, 1930–1960*. Dublin: Gill & Macmillan.

Feehan, J. 2012. "The Potato: Root of the Famine." In *Atlas of the Great Irish Famine*, edited by J. Crowley, W. J. Smyth, and M. Murphy, 28–40. Cork, Ireland: Cork University Press.

Ferguson, S. 1853. "Clonmacnoise, Clare, and Arran. Part I." *Dublin University Magazine* 41: 91.

———. 1879. "On the Ceremonial Turn, Called 'desiul.'" *Proceedings of the Royal Irish Academy* 1: 355–64.

Ferrando, F. 2019. *Philosophical Posthumanism*. London: Bloomsbury.

Fitzgerald, H. 2019. "Caring for Place, Constructing Common Worlds." *Building Material* 22: 137–62.

Fitzpatrick, E. 2006. "The Material World of the Parish." In *The Parish in Medieval and Post-Medieval Ireland*, edited by E. Fitzpatrick and R. Gillespie, 62–78. Dublin: Four Courts.

Flaherty, E. 2014. "Assessing the Distribution of Social-Ecological Resilience and Risk: Ireland as a Case Study of the Uneven Impact of Famine." *Ecological Complexity* 19 (September): 35–45.

———. 2015. "Rundale and 19th Century Irish Settlement: System, Space, and Genealogy." *Irish Geography* 48 (2): 3–38

Flanagan, M. T. 2010. *The Transformation of the Irish Church in the Twelfth and Thirteenth Centuries*. Rochester, NY: Boydell & Brewer.

Flannery, E. 2007. "Irish Cultural Studies and Postcolonial Theory." *Postcolonial Text* 3 (3): 1–9.

Flechner, R. 2017. "Identifying Monks in Early Medieval Britain and Ireland: A Reflection on Legal and Economic Aspects." *Atti delle Settimane di Studio Centro italiano di Studi sull'alto medioevo* 64: 805–44.

Forester, T., trans. Additional notes by T. Wright. 2000. *Giraldus Cambrensis: The Topography of Ireland*. Cambridge, Ontario: In Parentheses.

Forsythe, W. 2006. "The Archaeology of the Kelp Industry in the Northern Islands of Ireland." *International Journal of Nautical Archaeology* 35 (2): 218–29.

Fowler, E., and P. J. Fowler. 1988. "Excavations on Tòrr an Aba, Iona, Argyll." *Proceedings of the Society of Antiquaries of Scotland* 118: 181–201.

Fowles, S. 2010. "The Southwest School of Landscape Archaeology." *Annual Review of Anthropology* 39 (1): 453–68.

———. 2016. "The Perfect Subject (Postcolonial Object Studies)." *Journal of Material Culture* 21 (1): 9–27.

Franklin, M. 2020. "Enslaved Household Variability and Plantation Life and Labor in Colonial Virginia." *International Journal of Historical Archaeology* 24: 115–55.

Franklin, M., and N. Lee. 2019. "Revitalizing Tradition and Instigating Change: Foodways at the Ransom and Sarah Williams Farmstead, c. 1871–1905." *Journal of African Diaspora Archaeology and Heritage* 8 (3): 202–25.

Fraser, E. D. G. 2003. "Social Vulnerability and Ecological Fragility: Building Bridges between Social and Natural Sciences Using the Irish Potato Famine as a Case Study." *Conservation Ecology* 7 (2): 9.

French, B. M. 2013. "Ethnography and 'Postconflict' Violence in the Irish Free State." *American Anthropologist* 115 (2): 160–73.

Gaimster, D. 1997. "German Stoneware, 1200–1900: Archaeology and Cultural History." London: British Museum Press.

Gardiner, M. 2011. "Folklore's Timeless Past, Ireland's Present Past, and the Perception of Rural Houses in Early Historic Ireland." *International Journal of Historical Archaeology* 15 (4): 707–24.

Gardiner, M., L. Downey, and S. Ó Síocháin. 2020. "Sustainable Rundale, Runrig, and Northern English Open-Field Historical Farming Systems." *Béaloideas* 88: 101–31.

Gazin-Schwartz, A., and C. Holtorf. 1999. "'As Long as Ever I've Known it...': On Folklore and Archaeology." In *Archaeology and Folklore*, edited by A. Gazin-Schwartz and C. Holtorf, 2–23. New York: Routledge.

Gefreh, T. M. 2017. "Sun of Understanding: The Iconographic Programme of Iona's Free-standing Crosses." In *Islands in a Global Context: Proceedings of the Seventh International Conference on Insular Art*, edited by C. Newman, M. Mannion, and F. Gavin, 75–83. Dublin: Four Courts.

Gibbon, V. E., L. Feris, J. Gretzinger, K. Smith, S. Hall, N. Penn, T. E. M. Mutsvangwa, M. Heale, D. A. Finaughty, Y. W. Karanja, J. Esterhuyse, D. Kotze, N. Barnes, G. Gunston, J. May, J. Krause, C. M. Wilkinson, S. Schiffels, D. Februarie, S. Alves, and J. C. Sealy. 2023. "Confronting Historical Legacies of Biological Anthropology in South Africa—Restitution, Redress, and Community-Centered Science: The Sutherland Nine." *PLoS ONE* 18 (5): 1–23.

Glassie, H. 1993. *Turkish Traditional Art Today*. Bloomington: Indiana University Press.

———. 1995. *Passing the Time in Ballymenone: Culture and History of an Ulster Community*. Bloomington: Indiana University Press.

———. 1999. *Material Culture*. Bloomington: Indiana University Press.

———. 2003. "Tradition." In *Eight Words for the Study of Expressive Culture*, edited by B. Feintuch, 176–97. Urbana: University of Illinois Press.

Gleeson, P. 2012. "Constructing Kingship in Early Medieval Ireland: Power, Place and Ideology." *Medieval Archaeology* 56 (1): 1–33.

Gordillo, G. 2014. *Rubble: The Afterlife of Destruction*. Durham, NC: Duke University Press.

Gore-Booth, H. W. 1891. "The Basking Shark." *Longman's Magazine* 19 (109): 59–70.

Graham, B. J. 1994. "The Search for Common Ground: Estyn Evans's Ireland." *Transactions of the Institute of British Geographers* 19 (2): 183–201.

Grama, E. 2013. *Socialist Heritage: The Politics of Past and Place in Romania*. Bloomington: Indiana University Press.

Gravlee, C. C. 2009. "How Race Becomes Biology: Embodiment of Social Inequality." *American Journal of Biological Anthropology* 139: 47–57.

Gravlee, C. C., H. R. Bernard, and W. R. Leonard. 2003. "Heredity, Environment, and Cranial Form: A Reanalysis of Boas's Immigrant Data." *American Anthropologist* 105 (1): 125–38.

Gray, P. 2021. Was the Great Irish Famine a Colonial Famine? *East/West* 8 (1): 159–72.

Guinnane, T. W., and R. I. Miller. 1997. "The Limits to Land Reform: The Land Acts in Ireland, 1870–1909." *Economic Development & Cultural Change* 45 (3): 591.

Guyader, O. et al. 2013. "Small Scale Fisheries in Europe: A Comparative Analysis Based on a Selection of Case Studies." *Fisheries Research* 140: 1–13.

Haddon, A. C., and C. R. Browne. 1891. "The Ethnography of the Aran Islands, County Galway." *Proceedings of the Royal Irish Academy (1889–1901)* 2: 768–830.

Hadfield, A. and W. Maley, eds. 1997. *A View of the State of Ireland*. Oxford, UK: Blackwell.

Hadley, D. M. 2011. "Late Saxon Burial Practice." In *The Oxford Handbook of Anglo-Saxon Archaeology*, edited by H. Hamerow, D. A. Hinton, and S. Crawford, 288–311. Oxford, UK: Oxford University Press.

Hafstein, V. 2018. *Making Intangible Heritage: El Condor Pasa and Other Stories from UNESCO*. Bloomington: Indiana University Press.

Hall, Samuel C., and Anna M. Hall. 1841. *Ireland: Its Scenery and Character*, Vol 1. London: How & Parsons.

Hamlin, A., and T. R. Kerr. 2008. *The Archaeology of Early Christianity in the North of Ireland*. British Archaeological Reports Series 460. Oxford, UK: Archaeopress.

Handler, J. S., and M. C. Reilly. 2017. "Contesting 'White Slavery' in the Caribbean." *New West Indian Guide / Nieuwe West-Indische Gids* 91 (1–2): 30–55.

Haraway, D. 1988. "Situated Knowledges: The Science Question in Feminism and the Privilege of Partial Perspective." *Feminist Studies* 14 (3): 575–99.

Hardiman, J. 1846. *A Chorographical Description of West or H-Iar Connaught, Written A.D. 1684, by Roderic O'Flaherty, Esq., Author of the "Ogygia." Edited, from a Ms. in the Library of Trinity College, Dublin, with Notes and Illustrations, by James Hardiman, M.R.I.A.* Dublin: Irish Archeological Society.

Hardy, P. D. 1840. *The Holy Wells of Ireland, Containing an Authentic Account of Those Various Places of Pilgrimage and Penance Which Are Still Annually Visited by Thousands of the Roman Catholic Peasantry, with a Minute Description of the Patterns and Stations Periodically Held in Various Districts of Ireland*. Dublin: Hardy and Walker.

Harney, L. 2015–16. "Fasting and Feasting on Irish Church Sites: The Archaeological and Historical Evidence." *Ulster Journal of Archaeology* 73: 182–97.

Harrington, C. 2002. *Women in a Celtic Church: Ireland 450–1150*. 1st edition. Oxford, UK; New York: Oxford University Press.

Harrison, F. V. 2019. "Unraveling 'Race' for the Twenty-First Century." In *Exotic No More: Anthropology for the Contemporary World*, edited by J. MacClancy. Chicago, IL: University of Chicago Press.

Harte, A., and T. Ó Carragáin. 2020. "Land Tenure and Farming in Early Medieval Kerry, AD 400–1100: A Survey of Field Systems in the Lough Currane

Basin." In *Kerry: History and Society*, edited by M. Bric, 25–58. Dublin: Geography Publications.

Hartman, S., A. E. J. Ogilvie, J. Haukur Ingimundarson, A. J. Dugmore, G. Hambrecht, and T. H. McGovern. 2017. "Medieval Iceland, Greenland, and the New Human Condition: A Case Study in Integrated Environmental Humanities." *Global and Planetary Change* 156 (September): 123–39.

Hartnett, A. 2004. "The Politics of the Pipe: Clay Pipes and Tobacco Consumption in Galway, Ireland." *International Journal of Historical Archaeology* 8: 133–47.

Hauser, M. 2015. Materiality as a Problem Space. In *Practicing Materiality*, edited by R. Van Dyke, 196–214. Tucson: University of Arizona Press.

Hayes, G., and E. Kane. 2015. *The Last Blasket King: Padraig O Cathain, An Ri*. Cork, Ireland: Collins.

Hayes, S. 2011. "Gentility in the Dining and Tea Service Practices of Early Colonial Melbourne's 'Established Middle Class.'" *Australian Historical Archaeology* 29: 33–44.

Hennessey, M., M. Gill, and S. Ward. 2022. "Letter to Ciarán Walsh from the Old Anatomy Steering Committee." August 19, 2022.

Heraughty, P. 1982. *Inishmurray: Ancient Monastic Island*. Dublin, Ireland: O'Brien Press.

Herity, M. 1995a. "The Antiquity of An Turas (The Pilgrimage Round) in Ireland." In *Studies in the Layout, Buildings and Art in Stone of Early Irish Monasteries*, edited by M. Herity, 91–143. London: Pindar.

———. 1995b. "Two Hermitages in the Atlantic: Rathlin O'Birne, Donegal, and Caher Island, Mayo." *Journal of the Royal Society of Antiquaries of Ireland* 125: 85–128.

———. 2009. *Ordnance Survey Letters Mayo*. 1st edition. Dublin: Four Masters.

Higgins, J. 1987. *The Early Christian Cross Slabs, Pillar Stones and Related Monuments of County Galway, Ireland*. Oxford, UK: British Archaeological Reports International Series 375.

Hill, P. 1997. *Whithorn and St Ninian: The Excavation of a Monastic Town, 1984–91*. Stroud, UK: Whithorn Trust / Sutton Publishing.

Hobsbawm, E., and T. Ranger. 2012 [1983]. *The Invention of Tradition*. Cambridge, UK: Cambridge University Press.

Hogan, L. 2015. "Debunking the Imagery of the 'Irish Slaves' Meme." *Medium*. September 14, 2015. https://limerick1914.medium.com/the-imagery-of-the-irish-slaves-myth-dissected-143e70aa6e74.

Hogan, L., L. McAtackney, and M. C. Reilly. 2016. "The Irish in the Anglo-Caribbean: Servants or Slaves?" *History Ireland* 24 (2): 18–22.

Holloway, J. 2011. "Material Symbolism and Death: Charcoal Burial in Later Anglo-Saxon England." In *The Oxford Handbook of Anglo-Saxon Archaeology*, edited by H. Hamerow, D. A. Hinton, and S. Crawford, 81–90. Oxford, UK: Oxford University Press.

Holmes, M. 2023. "The 'Lamb of God' in the Early Middle Ages: A Zooarchaeological Perspective." *Journal of Medieval History* 49 (5): 701–10.

Hootan, E. A., and C. W. Dupertuis. 1955. *The Physical Anthropology of Ireland. With a Section on the West Coast Irish Females by Helen Dawson*. Papers of the Peabody Museum of Archaeology and Ethnology, Harvard University Vol. XXX, Nos. 1–2.

Horne, A. E. 1873. "Alleged Destitution in Boffin and Shark Islands." Constabulary Report. House of Commons Parliamentary Papers Online, Clifden.

Horning, A. 2007. "Materiality and Mutable Landscapes: Rethinking Seasonality and Marginality in Rural Ireland." *International Journal of Historical Archaeology* 11 (4): 358–78.

———. 2013. *Ireland in the Virginian Sea: Colonialism in the British Atlantic*. Chapel Hill: University of North Carolina Press.

———. 2017. "Crossing the Battlefield: Archaeology, Nationalism and Practice in Historical Archaeology." In *The Country Where My Heart Is: Historical Archaeology of Nationalism and National Identity*, edited by A. Brooks and N. Mehler, 172–201. Gainesville: University Press of Florida.

Hostetler, M. 1999. "Designing Religious Women: Privacy and Exposure in the *Life of Christina of Markyate and Ancrene Wisse*." *Mediævalia* 22 (2): 201–31.

Hughes, K. 1960. "The Changing Theory and Practice of Irish Pilgrimage." *Journal of Ecclesiastical History* 11 (2): 143–51.

Hull, K. L. 2006. "Forget Me Not: The Role of Women at Ballykilcline." In *Unearthing Hidden Ireland: Historical Archaeology at Ballykilcline, County Roscommon*, edited by C. E. Orser Jr., 140–60. Bray, Ireland: Wordwell.

Hussain, M., C. O'Neill, and P. Walsh. 2022. "Working Paper on Human Remains from Inishbofin held in the Haddon-Dixon collection at TCD." Accessed on January 3, 2024. https://www.tcd.ie/seniordean/legacies/inishbofinTLRWGworkingaper.pdf.

Hussain, M., C. O'Neill, and P. Walsh. 2025. "Trinity's Colonial Legacies. Transparency, Instrumentality, and Agency in an Engaged Research Project." In *Dealing with Complex Heritage: Revisiting University Pasts in Contemporary Practice*, edited by P.B. Larsen, M. Křížová and G. Plets., in press. Edinburgh: Edinburgh University Press.

Ingold, T. 1993. "The Temporality of the Landscape." *World Archaeology* 25 (2): 152–74.

———. 2000. *The Perception of the Environment*. 1st edition. London; New York: Routledge.

———. 2010. "Footprints through the Weather-World: Walking, Breathing, Knowing." *Journal of the Royal Anthropological Institute* 16 (s1): S121–39.

———. 2011. *Being Alive: Essays on Movement, Knowledge and Description*. New York: Routledge.

———. 2012. "Toward an Ecology of Materials." *Annual Review of Anthropology* 41 (1): 427–42.

———. 2013. *Making: Anthropology, Archaeology, Art and Architecture*. 1st edition. New York: Routledge.

———. 2014. "Is There Life Amidst the Ruins?" *Journal of Contemporary Archaeology* 1 (2): 231–35.

———. 2015. *The Life of Lines*. 1st edition. New York: Routledge.

———. 2017. "On human Correspondence." *Journal of the Royal Anthropological Institute* 23 (1): 9–27.

Ireland, C. 1997. "Penance and Prayer in Water: An Irish Practice in Northumbrian Hagiography." *Cambrian Medieval Celtic Studies* 34: 51–66.

Jackson, J. B., J. Müske, and L. Zhang. 2020. "Innovation, Habitus, and Heritage: Modeling the Careers of Cultural Forms through Time." *Journal of Folklore Research* 57 (1): 111–36.

James, S. 1999. *The Atlantic Celts: Ancient People or Modern Invention?* London: British Museum Press.

Johnson, M. 2019. *Archaeological Theory: An Introduction*. New Revised Ed. Oxford, UK: John Wiley & Sons.

Johnson, N. C. 1993. "Building a Nation: An Examination of the Irish Gaeltacht Commission Report of 1926." *Journal of Historical Geography* 19 (2): 157–68.

Johnston, E. 2016. "Exiles from the Edge? The Irish Context of Peregrinatio." In *The Irish in Early Medieval Europe: Identity, Culture and Religion*, edited by R. Flechner and S. Meeder, 39–52. London: Palgrave.

Joyce, R. A. 2004. "Unintended Consequences? Monumentality as a Novel Experience in Formative Mesoamerica." *Journal of Archaeological Method and Theory* 11 (1): 5–29

Kaul, A. R. 2012. *Turning the Tune: Traditional Music, Tourism, and Social Change in an Irish Village*. Dance and Performance Studies 3. Revised Edition. New York: Berghahn.

Kelechi Ugwuanyi, J. 2020. "Human-Nature Offspringing: Indigenous Thoughts on Posthuman Heritage." In *Deterritorializing the Future: Heritage in, of and after the Anthropocene*, edited by R. Harrison and C. Sterling, 266–88. London: Open Humanities.

Kelly, F. 1988. *A Guide to Early Irish Law*. Dublin: Dublin Institute for Advanced Studies.

———. 1997. *Early Irish Farming: A Study Based Mainly on the Law-texts of the 7th and 8th centuries A.D.* Dublin: Dublin Institute for Advanced Studies.

Kelly, H. E., A. A. Kowalsky, and D. E. Kowalsky. 2001. *Spongeware (1835–1935): Makers, Marks, and Patterns*. Atglen, PA: Schiffer.

Kennedy, J. P. 1847. *Digest of Evidence Taken before Her Majesty's Commissioners of Inquiry into the State of Law and Practices in Respect to the Occupation of Land in Ireland*.

Kenney, J. F. 1997. *The Sources for the Early History of Ireland: Ecclesiastical: An Introduction and Guide*. New York: Octagon.

Kinahan, G. 1870. "Notice of the Remains on the Island of Inishark." *Journal of the Royal Society of Antiquaries of Ireland* 1: 203–05.

Kinealy, C., ed. 2013. *Frederick Douglass in Ireland: In His Own Words*, Volume 1. London: Routledge.

Kinmonth, C. 1995. *Irish Country Furniture: 1700–1950*. New Haven, CT: Yale University Press.

Kirshenblatt-Gimblett, B. 1989. "Authoring Lives." *Journal of Folklore Research* 26 (2): 123–49.

———. 1995. "Theorizing Heritage." *Ethnomusicology* 39 (3): 367–80.

———. 2004. "Intangible Heritage as Metacultural Production." *Museum International* 56: 52–65.

Klein, N. 2015. *This Changes Everything: Capitalism vs. the Climate*. Reprint edition. New York: Simon and Schuster.

Knight, P. 1836. *Erris in the Irish Highlands and the Atlantic Railway*. Dublin: M. Keene.

Kohn, E. 2015. "Anthropology of Ontologies." *Annual Review of Anthropology* 44 (1): 311–27.

Kowalsky, A. A., and D. E. Kowalsky. 1999. *Encyclopedia of Marks on American, English, and European Earthenware, Ironstone, Stoneware (1780–1980)*. Atglen, PA: Schiffer.

Kuijt, I., M. Conway, K. Shakour, C. McNeill, and C. Brown. 2015. "Vectors of Improvement: The Material Footprint of Nineteenth- through Twentieth-Century Irish National Policy, Inishark, County Galway, Ireland." *International Journal of Historical Archaeology* 19 (1): 122–58.

Kuijt, I., R. Lash, M. Gibbons, J. Higgins, N. Goodale, and J. O'Neill. 2010. "Reconsidering Early Medieval Seascapes: New Insights from Inis Aire, Co. Galway, Ireland." *Journal of Irish Archaeology* 19: 51–70.

Kuijt, I., R. Lash, W. Donaruma, K. Shakour, and T. Burke. 2015. *Island Places, Island Lives: Exploring Inishbofin and Inishark Heritage, Co. Galway, Ireland*. Dublin: Wordwell.

Kurzwelly, J., N. Rapport, and A. D. Spiegel. 2020. "Encountering, Explaining and Refuting Essentialism." *Anthropology Southern Africa* 43 (2): 65–81.

Lans, A. M. 2021. "Decolonise this Collection: Integrating Black Feminism and Art to Re-Examine Human Skeletal Remains in Museums." *Feminist Anthropology* 2 (1): 130–42.

La Roche, C. J., and M. L. Blakey. 1997. "Seizing Intellectual Power: The Dialogue at the New York African Burial Ground." *Historical Archaeology* 31 (3): 84–106.

Lash, R. 2018a. "Enchantments of Stone: Confronting Other-than-Human Agency in Irish Pilgrimage Practices." *Journal of Social Archaeology* 18 (3): 284–305.

———. 2018b. "Pebbles and Peregrinatio: The Taskscape of Medieval Devotion on Inishark Island, Ireland." *Medieval Archaeology* 62 (1): 83–104.

———. 2019. "Movement, Materials, and Intersubjectivity—Insights from Western Ireland." In *Routledge Handbook to Sensory Archaeology*, edited by J. Day and R. Skeates, 130–48. London: Routledge.

———. 2020. "Leo on the Margins? Reform, Romanesque and the Island Monastery on Inishark, Ireland." *Romanesque Saints and Shrines: Proceedings of the 2016 British Archaeological Association Romanesque Conference*, edited by J. McNeill and R. Plant, 223–34. London: British Archaeological Association.

Lash, R., M. Chesson, E. Alonzi, I. Kuijt, T. O'Hagan, J. Ó Néill, and T. Burke. "Sensational Ensembles: Picnicking and Pilgrimage on Inishark Island, Co. Galway, Ireland, AD 1650–1960." *Current Anthropology* 64 (4): 380–409.

Latour, B. 2007. *Reassembling the Social: An Introduction to Actor-Network-Theory*. Oxford, UK: Oxford University Press.

———. 2014. "Agency at the Time of the Anthropocene." *New Literary History* 45 (1): 1–18.

Launay, R. 2018. *Savages, Romans, and Despots: Thinking about Others from Montaigne to Herder*. Chicago: Chicago University Press.

Li, Y. L., and C. Hunter. 2015. "Community Involvement for Sustainable Heritage Tourism: A Conceptual Model." *Journal of Cultural Heritage Management and Sustainable Development* 5: 248–62.

Liu, J., T. Dietz, S. R. Carpenter, M. Alberti, C. Folke, E. Moran, A. N. Pell, et al. 2007. "Complexity of Coupled Human and Natural Systems." *Science* 317 (5844): 1513–16.

Logan, A. L., and M. Dores Cruz. 2014. "Gendered Taskscapes: Food, Farming, and Craft Production in Banda, Ghana in the Eighteenth to Twenty-First Centuries." *The African Archaeological Review* 31 (2): 203–31.

Lucas, G. 2012. *Understanding the Archaeological Record*. Cambridge, UK: Cambridge University Press.

Macalister, R. A. S. 1949. *The Archaeology of Ireland*. New York: Methuen.

Mac Gabhann, F. 2014. *Logainmneacha Mhaigh Eo 2. Barúntacht Mhuraisce*. Baile Átha Cliath, Éire: Coiscéim.

MacLoughlin, B. 1942. "Material Concerning the Surviving Antiquities of Inish Airc (Inishark)." Irish Folklore Collection, Vol. 838 and 839, Irish Folklore Collection at University College Dublin.

MacLoughlin, D., A. Browne, and C. A. Sullivan. 2020. "The Delivery of Ecosystem Services through Results-Based Agri-environment Payment Schemes (RBPS): Three Irish Case Studies." *Biology and Environment: Proceedings of the Royal Irish Academy* 120B (2): 91–106.

Maddern, C. 2014. "The Cross-Slabs." In *High Island (Ardoileán), Co. Galway: Excavation of an Early Medieval Monastery*, edited by G. Scally, 176–200. Dublin: Wordwell.

Manning, C. 2005. "Rock Shelters and Caves Associated with Irish Saints." In *Above and Beyond: Essays in Memory of Leo Swan*, edited by T. Conduit and C. Corlett, 109–20. Dublin: Wordwell.

Marshall, J. W., and C. Walsh. 2005. *Illaunloughan Island: An Early Medieval Monastery in County Kerry*. Bray, Co. Wicklow: Wordwell.

Marshall, J. W., and G. D. Rourke. 2000. *High Island: An Irish Monastery in the Atlantic*. Dublin: Town House and Country House.

Marshall, Y. 2002. "What Is Community Archaeology?" *World Archaeology* 34 (2): 211–19.

McCarthy, B. 2013. "Monasticism and Its Limits: Rematerialising Monastic Space in Early Medieval Ireland." Unpublished PhD Dissertation. University College Cork.

McCarthy, D. and D. Ó Cróinín. 1987–88. "The 'Lost' 84-year Easter Table Rediscovered." *Peritia* 6–7: 227–42.

McCormick, F. 2008. "The Decline of the Cow: Agricultural and Settlement Change in Early Medieval Ireland." *Peritia* 20: 210–15.

McKittrick, K. 2010. "Science Quarrels Sculpture: The Politics of Reading Sarah Baartman." *Mosaic: A Journal for the Interdisciplinary Study of Literature* 43 (2): 113–30.

Meskell, L. 2020. "Imperialism, Internationalism, and Archaeology in the Un/Making of the Middle East." *American Anthropologist* 122 (3): 554–67.

Meyer, K. 2010. *Betha Colmain Maic Luachain: Life Of Colman Son Of Luachan*. Whitefish, MT: Kessinger Publishing, LLC.

Miller, D., ed. 2005. *Materiality*. Durham, NC: Duke University Press.

Mills, B. J., and W. H. Walker. 2008. *Memory Work: Archaeologies of Material Practices*. Sante Fe, NM: School for Advanced Research Press.

Moore, C. R., and V. D. Thompson. 2012. "Animism and Green River Persistent Places: A Dwelling Perspective of the Shell Mound Archaic." *Journal of Social Archaeology* 12 (2): 264–84.

Moran, G. 1997. "Near Famine: The Crisis in the West of Ireland, 1879–82." *Irish Studies Review* 5 (18): 14–21.

Moran, P. 2014. "High Island and the Cult of Saint Féichín in Connemara." In *High Island (Ardoileán), Co. Galway. Excavation of an Early Medieval Monastery*, edited by G. Scally, 16–27. Dublin: Wordwell.

Moran, P. F. 1907. *Historical Sketch of the Persecutions Suffered by the Catholics of Ireland Under the Rule of Cromwell and the Puritans*. Dublin: M. H. Gill.

Morehart, C. T. 2011. "Sustainable Ecologies and Unsustainable Politics: Chinampa Farming in Ancient Central Mexico." *Anthropology News* 52 (4): 9–10.

Morrissey, J., ed. 2012. *Inishbofin and Inishark, Connemara*. Dublin: Crannog.

Moyle, B. D., W. G. Croy, and B. Weiler. 2010. "Community Perceptions of Tourism: Bruny and Magnetic Islands." *Asia Pacific Journal of Tourist Research* 15 (3): 353–66.

Muhr, K. 1999. "Water Imagery in Early Irish." *Celtica* 23: 193–210.

Munsey, C. 1970. *The Illustrated Guide to Collecting Bottles*. New York: Hawthorn.

Murphy, E. M. 2011. "Children's Burial Grounds in Ireland (Cilliní) and Parental Emotions Toward Infant Death." *International Journal of Historical Archaeology* 15 (3): 409–28.

Murray, E., F. McCormick, and G. Plunkett. 2004. "The Food Economies of Atlantic Island Monasteries: The Documentary and Archaeo-Environmental Evidence." *Environmental Archaeology* 9 (2): 179–88.

Mytum, H. 2010. "An Archaeological Perspective from Rural Nineteenth-Century Pembrokeshire." In *Table Settings: The Material Culture and Social Context of Dining, AD 1700–1900*, edited by J. Symonds, 87–98. Oxford, UK: Oxbow.

———. 2017. "The Role of Historical Archaeology in the Emergence of Nationalist Identities in the Celtic Countries." In *The Country Where My Heart Is: Historical Archaeologies of Nationalism and National Identity*," edited by N. Brooks and N. Mehler, 154–67. Gainesville: University Press of Florida.

Nash, C. 1993. "'Embodying the Nation': The West of Ireland Landscape and Irish Identity." In *Tourism in Ireland: A Critical Analysis*, edited by B. O'Connor and M. Cronin, 86–112. Cork, Ireland: Cork University Press.

Neary, J. 1920. "History of Inishbofin and Inishark." *Irish Ecclesiastical Record* 15: 216–28.

Newman, C. 2011. "The Sacral Landscape of Tara: A Preliminary Exploration." In *Landscapes of Cult and Kingship*, edited by R. Schot, C. Newman, and E. Bhreathnach, 22–43. Dublin: Four Courts.

Ní Chonghaile, D. 2021. *Collecting Music in the Aran Islands: A Century of History and Practice*. Madison: University of Wisconsin Press.

Ní Ghabhláin, S. 2006. "Late Twelfth-Century Church Construction: Evidence of Parish Formation?" In *The Parish in Medieval and Early Modern Ireland*, edited by E. Fitzpatrick and R. Gillespie, 147–68. Dublin: Four Courts.

Nic Craith, M., and U. Kockel. 2016. "(Re-)Building Heritage: Integrating Tangible and Intangible Heritage." In *A Companion to Heritage Studies*, edited by W. Logan, M. Nic Craith, and U. Kockel, 426–42. Oxford, UK: Wiley Blackwell.

Nugent, L. 2020. *Journeys of Faith. Stories of Pilgrimage from Medieval Ireland*. Dublin: Columba.

Nugent, P. 2006. "The Dynamics of Parish Formation in High Medieval and Late Medieval Clare." In *The Parish in Medieval and Early Modern Ireland*, edited by E. Fitzpatrick and R. Gillespie, 172–85. Dublin: Fourt Courts.

Ó Carragáin, T. 2003. "The Architectural Setting of the Cult of Relics in Early Medieval Ireland." *Journal of the Royal Society of Antiquaries of Ireland* 133: 130–76.

———. 2005. "Regional Variation in Irish Pre-Romanesque Architecture." *The Antiquaries Journal* 85: 23–56.

———. 2006. "Church Building and Pastoral Care in Early Medieval Ireland." In *The Parish in Medieval and Post-Medieval Ireland*, edited by E. Fitzpatrick and R. Gillespie, 91–123. Dublin: Fourt Courts.

———. 2007. "Skeuomorphs and Spolia: The Presence of the Past in Irish Pre-Romanesque Architecture." In *Making and Meaning in Insular Art: Proceedings of the Fifth International Conference on Insular Art Held at Trinity College Dublin, 25–28 August 2005*. Dublin: Four Courts.

———. 2009a. "The Architectural Setting of the Mass in Early-Medieval Ireland." *Medieval Archaeology* 53 (1): 119–54.

———. 2009b. "The Saint and the Sacred Centre: The Early Medieval Pilgrimage Landscape of Inishmurray." In *The Archaeology of the Early Medieval Celtic Churches*, edited by N. Edwards, 207–26. New York: Routledge.

———. 2010. *Churches in Early Medieval Ireland: Architecture, Ritual and Memory*. New Haven, CT: Yale University Press.

———. 2013. "The View from the Shore: Perceiving Island Monasteries in Early Medieval Ireland." *Hortus Artium Medievalium* 19: 209–20.

———. 2014. "The Archaeology of Ecclesiastical Estates in Early Medieval Ireland: A Case Study of the Kingdom of Fir Maige." *Peritia* 24–25 (January): 266–312.

———. 2015. "Is There an Archaeology of Lay People at Early Irish Monasteries?" *Bulletin Du Centre D'études Médiévales d'Auxerre* Hors-série No. 8, https://doi.org/10.4000/cem.13620.

———. 2017a. "Altars, Graves and Cenotaphs: Leachta as Foci for Ritual in Early Medieval Ireland." In *Mapping New Territories in Art and Architectural Histories: Essays in Honour of Roger Stalley*, edited by D. O'Donovan, N. Nic Ghabhann, and F. Narkiewicz, 34–52. Turnhout, UK: Brepolis.

———. 2017b. "Vernacular Form, Monastic Practice in the Early Middle Ages: Evidence from Toureen Peakaun." *Anglo-Saxon Studies in Archaeology and History* 20: 67–81.

———. 2021. *Churches in the Irish Landscape, AD 400–1100*. Cork, Ireland: Cork Unversity Press.

Ó Conghaile, D. 2013. "The Role of Market Segmentation in the Future of Tourism Development on Inis Mór." Unpublished MA Dissertation in International Tourism. University of Limerick.

O'Connell, M., and E. Ní Ghráinne. 1994. "Inishbofin: Palaeoecology." In *Clare Island and Inishbofin*. Field Guide No. 17, edited by P. Coxon and M. O'Connell, 61–101. Dublin: Irish Association for Quaternary Studies.

Ó Corráin, D. 1989. "Prehistoric and Early Christian Ireland." In *The Oxford History of Ireland*, edited by R. F. Foster, 1–52. Oxford, UK: Oxford University Press.

Ó Cróinín, D. 2017. *Early Medieval Ireland 400–1200*. Second Edition. London: Routledge.

Ó Crualaoich, G. 2003. *The Book of the Cailleach: Stories of the Wise-Woman Healer*. Cork, Ireland: Cork University Press.

Ó Danachair, C. 1981. "An Rí (The King) an Example of Traditional Social Organisation." *Journal of the Royal Society of Antiquaries of Ireland* 111: 14–28.

Ó Dubda, S., M. Corduff, J. O'Dowd, T. a Búrca, S. Mac Thorcail, P. O. Díscín, B. Ní Chatháin, et al. 1941. "The Cake Dance." *Béaloideas* 11 (1/2): 126–42.

O'Flanagan, M. 1926. "Letters Relating to the Antiquities of the County Mayo Containing Information Collected During the Progress of the Ordnance Survey in 1832, 2 vols." Unpublished typescript, Bray.

Ó Giolláin, D. 2005. "Revisiting the Holy Well." *Éire-Ireland* 40 (1): 11–41.

Ó Gráda, C. 1995. *The Great Irish Famine*. Cambridge, UK: Cambridge University Press.

O'Hagan, T. 2012. "Cill Cáscan and 'De Controversia Paschali': Echoes of Early Medieval Ecclesiastical Controversy in the Irish Landscape." *Trowel* 13: 22–38.

O'Kane, F., and C. O'Neill, eds. 2023. *Ireland, Slavery and the Caribbean: Interdisciplinary Perspectives*. Manchester, UK: Manchester University Press.

Okasha, E., and K. Forsyth. 2001. *Early Christian Inscriptions of Munster: A Corpus of the Inscribed Stones*. Cork, Ireland: Cork University Press.

O'Keeffe, T. 1994. "Omey and the Sands of Time." *Archaeology Ireland* 8 (2): 14–17.

———. 2003. *Romanesque Ireland: Architecture and Ideology in the Twelfth Century by Tadhg O'Keeffe*. Dublin: Four Courts.

———. 2006. "The Built-Environment of Local Community Worship between the Late Eleventh and Early Thirteenth Centuries." In *The Parish in Medieval and Early Modern Ireland*, edited by E. Fitzpatrick and R. Gillespie, 124–46. Dublin: Four Courts.

———. 2023a. "Churches *in antis*: Skeuomorphism and Solomonic Iconography in Early Irish Architecture." *Peritia* 34: 181–210.

———. 2023b. "The Architecture of the *basilicae sanctorum* of the Seventh-Century Armagh and Kildare." *Peritia* 34: 145–80.

Ó Laoire, L. 2007. *On a Rock in the Middle of the Ocean: Songs and Singers in Tory Island*. Indreabhán, Ireland: Cló Iar-Chonnachta.

O'Loughlin, T. 2004. "Perceiving Palestine in Early Christian Ireland: Martyrium, Exegetical Key, Relic and Liturgical Space." *Ériu* 54: 125–37.

O'Meara, J. J. 1981. *Voyage of St Brendan*. Gerrards Cross, UK: Dolmen.

O'Neill, C. 2022. "'Harvard Scientist Seeks Typical Irishman': Measuring the Irish Race 1888–1936." *Radical History Review* 143: 89–108.

Orser, C. E. Jr., ed. 2006. *Unearthing Hidden Ireland: Historical Archaeology at Ballykilcline, County Roscommon*. Bray, Ireland: Wordwell.

Orton, C., P. Tyers, and A. Vince. 1993. *Pottery in Archaeology (Cambridge Manuals in Archaeology)*. Cambridge, UK: Cambridge University Press.

Ostrom, E. 1990. *Governing the Commons: The Evolution of Institutions for Collective Action*. Cambridge, UK: Cambridge University Press.

O'Sullivan, A. 2003. "The Harvard Archaeological Mission and the Politics of the Irish Free State." *Archaeology Ireland* 17 (1): 20–23.

O'Sullivan, A., F. McCormick, T. R. Kerr, and L. Harney. 2014. *Early Medieval Ireland, AD 400–1100: The Evidence from Archaeological Excavations*. Dublin: Royal Irish Academy.

O'Sullivan, J., and T. Ó Carragáin. 2008. *Inishmurray: Monks and Pilgrims in an Atlantic Landscape*. Cork, Ireland: Collins.

Ó Tuathaigh, G. 1991. "The Irish-Ireland Idea: Rationale and Relevance." In *Culture in Ireland: Division or Diversity*, edited by E. Longley, 54–71. Belfast, Ireland: Institute of Irish Studies.

Otway, C. 1839. *A Tour of Connaught*. Dublin: William Curry Jr. and Co.

Pantos, A., and S. Semple. 2004. *Assembly Places and Practices in Medieval Europe*. Dublin: Four Courts.

Patterson, N. et al. 2022. "Large-Scale Migration into Britain during the Middle to Late Bronze Age." *Nature* 601: 588–94.

Petts, D. 2019. "Ecclesiastical Tidescapes: Exploring the Early Medieval Tidal World." *Norwegian Archaeological Review* 52 (1): 41–64.

Picard, J.-M. 2009. "Miles Insulanus. Les Îles Monastiques Irlandaises et L'idéal du Désert Marin." In *Lérins, Une Îles Sainte de l'Antiquité au Moyen Âge*, edited by Y. Coudou and M. Lauwers, 301–17. Turnhout, UK: Brepols.

Plummer, C., ed. 1910. *Vita Sanctorum Hiberniae, Partim Hactenus Ineditae ad Fidem Codicum Manuscriptorum Recognavit Prolegominis Notis Indicibus Instruxit* (2 Vols), Reprinted 1968. Oxford, UK: Clarendon.

Power, M. J., A. Dillane, and E. Devereux. 2017. "'You'll Never Kill Our Will to be Free': Damian Dempsey's 'Colony' as a Critique of Historical and Contemporary Colonialism." *Musicultures* 44 (2): 29–52.

Power, R. 2015. "Walking the Spiritual Ways—West of Ireland Experience of Modern Pilgrimage." *International Journal of Religious Tourism and Pilgrimage* 3 (1): 46–54.

Preucel, R. W. 2010. *Archaeological Semiotics*. 1st edition. Oxford, UK: Wiley-Blackwell.

Quiggins, A. H. 1942. *Haddon the Head Hunter*. Cambridge, UK: Cambridge University Press.

Quinn, C. P., I. Kuijt, N. Goodale, and J. Ó Néill. 2018. "Along the Margins? The Later Bronze Age Seascapes of Western Ireland." *European Journal of Archaeology* (July): 1–23.

Rabinowitz, D. 2010. "Ostrom, the Commons, and the Anthropology of 'Earthlings' and Their Atmosphere." *Focaal* 2010 (57): 104–08.

Rajala, U., and P. Mills, eds. 2017. *Forms of Dwelling: 20 Years of Taskscapes in Archaeology*. 1st edition. Oxford, UK: Oxbow.

Ramos, A. R. 2012. "The Politics of Perspectivism." *Annual Review of Anthropology* 41 (1): 481–94.

Ray, C. 2011. "The Sacred and the Body Politic at Ireland's Holy Wells." *International Social Science Journal* 62 (205–206): 271–85.

———. 2014. *The Origins of Ireland's Holy Wells*. Oxford, UK: Archaeopress Archaeology.

Ray, C., and F. McCormick, eds. "Holy Wells of Ireland: Sacred Realms and Popular Domains." Bloomington: Indiana University Press.

Rebanks, J. 2015. *The Shepherd's Life: A Tale of the Lake District*. London: Penguin.

Richardson, J. 1727. *The Great Folly, Superstition, and Idolatry, of Pilgrimages in Ireland; Especially of That to St. Patrick's Purgatory. Together with an Account of the Loss That the Public Sustaineth Thereby; Truly and Impartially Represented*. Dublin: J. Hyde.

Robin, C. 2006. "Gender, Farming, and Long-Term Change: Maya Historical and Archaeological Perspectives." *Current Anthropology* 47 (3): 409–33.

Robinson, T. 2008. *Connemara: The Last Pool of Darkness.* Dublin: Penguin.

Rodgers, N. 2007. *Ireland, Slavery and Anti-Slavery: 1612–1865.* London: Palgrave Macmillan.

Rolston, B. 2009. "'The Brothers on the Walls': International Solidarity and Irish Political Murals." *Journal of Black Studies* 39 (3): 446–70.

Royle, S. A. 2003. "Exploitation and Celebration of the Heritage of the Irish Islands." *Irish Geography* 36 (1): 23–31.

Ryan, J. 1992. *Irish Monasticism: Origins and Early Development.* Dublin: Four Courts.

Rynne, C. 2000. "The Early Medieval Monastic Watermill." In *High Island: An Irish Monastery in the Atlantic,* edited by J. W. Marshall and G. D. Rourke, 185–213. Dublin: Town House and Country House.

Sackett, J. R. 2021. "Richard Murphy's The God Who Eats Corn: A Colonizer's Critique of British Imperialism in Ireland and Africa." *International Journal of English and Comparative Literary Studies* 2 (3): 1–15.

Said, E. W. 2003. "Afterward: Reflections on Ireland and Postcolonialism." In *Ireland and Postcolonial Theory,* edited by C. Carroll and P. King, 177–85. South Bend, IN: Notre Dame University Press.

———. 2014 [1978]. *Orientalism.* New York: Knopf Doubleday.

Scally, G., ed. 2014. *High Island (Ardoileán), Co. Galway. Excavation of an Early Medieval Monastery.* Dublin: Wordwell.

Scanlon, L. A., and M. S. Kumar. 2019. "Ireland and Irishness: The Contextuality of Postcolonial Identity." *Annals of the American Association of Geographers* 109 (1): 202–22.

Scott, R. E. 2006. "Social Identity in Early Medieval Ireland: A Bioarchaeology of the Early Christian Cemetery on Omey Island, Co. Galway." Unpublished PhD Dissertation. University of Pennsylvania.

Seifert, D. J., E. B. O'Brien, and J. Balicki. 2000. "Mary Ann Hall's First-Class House: The Archaeology of a Capital Brothel." In *The Archaeology of Sexuality,* edited by R. Schmidt and B. Voss, 117–28. London: Routledge.

Semple, S. 2013. *Perceptions of the Prehistoric in Anglo-Saxon England: Religion, Ritual, and Rulership in the Landscape.* Oxford, UK: Oxford University Press.

Seymour, J. D. 1921. *The Puritans in Ireland 1647–1661.* London: Clarendon.

Sharpe, R. 1984. "Some Problems Concerning the Organization of the Church in Early Medieval Ireland." *Peritia* 3 (January): 230–70.

———. 1992. "Churches and Communities in Early Medieval Ireland: Towards a Pastoral Model." In *Pastoral Care before the Parish,* edited by J. Blair and R. Sharpe, 81–109. Leicester, UK: Leicester University Press.

Silliman, S. W. 2014. "Archaeologies of Survivance and Residence: Reflections on the Historical Archaeology of Indigenous People." In *Rethinking Colonial Pasts through Archaeology,* edited by N. Ferris, R. Harrison, and M. Wilcox, 57–75. Gainesville: University Press of Florida.

Sims-Williams, P. 2020. "An Alternative to 'Celtic from the East' and 'Celtic from the West.'" *Cambridge Archaeological Journal* 30 (3): 511–29.

Slater, E., and E. Flaherty. 2009. "Marx on Primitive Communism: The Irish Rundale Agrarian Commune, Its Internal Dynamics and the Metabolic Rift." *Irish Journal of Anthropology* 12 (2): 5–34.

Smith, A. T. 2003. *The Political Landscape: Constellations of Authority in Early Complex Polities*. First edition. Berkeley: University of California Press.

Smyth, M. 1996. *Understanding the Universe in Seventh-Century Ireland*. Woodbridge, UK: Boydell.

Spivak, G. C. 1985. "The Rani of Sirmur: An Essay in Reading the Archives." *History and Theory* 24 (3): 247–72.

———. 2008. *Other Asias*. Hoboken, NJ: Wiley.

Stalley, R. 2014. "Irish Sculpture of the Early Tenth Century and the Work of the 'Muiredach Master': Problems of Identification and Meaning." *Proceedings of the Royal Irish Academy: Archaeology, Culture, History, Literature* 114C: 141–79.

Stancliffe, C. 1982. "Red, White and Blue Martyrdom." In *Ireland in Early Medieval Europe. Studies in Memory of Kathleen Hughes*, edited by D. Whitelock, R. McKitterick, and D. Dumville, 21–46. Cambridge, UK: Cambridge University Press.

Stephens, J. 1872. *Illustrated Handbook of the Scenery and Antiquities of Southwestern Donegal*. Killybegs, Ireland: McGlashan & Gill.

Stevens, P. 2012. "Clonfad—an Industrious Monastery." In *Settlement and Community in the Fir Tulach Kingdom: Archaeological Excavation on the M6 & N52 Road Schemes*, edited by P. Stevens and J. Channing, 109–36. Bray, Ireland: Wordwell.

Stokes, W. 1887. *The Tripartite Life of Patrick* (2 Vols.). London: Eyre and Spottiswoode.

Stout, M. 1996. "Emyr Estyn Evans and Northern Ireland: The Archaeology and Geography of a New State." In *Nationalism in Archaeology*, edited by J. A. Atkinson, I. Banks, and J. O'Sullivan, 111–27. Glasgow, Scotland: Cruithne.

Swift, C. 2003. "Sculptors and Their Customers: A Study of Clonmacnoise Grave-Slabs." In *Clonmacnoise Studies, Volume 2 Seminar Papers 1998*, edited by H. King, 105–23. Dublin: Dublin Stationary Office.

Symonds, J., ed. 2010. *Table Settings: The Material Culture and Social Context of Dining AD 1700–1900*. Oxford, UK: Oxbow.

Synge, J. M. 1966 [1907]. *Collected Works [of] J.M. Synge: Prose*. Oxford, UK: Oxford University Press.

Taylor, L. J. 1995. *Occasions of Faith: An Anthropology of Irish Catholics*. Philadelphia: University of Pennsylvania Press.

Thompson, T. 2004. "The Irish Sí Tradition: Connections Between the Disciplines, and What's in a Word?" *Journal of Archaeological Method and Theory* 11 (4): 335–68.

Thompson, V. 2002. "Constructing Salvation: A Homiletic and Penitential Context for Late Anglo-Saxon Burial Practice." In *Burial in Early Medieval England and Wales*, edited by S. Lucy and A. Reynolds, 229–40. Oxford, UK: Oxbow.

Timothy, D. J., and S. W. Boyd. 2006. "Heritage Tourism in the 21st Century: Valued Traditions and New Perspectives." *Journal of Heritage Tourism* 1 (1): 1–16.

Todd, Z. 2016. "An Indigenous Feminist's Take on the Ontological Turn: 'Ontology' Is Just Another Word for Colonialism." *Journal of Historical Sociology* 29 (1): 4–22.

Trigger, B. G. 1997. *A History of Archaeological Thought*. Cambridge, UK: Cambridge University Press.

Trouillot, M.-R. 1995. *Silencing the Past: Power and the Production of History*. Boston, MA: Beacon.

Turner, V., and E. Turner. 2011. *Image and Pilgrimage in Christian Culture*. New York: Columbia University Press.

Twiss, K. 2012. "The Archaeology of Food and Social Diversity." *Journal of Archaeological Research* 20: 357–95.

Vail, P. 2023a. "The Long Journey Home. Academic Research in the Anthropology of Europe." *Anthropological Journal of European Cultures* Blog. Last modified February 9, 2023. https://ajecblog.berghahnjournals.com/the-long-journey-home.

———. 2023b. "Skulls Return to Inishbofin." *Irish Echo*. July 19, 2023. https://www.irishecho.com/2023/7/skulls-return-to-inishbofin.

Van der Leeuw, S., and C. L. Redman. 2002. "Placing Archaeology at the Center of Socio-Natural Studies." *American Antiquity* 67 (4): 597–605.

Van Dyke, R. M. 2009. "Chaco Reloaded: Discursive Social Memory on the Post-Chacoan Landscape." *Journal of Social Archaeology* 9 (2): 220–48.

———. 2015. "Materiality in Practice: An Introduction." In *Practicing Materiality*, edited by R. M. Van Dyke, 3–32. Tucson: University of Arizona Press.

———. 2019. "Archaeology and Social Memory." *Annual Review of Anthropology* 48 (1): 207–25.

Van Dyke, R. M., and S. E. Alcock, eds. 2003. *Archaeologies of Memory*. 1st edition. Malden, MA: Wiley-Blackwell.

Velie, A. 2008. "The War Cry of the Trickster: The Concept of Survivance in Gerald Vizenor's Bear Island: The War at Sugar Point." In *Survivance: Narratives of Native Presence*, edited by G. Vizenor, 147–62. Lincoln: University of Nebraska Press.

Verkerk, D. H. 2014. "Feed My Sheep: Pastoral Imagery and the Bishop's Calling in Early Ireland." In *Envisioning the Bishop: Images and the Episcopacy in the Middle Ages*, edited by S. Danielson and E. A. Gatti, 157–79. Turnhout, Belgium: Brepols.

Vizenor, G. R. 1998. *Fugitive Poses: Native American Indian Scenes of Absence and Presence*. Lincoln: University of Nebraska Press.

———. 2008. *Survivance: Narratives of Native Presence*. Lincoln: University of Nebraska Press.

Voss, B. L., and R. Allen. 2010. "Guide to Ceramic MNV Calculation. Qualitative and Quantitative Analysis." *Society for Historical Archaeology, Technical Briefs in Historical Archaeology* 5: 1–9.

Walsh, C. 2022. "Don't Kick That Skull or the Dead Will Come After You!" RTE Brainstorm. November 30, 2022. https://www.rte.ie/brainstorm/2021/0825/1242817-ireland-folklore-skulls-human-remains-dead-bodies-graveyard-cemetery.

———. 2023a. *Alfred Cort Haddon: A Very English Savage*. New York: Berghahn.

———. 2023b. "'May They Rest in Peace Forever More': How the Inishbofin Skulls Finally Made It Home." *Irish Examiner*. July 21, 2023.

———. 2023c. "Normalising the Abnormal: Trinity College Dublin Decides What to Do with Its Collection of Stolen Skulls." Academic Research in the Anthropology of Europe / *Anthropological Journal of European Cultures* Blog. February 18, 2023. https://ajecblog.berghahnjournals.com/normalising-the-abnormal-trinity-college-dublin-decides-what-to-do-with-its-collection-of-stolen-skulls.

Walsh, P. 1989. "Cromwell's Barrack: A Commonwealth Garrison Fort on Inishbofin, Co. Galway." *Journal of the Galway Archaeological and Historical Society* 42: 30–71.

Waters, A. M. 2006. *Planning the Past: Heritage Tourism and Post-Colonial Politics at Port Royal*. Lanham, MD: Lexington.

Watts, C., ed. 2013. *Relational Archaeologies: Humans, Animals, Things*. 1st edition. New York: Routledge.

Webster, J. 1999. "Resisting Traditions: Ceramics, Identity, and Consumer Choice in the Outer Hebrides from 1800 to Present." *International Journal of Historical Archaeology* 3 (1): 53–73.

Westropp, T. J. 1911. Part 2. "History and Archaeology." *Proceedings of the Royal Irish Academy. Section C: Archaeology, Celtic Studies, History, Linguistics, Literature* 31: 2.1–2.78.

Whelan, K. 2004. "Reading the Ruins: The Presence of Absence in the Irish Landscape." In *Surveying Ireland's Past: Multidisciplinary Essays in Honour of Anngret Simms*, edited by H. B. Clarke, J. Prunty, and M. Hennessy, 297–328. Dublin: Geography Publications.

———. 2012. "Clacháns: Landscape and Life in Ireland before and after the Famine." In *At the Anvil: Essays in Honour of William J. Smyth*, edited by P. J. Duffy and W. Nolan, 453–75. Dublin: Geography Publications.

———. 2018. *Religion, Landscape & Settlement in Ireland: From Patrick to Present*. Dublin: Four Courts.

White, W. A. III. 2023. *Segregation Made Them Neighbors: An Archaeology of Racialization in Boise, Idaho*. Lincoln: Society for Historical Archaeology / University of Nebraska Press.

Whitelock, D., ed. 1979. *English Historical Documents c. 500–1042, English Historical Documents Vol 1.* Oxford, UK: Oxford University Press.

Whitridge, P. 2004. "Landscapes, Houses, Bodies, Things: 'Place' and the Archaeology of Inuit Imaginaries." *Journal of Archaeological Method and Theory* 11 (2): 213–50.

Wilde, J. F. E. 1888. *Ancient Legends, Mystic Charms, and Superstitions of Ireland: With Sketches of the Irish Past.* Boston, MA: Ticknor and Company.

Willerslev, R. 2004. "Not Animal, Not Not-Animal: Hunting, Imitation and Empathetic Knowledge among the Siberian Yukaghirs." *Journal of the Royal Anthropological Institute* 10 (1): 629–52.

Williams, H. 1997. "Ancient Landscapes and the Dead: The Reuse of Prehistoric and Roman Monuments as Early Anglo-Saxon Burial Sites." *Medieval Archaeology* 41 (1): 1–32.

———. 2006. *Death and Memory in Early Medieval Britain.* Cambridge, UK: Cambridge University Press.

Williams, H., J. Kirton, and M. Gondek. 2015. *Early Medieval Stone Monuments: Materiality, Biography, Landscape.* Rochester, NY: Boydell & Brewer.

Willmott, H., and A. Daubney. 2019. "Of Saints, Sows or Smiths? Copper-Brazed Iron Handbells in Early Medieval England." *Archaeological Journal* 177 (1): 336–55.

Wooding, J. M., ed. 2014. *The Otherworld Voyage in Early Irish Literature: An Anthology of Criticism.* Reprint edition. Dublin: Four Courts.

Woods, N. 2019. "Storm in a Teacup: The Life of a Nineteenth-Century New Zealand Settler Told through Her Tea Ware." *Historical Archaeology* 53: 702–21.

Wright, J. J. 2019. *An Ulster Slave-Owner in the Revolutionary Atlantic: The Life and Letters of John Black.* Dublin: Four Courts.

Yager, T. 2002. "What Was Rundale and Where Did It Come From?" *Béaloideas* 70: 153–86.

Yelling, J. A. 1977. *Common Field and Enclosure in England 1450–1850.* London: MacMillan.

Zacek, N. A. 2023. "How the Irish Became Black." In *Ireland, Slavery and the Caribbean*, edited by F. O'Kane and C. O'Neill. Manchester, UK: Manchester University Press.

Zaitsev, E. A. 1999. "The Meaning of Early Medieval Geometry: From Euclid and Surveyors' Manuals to Christian Philosophy." *Isis* 90 (3): 522–53.

Zhang, R., and L. Smith. 2019. "Bonding and Dissonance: Rethinking the Interrelations among Stakeholders in Heritage Tourism." *Tourism Management* 74: 212–23.

Index

Page numbers in italics refer to illustrations.

Abeyta, Kevin, 250, 264
agriculture: early medieval 60, 129, 155–9; nineteenth and twentieth centuries, 23, 173–82, 183, 203, 208; contemporary, 246–8
agri-environmental schemes/policies, 25, 245–8, 262, 275
alcohol, 56, 85 167, 171–2, 218. *See also* gin; whiskey; poitín.
Allies, Cyril, 179, 193–5, 203, 204
Anglo-Saxon Chronicle, 145
anti-Catholic, 32, 170, 192
anticolonial, 32. *See also* decolonization
anthropology: American Anthropological Association, 269; American anthropology, 33; anthropological collections, 267, 272; biological anthropology, 34; collaboration with stakeholders, 270, 273; colonial history and primitivist tropes, 22, 30, 33, 38; cross-cultural comparison, 183; ecological, 275; European Association of Social Anthropologists, 269; goal of the discipline, 20, 25. *See also* craniometrics

Anthropometric Laboratory of Ireland, 35. *See also* craniometrics; Haddon, Alfred C.; Cunningham, Daniel J.; Galton, Francis
Aran Islands, *xxiii*, 35, 218. *See also* Inishmore
archaeology: as a mode of remembering, 56; bioarchaeology, 273; collaboration with stakeholders, 270; colonial history and primitivist tropes, 33–7; experimental archaeology, 148; indigenous archaeologies, 39–40; stewardship of archaeological collections, 272; strengths, 48; with conservation, 248
ascetics, 68, 79–80, 95, 163
asceticism, 60, 93, 94, 105, 132, 140–2, 144–6, 153, 157, 163, 164, 172, 259; as preparation for death, 105, 140; role of archetypes, 136–7, 141, 145

Bald, William: map of Mayo, 55, 105, 122, 174
barking pan, 264–5
basking sharks, 178, 181, 219, 267, 270

305

Béal Cam, 29, 232–233
bells, 112, 130, 160, 210, 211; Clog Dubh, 112. *See also* St. Leo's Bell
belonging, xii, 21, 23, 24, 25, 39, 50–1, 125, 209, 215, 219–220, 230, 252, 259, 262, 265, 274, 276–8
Bia Bó Finne Food Festival, 217
birds, 10, 11, 157, 211; bird-watchers, 246, 7. *See also* corncrakes
biodiversity, 211, 237, 246–8, 275
Black Feminism, 273
Black Gate, 252. *See also* INISH Festival
Black Lives Matter, 232, 267
blow-ins, 236–7
boats, 4, 5, 27, 28, 29, 30, 56, 85, 104, 115, 148, 169, 178, 188, 196, 206–7, 216, 240, *241, 242*, 253, 254, 262, 269; *Ave Maria*, 220; *Ceol na Mara*, 216; of skin, 145; Galway Hookers, 43; *Maisie*, 220. *See also* currachs
Bofin Brewing, 216
booleying, 170
Bovril, 85, 197, 200
Bronze Age, 10, 158, 242
Browne, Charles R.: craniometrics, 35, *36*; folklore and antiquarian reporting, 62, 100, 101, 112–3, 115–6, 176–8, 181, 185, 190, 193, 195, 204, 210, 219, 229; photography, *36, 62, 201*
Browne, Howe Peter, 179; estate records, 179–80
bullauns (stone fonts), 43, 101, 106, *107, 108*, 117, 182, 191, 194
Burke, Ann Marie, 222, 223
Burke, Emer, 256
Burke, John, 4, 6, 8, 10, *16*, 27–30, *28*, 49, 220, 235, *241*, 244, 256, 257
Burke, Tommy, 4, 6, 8, 10, 27, 29, 59, 60, 76, 210, 211, 214, 220–5, 221, 222, 230, 232, 234, 235, 237, 245, 252, 256, 257, 264
buttons, 83, *84*, 102, 197

Caher Island, 114–115, 132, 133, *134*
cake dances, 88, 186
Cape Clear Island, 180
Catholicism: as heritage, 167, 172, 213, 232; authorities, 4, 44, 46, 124, 192–5, 202, 203, 208–9, 260–1, 277; Catholic Emancipation, 202; popular devotion, 32, 40–6, 170, 201; suppression of, 82, 112, 169–73, 192, 214, 231
cattle: medieval, 152, 157; nineteenth-century, 177; in oral history and contemporary farming, 237, 243–5, *244*, 247; re-use of church as cattle pen, 15, 100, 183, 191, 193; bulls, 223, 243, 245; calves, 243
Celts, 34, 37 celtic revival, 36–7, 44–5
cemeteries: cemeteries at early medieval monastic sites, 137, 155; cemetery at Inishark pier, 4, 6, 121–125, *122, 123*, 163–4, 260; cemetery at Teampaill Leo, Inishark, 99, *100*; cemetery at St Colman's Abbey, Inishbofin, 210–4, *212*, 265, 268, 270
cenotaphs: at early medieval ecclesiastical sites, 73, 76, 137–9, 160; on Inishark, 66, 73, *90, 91*, 95, 139–40, 163, 259
census, 174, 179, 228, 249
Centre for Experimental Archaeology and Material Culture (CEAMC), 148
ceramics, 23; seventeenth- and eighteenth-century, 80–2, *81*, 168–9, 171, 260; nineteenth- and twentieth-century, 83, 85, 95, 196, 197–200, *198*; as heirlooms, 200, 227; sea-delph, 226, 227, 260; spongeware, 85, *198*, 199; transfer-print, 85, *198*, 199
cereal crops, 9, 67, 106, 152, 154, 159, 176–7, 182
Chapel Island, *133*
Chesson, Meredith, 60, 197
children, 5, 11, 19, 207, 216, 220, 249; at monastic sites, 128, 143, 152, 155;

child minding, 249; children's burial grounds, 4, 123–4; childbirth, 160, 201; in relation to pilgrimage, 104, 183, 196, 197; at mass, 213; oral history project, 229; participation in rowing, 253–5; participation in farming, 248, 257, 258

churching, 201–2

cilliní. *See* children; children's burial grounds

Clare Island, 220

Cleggan, *xxiv*, 61, 104, 220, 230, 258

climate change, xiii, 47, 277, 278

Clocha Breca. *See* pebbles

clochán, 68, 117–9; *119*, 129, 141, 165; as caves, 136–7; as ascetic cells, 136, 140, 162; as associative relics of founders, 162. *See also* Clochán Leo Complex; Clochán Congleo Complex

Clochán Congleo Complex, 85–96; place-name 86–7; Congleo identity, 140; excavation, 88–93; *88, 89*; clochán, 85, *86, 88*, 91, 95, 137; cenotaph chamber, *90, 91*, 95, 140; carved cross, 92; as a shrine, 94, 138; quartz pebbles, 88–93, *88, 90, 93* 141–5, *142–3*; forgotten as a place of pilgrimage, 170

Cloherty, Pat, 220

Cloonamore, 242

Clochán Leo Complex, 54–85; Clochán Leo 8, *9, 18, 22*; *58, 62, 64, 65, 81*; excavation, 54–9, *57, 58, 59, 64, 65*; curvilinear feature, *66, 67, 69, 73, 74*; enclosure wall, *64, 65, 66, 67–8, 69*; cenotaphs, *66, 69, 70, 73*; wall crosses, 68, *81*, 83, 84, *168*, 172; cross-slabs, *59, 65, 69*, 74–6, *77, 81*, 171; leachta, *64, 65, 66*, 73–74; inscribed stone, *70, 71, 72*; granite cross pebble, *78, 79*, hearths, *65*, 80, *81, 82, 168*, 172; seventeenth- and eighteenth-century artifacts and activities, 80–3, *81*, 167–8, *168*, 171–3; 260; nineteenth- and twentieth-century artifacts and activities, 83, 84, 85, 191, 195–203, *196, 198*, 206, 208, 261; quartz pebbles, *57, 58, 59, 60, 70, 73, 74, 75, 78*–9, 80

Cnoc Leo, 117, 119, 121, 159, 182

Cogitosus, 162–3

Comhdháil na hÉireann (Irish Islands Federation), 8

Connerton, Paul, J., 51–2

Couey, Lauren Marie, 179, 181, 204, 206

Collectio Canonum Hibernensis, 153, 160

collectivity/collective action, xiii, 208–9, 276–8, 275; collective agriculture and land-holding, 23, 173, 180–4, 204, 260–1; collective creativity, 53; collective experience, 250, 260–1; collective heritage, 185–91, 193, 206, 209, 215, 260–1, 277

colonialism, 31–3, 172, 184, 232, 267, 273; colonial discourse/tropes/stereotypes, 31–3, 37–8, 47, 215; colonial dispossession and violence, 173, 183, 209, 278; colonial government, 170, 184. *See also* Trinity Colonial Legacies Project

Common Agricultural Policy, 245–6. *See also* European Union

commonage, 174, 177, 240; ritual commonage, 188–91, 260–1, 276

communitas, 159, 162–3

communities of care, 266, 272

Concannon, Andrew, 101

Concannon, Christy, 12

Concannon, Dermot, 56

Concannon, John, 244

Concannon, Kieran, 228, 264. *See also Inis Airc - Bás Oileáin; Inishbofin through Time and Tide; Inishbofin in Lockdown.*

Concannon, Matty, 235

Concannon, Pat, 56

Concannon, Seamus, 56
concentric boundaries, 130–5,*132, 135*; 153–4, 163
conflict, xiii, 169, 275; within small communities, 182, 189; within tourism, 245; within traditions, 201, 261–2
Congested Districts Board, 179, 181, 187, 203–6, 208, 261; houses, 204, *205*, 261
Congleo, 86–7, 140. *See also* Clochán Congleo Complex
Connemara, *xxiii*, 3, 60, 61, 98, 132, 133, 154, 194, 218, 225, 229; Connemara ponies 237
conservation, 11, 218, 236, 246–8, 275, 277
conventions, 30, 52, 63, 186, 188, 190, 200–1, 223, 237, 261–2
conversion to Christianity, 60, 130, 132, 144
cooperation, xiii, 20, 50, 166, 182, 184, 190, 208, 246, 261, 277. *See also* collective action; commonage
corncrakes, 211, 246–8, 275
cosmology, 33, 53; early medieval, 23, 60, 130–2, 153, 162; creation, 144, 146–7, 260
Covid, 24, 231, 250, 251, 256, 257, 263–66. *See also* pandemics
Coyne, Pat, 257
Coyne, Marie, 225–31, *226, 227, 228*, 253, 256, 257, 263, 264, 267, 269–70
Coyne, Ryan, 257–9, *258*
cults/saint cults, 61, 40, 76, 78, 111–3, 135, 139–41, 165, 170, 185, 188, 190–1, 203, 209, 259, 260–1. *See also* pattern days
Cultural Landscapes of the Irish Coast (CLIC), xii, xv, xvi, xviii, 22, 54–60, 61, 63, 89, 93, 100, 149, 155, 157, 168, 194, 197, 199, 203, 216
Cunnane, Bridget, 270
Cunnane, Veronica, 270
cursing, 104–5, 188–9, 202

currachs, 27, 29, 49, 115, 206, 253, 254, 255
Cunningham, Daniel J., 35.
craic, 250–1, 259, 265
craniometrics, 33–7, *36*, 229. *See also* Browne, Charles, R.; Haddon, Alfred C.; Dixon, Andrew
creativity: of heritage, xiii, 22, 24–5, 30–1, 45–6, 49, 50–3, 209, 252, 259, 262, 274; of islanders, xiii, 211, 216, 217; 252, 259, 262, 264, 278; creative expressions as a supplement to scientific analyses, 273
Croagh Patrick, 41, 42, 112. *See also* St. Patrick
Cromwell, Oliver, 234; Cromwell's Barracks/Old Barracks, 4, 5, 169–70, 231–2, 233, 262, 264; impact of conquest, 169–71, 214, 225, 260
cross-slabs, 73, 74–8, 77, *81*, 162, 165; production 147–151, *149, 150*, 157; lost cross-slabs 113–6, *124*; curation 82, 171, 183, 194; discovery 59, 60, 220
Crump Island, *133*

Davillaun *xxiv*, 27, 240, 241, 242
Day, Ann, 223–4
Day, Christopher, 269
Day Lavelle, Eamonn, 252
Day, Margaret, 213, 214, 216
Day, Miko, 216
Day's Bar. *See* The Beach: Day's Bar
Day's Hotel, 216
day-trippers, 214, 217–8, 253
decolonization 32, 39, 267, 273
deiseal, 42, 43. *See also* sun
demographics, 173, 251
Department of Irish Folklore. *See* folklore
de Valera, Éamon, 36, 206
division: arable fields, 177, 181–2, 204; ontological, 47, 247; social, 277; spatial, 153, 162; temporal, 210

Dixon, Andrew, 35, 211, 266, 268, 269
dogs: sheep dogs, xiii, 4, 5, 6, 10, 11, 12, 18, 20, 21, 28, 240, 256
Dolphin Hotel and Restaurant, 216
donkeys, 237
Douglass, Frederick, 33–4
drownings, 14, 76, 104, 138, 169, 178, 188, 207

early medieval Ireland: social structure, 151–2
Easter controversy, 139, 141
ecclesiastical communities/settlements, 42, 71, 73, 97, 112, 124, 128–35, 137, 151–5, 159, 160. *See also* monasticism
ecclesiastical reform, 139, 164. *See also* Easter controversy
elders, fears, 195; in burial, 4, 76, 123; in ritual, 212, 214, monastic elders, 76; social memory, 167, 182, 222, 235, 246, 264; speech patterns, 249; vulnerability, 207, 251, 263
embodied knowledge/skill, xiii-xiv, 21, 29–30, 48, 51–3, 148, 236, 248, 252, 255
enchantment, 26; as academic concept, 53, 250, 275
endurance, 21, 40, 105, 163–4, 207–9, 211, 259; dynamic endurance, 22, 30–1, 46, 48–50, 53, 272, 276–8.
ensembles, 11, 19, 128, 171, 210, 211, 250–1, 257, 278
erosion: coastal, 102, 121–2, 159, 265, 272
eugenics, 35, 37
European Union: regulations, 215, 219; subsidies 11, 215, 218–9, 245
Evans, E. Estyn, 37–8, 184

Fadden, Redmund Martin, Fr., 192
Fál Dubh, 245
famine, 32, 49–50, 169, 174, 178, 183, 184, 192, 213

farming: farming as heritage, 227, 229, 234, 236, 241–5, 247–8, 262. *See also* agriculture
Fawnmore, 234, 235
ferries, 11, 56, 216, 217, 218, 220, 230, 236, 249, 256–8, 263
fertilizer, 176, 238, 247
festivals, Inishbofin, 217, 250, 252–5, 262
field walls/systems/enclosures: prehistoric, 10; medieval, 155; nineteenth and twentieth centuries, 3, 11, 13, 20, 63, 106, 155, 190, 202, 204, 234, 255. *See also* mearing walls
fishing: medieval, 157; nineteenth and twentieth centuries, 8, 23, 35, 83, 104, 167, 177, 178, 180, 186, 195, 196, 203, 207, 219, 260, 264; contemporary, 11, 26, 30, 215, 216, 242, 249, 255, 257; as heritage, 227–9, 234; impact of super-trawlers, 215
Flannelly, William, Fr., 195
Flannery, John, Fr., 101, 207
folklore: as a discipline, 33, 35, 37–9, 40; Department of Irish Folklore, 61, 219; National Folklore Collection, xviii, xxi
foodways, 14, 23, 56, 85, 145, 182, 197–202, 216, 217, 257; food production and provisioning, 20, 49–50, 152, 153 ; food renders, 128, 152; food security, 184, 246. *See also* famine
fuaig a' Coinnleora, 87, *143*
funerals, 210, 211, 214, 269–70; wakes, 193

Galley Restaurant, 216
Galway: city, 252, 253, 256, 266; county, 225, 263; Galway County Art Office, 264; Galway County Council, 2–3, 229
Garbh, Máire, 102, 104
garden plots, 8, 97, 117, 154, 174, 176, 177, 182, 186, 206, 234, 260

gender, 50; in early medieval society, 151; at ecclesiastical sites, 137, 153, 154, 159, 160, 162, 260; at mass, 213; at the Maritime Festival, 254
genealogy, 222, 224, 228, 230, 235, 268, 270, 272. *See also* kinship
genetics, 268, 270, 272
geometry, 146–7
Gerald of Wales, 32
gin, 82, 167, 172
glass, 178, 195, 265; buttons and beads, 83, 95, 106, *108*, case glass, *81*, 167, 168, 171; cobalt blue glass, *84*, 85, 197; sea-glass, 225; stained glass 101
Glassie, Henry, 53, 184–5, 200
Glencolmcille, *41*
Gormgal, 76
Granuaile (Grace O'Malley), 225, 234
grass-ball, 258–9, *258*
gravel, 67, 69–72, 74, 90–1, 127, 138, 265
Great Blasket Island, 180
Griffith, Richard John, 181; Griffith valuation; 181

Haddon, Alfred Cort, 35, 211, 266, 268–9
Haddon Dixon Repatriation Project, 267, 268, 269, 270
Haddon-Dixon Collection, 267, 269–70
hagiography, 22, 60, 61, 78, 105, 106, 112, 128, 135, 136–7, 141, 145, 155, 157, 160
handheld X-ray fluorescence, 110
harbor, Inishbofin, 4–5, 27, 169, 191, 206, 210, 214, 216, 264; lack of infrastructure, 206, 240
Harbour Lights Bookshop, 216
Harvard Irish Mission, 36–7
hearths: as focal points for household hospitality, 14, 184–5, 200; at Inishgort, 157–8; open vs. closed hearths, 204. *See also* Clochán Leo
hens, 237, 275
heritage, 21 30, 236; creative heritage, 21, 22, 24–5, 46, 49, 50–3; 274; destruction of heritage, 235, 261;

enacted, 29, 245; heritage and belonging, 265, 276–8; heritage and legislation, 11, 40, 267, 272, 273; intimate heritage, 233–6; metonymic heritage, 231–3; timeless heritage, 38, 40. *See also* farming; fishing; tourism.
hermits/hermitage, 68, 73, 80, 105, 127, 136, 163
Hibernicus, Augustinus, 146
hierarchy, 33, 53, 131, 153, 159, 162–3, 274, 275
High Island, 12, 57, 59; monastic settlement layout *135*; cross-slabs 76, *135*; early medieval settlement agriculture and water mill, 154; pseudo-graves, 72, 76, 138
Hildebrand, Henry, 179–80, 192, 195
Halloran, Michael (King of Inishark), 181, 187, *201*, 219
Holleran, John, 181
holy wells. *See* pilgrimage; Tobar Leo
houses, 52, 102, 147, 176, 178–9, 182, 184, 201, 225, 227, 234, 236, 260; anchor-house, 140; architecture, 185–8, *186*, *187*; ceramics, 85, 199–200; Congested District Board houses, 204–6, *205*; landlord's house, 216; relationship to pilgrimage monuments, 98, 107, 109, 110, 117–9, 182, 186–91, 196, 203–4, 206, 208–9, 260–1; ruined houses, 2, *3*, 6, 8, 9, 11, *12*, 13–8, *14*, *15*, *16*, *17*, *18*, 20, 98, 168, 173–4, 223, 258; saints' houses, 86, 132
households, 3, 9, 23, 111, 176–7, 178, 179–81, 182–3, 185–7, 189–91, 197, 199, 201, 206, 208–9, 216, 227, 234, 237, 243, 247, 248, 260
housing, 247, 266
hospitality, 23, 152, 184–5, 200–2, 230, 267, 261

ideology, xiii, colonial, 30, 31, 33; ecclesiastical authority, 139, 153, 194–5,

208; of the past, 52, 215; political 38, 40, 51, 53, 141, 278
Igegeri, Dafe, 256–8, 258
Igegeri, Sean, 256
Illaunloughan, 57, 142–3, 153–4
imagined communities, 39, 277
indigenous groups/indigeneity, 31–3, 39–40, 232, 267, 270, 272, 274. *See also* Standing Rock Reservation
indigenous thought, 22, 38, 40, 47, 275. *See also* survivance
infrastructure: dwelling, 21, 176; farming, 155, 159; harbor, 206, 240; heritage as infrastructure, 24, 51, 166, 252, 261, 265; household, 111, 185, 190, 261; investment in, 4, 203, 206, 262; of belonging, 185, 190, 200, 217, 252, 255, 265; of political economy, 153, 159, 166; of social memory, 141, 166, 265; ritual, 76, 78, 79, 101, 141, 153, 159, 165, 166, 230, 259; ruins as infrastructure, 11, 18–21; tourism, 218
Ingold, Tim, 19–20, 47–9, 250
Inis Airc - Bás Oileáin (documentary), xviii, 186, 195, 206–7
INISH: Island Conversations, 217, 218, 222, 252
Inishark: place-name 26; evacuation 4–5, 14, 249
Inishbofin: place-name 26
Inishbofin Arts Festival, 217
Inishbofin Community Centre, 217, 249, 266
Inishbofin Community Services Programme, xviii, 255, 264
Inishbofin Darkness to Light, 217
Inishbofin Development Company, xviii, 217
Inishbofin Equestrian Centre, 216
Inishbofin Ferry, 11, 56, 216, 217, 218, 220, 230, 236, 245, 249, 253, 256, 257, 258, 263
Inishbofin Half-Marathon and 5K, 217

Inishbofin Heritage Museum and Gift Shop, 227, 228, 262, 263, 264, 269
Inishbofin in Lockdown, 264
Inishbofin Island Hostel, 216
Inishbofin Island Work Fund, 264–5
Inishbofin Maritime Festival, 217, 253–5, 254
Inishbofin Set Dancing and Trad Weekend, 217, 250
Inishbofin through Time and Tide, 228
Inishbofin Walking Festival, 217
Inishbofin Yoga Retreat, 217
Inishgort, *xxiv*, 147, 148, 156–7
Inishlyon, *xxiv*, 27, 239, 240
Inishmore, 110, 180, 218, 267. *See also* Aran Islands
Inishmurray, 45, 68; Clocha Breca, 78; leachta 45, 137–8, 154; kings 180
Inishskinny Beg, *xxiv*, 240
Inishskinny More, *xxiv*, 156, 240
Inishtrahull, 180
Inishwalla, 216
Iona, 68, 130, 136, 137–8, 139, 153. *See also* St. Columba
Irish American, 213, 231–2
Irish Free State, 36–7, 204, 206
Irish Land Commission, 206, 207, 208, 230
island development companies, 231

Joyce, Myles, 181–2

Kells (ecclesiastical site), 132
kelp 176–8. *See also* seaweed
Kinahan, George, 100–1, 115–6.
King, Liam, 252
King, Peadar, 252
King's Bike Hire, 216
kings in islands, 180–1, 219–20
kinship: academic subject, 33, 272; early medieval, 60, 128, 132, 151; on the islands, 8, 21, 104, 182, 184–5, 193, 200, 201, 208, 210, 223, 225, 230, 234, 235,

236, 249, 252, 265, 272. *See also* genealogy; genetics.
Knight, Patrick, 183
knitting 217, 222, 223–4, 227, 236, 262
Kuijt, Ian, 22. *See also* Cultural Landscapes of the Irish Coast (CLIC)

Lacey, Martin, 206
Lacey, Michael, 206
Lacey, Peter, 206
Lacey, Thomas, 14, 207
Lacey House, 6, 7, *14, 15, 16, 17, 18*
landholding, 167, 173, 179–84, 191, 203–4, 206, 208, 261, 274. *See also* commonage
landlords, 128, 167, 173, 178, 179–81, 183, 191–3, 195, 207, 208, 216, 261, 277
landscape: definition, 19, 48; daily encounters, 182, 248, 262, 277; Easter Controversy, 139; human livelihood, 49–50; island landscapes, 3, 25, 155, 167, 173, 225, 257; manipulation of, 154; marginal, 247; pastoral, 245; photography, 217, 229; relationality, 52, 128, 166, 215, 259; ritual, 43, 62; 68; 94; 106, 111, 117, 130, 134, 138, 140, 153, 155, 164, 194; rundale landscapes, 174; shapes, 87; social reproduction, 50, 153, 166, 190, 21, 265; stewardship of, 248; striping, 181, 203–4; temporality and memory, 21, 51, 128, 129, 166, 171, 190, 208, 215, 219, 232, 234, 247, 259, 262, 265, 277; timeless, 218, 236; visibility, 136, 142
language: notes on Irish, xxi; bilingualism, 180, 195; linguistic echos 181; prepositions, 27, 236
Lavelle, Marcais, *241, 242*
Lavelle, Stephen, 11
Lavelle, Willie, *241, 242*
Leaba Leo, 105–11, *107, 109*, 190, 206
Leac Leo, 101, 113–6, 117, 191, 193–5

Leac na naomh. *See* pebbles
leachta: as pilgrimage stations, 43, 45, 182; on Inishark, 65, 66, 69, 70, 73–6, 88, 89, 93, 95, 106, *107*, 182; as grave markers, 99–100; as cenotaphs, 73, 91, 140; as multi-functional monuments, 137; as evocations of distant times and places, 138–9, 259; as reminders of death, 140
Leata Mór, *120*, 121, 206
Levy, Zach, 257–9
LiDAR, 55, *187,* 205

Macalister, R.A.S, 37
Mackenzie, Murdoch: Maritime Survey, 173, 174, *175*
MacLoughlin, Brían, 61, 87, 105, 190, 194, 200, 202, 204, 206, 219; background, 61, 219; excerpts from his folklore collection, 10, 26, 61, 87, 88, 97, 102, 103, 104, 106, 116, 117, 118, 121, 123, 186, 189
Mahr, Adolph, 37
manaig, 152–5, 157–60, 162, 164
maps, *xxiii, xxiv,* 6, 7, 55, 56, 63, 101, 105, 106, 107, 112, 113, *114,* 116–7, *118,* 121, 122, 133, 173, 174, *176, 177,* 181, 185, 186, 190, 191, 227, 228, 260; mental maps, 27, 22, 144. *See also* Bald, William; Mackenzie, Murdoch; Ordnance Survey
marginality: cosmological, 130, 140; environments, 38, 173, 177, 183, 247; marginalized people, 38, 40, 232, 273, 275, 276, 277; practices, 124; spatial practices, 154; survival, 37
Martellaro, Linda, 56
mass, 68, 101, 112, 131, 132, 155, 162, 170, 182, 191–4, 201–2, 206; Assumption mass, 210–4, 216, 224, 231–2, 252
McDonough, Tom, Fr., 192
McMahon, Tara, 264

mearing walls: Inishark, 10, *156*; High Island, 154, 155; Omey Island 155, Inishgort and Inishskinny More, 156
Middlequarter, 245
migration, 34, 113, 167, 185, 174, 184, 191, 203, 206, 251, 262, 272
mills (water mills), 152, 153–5, *158*, 159, 234
monasticism, 21, 22–3, 45, 128–9, 139, 260, agricultural regimes 153; presence of women 153, 160–2
monks, 139, 141, 145, 151, 152, 155, 157, 159–64, 210, 214, 230, 259–60, 278
Moran, Gerry, 211, 214
Murphy, Richard, 220, 252
Murray, Caolán, 4, 6, *16*
Murray, George, 207
Murray, Luke, 29
Murray, Margaret, 216. *See* also The Doonmore Hotel
Murray, Martin, 61, 106, 121, 191, 194
Murray, Patrick, 117
Murray, Simon 4–6, 8, 10, 15, *16*, 20, 27, 29, 217, 231, 232, *238*, 239, 245, 256, 257, 258–9
music/musicians, 216, 249–52, 264, 265–6
Myles, Franc, *57*, 59

National Archives of Ireland, 56, 114, 118, 176
National Folklore Collection. *See* folklore
National Library of Ireland, 179–80
National Museum of Ireland, 270, 272
National School: Inishark, 174, 177, 181, 204, Inishbofin National School, 229, 250, 266
National University of Ireland Galway, 2015
nationalism, 30, 34, 36–9, 44. *See also* romanticism
navigation towers, 27, 29, 264

Neary, John, Fr., 116, 188, 192
nostalgia 248, 249, 251

Ó Carragáin, Tomás, 45, 129–30, 137, 138–9
Ó Cluanáin, Tomás, 104
O'Donovan, John, 105, 114–5
O'Flaherty, Roderic, 111–2, 135, 170
Ó Gallachóir, Conor, 104
O'Hagan, Terry, *57*, 87, 97, 113
O'Halloran, Cathay, 229
Oireachtas, 8, 20, 231
Old Barracks. *See* Cromwell, Oliver
Omey Island *133*, 155, 163–4
Ordnance Survey: field name books 86, 105, 123; maps, 55, *56*, 101, 107, *114*, *118*, 174, *176*, *177*, 181, 185, 186, 190, 191, 193
others/otherization, 10, 31, 51–2, 124, 277
other-than-human, xiii, 19, 24, 46–8, 52, 125, 128–9, 141, 146, 151, 165, 274–6

paganism, 32, 35, 44; neo-paganism, 45
Palestinian liberation, 232
pattern days, 41–4, 112, 200
pandemics, xiii, 19, 278. *See also* covid
pebbles: cloca breca, 78; Columba's stone, 136, 143; contemporary use, 265, *271*; granite cross pebble, *79*, 126, 141; Leac na naomh, *114*; nodules 109–111, *110*, 146, *147*; quartz, *57*, *58*, *59*, 60, 69, 70, 73, 74, 75, 78–9, 80, 88–93, *88*, *90*, *93*, 126, *127*, 141–5, *142–3*, 163, 210, 271
penal laws, 170, 191, 231
penance/penitentials, 45, 60, 105, 111, 128, 137, 145, 230. *See also* asceticism
photography, 178, 217, 225, 228–9
picnics, 196–202, 261
pier: Inishark, 4, 6, 121, 204, 206, 256, 257; old pier on Inishbofin, 4, 27, 227, 258
pigs, 154, 157, 177, 182, 236–7, 247

pilgrimage: circumambulation, 42–3, 52, 182–3, 210–11; cross-cultural approaches, 162; Irish traditions, 22, 31, 32, 40–6, *41, 42, 43*, 53, 61, 112, 117–21, 129, 141, 155, 166; pagan associations, 32, 42, 44–5; holy wells, 44–5, 170; on Inishark, 21, 23, 61–3, 73, 78–80, 82–3, 94, 102–4, 106, 138, 163, 164, 182–3, 196–7, 201, 203, 204, 230, 259–62; *peregrinatio pro amore dei*, 144–5, 260; persecution of pilgrimage traditions, 170, 260; tourism as pilgrimage 216, 230, 252. *See also* an turas/turas traditions

pilgrims, 4; in folklore, 41, 102, 117; medieval, 22–3, 24, 45, 73, 76, 78–80, 91, 126–8, *127*, 140–6, 151, 162–3, 230, 260; seventeenth and eighteenth centuries, 172; nineteenth and twentieth centuries, 45, 59, 82–3; 194; 200; contemporary, 42, 131, 211, 246

pipes, 82, 84, 171, 196

planning permission, 247, 266

poitín, 88, 172

pollen data, 154, 159

population: Inishark, 174; Inishbofin, 249

postcolonialism, 30–2. *See also* decolonization; anticolonial

posthumanism, 19, 22, 24, 31, 46–7, 247, 274–8

potatoes, xi, 8, 9, 13, 34, 49, 167, 173 174 176 178, 182 184, 190, 240, 260

priests 188, 191–5, 211–4, 212, 261, 278

primitivism, 259, 274; definition, 29–31, 31–40, 218, 278

Protestantism: observers of Catholic devotion, 32, 33, 44; Protestant ascendancy, 169–70, 172, 173; proselytization, 180, 192 (*see also* Hildebrand, Henry; souperism; penal laws)

psalms, 126, 210, 211

quartz. *See* pebbles

quern stones, 234

Rabbitte, James, Fr., 101, 191, 193–4

race: social construction, 38, 50; race-science/racism, 33–5, 38, 163, 168, 174, 183, 191, 193, 206–7, 261, 272

radiocarbon dates: Clochán Leo Complex, Inishark, 67, 76, 80, 139; Teampaill Leo, Inishark, 99, 168; Inishark cemetery, 125; High Island, 135; Illaunloughan, 143; Inishbofin cranial sample, 268; Inishgort, 157; Iona, 136

Rantala, Tuuli, 270

Reask (ecclesiastical site), 132

rectangular enclosures, Inishark, 85–96. *See also* western enclosure, Inishark; Clochán Congleo Complex

relationality, 46–7, 52–3, 128, 259, 274–6, 277. *See also* posthumanism

relics, 35, 73, 112–3, 129–130, 139, 142–3, 163, 170

remote working, 266

repatriation, 267, 269–70, 272–3

resting stone, 234, 235

re-wilding, 247–8

romanticism, 35, 37, 215, 245; romantic nationalism, 30, 34, 38, 44

rosary, 83, *84*, 197

ruins, 18, 20–1. *See also* houses; infrastructure

rundale, 173, 177, 180–4, 189–90, 261

Rural Environment Protection Scheme, 248

Salt Box, 216

science/scientific methods, 30, 31, 33, 34, 39, 248, 273. *See also* race-science; craniometrics

seascape, 260

seaweed, 157, 234; as fertilizer, 8, 176, 234; kelp, 176–8, 207; as food, 179

INDEX

sheep: gathering, xiii, 6, 7, 11, *12*, 13, 236, 245, 256–7, 275–6; hoggets, 29, 240, 242, 256; lambs, 8, 13, 18, 27–9, *28*, 127, 157, 221, 226, 237–8, *238*, 240, 243, 256–8; moving sheep between islands 240–2; sheep husbandry and monasticism 154, 157; shearing 3, 6, 12–8,*16*, 20, 101, 220, 237–9, 248, 255, 256, 258

shells: in pilgrimage, 103; limpets, 103, 157, 179; winkle 70, 157

Skellig Michael, 42, 68, 154

skeuomorphs, 130, *131*

slavery, 31, 33–4, 152, 232, 267; Irish slave meme, 232

Solas: Stories from Inishbofin, 229

souperism, 192

social evolutionism, 30, 33, 38, 39, 44

social media 228–30, 262, 263–5, 269, 274

social memory, 20, 51–2; forgetting, 8, 20, 22, 56, 63, 111, 117, 171, 121, 125, 167, 171, 227, 235

Special Areas of Conservation, 218

Special Protection Area 246

Spencer, Edmund, 32

Standing Rock Reservation, 232

St. Bede the Venerable, 139, 144, 219

St. Brendan the Navigator, 144–5

St. Colman: exile to Inishbofin, 139, 225. *See also* St. Colman's Abbey; St. Colman's Church

St. Colman's Abbey, Inisbofin: foundation, 61, 67, 123–5, 139; curation, theft, and reburial of skulls, 35, 268–70; associated mill, 159; memorial, 192, Assumption Mass, 210–4, 212; as metonym, 231, 262. *See also* cemeteries

St Colman's Abbey and Cemetery Inishbofin, 228

St. Colman's Church (medieval), 211, 212, 265, 268, 269, 271

St. Colman's Church (nineteenth-century), 191

St. Colman's Church (twentieth-century), 210, 212, 269

St. Columba, 132, 137; Columban monasticism, 139; blessed stone, 143–4, 146; hut on Iona, 136; *Vita Columbae*, 136, 141, 143, 160; as Colmcille, *41*

St. Féichín, 138, 155. *See also* High Island; Omey Island

St. Finian's Bay, 267, 270

stigma, 260. *See also* taboo

St. Leo: origins of cult, 135; papal connotations, 139, 164, 259–60; St. Leo's Day 62, 102, 139–40, 182–3, 185–6, 188, 190, 196, 201, 208, 261; footprint, 61, 196; protection of sailors, 104, 188; St. Leo's Bell, 111–113, 185

St MacDara's Island, *43*, *131*

stone: granite, 78, 79, 101, 106, 117, 127, 141; limestone, 4, 43, 192, 233; schist, 4, 20, 57, 60, 70, 74, 83, 85, 99, 122, 147–8, 151, 210; soapstone, 74, 97–9, 101, 161; quartz. *See* pebbles

stone-carving, 146–51

storms, 2, 16, 47, 115, 147, 148, 188–9, 258; of 2014, 4, 11, 252, 264

storytelling, 13, 223–24, 252; cautionary tales 104–5, 115, 118, 261–2

St. Patrick, 112, 115, 157, 213; *See also* Croagh Patrick

Straberger, Veronika, 229

St. Scaithín, 124

subsidies, 11, 215, 218–9, 245, 247, 262

Summer School Inishbofin, 217

sun: sun-wise movement, 42–3, 52–3, 210

survivance, 40

sustainability, 24–5, 40, 165, 207–9, 255, 276–8. *See also* endurance

Synge, John Millington, 35–6

synods, 210, 211; Synod of Whitby, 139

taboo 190, 201, 208. *See also* stigma
taskscape: definition 19, 47–8, 128; dwelling taskscape 48, 275–6; affordances of the framework, 274–5
tea, 196–7, 200, 202; teapots, 196, 198, 199, 200; teacups, 198, 199, 200
Teampaill Leo (St. Leo's Church), 12, 14, 15–6, 99, *100*, 163, 168, 174, 183, 191, 193, 206–7, 261; chronology, 96–101
textiles: production, 74, 128, 160; spindle whorls 74, *161*; woven, 82. *See also* wool
thatch, 176, 182, 185, 204
The Beach: Day's Bar, 216, 234, 249
The Doonmore Hotel (Murray's), 216, 249, 250, 251, 257
Tierney, Jim, 232
timelessness, xii, 38, 63, 218, 259, 272, 274
Tithe Applotment Books, 179, 181
tobacco, 29, 85, 171–2, 196–7. *See also* pipes
Tobar Leo, 102–105, *103*, 183, 191, 194–5, 202, 261
Tory Island, 180
tourism, 10, 211, 214–6; as pilgrimage 230; habitual tourism, 217–8; heritage tourism 21, 215, 218–20; 231–2, 262, 276; walking tours 222–5, *222*, 262; interaction with tradition and heritage, 215, 236–7, 242, 245, 249, 252–55, 262, 265; tourist season, 217, 237, 245, 250; tourist traffic, 237, 244–5, 263, 264
tourists, 3, 4, 11, 24, 213, 218, 223, 230, 278; interactions with islanders, 216, 230, 236, 245
Tower Cottage, 27
Trá Gheal, 206
tradition, 20, 38, 51, 201, 215, 220, 230, 247, 251, 252–5, 262, 272; dynamism, 40, 49, 50, 53, 248, 274; intellectual traditions, 30, 144, 146, 166, 275;
invented traditions 39, 272, 277; oral tradition, 13, 61, 117, 118, 225, 245; ritual, 9, 22–4, 31, 40–6, 49, 52–3, 56, 61–3, 78, 83, 102, 104, 111, 119, 136–7, 141, 160, 167, 170–1, 182, 190, 193, 195, 203, 213–4, 265, 269, 276; persistent 38, 50, 63, 236, 274; traditional knowledge 5, 8, 21, 23, 25, 30, 39–40, 51, 61, 113, 121, 219, 220, 223, 229, 233, 236, 240, 241, 245, 248, 252, 255, 259, 262, 273, 276
translation, 104
transliteration, 26, xxi
Triads of Ireland, 210–11
Trinity College Dublin, 263, 273; Old Anatomy Department and Museum, 24, 35, 267, 268, 270; Old Anatomy Steering Committee Letter, 268; Trinity Colonial Legacies Project, 268–9
turas/turas traditions, 22, 40–6, *41*, *42*, *43*, 48, 52–3, 78, 160, 166; on Inishark, 62–3, 83, 116–9, 137, 141, 167, 170–1, 182–3, 185, 188–90, 193–7, 202–4, 206, 208, 259–61, 274

Uaim leó/St. Leo's Cave, 105
University College Dublin, 37, 148. *See also* Centre for Experimental Archaeology and Material Culture

Vail, Pegi, 267, 269
Vizenor, Gerald, 40; see also survivance

wakes. *See* funerals
Walsh, Ciarán, 267, 270
water symbolism, 144; ocean, 60, 132, 144–5, 147
western enclosure, 86, *87*, 93–6, *94*, *95*; forgotten 170
Westquarter, 223

whiskey, 88, 167, 172. *See also* alcohol
Wilberforce, Henry William, 179, 181, 192, 195
Wilde, Jane, 104–5, 188–9
women: as pastoralists, 157, 170; as practitioners of hospitality and devotional practice 104, 201–2, 261; at monastic sites 127–8, 142, 153, 155, 157, 160–2; domestic labour, 182; regulation by priests, 201–2, 208
wool, 12, 29, 127, 128, 157; contemporary value, 237–8; felt art, 217. *See also* knitting; textile production

RYAN LASH is Teaching Fellow in the School of Archaeology at University College Dublin. He is author (with Ian Kuijt, William Donaruma, Katie Shakour, and Tommy Burke) of *Island Places, Island Lives: Exploring Inishbofin and Inishark Heritage, Co. Galway, Ireland*. He received his PhD in Anthropology from Northwestern University and has held postdoctoral fellowships at the University of Notre Dame and University College Dublin.

FOR INDIANA UNIVERSITY PRESS

Sabrina Black *Editorial Assistant*
Lesley Bolton *Project Manager/Editor*
Tony Brewer *Artist and Book Designer*
Anna Garnai *Production Coordinator*
Sophia Hebert *Assistant Acquisitions Editor*
Samantha Heffner *Marketing and Publicity Manager*
Katie Huggins *Production Manager*
Bethany Mowry *Acquisitions Editor*
Dan Pyle *Online Publishing Manager*
Jennifer Witzke *Senior Artist and Book Designer*